petals from the blossoms on the ground;

otherwise everything is exactly the same

as it was four nights ago, before you

came. What happened to the time

between, I do not know — it was _last_

night I was sitting here by my window;

there could not have been four days

between; the hours you were here have

slipped through my fingers like water,

and are gone. When you are gone, I feel

your absence all around me and I am

WAR WITHIN AND WITHOUT

Books by Anne Morrow Lindbergh

North to the Orient

Listen! the Wind

The Wave of the Future

The Steep Ascent

Gift from the Sea

The Unicorn

Dearly Beloved

Earth Shine

Bring Me a Unicorn — *college*

Hour of Gold, Hour of Lead —

Locked Rooms and Open Doors — *N. atlantic*

The Flower and the Nettle — *abroad*

War Within and Without —

WAR WITHIN AND WITHOUT

*Diaries
and Letters
of
Anne Morrow Lindbergh*

1939–1944

*A Helen and Kurt Wolff Book
Harcourt Brace Jovanovich
New York and London*

Library of Congress Cataloging in Publication Data

Lindbergh, Anne Morrow, 1906–
War within and without.

Continuation of the author's The flower and the nettle.
"A Helen and Kurt Wolff book."
Includes index.
1. Lindbergh, Anne Morrow, 1906–   —Diaries.
2. Lindbergh, Anne Morrow, 1906–   —Correspondence.
3. Authors, American—20th century—Biography.
I. Title.
PS3523.I516Z528   818'.5'209   79-21614
ISBN 0-15-194661-2

A limited first edition has been privately printed.

B C D E

Editorial Note

The diary and letter material in this book has been cut for repetition and corrected for readability. Since this is a personal rather than a historical record, the footnotes were kept, in general, contemporary with the diary and purposely brief, confined to information essential to understanding the text.

The following abbreviations have been used throughout:

D. W. M.—Dwight W. Morrow

E. C. M.—Elizabeth Cutter Morrow

E. R. M. M.—Elisabeth Reeve Morrow Morgan

C. C. M. M.—Constance Cutter Morrow Morgan

E. L. L. L.—Evangeline Lodge Land Lindbergh

A. M. L.—Anne Morrow Lindbergh

C. A. L.—Charles A. Lindbergh

I would like to give special thanks for help in this volume to Professor Wayne S. Cole, of the University of Maryland, for his detailed scholarly books on the period from which I have drawn heavily for information. I am grateful as well to Col. Raymond H. Fredette for his meticulous research and advice on the period, and to Miss Judith A. Schiff, Chief Research Archivist of Sterling Memorial Library at Yale University, for her help in research and advice on pertinent material.

ILLUSTRATIONS

Illustrations

INTRODUCTION

War Within and Without is the fifth and last of my published diaries and letters from 1922 to 1944, spanning the years between America's participation in two world wars in Europe. The 1914–18 war, starting when I was a child of seven, saw my older cousins in uniform headed for the trenches in France. The second war, coming in the middle years of my marriage, found my husband in fighter planes in the Pacific. Both wars cracked open the worlds from which they erupted.

I was hardly aware of the changes made by the first war. My sheltered world, held firmly within a warm and close-knit family circle in a small town in New Jersey, seemed secure and peaceful. My father, it is true, was away for months, serving under General John J. Pershing in London on the Allied Maritime Shipping Council. Also my mother, believing that women should carry their share, supported and visited the Smith College Relief Unit in Grécourt, France. But our everyday lives at home remained much the same.

By Armistice Day in 1918 a new era was already arising from the battlefields in France. Aviation was spawned by World War I. A farm boy in Minnesota was inspired by stories of the aces, and it was from surplus wartime equipment that Charles Lindbergh purchased his first plane, in Americus, Georgia, in 1923. His father, Progressive Republican Congressman from Minnesota for ten years, was an important figure in the American reform movement for improving the conditions of farm and industrial labor.[1]

Great and hopeful changes were in the air in the 1920's. Wilson's Fourteen Points and the League of Nations were to replace armed conflict. "National self-determination" and "peaceful arbitration" were to remove the causes of combat. The Kellogg-

Briand Pact had outlawed war. My parents were dedicated to the power of education and service to community and mankind. They believed strongly in progress; and in their eyes civilization had apparently advanced to the stage of international cooperation.

Following my parents' example and advice, I was deeply absorbed by my studies in history, literature, and writing. Smith College (1924–28) under President William Allan Neilson was an enriching experience recorded in *Bring Me a Unicorn*. One of my professors, Sidney B. Fay, published in 1928 his *Origins of the World War,* raising doubts as to Germany's presumed "total responsibility" for World War I. In these years Erich Remarque's *All Quiet on the Western Front* converted me early to a pacifist point of view. The Nazi era was still in the future, and I had yet to learn that there were worse things than war. In college I read history but seldom saw a newspaper. When Lindbergh flew the Atlantic, I was buried in the Smith College library writing a paper on Erasmus, in whom I saw a resemblance to my father, a moderate and a peacemaker.

When I came up from the stacks, I asked who was this Lindbergh everyone was talking about. I was told but did not grasp the far-reaching consequences of the flight until I met the flier the next Christmas in Mexico City. After his record-breaking flight over the Atlantic in 1927, Charles Lindbergh was invited by my father, then U.S. Ambassador, to fly to Mexico City to aid relations between the two nations.

Six months later, the celebrated airman took me out flying from a Long Island meadow and asked me to marry him. For me, the gentle world of literature, books, and poetry was eclipsed by the new drama of the airplane and its crusaders.

After our marriage in 1929, we continued my husband's role in surveying routes for the not yet established passenger airlines. Our flights opened up mail routes around the Caribbean, across the United States for Transcontinental Air Transport (now TWA). Our subsequent flight (*North to the Orient*) surveyed the Pacific for future airlines to Alaska, Japan, and China. In *Locked Rooms and Open Doors,* I described the circle we flew around the North Atlantic, spanning Greenland, Iceland, Norway, Ireland, the Azores, and across the ocean to Brazil for Pan American's overseas service. Sitting long hours in the back cockpit, operating an old-fashioned key radio and using a bubble sextant to check navigation, I did not realize we were part of the revolution in twentieth-century transportation.

Life in the air was beautiful, limitless, and free—if often hazardous—but life on the ground married to a public hero was a full-cry race between hunter and hunted. We were the quarry. We were unable to lead our private lives without being hounded on most occasions by reporters, photographers, and celebrity seekers. The climax came when our 18-month-old baby was kidnapped from our first home, near Princeton, New Jersey, in 1931. *Hour of Gold, Hour of Lead* covers the weeks of anguished searching before the child's body was found in the woods near our home. In our bitterness we felt that the spotlight of publicity focused upon us was largely responsible for the tragedy. When our second son was born and we were again pursued for photographs and news stories, we decided to leave for a secluded life in Europe.

The years abroad in England and France were portrayed in *The Flower and the Nettle*. We found private peace and happiness in two temporary homes: first in Long Barn in the rolling fields of Kent, the former house of Harold and Victoria (Vita Sackville-West) Nicolson. Later we moved to France, onto the wild rocky island of Illiec, off the coast of Brittany. On the neighboring island, St. Gildas, lived Dr. Alexis Carrel, with whom my husband had worked on biomedical research in the Rockefeller Institute of New York.

With civil war raging in Spain and the Nazi power rising in Germany, we became increasingly aware of the cloud of danger looming over Europe. In 1936, while living quietly and anonymously in Long Barn, my husband was asked by the U.S. Military Attaché in Berlin to make a trip to Germany to assess the growing Nazi air power. His assistance was sought because official observers were having difficulty obtaining accurate information about military aviation. There followed the United States–instigated invitation from Marshal Hermann Göring, head of the

German air force, and several trips to Germany.[2] Using Lindbergh's fame and presence as an opening wedge, U.S. Intelligence obtained the coveted estimates. The Nazis were delighted to show off their air strength, and they even let my husband fly their newest planes.

Charles Lindbergh's survey of European military air installations was not, as is sometimes implied, for the benefit of any foreign power. It was to inform his own country's air command, and he carried out his mission as requested. Inevitably, the information he obtained for U.S. Army Intelligence filtered down to world news services, causing a flurry of false or exaggerated stories. His estimates of comparative European air strengths were rumored to have influenced Prime Minister Neville Chamberlain in his decision to go to Munich and to persuade the Czechs to yield to Hitler's demands. The truth is that Lindbergh never spoke about German air power to Chamberlain or to the Secretary of State for Air, Sir Kingsley Wood. His reports to other air officials were no doubt repeated, but there is no evidence that these were influential in the decisions at Munich.[3] The British, in fact, had long ignored other warnings from aviation experts and those of Winston Churchill.*

After Hitler's annexation of Czechoslovakia in 1939, my husband felt he should return to his own country in order to contribute to the critical expansion of U.S. army aviation installations, which alone, he felt, could match German air strength.

This volume deals with our life during the prewar period in America. My diary starts in the spring of 1939, when we returned home from two and one half years in Europe. My husband preceded me on the voyage back. While still on the boat, he received a radiogram from General Henry H. Arnold (then Chief of the Air Corps), asking to see him as soon as possible after his arrival. Two days later, my husband reported to Arnold on the aviation developments in Europe, particularly in Germany —a report which Arnold later described as "the most accurate

---

* This prewar period in Europe is so thoroughly covered in the Introduction to *The Flower and the Nettle* that I have not repeated the information here.

picture of the Luftwaffe, its equipment, leaders, apparent plans, training methods, and present defects [he had] received up to that time."[4] Arnold wanted him immediately "to go on active duty, to make a study of and attempt to increase the efficiency of American [aeronautical] research organizations."[5]

My husband was already deeply involved in this mission when I arrived a fortnight later with our two children to stay temporarily at my mother's home in Englewood, New Jersey. Since his work for the air force involved constant traveling over the country on inspection trips, with Washington as his home base, we considered moving to the Capital for the summer, but finally decided to rent a house on Long Island, not far from an airfield, from which he could take off on his trips. He continued his air force work up to the time he gave his first speech against United States involvement in the European war (Sept. 15, 1939). General Arnold was consulted and did not object to this speech, but suggested that Lindbergh should return to civilian status if he became involved in anti-war activity.[6]

Despite the violent extremes of opinion expressed among people of the United States for and against involvement and the countless efforts since then of scholars and historians, the prewar period has almost disappeared from the national memory. The intense feelings and bitter conflicts of the time were engulfed in the vast events which followed Pearl Harbor. Today, hardly anyone gives much thought to what was once called "the Great Debate" over the question: Should we or should we not enter World War II? The general conclusion today is that we waged a just war against evil forces and that we won. Interventionists and noninterventionists alike can agree on some such formula. As the historian Bruce M. Russett has put it succinctly: "Participation in the war against Hitler remains almost wholly sacrosanct, nearly in the realm of theology."[7]

Few of us question what preceded Hitler or examine critically the conditions that caused his rise to power. Few stop to consider what consequences followed our enthusiastic embrace of Stalin and, inevitably, of his aims and ends. Except in the minds of historians, World War II stands like an isolated peak in history: its approaches and descents remain practically unnoticed. Wartime emotions clouded contemporary accounts—including mine. In popular opinion, that period is largely remembered from front-page columns in daily newspapers.

What justification can there be in reviewing the prelude and the course of those years? Brief as it was, the prewar period is still a crucial link in the history of the United States. Its conflicts, its doubts and problems have recurrent implications for the present and the future. The country was deeply divided on the question of participation in World War II. Historians and biographers must continue to examine this conflict and the figures prominent in it. Firsthand accounts will be looked into—even those limited by personal and biased views. Numerous diaries and memoirs, chiefly from the interventionist side of the debate, have already been published. My own diary is frankly biased. It could hardly be otherwise. It gives a subjective view of the temper of the times and the personality of one of the chief protagonists of the debate.

My introduction and notes are, however, written today, with the benefit of hindsight and almost forty years of reflection, study, and reading. I have tried to be accurate and objective, a necessary and crucial effort. Facts and figures have blurred in the mists of propaganda from both sides. Who were the non-interventionists—or isolationists, as they were called by their opponents? It is a rare individual who remembers anyone but Charles Lindbergh. The widespread impression remains that only a small minority of reactionaries and bigots opposed the United States entry into the war.

Actually, the majority of Americans were against entry into the war, while overwhelmingly opposed to Hitler's Germany and desirous of a British victory. Joseph P. Lash, in his recent sympathetic book on Roosevelt and Churchill, describes F.D.R.'s genuine concern before his third-term election over public-opinion polls which showed 83 per cent of the voters opposed to U.S. entry into the war, although a high percentage favored aid to England even at the risk of war.[8] The actions of Congress are an indication of the sentiment of the country. The Selective

Service Act, extending the draft, was renewed in the summer of 1941 by a majority of only *one* vote. The repeal of the Neutrality Act, three weeks before Pearl Harbor, passed the Senate but narrowly escaped defeat in the House. Interventionists at this time frankly admitted, and deplored, the reluctance of the American people to enter the conflict.

"The isolationist viewpoint," according to the reputable historian Manfred Jonas, ". . . cannot be dismissed as simple obstructionism based on ignorance and folly. Isolationism [in 1940–41] was the considered response to foreign and domestic developments of a large, responsible, and respectable segment of the American people."[9] Rightly or wrongly, isolationism was one of the chief tenets of early American foreign policy. Its roots lie deep in the foundation of our nation.

Walter Lippmann, a convinced interventionist in World War II, further explains and defines, in a series of lectures delivered in England, this American tradition:

"The term isolationist, and the mythology which has grown up around it, suggests passivity and lethargy. The word isolationist conceals the dynamic and expansionist energy of the American nation. . . . Those whom we now call isolationists are the true believers in the foreign policy of the men who conquered and settled the American continental domain."[10]

The America First movement and the long list of historians, international lawyers, scholars, and citizens in public and private life who followed its leadership were continuing a traditional mainstream of American foreign policy. The organization was started in September of 1940 by two young Yale graduate students, R. Douglas Stuart, Jr. (later president of Quaker Oats), and Kingman Brewster (later president of Yale and Ambassador to Great Britain), and headed by General Robert E. Wood, manager of Sears, Roebuck, who was noted for his war record in the Philippines and World War I. It was formed to give voice to both pacifist and other noninterventionist sentiment in the country and to provide a platform for anti-war speakers, senators, congressmen, and many private individuals like my husband. The crowds at their meetings were "grass-roots" gatherings: they sprang up spontaneously throughout the country.

Briefly, the purpose of the America First Committee was to keep America out of the war in Europe, to urge a negotiated peace, which it was hoped could avoid the continued destruction of Europe and allow Britain to keep its navy and its empire, and to permit Germany free economic control of western Europe. To a large extent, the movement was conservative, traditionalist, and Middle Western, but not primarily pacifist, despite the inclusion of pacifist groups. The committee's platform was not anti-defense, anti-British, anti-Semitic, or anti–Aid to Britain, although inevitably at times it attracted followers who held some of these views. The members of America First were not necessarily opposed to the New Deal. Stuart supported President Roosevelt's New Deal program, for example, as did many left-wing liberals, inside and outside of the committee, among them John T. Flynn, Senator Burton K. Wheeler, Norman Thomas, and Robert and Philip La Follette. "Rather than enter the war, committee spokesmen declared that the U.S. should perfect its own democracy and solve its own domestic problems."[11]

Perhaps education was the most important function of America First, and consequently the most vital issue brought up in its short career (1940–41) was that of protecting representative government. Isolationists took the stand that the American people, according to their constitutional government, should have the right to vote through their elected representatives on the question of declaring war or withholding from it.

There seems little doubt today that President Roosevelt, who was sincerely convinced that a British victory was essential for American security and welfare, pressed the people of the United States into participation in the war, and that he used every instrument at his hand to persuade them to that course. His tactics are readily admitted by his apologists, one of whom has explained: "Franklin Roosevelt repeatedly deceived the American people during the period before Pearl Harbor. . . . He was like the physician who must tell the patient lies for the patient's own good. . . . The country was overwhelmingly non-interventionist to the very day of Pearl Harbor, and an overt attempt to lead the people into war would have resulted in certain failure and an almost certain ousting of Roosevelt in 1940."[12]

Since "an overt attempt to lead the people into war" was politically inexpedient, a gradual approach was followed toward this ultimate aim. By "steps short of war" and a series of naval "incidents," Roosevelt was able to arouse and convert a reluctant public and Congress to force him into action. The culminating event which propelled us into war was, of course, the bombing of our fleet at Pearl Harbor by the Japanese. In the meantime, our own navy had been carrying on an undeclared war in the Atlantic for months beforehand, convoying British ships, with orders from our President to "search and destroy" and to "shoot on sight."[13]

Up to Pearl Harbor, "the Great Debate" continued with the arguments on both sides becoming more and more vehement, the language increasingly bitter. My diaries are full of passionate and indignant denials of the accusations hurled against my husband. Although I disagreed often with the emphasis he made in his speeches, I believed completely in his integrity. I was naïvely unprepared for the smear campaign which attacked him. Repeatedly words were torn out of context, main points were omitted, and public opinion was misled in order to make a distorted cartoon that suited the cause of the opposition. Guilt by association, by omission, by unfounded accusations, so cleverly developed later in the McCarthy era against the so-called Liberal Internationalist Establishment, was a relatively new weapon at the time.

Rereading the diaries almost forty years later, I am appalled at my innocence of politics and the violence of my indignation. Over the years I have gained some objectivity. I can see and admit my own mistakes and those of my husband. With hindsight, I can also see where his vision was clear and his prophecies correct. In my study of the historical accounts of the period, I have also come to feel much more understanding of the Administration's point of view and the difficult decisions it faced.

Reading these accounts I can well understand the Administration's misinterpretation—indeed, panic—on observing my husband's prewar role. Here was a man who could not be "bought." At the outset of the debate, the office of the Secretary of War offered him an especially created secretaryship for air if he would refrain from speaking in opposition to the United States entry into the war.[14] He refused. He was also a man who could not be intimidated. The Administration and the pro-war groups threw their heaviest abusive bombardment against him from their most gifted writers and speakers, ranging from Secretary Harold L. Ickes to President Roosevelt himself. F.D.R. derided him publicly as "a Copperhead" (see p. 179), to which charge Lindbergh responded by resigning his commission in the army. The F.B.I. tapped his phone, and the Administration tried to silence or dismiss from government positions friends who were thought to be writing his speeches. He wrote his own speeches and, to the dismay of friends and foes alike, took no one's advice. His "stubborn Swedish" character held fast. Disregarding all attacks, he continued to draw enormous and enthusiastic crowds whenever he appeared. Many of these crowds, much to his discomfiture, broke spontaneously into calls of "Our next President!"

The Roosevelt Administration and the pro-war groups were actually in an extremely critical position in 1940–41. The Democratic President was about to run for an unprecedented third term in office against Republican nominee Wendell L. Willkie. There was strong pressure within the Republican party to make Willkie the pro-peace candidate. Because of the solid anti-war sentiment in Congress, neither candidate would risk running on a pro-war ticket. F.D.R. felt himself obliged to strengthen his position in a campaign speech by repeating his hardly ingenuous promise to the American people: "Your sons are not going to be sent into any foreign wars." At this juncture, with Lindbergh speaking to cheering America First crowds, his was undoubtedly the strongest voice in the opposition to the President. If he could not be silenced, he had to be discredited.

I cannot believe that his most bitter critics were convinced by the absurd accusations leveled irresponsibly at him: the appellations of "traitor," "Nazi," "Fascist," "knight of the German Eagle," or the demands for his expatriation, and the assertions that he was already picked out as Hitler's "Gauleiter" for America (after conquest!). Certainly he must have seemed to the Administration not only an effective deterrent to the crusade against evil, but also a potential threat to the party's political power. With such crowds and applause and an apparent following, it was naturally assumed he was after political position and leadership. No one could believe that a man could take his stand out of personal conviction alone, unmoved by political ambition.

Implausible as it seems, this was the truth. Throughout his life, Charles Lindbergh consistently turned down all suggestions that he take part in political life. He seemed to know he was unfitted for such a role. Possibly the unhappy experiences of his father in politics during World War I had influenced him early against a similar career. The elder Lindbergh as Congressman from Minnesota had opposed World War I. Despite strong support from the farmer-oriented Nonpartisan League, he was overcome by a wave of pro-war fever. He was run out of town, stoned, called a friend of the Kaiser, and was hanged in effigy. Undaunted by the criticism, he stood by his position until defeated for re-election in 1920.[15]

It is clear that the younger Lindbergh was not by nature a political leader. As a public figure, his appeal was emotional, but he always resented and denied that aspect of his personality. He bent over backwards to be rational and to persuade people to use their minds and not their emotions. He never wanted to be regarded as either a hero or a leader. Never did he wish to, or in fact did he, lead a movement—not America First, not any of the aviation organizations with which he worked, not the conservation groups among which he ended his career.

If only, I have often thought, he had been more of a politician, he would not have made the mistakes that trapped him in his prewar speeches. But if he was not a politician, why did he draw such crowds? Certainly not by his oratory. I have to agree with one of his critics, who ridiculed the "cold schoolmarm tone" of his wartime addresses. The Lindbergh speeches for the most part were logical and technical. He saw the war through the lens of aviation, and justifiably believed aviation was probably the decisive element in its outcome. His anti-war stand was in part, I believe, a last expression of his early faith in the invincibility of aviation. Even here he was not emotional but factual. His Fort Wayne speech in the fall of 1941 reveals his approach as a speaker:

"In making these addresses, I have no motive in mind other than the welfare of my country and my civilization. This is not a life that I enjoy. Speaking is not my vocation, and political life is not my ambition. . . . I am moved by no personal interest or animosity. I do not speak out of hate for any individuals or any people. But neither have I tried to avoid facts in order to have my speeches politically popular. I have tried, and I shall continue to try, as long as it is possible, to give you the truth without prejudice and without passion."

What a platform from which to appeal to the crowds in an impassioned wartime debate! He refused to stoop to demagoguery or rabble-rousing, and was astonished when some of his "factual statements" were seen in that light. It was not his "message"—essentially differing little from that of other isolationists—that drew the crowds. It was certainly not his oratory, not his facts and logic. I believe it was something far less tangible. Lindbergh struck a chord precisely because he was not a party supporter, because he was obviously not a politician. Audiences cheered not so much his message as his honesty; not so much his words as his character. His integrity, however often openly and constantly attacked, was never questioned by most people in the country, even if some thought him in error. A Gallup poll conducted on Lindbergh in May, 1941 (almost at the end of the debate), shows that "approximately two-thirds of the voters interviewed, who are familiar with Lindbergh's views on foreign policy, disagree with these views . . . virtually none of the voters interviewed questioned his sincerity or his right to speak."[16]

My husband did not have the advantage of hindsight open to historians of today. The full horrors of the Nazi crimes were not generally known to the world at the time he gave his anti-war speeches, and the appalling details were revealed only at the end of the war.[17] Without doubt he was overly pessimistic about a British victory. He did not know that the British had cracked the German secret code ("Ultra") soon after the onset of hostilities, nor did he know about their discovery and use of radar. Neither he nor others closer to the scene could know beforehand that Hitler's invasion of Russia would bring the U.S.S.R. to the Allied side in 1941. He overestimated the psychological effect of air bombing (not the technical), and he underestimated the morale of the British when under attack and the miraculous courage and brilliance of the British air force in defense. He was not wrong on his estimate of German air power and production,[18] nor was he wrong in foreseeing that the U.S.S.R. would emerge from the war with the greatest territorial gains in Europe.

Lindbergh's isolationist stand and that of most of the isolationist speakers, as Wayne Cole has fairly analyzed,[19] was backward-looking to a younger and pioneering America whose image was self-reliant and self-sufficient. The Lindbergh speeches are full of the character, the stories, and the cadence of the old West. Although their factual content rests firmly on "the capabilities, limitations and consequences" of the air power of his day, the emotional thrust and language are those of his father and grandfather. One recognizes the rhetorical tone of those hardy immigrants who had left Europe behind them for the "new world of the West"; the America with an "independent destiny" which would not be "forever entangled in these endless wars of Europe." Lindbergh had his ancestors' staunch belief in our representative government, an issue that he felt was "even more fundamental than war itself."[20] He was quick to perceive that the powers of Congress were being abrogated and the people of America led into an undeclared war, without the opportunity to voice their decision.

The explosive issue of a President's right to wage an undeclared war has pursued and haunted us through five administrations. The parallel with Korea and Vietnam is fresh in our memory. The cries of "the Imperial Presidency" still echo in our ears.

Lash expanded on this subject in a chapter called "Undeclared War in the Atlantic": ". . . after a generation of presidential wars it is possible to see that, in the hands of Roosevelt's successors, the powers that he wielded as commander in chief to deploy the army, navy, and air force as he deemed necessary . . . in distant waters and skies . . . led the nation into the Vietnamese quagmire." Quoting Senator J. William Fulbright, he concluded: "The fact that Roosevelt and Truman . . . were substantially right in their assessment of the national interest in no way diminishes the blamefulness of the precedents they set. F.D.R.'s deviousness in a good cause made it much easier for LBJ to practice the same kind of deviousness in a bad cause."[21]

World War II, ending with Hiroshima and Nagasaki, marked a watershed in our history. Some of the inevitable consequences of the war were those Charles Lindbergh foresaw and about which he tried to warn his countrymen.

My diaries and letters are not entirely taken up with the prewar fight in the United States, which covers a bare two years' time in this five-year story. After Pearl Harbor, Lindbergh immediately stopped public speaking. He made only one public statement: "Now it [war] has come and we must meet it as united Americans regardless of our attitude in the past toward the policy our government has followed. . . . We must now turn every effort to building the greatest and most efficient Army, Navy, and Air Force in the world. . . ."[22]

He tried to follow this advice personally, offering his services to the air force. He was turned down by the Administration. Secretary of the Navy Frank Knox suggested that he "would offer Lindbergh an opportunity to enlist as an air cadet, like anybody else would have to do." Secretary Ickes advised Roosevelt that Lindbergh's actions were "coldly calculated with a view to attaining ultimate power for himself" and called him a "ruthless and conscious fascist." Roosevelt agreed. The New York *Times,* although critical of Lindbergh's stand, broad-mindedly took an opposite view and thought his offer should be accepted. His attempts to help the aviation industry were also rejected because of Administration pressure on companies that had government contracts.[23]

In 1942, he was, however, asked to be a technical consultant to the Ford Motor Company for the mass production of war planes at the Willow Run bomber plant in Dearborn, Michigan. The Ford production was too indispensable to the war effort for the Administration to object. (This job brought about our move to the suburbs of Detroit.) On his own initiative, Lindbergh became the equivalent of an air cadet. In his *Wartime Journals* he wrote, "In a sense, I am learning to fly all over again here at Willow Run." He was coached in the techniques of the most advanced war fighters, which he ended up flight-testing. In addition, he explored a new and then unknown and dangerous field by studying the effects of high-altitude flying with Dr. Walter M. Boothby at the Mayo Clinic's Aeromedical Unit in Minnesota. He spent two weeks in the clinic, becoming himself a "guinea pig" in an altitude chamber to test the effects of loss of oxygen. Owing to his experiments, he was able to develop better equipment for emergency parachute jumps at high altitude.[24]

In 1944 he was asked by the Chance Vought Division of United Aircraft to inspect the Pacific war areas as a civilian adviser and observer of the planes he had been testing. During this mission he developed fuel-conservation techniques to increase the range of the P-38 fighter plane by hundreds of miles. While on his tour of duty, although technically an observer and by regulations overage, he flew with marine and air force squadrons, completing fifty combat missions. After his death one of the pilots in his group wrote of him, "As an observer he didn't have to fly with us, but he came. He shared the discomforts of life in camp and the strains of combat. There was never an occasion when he was not one of us."[25]

This volume ends with my husband's return to the United

States after his tour of duty, but the story is unfinished. Immediately after Germany's surrender on May 7, 1945, he was sent on a naval technical mission to Europe and was driven to Nordhausen, the German underground factory for V-1 and V-2 rockets. Nearby he saw Camp Dora, an ex-German prison camp, whose inmates were used as forced labor in the factory. Some of the barracks were still occupied by Poles, Russians, and Czechs. It was here that he faced for the first time the horrifying remains of the Nazi death factories, about which he then wrote in his *Wartime Journals:* "Here was a place where men and life and death had reached the lowest form of degradation. How could any reward in national progress even faintly justify the establishment and operation of such a place? When the value of life and dignity of death are removed, what is left for man? . . . It seemed impossible that men—civilized men—could degenerate to such a level."[26]

I started this volume in order to leave a record as I saw it of the period my husband and I lived through in the prewar years. I wanted to show the unwritten side of his *Wartime Journals,* to say the things he could never say. By looking at the inner side of a tapestry, one can often uncover patterns and colors that reveal a complexity and meaning invisible on the surface. I find, in the end, I have revealed, not an annotated record of those years, but simply an intensely personal story of two individuals: a complex man and his struggle to follow what his background, his character and integrity demanded; and a complex woman of quite a different background, who must reconcile her divided loyalties in a time of stress. It is not so much history or a factual wartime record as it is simply a personal story. It is, I realize, more personal, more open, and more vulnerable, and, because of this, ultimately more honest than any of the preceding four volumes.

This collection of five volumes in a sense has come full circle. The complete story takes us through turbulent years: fame, romance, and popularity in *Bring Me a Unicorn;* adventure, crime, sorrow, and the sympathy of the world in *Hour of Gold,*

Hour of Lead; a beginning again of a flying career in a wider world in *Locked Rooms and Open Doors;* in *The Flower and the Nettle,* our self-imposed exile in Europe and coming to grips with world problems; and in this final volume our combined and differing attitudes to these crises and, in the process, facing and enduring criticism, rejection, and calumny.

The story gives a dramatic example of a familiar American cycle of an individual's reputation passing from the heights of adulation to the depths of contempt and ostracism. In this country we seem to enjoy, as a child playing with blocks, building up our heroes overnight, only to knock them down again almost as quickly. It is a recurrent theme in American mores and manners, present to this day. We worship success but tend to resent the successful. One suspects that our egalitarian ideal both inspires and troubles us.

For my husband, the cycle turned again swiftly. Even before his war record was known to the general public, his services to his country were sufficiently recognized by the military to bring him an assignment to Europe immediately after V-E Day. Returning home, he took part in the postwar reorganization of the Strategic Air Command. As special consultant to the Secretary of the Air Force, he inspected air force units and facilities around the world. He was trusted to serve on the distinguished committee headed by John von Neumann which advised the air force and the Secretary of Defense on the top-priority development of long-range ballistic missiles. In 1954 President Eisenhower restored his military standing, raising him to the rank of brigadier general in the Air Force Reserve.

Looking back on his life today, one sees that his vision was not intrinsically isolationist. His global point of view in later postwar years proves the opposite. In the 1960's and 70's he had no reluctance in working with British, French, Spanish, Russian, Japanese, African, and other nationalities on the protection of endangered wildlife. He was one of the first to realize that one cannot be an "isolationist" in the preservation of our planet.

The story of these five volumes comes full circle on another level, in this last volume, in a more personal way. It is the story of a marriage. One might say it returns to a love story, not in the sense of the romance of *Bring Me a Unicorn,* but as a picture of a marriage which weathered the differences and difficulties and survived whole and fruitful. One of my letters written at the time, to my husband in the Pacific (copying a letter written in another age about another marriage) expresses it all.

"How are the waters of the world sweet—if we should die, we have drunk them. If we should sin—or separate—if we should fail or secede—we have tasted of happiness—we must be written in the book of the blessed."[27]

[1] Bruce L. Larson, *Lindbergh of Minnesota* (New York: Harcourt Brace Jovanovich, 1973).

[2] *Air Intelligence Activities,* Office of the Military Attaché, American Embassy, Berlin, Germany, August, 1935–April, 1939, pp. 19–26.

[3] Lt. Col. Raymond H. Fredette, USAF (Ret.), "Lindbergh and Munich: A Myth Revived," *Missouri Historical Society Bulletin,* April, 1977.

[4] H. H. Arnold, *Global Mission* (New York: Harper & Brothers, 1949), pp. 187–89.

[5] *The Wartime Journals of Charles A. Lindbergh* (New York: Harcourt Brace Jovanovich, 1970), p. 184.

[6] *Ibid.,* p. 254.

[7] Bruce M. Russett, *No Clear and Present Danger* (New York: Harper & Row, 1972), p. 12.

[8] Joseph P. Lash, *Roosevelt and Churchill, 1939–1941* (New York: W. W. Norton, 1976), pp. 242–43.

[9] Manfred Jonas, *Isolationism in America, 1935–1941* (Ithaca and London: Cornell University Press, 1966), p. viii.

[10] Walter Lippmann, *Isolation and Alliances* (Boston: Little, Brown, 1952), pp. 10, 11.

[11] Wayne S. Cole, *America First: The Battle Against Intervention, 1940–41* (New York: Octagon Books, 1971), p. 39.

[12] Thomas A. Bailey, *The Man in the Street* (New York: Macmillan, 1948), pp. 11–13, quoted by W. H. Chamberlin in *America's Second Crusade* (Chicago: Henry Regnery, 1950).

[13] See text, pp. 208 and 221.

[14] Lindbergh, *Wartime Journals*, p. 257.

[15] Larson, *Lindbergh of Minnesota*.

[16] New York *Times*, May 20, 1941.

[17] Russett, *No Clear and Present Danger*, p. 42.

[18] Fredette, "Lindbergh and Munich."

[19] Wayne S. Cole, "Charles A. Lindbergh and the Battle Against Intervention," Symposium, National Air and Space Museum, May 20, 1977.

[20] Quotations from Charles A. Lindbergh's wartime addresses.

[21] Lash, *Roosevelt and Churchill*, p. 421.

[22] Wayne S. Cole, *Charles A. Lindbergh and the Battle Against American Intervention in World War II* (New York: Harcourt Brace Jovanovich, 1974), p. 209.

[23] *Ibid.*, pp. 213–17.

[24] Lindbergh, *Wartime Journals*, pp. 720–30.

[25] Letter to A. M. L.

[26] Lindbergh, *Wartime Journals*, pp. 995–96.

[27] *John Jay Chapman and His Letters*, M. A. De Wolfe Howe, ed. (Boston: Houghton Mifflin, 1937), p. 87.

1939

When this diary starts, I and my two children are on the boat in New York harbor, returning from our self-imposed exile in Europe. I knew my husband was glad to be back serving his country in its defense preparedness, a role for which he was well fitted after his two-year investigation of military installations in Europe.

I, too, was happy to be back in the United States after the years abroad. There was much to look forward to: seeing my mother, my younger sister, Constance, my brother, Dwight, my sister-in-law, Margot Loines Morrow, all of whom were living at that time in the family home, Next Day Hill, in Englewood, New Jersey. I was eager to have them see my toddler son, Land, who had been born in England. I was anxious for my seven-year-old son, Jon, to find his place in American schools and friendships. I wanted to discover my own roots again in family, friends, and the dearly loved landscapes of my own country.

There were readjustments, too, in returning to America. My husband had sent a note to the boat warning me of the pressures from newspapers and photographers we would face on our arrival at the dock. From such pressures we had been free during our two years of private life in England and France. We were also aware of having left behind us the mounting tensions of an impending war crisis in Europe. Many of our French and English friends were living under unbearable suspense and danger. America seemed appallingly unaware of trouble and astonishingly carefree. People brushed aside the possibility of imminent war. It was the year of the New York World's Fair. "The World of Tomorrow" bloomed exuberantly that summer with its towering trylon and bulbous perisphere in Flushing Meadow. Although a returning pilgrim to the New World, I felt myself also an exile from the Old and missed many of its aspects I had learned to love. I had a stake in both worlds, I realized, which would heighten the conflicts I was to face in the coming crisis.

Friday, April 28th [*On the* Champlain]

Wake at 4:30 or 5, to find us coming quietly up the river. It is cold, overcast, and drizzly. Breakfast in our rooms because there are already strangers and press men on board.

Before we are through, the Immigration officer comes on and does our papers right there (very nice man, and nice of him and the French Line to arrange it). Also the customs man. I give up the keys and tell him about the dutiable things. They want us to get off quickly. Hurry the children into their things, hats pulled down over eyes, out quickly. Policemen, flash bulbs, quickly into Burke's [the chauffeur's] car and we rush out of the dock, police sirens shrieking ahead of us. It is rather breathless and I don't feel very comfortable. But at least it was swift and I don't think much picturing of the children.

Englewood, with flowering trees, magnolia and forsythia and daffodils—a month behind Paris. And *huge* robins!

Mother and Margot at the door. Mother with a cane (her knee), looking rather tired. Margot slim and pretty.

C. in bed tousled and tired, asleep after driving up from Washington last night. He is very happy and full of life and his new job.[1] It is wonderful to see him like that—absorbed, active, putting his energy into something successfully. (Although it always amazes me how happy he is "inactive"—or supposedly inactive—as in Paris. He has the most extraordinary resources, like writing his life in Paris this winter, or studying mathematics or history or science.)

The day goes in a kind of tired daze. Settling the children in the new wing. Seeing the house—full of flowers, magazines,

[1] See Introduction, pp. xvi–xvii.

comforts, luxuries, and steam heat, in a rather overpowering way; Margot's baby (Stephen Morrow) eager and active and responsive; talking to Mother.

In to the hospital to see Con[1] and her tiny little girl (Saran Niel Morgan). Dark little kitten with a dreamy intensity in her mouth. Con, so young and natural and matter-of-fact, but so calm and happy, released and relaxed, surrounded by flowers.

Saturday, April 29th

Wake up still very cold-y and with a headache. I feel terribly overstimulated here, as though my head would burst.

The dogs arrive—Thor quite thin but well and galloping around us; Skean alert and not too fat, rather gray about the face. The red collars I bought for them in France fit quite well and are gay and nice.

Curious how the weight of war drops from your shoulders in America. I no longer think of bombers when I hear airplanes in the sky. Nor are the small details in the newspapers so vital now that I am not in Paris, wondering whether to move the children to Brittany or not.

I feel on the whole rather shocked by the material shell of America, the impact of it as you first land. The speed, the brightness, the flash and advertisement. Nothing solid or real or quiet (at least in New York). I feel outcast by it and a stranger. I know I shall get accustomed to it, get acclimated. But I don't somehow (sneakingly) *want* to. I want to hang on to France, the maturity of life there, the sense of tasting and touching and relishing life as it goes by. Here you can't. It goes by too fast. And yet, I don't want to be one of those strange homeless creatures—"a Henry James American."

The *Expression* of America seems so false. The good part of America does not seem to find any expression. I see only false high-pressuring newspapers and magazines, flashy and cheap;

[1] Constance Morrow Morgan, A. M. L.'s sister, married to Aubrey Niel Morgan, first married to her sister Elisabeth, who died in 1934.

racy and material advertising; sex-appeal movies; blustering politicians. I want to find the America I dream of when abroad.

Monday, May 1st

Take Jon to the Little School.[1]

Connie tells me that she is delighted with Jon. That he read out of a primer he never saw before and shows real understanding of reading and that I am a splendid teacher! I am really pleased that all my tutoring work last fall at Illiec was not in vain.

Tuesday, May 2nd

Dinner in town with the Millers and Carrels.[2] We talk about how New York strikes us—so loud and fast and flashing—and the *richness* of it. "You keep thinking it's all a façade," as Mrs. M. said, "but the same show is going on every day!"

The Carrels come in. She, warm and sympathetic. He, bright, sparkling, and quick. He is pleased that C. has this job, says it is a very good thing (counteracting the bad publicity). I wish he would not stress this side. I am so full of C. being happy in *useful action*. I hate to see it put in another light. He tells me how bad the feeling, the papers, etc. were against him. I said: I know. But I do not argue, because Dr. Carrel makes all argument impossible. He does not say mildly or sympathetically: "I think you don't understand" or "I think you are mistaken." It is always: "No, you are quite wrong about that," and there is nothing more to say unless you get angry and say the "Pardon-me-sir-but-my-opinion-is" sort of thing.

Downstairs they talk politics. They are all gloomy. Mrs. Miller

[1] A nursery and elementary school started in Englewood by Elisabeth Morrow Morgan some years earlier and continued, after her death, by her friend and associate Constance Chilton (Connie).

[2] Harlan Miller, formerly of the U.S. Embassy in Paris, and his wife, Harriet; Paris friends of the Lindberghs. Dr. and Mme Alexis Carrel; Dr. Carrel, French Nobel Prize winner, scientist, and author, with Charles Lindbergh, of *The Culture of Organs*. Both were close friends of the Lindberghs. See also *The Flower and the Nettle*.

says Hitler's speech is the speech of a madman. Harlan Miller says it is all untrue, "practically all of it."

Dr. Carrel is convinced that Hitler will turn on France, take back Alsace-Lorraine. ("Just because he says he won't," Mme C. adds.)

"At the time of the [first] war," says Dr. C. gloomily, "I predicted that the struggle would last at least fifty years."

"Yes," said Mme C. from across the table, "yes, you did. . . ."

"Perhaps more," adds Dr. C. ominously.

"Another One Hundred Years' War."

They also all fall on me when I broach our plans of getting a place near Washington for the summer. They say it is *impossible* to take the children there.

Wednesday, May 3rd

Almost didn't catch the train [for Washington] at Pennsylvania Station. I feel suddenly that it is all terribly foreign to me and that I would feel less strange on a French train.

Going down on the train I think: If the adjustment after a year, or even three years, is upsetting to me, think what it may be to Jon, after a childhood spent in England and France. Is it fair to give him this rootless impermanent feeling of where do I belong? whose child am I? what people are mine? And yet, what else can we do?

I am won by the light-hearted friendliness of people—conductors, porters, travelers. How free they are, and young. "Youth is life as yet untouched by tragedy," yet we have had the Civil War, the Great War.

And the light effects are very beautiful in America, so clearcut, so far, so bright.

Taxi to the Lands,[1] where C. is and where we have a very American supper—chicken, mashed potatoes, peas, hot rolls, asparagus, and strawberry shortcake.

In the morning I am seeing the girl who may be our secretary.

[1] Rear Admiral Emory Scott ("Jerry") Land, cousin of C. A. L., and his wife, Betty.

Thursday, May 4th

Headlines that Litvinov[1] has been pushed out by Stalin; no one knows what that means. Because the negotiations were going too slowly with England and France? Or does Stalin want a rapprochement with Berlin, as some of the rumors suggest?

See Christine Gawne at 9. She is very young, sweet, and intelligent, might come temporarily, too pretty to stay long. Betty Land and I go off and look at houses.

Tea with Betty and Jerry at their friends' the Merrills'. I get the impression from all the beautiful homes, expensively stone-built and luxuriously bathroomed, exquisitely landscaped, that Washington is full of "Nice People," all the same class, all well dressed, well gardened, well homed, busy and social. I am not sure that I like it. There is something insipid about it, too much pink ice cream.

America looks so rich—I can't get over it. I know it is poor, too, but what is poor looks less abnormal than the rich.

The evening papers full of tension again. There are evidently frantic efforts on the part of France and England to put pressure on Poland not to slam the door in Germany's face; and equally frantic efforts on the part of Mussolini to urge moderation on Germany. (Evidently they don't wish to be dragged into a war about Danzig.) I think it looks very bad.

C. is off at 4:30 to start a coast-to-coast survey. He packs his army uniforms.

Friday, May 5th

C. up in the middle of the night, so it seems, to leave.

Betty Land and I drive out to a place on a bluff among trees above the Potomac about nine miles from Washington. It is cool; a big roomy, careless, Victorian lived-in family house. It would be perfectly workable, though on the large side, but I feel more and more uncertain about uprooting and bringing the children here. If C. is away a lot, why not stay in Englewood? Where there is a pool and a tennis court and we would not have

[1] Maksim Maksimovich Litvinov, Russian Communist leader and diplomat, People's Commissar for Foreign Affairs since 1930.

to move all our things. Of course if C. is going to be there a lot, that is different.

Monday, May 15th

C. and I decide to leave the children in Englewood, where they are well and happy, get two rooms in Washington, I to ferry back and forth—and simply tread water about a house for a month.

Feel much relieved. As C. says, we have moved or tried to move (gone through the business of looking for houses) four times since last May. Perhaps it is better to take the line of least resistance at this point and stay where we are.

Englewood, Monday, May 22nd

It is strange how hard it is to live in Englewood. One keeps trying to justify oneself (for the big house, for the material-ness and comfort of life here) by having people out, by being busy, by trying to be sympathetic, do good deeds.

And it all tends to make life more and more material, more rushed, with less and less time for real talks or real thought.

Of course, there are too many of us—all with our own lives and problems, trying to fit them into one routine and one place.

The hours spent arranging what nights are free for whose guests and what cars will take who in to town, etc.!

Tuesday, May 23rd

Afternoon spent having a permanent. (This always makes me feel like renouncing the world and going into a nunnery. A spirit of angry and impotent rebellion sets in. Is it worth it? And yet I like to look nice and dress well.)

Home late. Nice quiet evening with Con, Aubrey, and Mother. Discuss [David Cecil's] *Lord Melbourne,* an enchanting book (which has "saved" this day for me). I read it while my hair was drying and it lifted me out of this cheap magazine-advertisement world I have been living in. It has quality, precision, and delight.

Wednesday, May 24th

The morning goes as usual, in plans. I do not know exactly why. It is a part of this Englewood circle. Con says that when we *do* get a "quiet" morning we spend it making plans to complicate *other* mornings.

I go up to Mother's room after I come back from school. Mother, naturally, has the threads of the day in her hands. How many people for lunch? Who is going in to town? Who will be here tonight? These questions must be answered. We as a family all want to be together, have meals together, and trying to do this complicates things.

Then come the questions about guests. When can I ask the Vaillants,[1] the Stevenses,[2] the Lin Yutangs[3]? The Vaillants will not want to come unless C. is here, or the Lin Yutangs. Also I want Mother and Aubrey here for them. The complications appear so great that it seems better to have no guests or friends.

Sunday, May 28th

I call Mrs. Platt, on Long Island. The "lovely house" Thelma[4] saw is still unrented. I plan to see it Tuesday. Feel we must have a place of our own.

The Lin Yutangs out for dinner, a little shy at first. Then conversation goes from China and the war and politics, somehow, to concubines! C. with his tongue in his cheek, Lin Yutang very earnest, Dwight and Aubrey amused and eager listeners.

[1] George Vaillant, then associate curator of Mexican archaeology at the American Museum of Natural History, author of *Aztecs of Mexico,* and his wife, Susanna, old family friends.

[2] Laura Stevens, friend and roommate of A. M. L. at college, and her husband, George, a writer and editor.

[3] Chinese-American writer, author of *The Importance of Living,* and his wife.

[4] Thelma Crawford [Mrs. Brooke] Lee, friend of A. M. L. and E. R. M. M., who lived in Washington and, in the summer, on Long Island.

But, as Aubrey remarked, a strange lack of animation on the faces of all the women!

Lin Yutang's thesis was: If a marriage is unhappy, there is no real solution, but in China concubinage is a better solution than divorce.

He also translates the Chinese screen in the Mexican library. It portrays some writers, philosophers, artists who are taking tea and discussing together, and how rare such discussion is in such beautiful surroundings, far from the turmoil of business and material life.

It was a very nice evening and Mother really did enjoy it. I was happy about it and felt that there, at least, we were giving her something.

Tuesday, May 30th, Decoration Day

C. and I to Syosset, both very happy and holiday-feeling to go off together. He starts planning how he could quite well base on Long Island, use Mitchel Field. I say: Wait; you haven't seen the house yet. It may be awful.

Mrs. Platt meets us at a country station. She is very natural and I like her. We drive quite a long way, reach the Sound, hazy with heat and blue into the distance. Lovely sounds of horns and bell buoys, and the smell of the sea. Lloyd Neck. Into a kind of private property. "There is the house, up there." I take a breath and expect not to like it. But I do. It is not too big, white clapboard, freshly painted, and when you walk in you see right through the hall and out the door over a terrace, a lawn, down a slope to the Sound.

It is nicely furnished and all brand-new and clean—summer rugs, cool, and space. We see the beach and the garage down the hill (where I can work). I begin to people the rooms—Jon here, the baby, Christine, C.'s office. But it is chiefly the high cool perch of the house and that view through two big shady oak trees down to the sea below you.

C. and I drive back happy, decide we must take it. He says it is entirely my find and he would never have looked at it if I hadn't pressed it, and yet it is perfect and will do for us very well.

It is another example of one's solution coming to you from another angle than you expected—not conforming to preconceived plans but to one's plans having to conform to it because it is lovely and right.

Sunday, June 4th

Auntie Paul[1] and the Allan Dawsons[2] here for lunch. (What a combination!) Allan is very interesting on Germany (just back from two years in Hamburg), but one can't listen to him because at least two people at the table are not content just to listen, but feel they must assert their personality: Auntie Paul, who chats in a high voice with no knowledge but a superficial average newspaper one and asks questions just to ask questions, and Allan's wife, who interrupts and contradicts Allan and carries on a private conversation on the same subject with C.

C. is seated between these two women and, I can see, is driven nearly crazy. Finally he just blatantly and rudely listens to Allan across the table.

Con and I talk to Mother on finances. It is difficult because she hates to discuss it (like me).

After we get through I talk to her about writing her life. She makes all kinds of objections but I think would like to do it really (if only she felt she could) and is pleased. (She said about an old friend's funeral: "There is no consolation for loss, except the realization that one has had a rich life.")

Poor Mother. She gives and gives and is still hungry inside, terribly sad and hungry—ever since Daddy's death, and Elisabeth's, of course. She unconsciously, I think, fills up their loss with all these other things, but I don't think it can be done. A really *personally* creative thing like writing might help.

Monday, June 5th

C. leaves early; I take the children to school. The morning goes in details. All mornings here do. It is what C. complains of.

[1] Pauline Dillingham, cousin of E. C. M.

[2] Allan Dawson, Third Secretary at the U.S. Embassy in Mexico City under D. W. M.

Refusing invitations, writing notes (and I write so few, only the ones that must be written). I sit in the sun and go over the inventories. Margot sits with me, later. She and Dwight are going on the cruise,[1] after all the indecision.

Rest in the afternoon after going over the attic for blankets, sheets, linen, etc. for the new house and finding some things for the children. I am depressed by the burden of *things* in this house—so cluttered, heaped, stifled with *things*. I wish sometimes all mine would burn up.

I have done no writing, and can't (this is the frustrating thing) until we are in our own house on Long Island.

Tuesday, June 6th

Dwight and I alone for supper. He quite restless and anxious to go out. So we drive to the [World's] Fair, go round in a bus, eat hot dogs and crêpes suzettes (D. the hot dogs and I the crêpes) and then drive home. It was quite gay and fun—the kind of thing that is nice to do with D.

Coming home I see a man and a girl walking up Madison Avenue—walking home after the theater or a movie, probably. I am struck by them. They are very nice looking. But what makes you look at them is their jaunty, casual, completely assured little walk. They are obviously in love and oblivious of the outside world, but not tensely so. They are happy, though it is not the happiness of ecstasy, but, rather, the happiness of security, familiarity, understanding, and ease. *Security*—that was what struck you about them. It was late. There was hardly anyone else on the street, but they were not hurrying—arm in arm, their heels sounding on the pavement rhythmically, his casual gray felt hat tipped forward a little, her silk pleated skirt swinging slightly, not talking, not laughing, not looking at each other. Self-absorbed, they sauntered on into the darkness of a spring evening, as though keeping time to a tune in their minds.

[1] A six-month cruise planned by Dr. Samuel Eliot Morison, historian, to follow routes of Columbus.

And I, feeling alone, turning my head to watch them as I passed, felt a pang of envy.

Wednesday, June 7th

A nice day—at home all day. Take the children to school. (Land always sings on the way down.) A walk with the dogs. The big pink poppies are out, making me long for Long Barn.

At night, M. Monnet[1] and Copley Amory[2] come for dinner. We eat outside, in the growing dusk.

I enjoy very much talking to Jean Monnet, about the world of tolerance we are leaving, about how everyone is labeled today. (He thinks the tendency so dangerous and insidious—as I do—that it is one of the factors that make war inevitable.) I always enjoy him. He pulls me up to the best kind of thinking and talking. One can't be careless or lazy or undiscriminating, and when you take the trouble to be the best you are, you are sure of being met with his wise, acute, civilized understanding. And I *love* his humor, which comes from understanding, wisdom, and a kindly but *somewhat* disillusioned observation.

I enjoy Copley, too, though I always feel he is talking to me and looking at me through very very thick-lensed glasses. The conversation is filtered through lenses, too.

This has been a rich day, though I haven't "done" much. Full of sun and leisure and out-of-doors and children, quickened at the end by the spark of human contact (intellectual understanding).

Saturday, June 10th

Jon and I watch all afternoon for C.'s plane. One goes by about 7. Jon calls for me to see it. "It looked like Father's plane—the wings slanted up."

Shortly after, C. drives in. (It was not his plane.) C. very happy in his work and happy about the summer.

---

[1] Jean Monnet, French political economist; worked with D. W. M. on the Allied Maritime Shipping Council; later responsible for the Monnet Plan and the European Common Market.

[2] Member of the U.S. diplomatic corps, 1920–29.

Sunday, June 11th

Jon proudly shows C. that he can swim alone. He starts out by swimming a few yards around the edge of the pool, but before we leave he is swimming to C. in the center of the pool. He also "dives" in, falling headfirst into the water after C. When he comes up he is not quite sure whether it was nice or not. So I say quickly (while he is still drowned-rat-like, streaming hair over eyes), "Now you are really grown up. You can swim and you can dive. You'll be able to play by the pool by yourself." And his face breaks into a smile and he promptly "dives" in again and again! C. is terribly pleased. It is like Land learning to walk, suddenly walking out of the room.

Decide to go up to West Point to see C. off. Take Con and Aubrey along. C. is pleased to show us the plane, which is very beautiful—a silver-winged fish; he dives over us and then climbs effortlessly into the sky and out of sight in no time. I get a thrill from it.

Thursday, June 22nd, "At 33" [A. M. L.'s birthday]

After an hour or two of frantic packing and loading, off for Long Island, stopping for the two maids at Mrs. James Roosevelt, Jr.'s. They are thrilled to come out to the country.

Then a day of unloading. But the house looks lovely—all the changes made, and the little study sweet, clean, and painted. Christine takes the cook shopping while I unpack, get things settled.

Back late but happy to Englewood.

Mother and I have a peaceful evening alone.

Friday, June 23rd

Up early. Jon into my room. It is raining and he is very disappointed. I tell him, "Rain before seven, clear before eleven." It pleases him, not only the thought but also the sound of it. I can see he feels it is an incantation. And soon the sky lightens.

Last packing. Finally we are off—Christine driving Land

and Soeur Lisi[1] and a load of things, and I taking Jon with me on the front seat, and the dogs behind.

When we get to Lloyd Neck the dogs leap out. The maids are there and lunch is good. Land and the dogs take to the place as though it belonged to them, but Jon is still new and excited. "It isn't like Illiec," he says, with some homesickness.

After a restless nap he finds a cherry tree he can climb, while I unpack. Then we go swimming—which he loves and does fearlessly—with a raft.

A terrific storm comes over the bay, white and blind with rain and the trees tortured and twisting. People run to shut windows, and there is the sound of sheets of water. The evening is misty and cool. The tall trees drip a summer mist; the bay is satin smooth and full of light.

Soeur Lisi and I eat outside and then I sit in peace, hearing Jon murmuring, "Rain before seven—clear before eleven," over and over. The bell buoy is chiming and some sheep baaing. I cannot work, read, unpack, or write, but just sit in peace, relaxed, and pray I can keep this place as peaceful as it seems to me tonight for C., and that I can accomplish something here.

June 24th

Morning spent on ordering meals, getting room ready for Mother.

When I get back from taking Soeur Lisi to the station—it is her day off—C. is there, just arrived in an army car from Mitchel Field. Also, almost immediately, Mother and a load of pictures (I wanted to have them all up for C.), tables, etc.

We have a very good lunch. C. is in fine form. Put the children to bed after lunch. We take a swim after they wake, Land sitting with Mother throwing shells. C. and Jon, a tall figure and a small one but both lean, going in shorts up the beach side by side, with the air-float. They swim out together. C. is very pleased with Jon's progress.

Later C. goes into town for supper with Carrel. Mother and I have supper alone on the porch.

[1] A Swiss nurse brought from Paris.

Monday, June 26th

Write letters in my room. C. says, "Third morning gone on letters!" He feels letters are a waste of time. At least, spending so much time on them, as I do!

C. has bought a *very good* radio-Victrola and the Ninth Symphony for me! He is sweet and pleased about his purchases. Also a good oil-painting box and a book on the techniques of oil painting—which he persists in thinking I can do, for some reason.

Thursday, July 6th

After their rest (I rest, too) I take the children over to Mrs. Wood.[1] She is a nice brown, lean, twinkly person, kind and good. She takes us to the beach, where I meet the "young marrieds" who live on her place: May Swords Hoppin (I knew her at Miss Chapin's School), Evelyn Ames, and a Mrs. Potts— all nice, with young children of Jon's and Land's age. I am very pleased. I practically throw my arms around M. S., who has vastly improved in looks and dress (I wonder if she feels the same about me!), for the sake of her three little boys, who can play with Jon and Land, and her French governess, who will talk to Soeur Lisi. Land up the big slide by himself, with glee!

Saturday, July 8th

Take Soeur Lisi and children to Mrs. Wood's beach to introduce them to the group. Better to do it now, before C. comes back, when I shall be busy.

Back to the house, very satisfied with the afternoon.

Jon just gets to bed when a car drives up. I wonder who it is —and C., in uniform, gets out! Jon, lifting up his shade and peering out, says *momentously* in a loud child's voice that echoes down the drive, "Mother, *Father* has arrived!"

---

[1] Mrs. Willis Wood, neighbor, old-time resident and owner of much of the property on Lloyd Neck, friend of the Morrows.

Sunday, July 16th

Work mornings in the garage (I sink into its quiet—another world, another time, other people). Swim at the beach. A big raft has been washed ashore, big enough to stand on and dive off—great excitement for Jon.

Margot and Dwight arrive for lunch. Various people telephone—feeling of pressure immediately—very nice people, but when you want *no one* else, *anyone* else gives you claustrophobia. Just what I want to protect C. from.

Tell Jon, "Mr. Newton,[1] a friend of Father's, is coming for supper."

"So many friends," says Jon, a little wearily and confused. "Why are there too many friends today?"

I know just how he feels. Too many nice people in the world, sometimes.

We have a big cold supper, spread out by Mrs. McAvoy, a little wide-eyed with all the company. It is good, though, and goes well.

Newton is very American, that nice, open, alive, gay, and childlike quality—and *good*—pure and good. But *practical*, too, a rough-and-tumble independent American quality.

Thursday, July 20th

Soeur Lisi "off." I again get all my things on the porch to write at least in my diary while watching the children. But they fight or come up to me and talk and demand attention or get caught in the door, or have to go to the bathroom or have orange juice, and I do nothing. In desperation I order a wading pool over the telephone (not *expensive,* but extravagant, because, after all, they have the sea), thinking they can play in it on hot days instead of playing on *me!*

After supper—the children in bed—I am tired but satisfied, only hungry for something concentrated, not diverse and dis-

[1] James Newton, close friend of Dr. Carrel and the Lindberghs. See *The Flower and the Nettle.*

tracted. I start again on the letters.[1] I am absorbed by the warmth and richness of my relationship with Elisabeth, poured out recklessly and never to be recaptured. Many many letters back and forth. Also my letters to Con at the time C. first came out to see me—that swift horizon-cracking week. I am overcome with the romance of my own life, my own youth.

I cannot break myself away from it—stay up too late.

Saturday, July 22nd

Get Frank [a temporary hired man] to move a desk and chair up into a room for Mrs. Lindbergh's brother.[2] Jon catcalls to me to come, that "They're here!," excitedly. Mrs. L. and her brother in the hall, surrounded by Jon and Land.

The rest of the morning goes in the excitement. Everyone happy. Mrs. L. opens her suitcase on the front steps and lets Jon pull things out of it—all toys for Jon and Land. It is such fun to watch the children, especially Land, who is not used to toys, bending forward, his hands on his fat knees, incredulous delight on his rosy face at the Mickey Mouse mechanical toy turning over and over on the floor at his feet. (Handsprings.) In the end, though, there are two toys which win out. With Land a yellow canary which you wind up and it twitters; he likes to hold it in his hand and feel the vibrations. And for Jon a battleship and destroyer. When you shoot a small "rocket" at a mark on the battleship, the "rattrap" in the inside jumps up and the ship flies to pieces. Jon cannot be torn from this and does it steadily all morning.

Sunday, July 23rd

Nice talk with Mrs. L. before supper. Says she feels strange with women (especially in the East) and has no "woman's talk." I understand so well. Every person has her own brand of shyness.

[1] A. M. L. was considering a book of reminiscences of her sister Elisabeth.
[2] Charles H. Land, Jr., referred to as "B."

Tuesday, July 25th. Very hot and humid

After breakfast Mrs. L. and B. leave. I think they have had a happy time. They are both worried about its being too much trouble. Very sweet about it.

Also C. leaves, saying he will try to come back for dinner with the Davisons.[1]

At four I call Mrs. Davison. C. not coming, evidently. I must go alone.

Bathe and dress and drive to the Lloyd Smith dock, where the Davison speedboat meets me and slaps over the water in fifteen minutes to Peacock Point. Mrs. Davison meets me at the dock, sitting up very straight in an old-fashioned "electric," the only car she can drive. She is a grand person, of another era. She drives me around the place showing me what trees were lost in the hurricane, the garden, the new spraying system for the lawns. The garden was lush, fresh, and green as England (in the middle of this drought!). A large family and all its connections, all leisurely, all living about the mother-house. Children sprawling on the lawn with a new puppy. Security, plenty, ease.

A huge table in the dining room, white roses on the sideboard underneath the Gainsboroughs. Plenty to eat: oysters, chicken, tomato ring, pêche melba, wine. Sitting on the terrace afterwards in cushioned terrace furniture.

Then home in the cruising motorboat with Harry. (It is foggy and we cannot see the dock!)

I think the D.'s are a wonderful family. They are very American and have contributed a great deal to American life. The boys really have a sense of duty about public service (and so of course did the father and mother), and yet there was something terrifyingly secure about them—a calm island in the midst of rolling seas of trouble. I felt: How long can it last? The lush lawns in the midst of the drought are somehow typical.

---

[1] Mrs. Henry P. Davison and her family, old friends of the Morrows and partners in J. P. Morgan & Co.

Thursday, July 27th

Every morning Jon calls in to me, "Can I come in yet?" in a high eager voice. I turn over and say sleepily, "Yes, if you're *very* quiet." Then he leaps in in his blue pajamas: "How do you think I can make a net to catch oysters?" and then the questions start. But I am always fooled and let him come. When there is enough noise Land trots in, too, throwing his green *tortue* ahead of him and climbing on top of me.

Thursday, August 3rd

Work A.M. Depressed. I must find something to make me forget this, forget that I want another child. I have so much—C. and two such wonderful children. Early lunch and drive to town, meet C. on the road and change cars. Can't get mine started (C. has left). I call him from a house on the road. He comes and fixes it. How like C. this is—and my faith and dependence on him!

Friday, August 4th

C. hands me a letter and preface by Antoine de Saint-Exupéry[1] to my (French) edition of *Listen! the Wind*, just sent here. I start to read it through supper. The letter says that he had agreed to write a one-page preface before he had read the book but after reading it he had written nine pages, and here it was. I read haltingly; the French is very subtle and full of meaning. I am much absorbed, not only with the importance he attaches to the book and his analysis of it—which is intensely beautiful— but I am startled by what he has seen of me.

"Il est ainsi une petite fille qui court moins vite que les autres. Là-bas les autres jouent. 'Attendez-moi! Attendez-moi!' mais elle est un peu en retard, on va se lasser de l'attendre, on va la laisser en arrière, on va l'oublier seule au monde. Comment la rassurerait-on? Cette forme d'angoisse est inguérissable." ("There is a little girl who runs more slowly than the others. Over there

---

[1] French flier and writer; his *Wind, Sand and Stars* had just been published in America.

the others are playing. 'Wait for me! Wait for me!' Already she is late, they will get tired of waiting for her, they will leave her behind, she will be forgotten and left alone in the world. How can she be reassured? This kind of anguish is incurable.")

Did I so strip myself in that book? I had no idea that was there—or even in my life—that *"angoisse légère."* But it is, of course, that feeling of pressure (that C. tries to cure), inner pressure, that I have not learned to harness. "Chariots at the breast." But it has colored the book. It has crept out. I am rather upset. The note from the publisher says that he [Saint-Exupéry] would like to meet me. C. is going to call the hotel tomorrow. I am rather afraid to meet him.

I get down *Wind, Sand and Stars.* It is incredibly beautiful and gripping. It is all I ever wanted to say and more of flying and time and human relationships.

Saturday, August 5th

We call Saint-Exupéry. He is there, he speaks *"pas un mot"* of English. I have to talk to him. Heavens! What a prospect! Yes, he would be delighted to come out for dinner and the night. C. is going to pick him up in town. Then C. leaves for upper New York to see Miss Nute[1] on his father's life. Will pick St.-Ex. up on his way home.

I don't try to work, but read and try to figure out words in the preface I don't know.

At 3, in the middle of my nap, C. calls from upper New York, says he can't make it, and will *I* call for St.-Ex. And I had counted on that time to finish the book. Now *what* would I talk to him about?

The car is being fixed for flat tires. I tear into town, rather cross to be late—*"toujours un petit peu en retard!"* M. St.-Ex., they say, is in the bar. (Heavens, I think, he is one of those drunken aviators—*why* did we do this?) He appears, tall and stooped and a little bald, beginning to be not as young as he

[1] Dr. Grace Lee Nute, historian.

once was; an inscrutable sort of face, not at all good looking, almost Slavic in its solidity and inscrutability, and his eyes turn up at the corners a little.

Oh—it's *that* man, is it? I think, with a confused dream feeling that I have seen him often before—met him before, even. I recognize him immediately. (I must have seen him somewhere, perhaps in Paris.) I apologize for C. and my lateness and we go across to the car and start out. We hardly get around the block when the car stalls and will not start again. And all this time we are talking at top speed with a kind of intensity (at least on my part) that precludes any attention to practical details. He is talking about the book, how he had not read the first one, how he intended to write simply a polite page about flight or what the name stood for. How he read the book on the boat coming over, how it astonished him ("You know how rare it is to touch in a book . . ." he said), how he telegraphed the publisher that he must say something more. I was trying to talk back in French, always an effort, talk to a taxi driver who was pushing us, and explain what was wrong with the car in French and then in English, all at the same time.

"But perhaps you do not like the preface . . . ?"

"Ah oui—mais vous avez si bien vu . . . trop vu . . ."

I tell him how I tried to translate it for C. But it was difficult and subtle and how C. did not understand my being always *"un peu en retard."* He laughs and says he would have said it slightly differently—"a hesitancy. . . ."

Finally we pull up to a repair shop, where a group of taxi drivers decide that it is the pump and that it will take two hours to fix! I leave it, in Christine's name; we get into a taxi and start for Pennsylvania Station—still talking furiously. He talks about the rhythm in writing, which he thinks is almost the most important thing in a book—as I understand it. That only the *conscious* gets across in words, the unconscious in the rhythm.

I tell him how much we liked his books and wanted to meet him. How C. read his book and liked it, about his being a spectator and actor at the same time, and how the only other person I could remember having that combination was T. E. Lawrence.

He says he felt the separation between action and vision was less than people supposed—a theory I don't quite believe.

"But life itself is always pulling you away from the understanding of life," I say.

"Yes—that is always the trouble," he answers.

Then we were at Pennsylvania Station, I almost as much a stranger as he. We had an orangeade at a counter, still talking, like children on those high stools. (He can count in English, up to ten.)

"But how do you get on by yourself?"

"*Très bien* . . ." on the theory that when one cannot speak at all one meets on a different level—of human kindness and understanding—which is true. I felt gay, freed and happy. I and this absolute stranger who understood so well everything I said and felt!

Then, onto the train—a funny little train with basket seats. And we go on talking all the way to Huntington, in French, oblivious of the people around us who look askance at us, thinking we are two foreign visitors to the Fair.

It was very exciting. Perhaps it was only because it was almost the first time anyone had talked to me purely on my *craft*. Not because I was a woman to be polite to, to charm with superficials, not because I was my father's daughter or C.'s wife; no, simply because of my book, my mind, my *craft*. I have a *craft!* And someone who is master of that craft, who writes beautifully, thinks I know enough about my craft to want to compare notes about it, to want to fence with my *mind,* steel against steel.

He pulls the preface out of his pocket and we go over the words I didn't understand. "*Mais ça . . . comme c'est beau!*" I say.

"And here—only, you know, it is not my husband, that. *C'est moi, ce n'est pas mon mari. Il n'a pas peur. Il n'est pas timide. Il ne pense pas à ça. . . .*" He smiles. "*Je sais—je sais.*"

My heavens, what a joy it was to talk, to compare, to throw things out, to be understood like that without an effort. Summer lightning.

Of course, I was warmed by the praise and opened to it, as one does. He said there was something classical about the book, something fundamental, like a Greek play. And he was astonished to find it in America.

I said perhaps the reason it appealed to the layman was that Aviation was not my world. I was a foreigner to it.

He said that had nothing to do with it whatsoever. That the writer, like the bee, gathers honey from whatever circumstances he happens to be in, and I had done that and it would not have mattered *what* I had written about.

And somewhere we were talking about Aviation—I telling him that C. thinks it is encouraging that the tools of war require more and more intelligence and in that there is hope. But he countered: *"Mais je ne suis pas tout à fait de son avis."* ("But I don't quite share his opinion.") And I said, desperately, "It seems that nature is always pushing us down onto all fours again. As soon as a nation is civilized . . ." "But man has always succeeded in rising again," St.-Ex. said.

I talked about flying, too, how it did not separate you from the elements but, rather, bathed you in them.

I said, looking up at him, astonished, "But *you* have said that." "Yes, I have said that. . . ."

I told him about Illiec, how it was the same thing—one was cradled in the elements.

We talked of Americans and the Puritan background. Perhaps it is *that*, I said, that gives us our sense of *pressure*, of hurry, of being late.

Talking in French about ideas that are so deeply rooted in me in English, ideas that are barely communicable in your own language, to say them in a foreign language you are not the master of, was really a kind of anguish. I beat my wings against it in vain. Never have I felt so frustrated by that wall of incommunicability. And yet it was amazing that we could communicate at all.

Of translations—the difficulties of: "There is a German poet I like very much, who excites me more than anyone I have read in a long time," I start to say.

"Rainer Maria Rilke," he finishes quietly for me.

"But how did you know?" I ask, astonished. He just waves his hands a little and smiles.

"Il a pris le chemin intérieur" ("He has chosen the inner road"), I say.

"Oui," again smiling, with perfect understanding.

It is his life that interests me, I say, his inner struggle, and Van Gogh's, too. What I don't like in Van Gogh, I say, is that he *forces* it on you, does it with the fist. It is German, whereas Cézanne simply holds it out in his hands, to take. (But he thinks Van Gogh has more.) But still, I finish, perhaps it isn't fair to say that—so much of one's judgment is the stage of life. . . . He finishes for me. "The stage one happens to be in oneself."

And all this time stopping at stations, peering out, asking the conductor, who guided us off at Jamaica like the two foreigners we were.

I realize now, looking back, that I talked too much. It ran over like joy—like a child, like Land showing me his treasures. *"Regarde, regarde!"* Like talking to Margot, the first time I met her, or to Mrs. Hand[1] when I discovered her—the desire to throw out the rope and see how much they'll take. Is it slack? No, it's taut—all taken!

"I feel as though I had been sleeping for years or had lain in the lowest hold of a ship that, loaded with heavy things, sailed through strange distances. Oh, to climb up on deck once more and feel the winds and the birds, and to see how the great, great nights come with their gleaming stars . . ." [Rilke]

This I wrote down of talking to Mrs. Hand the winter of 1935.

That strange childish desire to give it all—"It is so vast an alleviation," as V. Woolf says.

Of Americans being closer to the French than to the English. Of the childlike quality of Americans I noticed everywhere on coming back from abroad. He agreed: "Yes, but that I find very refreshing."

[1] Frances Hand, wife of Judge Learned Hand; old friends of the Morrows.

Of living abroad and how it dislodges you for good. Of the French being closer to the soil, able to revive, come back. The separation in England between classes.

Of flying—had I taken a license? I found I was saying, "Before I was married I had not lived in the world of action at all. Then I felt it was the only world and that my world must be thrown away—it didn't count for anything; only action counted, and so I did all that . . . but now . . ." He smiled, *"Oui,"* and went on to ask had I gone into biology, too. No, I hadn't, I answered, adding that I thought there was a danger when husbands and wives were in the same profession. I quoted D. H. Lawrence saying of marriage that man and woman should be like the two poles which hold the world between them. *"Oh— pas si loin que tout ça!"* ("Oh—not as far off as all that!") He laughed, and then gave a definition of his own, an image of the bees, gathering honey from different sources, and each bringing it home to the hive.

At some point I talk to him about [Alfred North] Whitehead and his *Adventures of Ideas*. I quote, "Adventure rarely reaches its predetermined end. . . ."

"It never reaches it," he interrupts, with a sigh. But I go on trying to translate the place in Whitehead where he speaks of the waves of new ideas beating on civilization, adventure being always part of the new idea: "Without adventure a civilization is in full decay." But I find it hard to translate, from memory, too, and finally I say in discouragement:

"Mais, je dis les choses banales." ("I am just saying banalities.")

"Oh, non—moi, j'avais toujours eu ces idées, mais je ne les ai jamais vues autre part," he reassures me. ("Oh, no—I, I have always had these ideas, but I have never seen them anywhere else.")

By the time we got to Huntington, looking at each station hopefully, I was beginning to feel terrified that this pitch would break and worried about talking too much and boring him. I hoped against hope that C. would be at the station. But he wasn't. We took a taxi. It was cooler and the trees smelled fresh, of rain and honeysuckle. When we got to the house (Thor barking and leaping, Jon calling from the window, "Did you find a turtle?") I was really dashed to find that not only was C. not there, but there was no word from him. I felt wilted. Will we have the whole evening alone? If *only* C. were here.

I go ahead with supper, talking about Russia and aviation—that's safe! He talks about desert flying, the variety it had, in the sands. And I quote T. E. Lawrence saying that he liked the "variety of taste" in water. Water, which seemed so much alike to most people, had more variety than the Alps.

"Oui," he says, "I felt just like him about the sands." He goes on to speak of the beauty of the desert and how enhanced it was by danger. He tells of returning on a flight over the desert when it was safe. It seemed to him flat and uninteresting until he was shot at—and then suddenly it was beautiful again.

I am feeding the dogs when C. finally appears—it is almost 10. I drop back in relief, I am so glad he is there. We (St.-Ex. and I) both leap at him with the relief of thirsty travelers needing water. C. blows in like a sea breeze. But he is tired, driving all day in traffic. However, he takes his supper on a tray and over the tray carries on the torch of conversation, which immediately goes up a level, takes on a higher, less feminine tone. I sit back and translate. They compare notes, on that thrilling period in Aviation which is past. "But I never know," St.-Ex. says, laughing, "whether it is not my own youth I am regretting."

They discuss the place of the machine in modern life. St.-Ex.'s theory is that it is not directly the fault of the machine that man has become more material, but that it is due to a combination of things which have so changed his world that he is like a foreigner in it—more a foreigner than the early English transplanted to America. And it has taken them 300 years to begin to have a culture. He is optimistic that man will come out on top of the machine—use it as a tool for greater spiritual ends.

The trend toward a spiritual revival is already here, St.-Ex. says, witness the return to nature, camping, etc., witness even these movements like Communism and Fascism (which he dislikes but which he regards as a symptom). And what man seeks and wants he will find—he always *has*.

C. is less hopeful, or, rather, more practical, taking a nearer view of it and the suffering involved, and what road to choose.

And all this from French into English and vice versa, my mind panting in the traces.

All this discussion reminds me of the talk we had with Père [Teilhard de] Chardin in Paris. The afternoon, rather, that he simply stood and talked for hours in terms of *"man"* and his past (archaeological) and his future—*man,* and not *men*—and I went home inspired with his hope and his vision, which could overleap the sorrows and confusion and misery of this age we're going through.

Finally, after ginger ale and milk and questions about his plans for tomorrow, he says he must see a sick friend on Long Island. *Where?* we say dubiously, foreseeing a long drive to East Hampton, no Sunday trains. He says he doesn't know and pulls out of his pocket a slip of paper which he unfolds and reads slowly, in his French accent: "Hunt-ing-ton."

"Huntington!?" [the nearest town] we shout, incredulous. Yes, Huntington. We all sit back and laugh—helplessly. What an incredible day!

Sunday, August 6th

M. St.-Ex. comes down while we are all at breakfast and tells us with some amusement that when he went to bed last night he didn't notice there were two doors to his room. This morning he got up, went out the wrong door, and could not find his way about. "The bathroom was the second door on the right . . . but there is no *right . . . je suis fou!"* Land comes in—a cherub with golden hair. St.-Ex. looks at him, overcome, it seems to me, with his beauty.

Jon takes him out to see the *tortues* and talks French to him. *"Mais, il parle très bien le français!"* says St.-Ex., delighted.

We talk all morning on the porch, C. and he on Aviation, Germany's strength, England's next move, France's inherent strength, war tactics. Of war: it is so terrible, I say, it must be avoided at almost any price, and he agrees.

Also, C. tells the Göring lion story[1] and at the crucial point Land hands St.-Ex. a turtle, which proceeds to act. *"Tout à fait comme le lion de Göring!"*

There is really nothing to say at this point but *"Heureusement que vous n'êtes pas dans un uniforme splendide!"*

I ask him to write in our copy of *Wind, Sand and Stars,* which he does—something polite besides his name—and C. says then that I must write something in *Listen! the Wind,* which we have given him. I can think of nothing to write except, "In gratitude for the adventures he has given us" and then a quotation from Whitehead on adventure (in English, of course).

We go swimming at 12, and then C. and I take him to his friends outside of Huntington. I don't know exactly how we find the way, because he is talking all the time about a crash he was in, under water and almost drowned. (He has been in an *incredible* number of crashes—bad ones—but I don't see how a man who is that much of an artist can fly *at all.*)

We ask him if he will come back again and he says he'd love to come back for supper. So we plan to come for him at 5. C. and I talk about him, going back. I am convinced he is going to be killed if he goes on flying. C. talks of the impossibility of being absolutely first-rate—perfection in the world of action— and being anything else (at the same moment). And I suddenly remake an old discovery. It is the striving after perfection that makes one an artist. It is the sense that one is imperfect, unfulfilled, unfinished. One attempts by a superhuman effort to fill the gap, to leap over it, to finish it in another medium. And one creates a third and separate thing: "Adventure rarely reaches its predetermined end. Columbus never reached China. But he discovered America."

The stutterers (or those who cannot speak well or quickly, like me) write. But it is not enough to be a stutterer. One must also have glimpsed a vision of perfect articulateness which presses one on to compensate for one's inadequacy.

[1] See *The Flower and the Nettle,* p. 98.

After a quiet lunch I lie in the sun, try to comfort my body after these intense hours of living only in the mind.

Then we go for St.-Ex. at 5. He is doing card tricks on the porch with his friends. One man is so ill that it makes me tremble to be near him, to feel his tremulous nearness to Death. I am so conscious of him and his lassitude—life flowing out of him and the gap between us and him, and also of his wife's tired, carved, sharp and patient anguish—like an old hurt—that I can hardly pay attention to anything else. Is there as much of a gap between life and death?

Then we come home and swim—only I can hardly immerse myself in it; my mind is going so hard, is so quickened, that I can only think of more and more things to say. I can only feel horizons breaking and then breaking again in my mind, like the locked ice pack in the spring—pieces breaking off and flowing away, with a tremendous roaring.

And all the time the sense of life being so precious and running away so fast that not one fraction of a second must be lost.

Coming home in the car we talked—he and C. really, I translating—of missing the desert, of desert weather. How danger and solitude are the two factors that go to form a man's character, that do the most for him. There is a kind of mountain-top, clear, cold-air austerity about him that reminds me of Carrel or of a monk, dedicated to something—what?

He says he can talk to us as to his own family, and how quickly one recognizes that one is on the same level. *"Je comprends tout ce que vous dites."* ("I understand all you say.") "There are the people one can talk to and there are the people one cannot talk to—there is no middle ground." The three greatest human beings he has met in his life are three illiterates, he says, two Brittany fishermen and a farmer in Savoy.

"Yes," I say, "it has nothing to do with speech—quick brilliant speech—though one *thinks* it has when one is young."

"Oh, yes," he says, "mistrust always the quick and brilliant mind."

And then he goes on to say that the great of the earth are

those who leave silence and solitude around themselves, their work and their life, and let it ripen of its own accord.

I believe this so utterly that it is like my own thought.

Of the Despiau[1] head he says that it is a *chef d'oeuvre* because it does not say it all the first time one looks at it but bit by bit. And that he had thought from my writing that I could sculpt!

We have supper on the porch—with a very red sea and very green trees—and they talk about the state of France, what is wrong with it, various ills, alcoholism. We talk about Dr. Carrel, too, and how they must meet. (And we get bitten by mosquitoes.) A little June bug gets caught in my hair. I take it out hastily, a little afraid, and then put it on the table. (If you kill it . . . I think.) But he picks it up gently and looks at it. "It is trying hard to take off," he says, and when it does, only to land on his arm, "It was hardly worth taking off for such a short flight!"

Then we walk down to the beach. He talks about the south of France (the interior), where he says we must go and which we would like, and people he would like us to meet.

I say of La Grande Chartreuse: *"Quelle vie admirable!"*

And we talk of Illiec, where we want him to come. Though in this changing world I fear neither of those things will come true. We are living in a dream interlude—before what cataclysm, I don't know but fear.

We walk home through the heavy drowning sea of cricket song.

St.-Ex. talks of Baudelaire, his life, his poetry. He says that Baudelaire was great not for what he said but because he was one of those who knew best how to knot words, and he recites some of his poetry to me and goes on, about his theory of style— that the same words arranged differently became banal, did not mean the same thing. The unexpressed finds expression in style, rhythm, etc.—words carry only half the freight. Of how inverted words sometimes gave quality.

[1] Charles Despiau, French sculptor, who did a head of A. M. L. in Paris.

Yes, I say, it is the breaking of rules, but cannot explain all I mean by that, which is much more—a union of the familiar and the strange which makes for an artistic creation—in fact, for any creation.

Then he talks of the poetic image—what it is, technically—very exciting. He describes how in comparing things one has one object and another object and a bridge with which they are linked—so-and-so is like so-and-so. *Like* is the bridge. But sometimes one has no bridge. The mind must vault the gap; one's mind *creates* the bridge. It creates a new thing entirely. A whole new civilization—in the case of "Les Archevêques de la mer" one's mind imagines a whole hierarchy of things, an imaginary world.

"But perhaps this doesn't interest you?"

"Oh, yes . . . yes!"

Then he takes the example of the stereoscope—two pictures of the same thing taken from a different angle—you put them together and the mind makes the adjustment. The mind supplies a third picture.

I tell him about the missionary in Baker Lake, translating the 23rd Psalm—the Lord is my shepherd—to the Eskimos in terms of reindeer and whale blubber. He asks about the Eskimos— were they interesting people? I talk a little about their rigid codes. C. disagrees and cites their changing of wives.

Yes, I say, but for *utilitarian* reasons, not for *pleasure*. Is that more moral? C. asks. Of course, St.-Ex. and I answer together, looking at C.

I hardly know, looking back, which are my thoughts and which his, for he would start a train of thought and I would go off on a line of my own, jumping ahead, finishing his thought, whether correctly or not I can't tell.

All of this, of course, is not accurately stated, because it has been translated and filtered through my mind. I wonder if it would not be the same if I met any of the people whose minds have touched mine in books—Rilke, or Whitehead (but no, I could not talk to him), V. Woolf (when I most admired her), L. H. Myers (for his preface to *The Root and the Flower* and

Strange Glory), Thornton Wilder, for his *Our Town*. The
man who wrote *They Came Like Swallows*. Victoria Lincoln
for Jenny in *February Hill*. Perhaps my excitement comes because so rarely do I tap that world (my world—even if I am
not a master in it—world of artistic vision). I have not yet found
my circle, my friends, my nation. If this is true, then "O brave
new world, that has such people in 't!"

What a commentary it is on human communication in this
world. How impossible it is to know other people. When one
finds a person who has the same thought as yours you cry out
for joy, you go and shake him by the hand. Your heart leaps
as though you were walking in a street in a foreign land and
you heard your own language spoken, or your name in a room
full of strangers.

We get ginger ale and milk and C. and he talk on what he
wants to do in this country and see—planes, factories, etc.
St.-Ex. says he wants to see the Grand Canyon!

Then to bed, very tired. What a comfort is C.'s unspoken
understanding. "Give us this day our daily bread."

Monday, August 7th

C. and I into town with Saint-Exupéry, he talking to C. all the
way, and I translating feverishly. We talk about the problems of
the world, men's talk, and my mind is stretched, takes deep
breaths.

We talk somewhere of faith, of the times in a plane when it
is black ahead and one must go on only by that patch of green
off to the right, like a thread. How one must have faith, like a
child. *"Il faut être enfant,"* like the Bible, faith like Gideon at
Jericho.

He says yes, and from that goes on to tell the story of Esau
selling his birthright, as he interprets it. He is sure that Esau
was dying of thirst when he did that. They had been out in the
desert and they had missed their wells and they came back
dying of thirst. He went on to explain how in the desert if you
go for a long time without water the throat finally hardens and
closes and one can no longer be saved even if at last one finds

water. But the people who live in the desert have discovered that if you make a paste from beans or some farinaceous vegetable and stuff it in the mouth and throat and around the neck of the sufferer, little by little the moisture seeps into the throat and a tiny thread is opened and water, one drop at a time, can finally be let down it, and the man is saved.

The mess of "pottage" was "lentils" and it was *that* that Esau craved. It was a death cry: Give it to me "or I die"! It was a holdup on the part of Jacob.

St.-Ex. says that for the problem of the machine age there are two general answers. The one is simple, too simple, he feels —the answer of Gandhi. The machine has destroyed man, or, rather, man was happier before the machine age. Therefore we must go back to the time before the machine, weave by hand, etc. If man can be saved only by his going backwards, then he is doomed, St.-Ex. thinks.

The other answer, which is complex and not clear, is that man must somehow learn to dominate and use the machine. The answer, he feels, is not simply in denying the fact of the existence of the machine. Then he tells a fable—a true story but a fable—of sheep farming in Patagonia, to illustrate the thesis that you can never apply logic to the future, only to history, never to judge about what is to come. They calculate 1 sheep to a hectare, 100 sheep to 100 hectares. But in reality they can raise only 85 from 100 hectares, because of the wolves that kill the sheep. Then they see the solution to this problem and kill the wolves. And then they find to their amazement that instead of getting 100 sheep to 100 hectares, as they hoped, they now get only 65 sheep to 100 hectares—for this reason:

It is true that the wolves ate the sheep, but not nearly as many sheep as guanacos. And when there were no wolves, the guanacos multiplied so fast that they ate the sheep out of house and home. And one could not foresee this problem, St.-Ex. went on, because while the wolves were there the guanacos were so few that no one dreamed of their ever encroaching on the sheep.

We do not know what is the guanaco of the machine age, he continued.

We all get so enthralled by this discussion that we never look at the road or see what is happening. By now we are at the bridge. Just as we turn to get onto the ramp the engine sputters and we discover we have not a drop more of gas! C. has gotten so absorbed that, though knowing when we left home that we would have to get gas, he has passed two stations. This is very rare and embarrasses him. But one cannot get so absorbed in an argument and keep practical. We draw up to a fuel station, have to prime the carburetor. For the second time in two days St.-Ex. stands bent over the hood of an engine of a Lindbergh!

Finally we get started again and get him to his hotel—*"merci infiniment"*—and there it is and I have not had time to thank him for being so nice about the book or talking to me about writing and being so good about my bad French. I have not been able to apologize for talking too much.

But then perhaps it is just as well. One can't thank for those things, one can only be grateful, terribly and humbly grateful, and then the obligation is to take what has been given you, and make something out of it and give it back—not to them, oh no, they don't need it—hand it on.

My mind has been quickened, and my sight and feelings. For a week now the world has been almost unbearably beautiful. It cries out everywhere I turn. A twisted branch tears at the heart. The tendril of a dried vine is infinitely pathetic. A driving white rainstorm gives me wings, and trees steeped in the drowsy dusk of evening stand up like rooted gods, reaching for the sky.

It is too much. And I think of the Greek myth in Thornton Wilder, of the hero who returned to the earth for one day but only in a "difficult and painful condition," "with a mind divided into two persons, the participant and the onlooker." "Suddenly the hero saw that the living too are dead and that we can only be said to be alive in those moments when our hearts are conscious of our treasure; for our hearts are not strong enough to love every moment."[1]

I pick up the car at the repair shop and drive it home, C.

---

[1] Quotations from *The Woman of Andros*.

following me. It is very hot and we get home late for lunch. After lunch I take a nap and a swim. C.'s army friends come to dinner. They are nice simple people, but it is terribly difficult to talk to them. Conversation lags and I almost fall asleep.

To bed dead tired.

Tuesday

C. plans to leave. I go down to the garage and try to work—ideas pounding through me too fast to put down. I hear Jon outside in a tree. He has climbed up to the top and is singing in ecstasy—the little chant he made up at Long Barn climbing the cherry tree: "Higher than the coal shed, higher than the apple tree," interspersed with high childish caroling yodels, just for sheer joy in between. I know just how he feels. I run out and call to him and wave.

C. can't leave, plane down, works with Christine and brings me that terrible folder of demands, requests, letters that swarm upon me and that I cannot even bear to look at or think about, that gives me such a feeling of guilt, and yet I know that if I dealt with them all I would do nothing else.

But I cannot choose—like C.—and deal only with a few; so I neglect them all and try to forget them until C. brings them up.

What a torture it is, what a nailing to the boards to have to answer a formal letter!

Must get back to life after these days spent living in a world of the mind alone.

Wednesday, August 9th

There is a lovely storm in late afternoon. I go and sit out under the big umbrella to watch the different trees and leaves take it, the oak torn this way and that in a struggle against it but the birch all ashimmer with it, part of it. Wonderful sound, too. Thor sits out with me in a kind of patient and completely non-understanding devotion. "I don't know why my mistress wants to sit out in the rain but if she does I am going to sit with her!"

C. also, in amusement, comes out and sits with me. After supper we walk outside and down to the beach and far along it. It is intensely beautiful. I am very happy.

I show C. a twisted branch that I say has a certain passion in it, and he says the branch is that way because it was broken off and a side branch forced itself to grow past that break. "It is the *will* to live past Death." I say he saw far more than I, that he has taught me to see.

The branch has tried to compensate, even in direction, for its sister branch.

Thursday, August 10th

After supper with C. I finish *Wind, Sand and Stars*. Mrs. Reid[1] has tried for two days to get hold of C. to speak at her Women's Conference. C. has already seen her in Washington for lunch, written her, and called her on the telephone. She is still persisting that he does not mean it when he says he doesn't want to speak. Tonight, unable to get him on the telephone, she has sent a special messenger with a to-be-personally-delivered packet out here. I feel annoyed—and hunted. I think in impatience that I never *never* press myself on anyone; but perhaps I do, without knowing it, in other ways. In talking too much, perhaps, like this weekend. I must try to remember how dreadful it is. It is a sin to intrude where you are not wanted, pressing in on that ring of silence around each personality.

No American can understand the need for time—that is, simply space to breathe. If you have ten minutes to spare you should jam that full instead of leaving it—as space around your *next* ten minutes. How can anything ripen without those "empty" ten minutes?

Thursday, August 17th

The news in the papers very black. Germany's demands, Danzig and the Corridor. Absolute refusal on both sides of any negotiation and a kind of unmistakably genuine rumbling on the German side that means Storm. "A matter of days." They want a showdown.

[1] Mrs. Ogden Reid, owner of the *Herald Tribune*.

That the Vatican "takes a grave view" depresses me almost more than anything else. I don't know why. But I feel they are above it and yet know all there is to be known. I feel I have heard the verdict of the great specialist from the Mayo Clinic and it is: "The patient cannot survive."

C. calls up and is coming home. I decide to meet him. It is cool and a lovely evening. I wait at the field. And when he comes over the field I recognize him even though I did not know what plane he was flying. It gives me such a thrill. How strange it is—how people are like themselves! C. coming out of the sky with a kind of directness, a kind of magnificence that is only his. And when he banks his plane around the field, with that slow and absolute grace, it is as much him as a gesture of his hand. It catches my breath. I have always taken it for granted. But to see it in the sky . . . it is an act of creative beauty, a work of art.

We drive home. C. on war, on trouble in this country. He is much stimulated by his contacts in Washington and feels, I think, that he is with his own people, can really work to the best of his ability, to the most useful ends. We talk all evening.

I am happy for him at first, but later, at night, I am afraid. I am afraid of this turmoil we are facing, not war only but worse than war—a struggle in this country perhaps, a struggle of the immoderates. I see no place for me in that, no place for the moderates, no place for the middle ground (when things get so terrible one is forced to take sides, for survival alone). I who do not want to take sides, I who do not want to fight, who do not want to force myself—even intellectually, even spiritually, even emotionally—on another human being.

And it is not just for myself that I am afraid; if I were all alone it would be no problem. The middle ground is always automatically disposed of in these periods. They flee either to convents or into nervous breakdowns or they are simply shot standing still in their no man's land. It is because of C. that I am afraid. Can I follow him? How can I follow him? That is the nightmare—separation from him.

Of course I used to feel like this looking forward to the great flights—a dread, a fear that I could not follow him, that I could not keep up in strength, in courage, in ability—that was the real nightmare. Suppose I should fail him. And yet that was only physical, really, and I found my place.

This is mental and spiritual. I feel bitterly alone. But it is no good trying to guess the future.

Christine tells me that when people ask her, "Are the Lindberghs really as divinely in love as one always thinks of them?" she always answers, "Oh, yes, even more so!" What an odd picture one gives to the outside world and what strange standards young people have. As if marriage weren't a thousand times more enthralling, gripping, demanding, complex, paradoxical, subtle, and real than being "divinely in love." Though I suppose if I see C. in the turn of a wing in the sky perhaps that might be called being "divinely in love."

Friday, August 18th

The newspapers are terrible. The Germans all seem ready. What are they waiting for? England worries me, though, more than Hitler. She will fight, I think, even if it is mass suicide. Is this courage or is it stupidity?

Saturday, August 19th

Germany has taken Slovakia. Things are closing in. There are no diplomatic channels left. They are going to strike. It is so strange. I cannot feel the way I felt last fall or this spring, partly of course because it is not so imminent on this peaceful summer Sound. But partly, too, that one has been dreading it for so long that one has become numbed to crises.

And partly that right into the face of such a catastrophe one cannot look. The mind can't grasp it.

C. writes and thinks all day—on war?

Sunday, August 20th

C. reads me some of his writing. It is very beautiful and strong and strides ahead—far ahead in the future. But there are implications of trouble in it that make me tremble a little. There are challenges.

Monday

The war talk and complications plunge on, deeper and deeper. One lives in a kind of hopeless suspense, wishing one knew, either one way or the other, and yet one dare not give up hope.

It looks as though it may go on like this until the middle of September.

Tuesday, August 22nd

The Russians and Germans have signed a nonaggression pact, right under the noses of the English and French mission sent to get Russia into the "Peace Front." England is aghast. She has again been double-crossed. Now there is *no* way to defend Poland at all. No one knows what is behind it. They already have a trade agreement. Germany has tapped vast resources and gained protection, if not actually made some other hidden bargain underneath—partition of Poland?

Japan has been double-crossed also. Germany certainly is a ruthless and brilliant diplomat. The Poles are saying they will still fight, and England and France, though desperate, are not backing down at all. I see no way out. The only slightly lighter patch in the gloom is the account saying that Rome is the only capital not under the most urgent war pressure. What does this indicate? Italy always gives the game away. Does she intend to stay neutral?

Laura and George [Stevens] meet me at the ferry and we drive to their nice rambling old house in the middle of old trees, woods, and quiet. We talk, chiefly books (not war at all!) and a little about the future, but vaguely, vaguely. I am having a very good time, but it is a frightening kind of happiness. I feel as though it were the last time I should ever talk like that to them —in complete confidence, innocence, and love between us. While we are talking, that serene world of peace and faith is crashing about us, and we don't know it. George is wrapped up in his work, vaguely distressed at the world, vaguely feeling he should get into it, take some responsibility for his community. Laura is wrapped up in George and children. I dread what there may be in store for all of us, the struggles that are going to separate us from each other and this kind of understanding. Sleep badly.

Wednesday, August 23rd

Thelma [Crawford Lee] calls up. She is in a terrible state on the war. Brooke has been telephoning her from Washington: "It's come—it's here," etc.

Later she comes over and talks to me—about war. She was seventeen when the last one started. She is white and upset and very shaken. We talk a little, of my dread of war and its consequences, entering into every family, rending brother and sister, husband and wife, friends.

Friday, August 25th

Margot here in the morning. We wait for C. to come from Washington, to get war news. The papers are bad, full of blasts and terrible details all leading to war. Roosevelt and the Pope both broadcast appeals for peace. "Nothing is lost by peace; everything may be lost by war," the Pope says. Paris is evacuating its people, more reservists are called up. Britain's navy to stop up the Baltic. Danzig and the Poles are firm. Hitler locked up with his aides. Foreigners here rush home. Saint-Exupéry, I read, went yesterday on the *Ile-de-France*.

C. comes back. He is not so gloomy. He talks to us about the military angle. There is still nothing that England and France can do to save Poland, and no place they can attack Germany easily anywhere. Therefore some other solution will be found.

C., I fear, is arguing logically. He does not see that the issues have become so wound up that nothing *logical* will affect them.

Saturday, August 26th

Things look a little better in the papers this morning—as though Germany were willing to talk, though she still demands Danzig and the Corridor.

C. and I go to the B.'s for dinner, rather social and quite a lot of people. Everyone is very casual about war—sure it won't come. They talk with that careless assurance that reminds me of outsiders talking about someone very ill in your family: "Of course they're going to get well." They can afford to be sure because it doesn't matter vitally to them.

Sunday, August 27th

News is still in suspense. Hitler's demands include Danzig, England's dropping of the Polish pact, and a corridor across the Corridor. England will probably reject these but does not wish to slam the door. In the meantime everything steams ahead full blast—with terrifying weblike thoroughness.

Monday, August 28th

Con telephones me. She and Aubrey are coming out tonight.

I go down and work on the review.[1] In the middle of the morning C. comes down with quick sharp steps. He says he has had word from Washington. Things are worse. The chances are now 80/20 for war. It is hopeless then—80/20. What has happened?

We listen to the radio. There is something terrible even about the announcers. This mad whooping up of the news, the terrible excitement in their voices, their personal pride in being the ones to deliver this bad news to you. The sickbed details they feed you with: "The Prime Minister called on His Majesty the King this morning," etc.

It doesn't mean anything. I can only think: 80/20, 80/20. I go to bed with it on my chest at night—a lump, a heavy lump—and the first thing in the morning when I wake, I feel it is there. What is it? Oh, 80/20.

Tuesday, August 29th

There is a storm outside. It is dark and cold. The doors are shut. You can hear the rain and the wind. We are separated

[1] A. M. L. was writing a review of *Wind, Sand and Stars,* later published in *The Saturday Review of Literature.*

from the summer, from that peaceful world. We are unsteady, rocking in a storm.

Aubrey comes for a late lunch to talk with C. on the situation.

Wednesday, August 30th

The storm is still with us, blustering and cold and the wind crying. Russian troops are massing on the Polish border. Will Poland give way to pressure from both sides?

King Leopold and Queen Wilhelmina offer to mediate. They say the door is still open to peace, but everything closes in on it. The Poles will never give in, the Germans never come down in their demands, and the English never back down.

Con and Aubrey come for supper. We listen to the radio. It has become a physical pain, Con says, those voices of the radio announcers. Poland mobilizes. Britain refuses to force her to Hitler's terms. But I keep thinking *something* may be happening underneath. Beck[1] may go to Berlin, something may break. C. says the percentage has gone up to 50/50.

Thursday, August 31st

Con leaves. The papers are black. Hitler has called a meeting of the Reichstag for tomorrow morning, when he will announce his decision. I see no crack of light anywhere. The storm is still on, wind and rain and gray clouds moving over us—constantly a changing world. And that terrible suspended sound of the wind, like our suspense. It seems to have been going on—the storm, the suspense—forever.

Friday, September 1st

I wake up thinking: Now we know. What did Hitler say? War, I think.

From the radio downstairs I find that the German army has already started through Poland. Hitler, putting on his great army coat, says he will not take it off until they have won, even if it takes ten years.

[1] Józef Beck, Polish Minister of Foreign Affairs, 1932–39.

The storm has cleared and it is beautiful again—brilliant sunshine, a clear, shining world, blazing white sand, shimmering green leaves, a smooth bay.

I spent the morning walking down on the beach, trying to grasp it, trying to accept it.

Saturday, September 2nd

The Germans are steaming ahead into Poland; all negotiations are off. Even the news becomes not diplomatic but military, not subtle and various and human but clear and cold and metallic. But it is almost a relief to have it so *practical,* after the hysteria and suspense. This long and terrible week is like the week before Elisabeth died, a week of piling up hopes and then fears, a week of listening at the radio, trying to sort out truth from lies, of terrible clinging to one straw and then another, of seesawing with each new word, up and down, of telegrams from Washington and phone calls, and not sleeping, and talking, passionately arguing, first this way, then another, but all this against war— war which is now upon us. For the German army is now pressing toward Warsaw, the German navy is in command of the Baltic, the German air fleet is bombing Polish cities. Poland has invoked the Anglo-Polish pact and the French-Polish pact. England has sent a last telegram to Hitler asking him to cease hostilities or she will fulfill her obligations to Poland.

I look at the newspapers piled up on our table, fruitless words, fruitless telegrams, letters, meetings, negotiations, airplane trips of diplomatists, words of pleading, of hope, prayers. All useless. It makes me think of Hopewell—that tremendous machine set going: state troopers, handwriting experts, ticker tapes, telephone services, detectives, specialists, politicians, friends, reporters, letters. . . . For what use, for what purpose?

The child is dead.

The child is dead in Europe.

C. is not, to my relief, speaking.[1] There is no use now the war

[1] C. A. L. had considered a radio address.

has started. His vigorous practicality appals me in a way. N
that war is here one has to look at it.

I go down and write in my diary in the garage. We are in a
suspended period again.

Come up for lunch. Find a letter from George [Stevens]—
Saturday Review. They like my "piece" on *Wind, Sand and
Stars very* much and want to print it, don't want to cut or
change a thing. George says it's a fine piece of writing. All this
would have made me so happy a few weeks ago, and it does
please me now, though it seems to be a voice from another world.
The review now seems to me to have an incredible lightness and
joy that does not belong to this period.

Aubrey comes out in the late afternoon. We listen to the radio.
Mussolini is pressing France for some kind of a Five Power
Conference. England, though she has delayed any announcement
of war, says she will make her final decision tomorrow at noon.
Chamberlain has spoken to the Commons, who are impatient
and suspicious of a new Munich. And Halifax has spoken to the
House of Lords. They have so tied themselves up in promises
that they can never get out. They won't arbitrate until Germany
withdraws all her men from Poland and stops fighting, which of
course she'll never do.

I go to bed early with a splitting headache and lie down with
hot cloths on my eyes. But it goes on. I hear guns booming dis-
tantly. I would think it my imagination or the headache, but C.
hears them, too. Finally I go into confused dreams. I wake
about 3 or 3:30. And I feel certain—with the certainty of morning—that war has been declared. I feel I cannot lie in bed any
longer—not the eyeache now but as though something would
burst inside of me. I get up and go to the window, quietly, so
as not to wake C., and sit on the arm of a chair and look out. It
is cool and very tranquil. The ground is dappled with moonlight, though I can't see the moon. The trees, that wall to the
west, stand up in the moonlight dimly, drowsily. The air is full
of that thick curtain of sound of crickets—a drowning noise, like
sleep. It is calm and peaceful. I can see the broken pier down

by the water and the dark water beyond, through the trees, and the dim lights—warm gold—of Connecticut on the opposite shore, and I can see two stars in the sky—Arcturus? And this terrible ache in my chest—that I can do nothing about.

And then I find that I am praying, as I have not prayed since little Charles, and perhaps it is the same, for it is not exactly for myself that I pray, not even as much as when I prayed then. Though I cannot exactly explain this. And I am, in a miraculous way, emptied of all anguish, empty and free, exactly as if there had been bars against my heart and suddenly they had cracked and heart and spirit were free and could leave my body—like death.

And not only that. I felt almost with as much reality as I felt the wind, softly rising, on my lips—a change of wind, the morning's. I felt something come into me as though from the outside, answers to my questions and doubts. I suppose my own answers inside of me, and yet they felt as much from the outside, as objective as that change of wind on my lips.

Then I knew it was over and that I must go back to bed, my heart full of gratitude, and I slept.

Sunday, September 3rd

I wake up early, very exhausted and still with the embers of a headache. C. goes downstairs and finds out that Chamberlain has declared war. But it is no shock. Aubrey comes down and we eat in silence, or, rather, I don't eat because of the headache. Aubrey says only, "No *further* news?" As though there could be anything "further"!

I go out and sit with the children. That is the thing to do, I think, absorb yourself in the children. I sit on the steps and peel unripe chestnuts for Jon. Land climbs over me as I work. I hardly feel that they are my children, but only dully that I must go on peeling chestnuts.

Aubrey has had the radio on all morning. It is all so much water rushing over the dam. Chamberlain's bitter bitter speech —the world cracked around him.

It is like the morning after a death, full of telegrams of sympathy, coming too soon. Only these are not telegrams of sympathy. They are expressions of loyalty coming in from all the British and French colonies. I wonder how much comfort they are to Daladier and Chamberlain. From now on it is going to be all emotion—no facts, no truth, no objectivity. The light of the world has gone out and it will be impossible to see through the gloom.

Aubrey turns on the King's speech at lunch. It is quite simple and moving. My heart is so moved by these people and my mind so disillusioned.

In the afternoon Aubrey goes. I go up to bed with relief. I don't have to keep up such a face any more. The children are at the beach, C. is writing, Aubrey gone (Aubrey who has so much more to face). Then I lie down and try to face this war—all of it at its worst—what it means. I don't believe it will be a short war. I dismiss the hope that after Poland is conquered in a few weeks, Germany will bid for peace. Neither do I have any hope of its being a "humane" war. I place no faith in the objectivity (Aubrey extols) of the British at this point, or in the promises of the Germans. Wars start out humanely—rules about noncombatants, not sinking nonmilitary ships, not bombing nonmilitary objectives.

But one is led little by little into the full horror of it. By little shocks, by little horrors, by small doses, one is led at last into the final draught of poison. And I suppose it is the kindest way. And yet I want to face it all now—like seeing little Charles, his head bashed in, dead, laid out before me, in that first flash of realization that he was gone; or Elisabeth lifeless, at the first word of pneumonia.

Yes—but the mind won't take it. It takes it—then rejects it again. One is weaned little by little away from the truth. The truth is hard to stay faithful to, hopes creep in, dreams creep. Little by little one is lured on into a false world, onto a false ledge, and when that is knocked from under you, you go to another. I want to steel myself against these hopes, these dreams.

Poland will be conquered. Hitler will—rather superciliously, pompously, and stupidly—offer peace to England and France. They will refuse unconditionally at once. Paris and London will be bombed mercilessly. The English and French air forces will be wiped out completely. The English fleet will survive doggedly —but helpless. It will go on and on; all the people we love will be separated, bombed, gassed. All the things we love will be destroyed. It will be a new Spain.

America will be shocked out of its senses and will, in a wave of emotion—after a terrible fight internally in which C. will be in the forefront and be extremely unpopular—go in at last, not wanting, emotionally, to see England and France go down (which I will feel, too). The conflict will be prolonged. We will never see peace again, even after "war" ceases. The world will be in turmoil, revolution, terror. My husband and my friends will go in the beginning of this long struggle and my children in the end of it. I am an old woman already.

But not only in the *"big,"* in the *"little"* I see war—women gassed, babies with legs blown off, men with their brains blown to bits. One cannot conceive of the horror, only I feel that I must. I have always felt it. If there is such horror in the world and other human beings have suffered it, then it might be mine, too, it must be mine. I felt it as a child reading of Christ crucified, Joan of Arc burned at the stake, Catherine crushed on a wheel. Mother might gloss over it by saying that those were things that happened only to a few rare people—saints and martyrs. But I felt, in terror: If such horror exists in the world, · it is as if it were mine. And it did no good to look the other way. You must face it. I had forgotten—or lost faith in—my vision of the night before.

All afternoon I thought and thought, and weakly too, personally. I thought of all the people I loved, of all the places, all the things in Europe, and all my own plans, dreams, hopes of the future (I had not realized how wrapped up in Europe they were, how Europe is the mecca, the spiritual home, of so much I love). Paris and Illiec, Chartres and Mont-St.-Michel, little stone churches in Brittany and crosses at the corners. And the English countryside—Long Barn and peace—and the oaks in that field, and our old life, our old happiness. And people—all the people I love—I saw them tortured, torn, dead, cut off before their time (or even if not killed or tortured—embittered, turned to ashes inside), before their work, their dreams are finished—wasted, spilled out for nothing.

I knew I had no right to feel so badly. I was at peace, *my* children were not in danger of being gassed, *my* husband was not to be sent off to be shot down by antiaircraft. And it was not right to "take on" so, for a world that was not my world. My world was here with my husband, my children; I must keep to that, do my little job there as best I could. But how leadenly, how heavily, how dully I should do it, I felt.

Yes, I can do it, I have done it before; tomorrow I will start, I will live with the living, but today I am sitting up with the dead.

Charles came up and asked me how I felt, and then: "But, Anne, what *is* it? What is the matter?" not understanding. "The war," I say, "just the war," and then I cry and cry at last and he is very sweet—not stern, as he should be, calling me back to life—and he understands and is very gentle and says only, "You see it all too clearly, Anne." And he does not, thank goodness, try to comfort me with words, but only with his understanding.

And then finally I rest and later in the afternoon Jim Newton comes and I get up and wash my eyes. Newton has brought an *enormous* turtle for Jon from Florida. C. sticks it in on my bathroom floor. It is like a dream of the *Alice in Wonderland* illustrations come to life. I half expect it to get up, offer a fin, and dance a quadrille with me! I dress, powder my face, comb my hair, put lipstick on (yes, I do look old today in the mirror), and go downstairs. Newton looks white and tired and tells me he has not been able to sleep.

He stays for supper and talks to C. about what we can do next—keep America out, build up our own strength, attend to our own troubles, straighten our house, save it from the storm.

It is a great comfort to see him tonight, not only because he is understanding and sensitive and feels as badly as we do about what's happened but because in a strange way I feel, looking at him: Here's hope for the future. This is spiritual America, sensitive, aware, but also healthy and young and boyish. This is the counterpart to what you have said good-bye to, all afternoon, in

Europe. This is what you must build on here, in America. The child of Europe is here—not *he,* of course, but what he represents, what he is striving after, what he is dreaming of.

It made it a little easier to think about, to start living the new life here in America.

We hear Roosevelt talk. Evidently he feels that most of America wants to stay out of war. "Let no man or woman thoughtlessly or falsely talk of America sending its armies to European fields. . . . This nation will remain a neutral nation, but I cannot ask that every American remain neutral in thought as well. . . . I hope the United States will keep out of this war. I believe that it will. And I give you assurances that every effort of your government will be directed toward that end."

Lloyd Neck, Monday, September 4th, Labor Day

Come down to breakfast. There has been a boat torpedoed, off the coast of Scotland. A passenger boat, Americans and Canadians chiefly. The horror hardly strikes one, except to think: So soon. And this is only the beginning—a foretaste.

Supper alone with C. We hear over the radio that the French are attacking the Siegfried line. I can no longer feel anything. But C. paces the floor and says France can't stand that. They'll pour the blood of France out on that line—a human wave breaking. If they start doing that, there's no hope of an early peace.

Only the first day of the war. How time has slowed up! Time, which was rushing away at breakneck speed last week, is now slowed to a snail's pace. It will be like this until war ends. Two years, three years, four years, ten years. And this only the first day. If it lasts ten years Jon will be in it. There'll be another war by then, C. says. But what is it all about? I say. Why have children, each generation, in order to have them killed at 17, 20? Why should civilization go on?

It always has, says C.

Tuesday, September 5th

A beautiful letter from Dr. Carrel to C. from St. Gildas [Brittany]. They sit there waiting for the tocsin to sound (announc-

ing war) in the little church on the hill opposite them on shore.
". . . comes simply—like all great tragedies."

Saturday, September 9th

Cold and clear—a Maine day. The papers say the French are
advancing, fighting on German soil (they have said so for a
week, interpreting the brief communiqués), that they have
pushed forward nine miles (but this is land *between* the two
lines—not *beyond* the Siegfried line).

I go down to the garage to write in my diary. Newton and
a retired English General come to see C. C. says that the General agreed with him quite amazingly in a number of things,
even saying that we should stay out of this war.

In the evening we go to the G.'s for dinner. I like them both,
especially him, who is not as isolated from life as most of his
class, has a contact with the earth (from his flying experiences
during the war?) even though he is a New York banker. But
on the whole it is like most evenings here, nice people but
separated from life. For instance they say, "You're not allowed
to talk about war!" As if one could help it. I am bored to death
with the women (and feel I shouldn't be—nice upstanding attractive American women). Almost everyone I meet carelessly
thinks it will not be a long war because Germany will collapse
internally. What wishful thinking!

I feel about the whole evening like Myers: "The *unawareness*
of most people made children of them; they were children playing with brittle toys, children running hither and thither on a
thin and brittle surface through which, one and all, they needs
must break at last—to fall, after a profitless life, into an empty
death. Reality, significant and dark, stretched above them and
beneath them, and they regarded it not."[1]

The only "aware" person is [Simon] Elwes, the painter, and
he successfully covers it up with that incredible parlor chatter
the English always produce at the worst moments. I feel shy
with him and do not dare to look at him lest he should see what
I am looking at in him—a man who is about to die.

[1] L. H. Myers, *Strange Glory*.

C. says, going home, that he is in a tank division but has not yet been called back to England. The waste of an artist in a tank division!

Sunday, September 10th

We have had a week of war. Twelve merchant vessels have gone down. The English bombed Wilhelmshaven. There has been artillery bombardment on the Western Front and some action between the lines. Lots of propaganda war but nothing definite—except in Poland, where Warsaw is surrounded, but not collapsed, and the Polish army cut off.

C. reads me his speech[1] and also his article. The speech is good—simple and direct. The article is beautiful and far-reaching. Very much C. at his best—most visionary and yet practical.

Newton, Con, and Aubrey for lunch. In the afternoon Jim and C. go off to discuss procedure on article and speech.

Aubrey says even if the French collapse or make a truce with Germany, England will have to go on alone. He says that although every Englishman is fighting to preserve "the English way of life," he doubts very much that, at the end of war, it will still exist. He is quite right—but no one in England realizes this.

Con seems calmer. In fact we all seem calmer than a week ago.

At night after they go Jim talks to me. (I have been arguing with C. that there is no chance for peace.) Jim says he thinks there is a chance: "There is something strange about this war. There is an unreality about it. . . ."

Monday, September 11th

I read C.'s speech and the article.[2] The speech is good but not as good as the article, which is his deepest, best thinking. I say

[1] C. A. L. was preparing an article and radio address opposing American entry into a European war. "I do not intend to stand by and see this country pushed into war if it is not absolutely essential to the future welfare of the nation."

[2] "Aviation, Geography, and Race," published in the *Reader's Digest,* November, 1939.

the end (of the speech) needs to be on a broader and higher note. I write a page for an ending as I feel he means it and take it up to him. He says it is very good and he will use part of it, changing it slightly.

Tuesday, September 12th

I read C.'s new ending—better. He is going to Washington to-night. I feel low and discouraged, with the taste of false hope in my mouth that I let creep in from time to time despite my strong resolutions.

There is not a breath of air today and no sunshine. The world is so still, so dead, one feels one could almost, if one listened hard, hear the guns in Europe.

Jim Newton, C., and I for supper. After supper Jim reads C.'s speech. He thinks it is much better and that the new end lifts it, gives people something constructive to carry on. I am relieved. I tell Jim my doubts about it, that it will be confused, it will be smeared politically and brought down to the level of the Neutrality Act issue.[1] (Though I realize it will be too late if he waits till *after* the act is repealed.)

But it is worth trying—1) to give people here a real path, a real staff, and 2) on the chance of influencing Europe indirectly.

Jim says he has hoped this *could* be said before the lull there is over—after Poland and before the real storm—in case it might influence them. I say I think no one will pay the slightest attention over there unless it raises a wave of neutrality feeling here. But that C. must take that chance (even though he will be terribly criticized for it both here and over there). "We took him in when he was exiled from his country and this is the way he rewards us!" (The British will be wild—think of Lady Astor!) "We'll never be able to go back to France!" I say, half joking, to C. "We may never, *anyway*," he answers grimly.

[1] Roosevelt was then trying to amend the Neutrality Act in favor of exporting arms to the democracies. On November 4th he succeeded. The embargo on arms to belligerents was repealed.

They go off together, C. to the train. I walk outside and stand under the trees, my back against a trunk, looking up—but there are no stars. I think I must go to Washington on Thursday.

Wednesday, September 13th

The sky is that dazzling, quivering, all-embracing blue. I cannot hold it all in my heart. I decide even my grief about war is a selfish one. "Love *all* God's Creation—both its whole and every grain of sand."

It is a beautiful day and they are skywriting. *Pepsi-Cola,* I guess it is. It seems a shame to write only Pepsi-Cola with such a medium. Some splendid truth might be written on the sky—"God is Love"—or even those things plastered on rocks by religious zealots: "He died for you," "Christ is Risen!"

After lunch go to town, then out to Englewood. Con and I sit on the porch and discuss war and babies. As she says, there is nothing in between the two now.

After supper Aubrey comes. He is very tired, I gather, and rather discouraged. He says his chief[1] says (of this war), "Why, we're just sitting listening to the orchestra, waiting for the curtain to go up!" which is exactly it.

Aubrey talks of the English and French, most of them believing that America was coming in, and how he was doing his best to show them that this was by no means a certainty. He wished someone would tell Lothian[2] to stop assuming that America would go in.

I said, rather grimly, *"Charles* will tell him!"

"Is Charles going to see him?"

"No—he'll probably never see him again—but he may speak."

"Where?"

"He may speak in Washington this week, on the war."

[1] Angus Fletcher, Director of the British Library of Information in New York, 1928–41 (later Sir Angus).

[2] Philip Henry Kerr, 11th Marquess of Lothian, British Ambassador to the United States in 1939.

Thursday, September 14th

Call C. but cannot get him in Washington. I leave word that I am coming in the late evening unless he telephones to the contrary. But I hate not to talk to him, get his assurance that it is all right to come.

After lunch I take the car to town, just make the train to Washington. Read Tolstoy's *Resurrection* on the train, excited to find a new "good-bye" in it—Katyusha's good-bye to Nekhlyudov; she said not "good-bye" but "forgive me," and the note at the bottom of the page says the two words (in Russian) are *practically interchangeable!* It is the profoundest, the last good-bye. After that there is nothing more. I was terribly happy at finding it. It gave me a kind of assurance, and all the doubts and fears of the day vanished for some strange reason. I knew that I had done right to come to Washington to be with C., *one,* because I believed in him and his stand (no matter how hard it was emotionally to turn one's back on Europe), and *two,* because it might please him, help him a little—release him to talk—give him a better sleep. And that in spite of all the criticism it might call forth—it was right to give the speech. That it was beautiful and stood on C.'s integrity and not on anything shaky. It was above politics and intrigue. It was truly him.

C. was not at The Anchorage[1] when I got in but came in later. I felt very happy and "married." The two of us alone in that little apartment. C. in good spirits. The now-he-is-in-the-fight-he-means-to-enjoy-it sort of attitude.

The Administration is terribly worried. They don't know what he is going to say and would give anything if he wouldn't. They evidently think he will wreck the Neutrality [Act] repeal, take power from them. C.'s talk is above all that but they don't know it; they are afraid of his power.

We talk about the war—I discouraged as usual. But he says there has been no major battle as yet, few casualties, and he feels there is still a chance it may not be a long war. I feel immensely

[1] Apartment house in Washington where C. A. L. had rented a *pied-à-terre.*

cheered, and happy to be there. C. is *so* pleased I came—proud of finding the apartment, pleased I liked it. He said, "Of course I didn't telephone back. Why should I—I wanted you to come."

C. had arranged first to do this on one small broadcast system but two others have called up asking if they can have it, too. It will be nationwide!

Friday, September 15th

C. tells me Newton is here and is looking up quotations for him in the library. How like Jim—he never waits until someone asks to be helped. He just is there quietly, in the place where one needs help.

After breakfast, a leisurely one, C. goes off to a meeting and leaves me two pages of the speech to recopy on the typewriter and to make four copies of it.

I have not touched a typewriter for years, and didn't know how then. But I am *so* pleased to be useful, especially in a practical way, that I start out with zeal. What a morning! I am so anxious to do well that I am all thumbs, make countless mistakes; also I am interrupted all morning by calls for C. Finally after wasting a good deal of paper I get going pretty well and decide to copy it all, for good measure. However I am still typing when Newton comes for lunch at 12:45. C. comes in at 2. All the telephone calls descend on him. He asks Fulton Lewis[1] to have lunch with us. Also Truman [Smith][2] comes in, looking very tall and terribly thin, a ghost of himself in Berlin; but it is very good to see him. I feel warmed by it. "Well, here we all are again," he says joyfully, sitting down. "Yes," I say a little ruefully, "only we are not in Paris, about to take a motor trip to Chartres."

"Oh, we'll be there again!" he says cheerfully and then sits down to talk about the war. He says there's been—on the Western Front—no action so far and that the French *aren't* "all tied up"

[1] Radio commentator and journalist, who for many years spoke on national affairs for the Mutual Broadcasting System.

[2] Lieutenant Colonel Truman Smith, Military Attaché with the U.S. Embassy in Berlin, 1935–39. See also *The Flower and the Nettle*.

with the British policy and are not hurling men across that front to be slaughtered.

I long to talk with him and drink down more of these words of hope which my heart doesn't dare believe. After they all go (having read the speech and all liking it very much), C., Newton, and I go out for a walk in Rock Creek Park. We are quite gay. I because Truman has sent my hopes up in spite of myself, C. because he is in a fight, and Jim because he is unselfish. Besides, it is a nice day. I like the tired, calm, faded end of summer.

Go out at 6:30 for supper with the Fulton Lewises. When we return to the hotel we have to walk across a lobby full of photographers. Flashes and faces—I feel grim. Upstairs to a small quiet suite full of people and equipment, but quite nice people. It takes a long time. C. is photographed. The atmosphere is restrained and quiet, not like downstairs. I feel very tired. C. looks white to me but not to the others, who remark on his "schoolgirl complexion." At last he starts to speak. I shut my eyes. His voice sounds unnatural, slightly, though it is strong and even and clear—just slightly unnatural. I sit and think and pray people will understand. They can't all. They can't know how *hard* it is for him to give it, how *hard* to say how much he loves France and how much I do. Oh, how *can* they understand?

He views the war as "an age-old struggle between the nations of Europe." "Our safety does not lie in fighting European wars. It lies in our own internal strength, in the character of the American people and of American institutions. . . . If Europe is prostrated again by war . . . then the greatest hope for our Western Civilization lies in America. By staying out of war ourselves, we may even bring peace to Europe more quickly. Let us look to our own defenses and to our own character. . . ."

When it is through, everyone congratulates him—wonderful speech, the delivery splendid, etc. Newton beams from a corner. At last we go out, down into that mob of photographers with flash bulbs who chase us through the hotel and out and down three blocks, stopping traffic, jumping, hopping, grimacing ahead of us—a nightmare world, a dream in which nothing is real except them. Cars won't run you down, traffic lights don't matter; only taking the picture matters.

We go back to Fulton Lewis's house, where we listen to a bad record made of the speech. C.'s voice was much clearer. It bothers him. I wish I could get him alone and tell him so. Newton, C., the Lewises, and I sit around. F. L. plays with the radio, trying to get news broadcasts of the speech, which emphasize the political significance. It will be taken as a blow to the repeal of the Neutrality Act, a blow to the Administration. But it is much bigger than that.

Finally to the station. We get on the train. The porter has just made up the beds—I am dropping with fatigue.

Bad night as usual—in early.

Saturday, September 16th

Buy papers. Speech is headlines in *Tribune,* front page. All very fully given; evidently made tremendous impression. We are much surprised it is given that much attention.

At lunch there are hundreds of telegrams—almost none from people we know—full of enthusiasm, direct response; only one, so far, anti. It is very impressive.

After our supper C. and I drive to Oyster Bay to get more papers. On the whole all favorable, and much stirred up. People are thinking, really thinking. The telegrams continue to pour in —in huge proportion favorable, as though C. had cut through to some real core of feeling in the United States.

Sunday, September 17th

Read papers all morning. Very exciting. C. is praised by both sides—at least each respects his integrity and sincerity. Criticism from paper in England (ungrateful for refuge given, etc.). That was bound to come.

Aubrey for lunch. I call Kay [Mrs. Truman] Smith and ask her and Mother for supper. Aubrey says speech was beautiful though a blow to the British. Mother also telephones to say it was beautiful.

We talk war all evening. Kay talks well. It is a relief to talk to someone with as mature a mind, someone who has lived in Europe and feels it and sees it. No one here does, really, and I feel so much older than everyone here. I don't mean old and tired and broken-down. Not *that* kind of "old"—but old, mature, having lived, "old" as Europe is old compared to America. She says she does, too. She talks tactics, what will happen next. Breakup of British Empire.

Monday, September 18th

Cold and clear—wind.

After lunch, to tea with Evelyn Ames[1] in the old Manor House. The wind is cut off here, its back to the hill. There is a walled garden, sunny and still, and a glimpse of the sea, and sun and fallen yellow leaves. I am warmed by it and by the old house and by Mrs. Ames's nice young American friendship. We go through the house. It comes out to you, like Long Barn.

Tuesday, September 19th

Take C. to see the Manor House. He likes it very much and sees what I mean—says we should try and take it [for the winter].

Wednesday, September 20th

Dorothy Thompson[2] has hit at C. in her column. It is a petty, personal, and bitter mudslinging. I expected this, but not from her.[3]

In the evening the B.'s and the L.'s and a friend from the West come for supper. It is not a dinner party (I have never given one) but it goes all right. They are very nice and we talk politics heatedly. The Embargo Act, etc. The L.'s are conservative and have nothing constructive to offer and do not see ahead or even behind very clearly. The B.'s are less conservative, see behind quite well, and ahead, too, but feel it is hopeless to do anything about it. In other words they all wish we could keep out of war

---

[1] Mrs. Amyas Ames, later writer, poet, and conservationist.

[2] Journalist and columnist for the New York *Herald Tribune*.

[3] C. A. L. was portrayed as a "pro-Nazi recipient of a German medal."

but feel "inevitably" that we'll be drawn in and it's hopeless to do anything about it. C. argues firmly against this stand.

The extra man from the West does not agree with any of us. He thinks England and France are dead right all along and that we should get in and help them as quickly as possible. I don't agree with him intellectually but I admire him—at least he has the courage of his convictions. He is more of a man, has more guts than anyone there but C. And in a strange way is really closer to C.

C. goes to bed very discouraged. "No hope there—no use looking for help there." I also feel dashed and low. Mrs. B. tells me she has heard from the wife of the British Ambassador (just left) that the French lost 12,500 men during the first week of the war. I can't think of anything else, the whole evening. C. says he doesn't believe it's true, but that if this war really gets started that will be only a drop in the bucket.

Northampton, Monday, September 25th

After lunch and packing C. drives me into town, meet Con at Cosmopolitan Club and we go on to the station.[1] (C. is going to Washington.)

Mother meets us at the Northampton station. She is gay and young and fluttering (nicely) about the opening tomorrow. It feels far from war.

We go up to Mother's room in Ellen Emerson. Then over to Miss Chase and Miss Duckett's[2] little New England house.

Tuesday, September 26th

Up early. After breakfast I run across to say good morning to Mother and send her off with a kiss. She looks like a girl, shy

---

[1] A. M. L. and C. C. M. M. went to Northampton for the opening of the Smith College year. Mrs. Morrow had agreed to act as interim head of the college after President Neilson's retirement, pending the selection of a new president.

[2] Mary Ellen Chase, author and professor of English literature; Eleanor Shipley Duckett, Latin professor and author.

and pretty. I stick hairpins into her hair in back and we start off, up Paradise Road and across the President's yard, as I used to go freshman year from Ellen Emerson under the dripping elms and the yellowing leaves. Chapel is full of girls. I am overwhelmed by it. They are *so* young and pretty. It is very rare that one sees so much youth, that careless glow of youth all at once. I realized in one dashed moment what youth was and how far I had come from it.

This sense of being far from "youth" is not exactly physical—in fact, it is hardly physical at all. It is what I feel with the young marrieds on Lloyd Neck. Europe has done it and now the war. For I *feel* Europe, I feel Europe's tragedy, and they do not. There is an incredible insouciance about them all that separates me from them. Con is mature, too, like me, but *not* European. The girls seem about the same to her; they might be her friends. They couldn't be mine. The hair has completely changed. It was buns then, or very short bobs. Now it is everywhere the same—Garbo. Also we were not as well dressed. But the greetings and chatter were much the same, and the stares; (I felt conscious of my wrinkles and my sadness written all over my face).

The sadness, though, is the war and not my life. My life has been much happier since I left college, much happier than I then thought it would be. It has grown happier all the time—a strange thing to say, but it is true. I wouldn't go back, not for anything would I go back to youth; what would I take for my "having lived," for understanding, for feeling, even feeling sad? Nothing, nothing at all.

The girls next to us were saying, "My, doesn't it seem strange not to have President Neilson here!" For the faculty were now coming in. *They* looked just the same—once you lose youth, perhaps you don't change much. The President's chair was empty. And the whole college felt empty, too, not integrated, confused and at sea.

Then Mother came in, little and soft and gray, in her black robes, very petite and gracious. I felt I saw her at that moment as Harold Nicolson[1] saw her. The Dean opened college with crisp facts and rather a comforting practical carrying-on. There was the reading of the Bible verses. It all seemed strange and terribly vivid to me—through the double vision of my memory and the present.

"A thousand shall fall at thy side, and ten thousand at thy right hand; but it shall not come nigh thee."

I can remember as a child taking that absolutely literally, with perfect faith, and in college, if I didn't take it absolutely literally, I still believed it with my heart, in a superstitious, egotistical way. But now I don't any more, except perhaps in the way it was intended ("He shall preserve thy soul") and I even have my doubts there. And then the hymn always sung at first chapel, that I sang so many times, the first time with Elisabeth. "From hand to hand." It is a lovely hymn, full of the feeling of the eternity of the spirit. What can these girls know about that? When I am just beginning to learn. "The sense of life that knows no Death." Only the young have that—physically—until it is broken and one slowly tries to build it up on a different basis.

Then Mother got up to speak, quite girlish in spite of that soft gray hair, girlish because she is small and wistful and gracious. She gave a superb speech, dazzling in its perfection; one was seduced by its artless simplicity, which was utter skill and control—of herself, her audience, and her words. She is a real artist here. Though no one thinks of a speech as demanding that much artistry.

She got them laughing first—delicate and pointed humor, gradually building up to the serious structure—so that one was pulled up in spite of oneself and, quite by surprise, left challenged, inspired, integrated.

It was not at all personal. I have seen Mother magnificent before but usually it has been a kind of personal thing. Here she was herself and yet not herself. She was humble (I, the bridge, I felt her to be feeling). And in this humility before her

[1] English career diplomat, biographer, and critic; friend of the Morrows and author of *Dwight Morrow,* a biography of A. M. L.'s father.

Charles Lindbergh
after going on active duty
as a colonel
on return to the U.S.,
1939

Left to right: Jon, Anne Lindbergh, Land, Mrs. Dwight W. Morrow,
Constance Morrow Morgan with Saran Morgan, Margaret Loines Morrow
with Stephen Morrow, Next Day Hill, Englewood, May 29, 1939

Anne Lindbergh, 1939
Photo Charles Lindbergh

Mrs. Dwight W. Morrow with William
Allan Neilson, President, Smith College

Mrs. Dwight W. Morrow
as acting head of Smith College, 1

Anne Lindbergh with Land, summer 1939

Manor House, Lloyd Neck

Mrs. Dwight W. Morrow with Land, Lloyd Neck

*Land and Jon,
Lloyd Neck, 1939*

Land, Charles Lindbergh, and Jon, Manor House, Lloyd Neck, 1940

Charles Lindbergh with Ambassador John Cudahy, September 1940

*Charles Lindbergh
with Igor Sikorsky
and early helicopter,
October 18, 1940*

Founded
January 28, 1878

NEW HAVEN, CONN., THURSDAY, OCTOBER 31, 1940   Price, Five Cents

"... You Inherit the Problem ..."

Colonel Charles A. Lindbergh, as he addressed a crowded Woolsey Hall audience last night. Members of the Yale America First Committee are seated in the rear.

Lindbergh Sees U. S. Unprepared To Change Course of War Abroad

Christmas Jobs Ready For Local Eli Students

There is a limited number of employment opportunities available to Yale students living in New Haven during Christmas Vacation. Those interested should register immediately with Miss Little at the Bureau of Appointments, 123 Wall Street.

Yale Will Welcome Alumni Tomorrow

Seymour's Speech, Luncheon Will Feature Gathering Of Various Groups

Yale University's Alumni Board will play host to members of the Class Secretaries Association, officers of the University Alumni Fund Association, and officers of the Association of Yale Alumni in Medicine at a luncheon meeting in the Sterling Hall of Medicine at 1 P. M. tomorrow. About 60 are expected to attend.

Francis G. Blake, acting dean of the School of Medicine, will introduce President Charles Seymour, who will speak on the position of the Medical School in the University. Following luncheon, a tour of the medical school, its laboratories and classrooms, and conducted by Medical School students.

Dinner on Schedule

The guests will again meet for dinner in the President's Room in Memorial Hall at 7. Speakers will be Dr. Milton C. Winternitz, professor of Pathology and former dean of the Medical School, and James Hamilton, director of the New Haven Hospital; John B. Dempsey, 1911, of Cleveland, Ohio, chairman of the Alumni Board,

HITS 'VACILLATION'

Bissell Introduces Speaker, Defines Current Issue Of Foreign Policy

CAPACITY AUDIENCE

America First Committee Sponsors Meeting

The full text of Colonel Lindbergh's speech may be found on page three.

Charging American foreign policy with confusion and vacillation, Colonel Charles A. Lindbergh warned an overflow Woolsey Hall audience last night that America is totally unprepared to enter any war under present circumstances. His speech was the first in a series sponsored by the Yale Chapter of the America First Committee.

In a survey of United States postwar policy, the speaker showed its vacillation between Wilsonian idealism and strict neutrality, with the result that the present interventionist trend of the government finds our military forces, allowed to dwindle after the war, unequal to the task which recent diplomatic moves are setting for them.

"Utter Confusion"

Pleading for a clear-cut policy towards foreign nations as well as internally, he said, "Due to our vacillating policies we are now in a position of utter confusion. We have not been able to send enough assistance to Europe to change the course of the conflict. Although the people of our country are overwhelmingly opposed to war, and while we are utterly unprepared for it as a nation, our gov-

Counsel for Defense Wins Jury Decision In Barristers' Union

In a Thomas Swan Barristers' Union trial last night, involving the case of Oliva v. Hartford Flour Company, the jury brought in a unanimous decision in favor of the defendant. The case, which was presided over by the Hon. Carrell C. Hincks, of the United States District Court, was an action of tort to recover damages for illness brought about when the plaintiff ate some of the defendant's flour in which was found a quantity of arsenic.

Counsels for the plaintiff, John Pohlman, of Mississippi College, and Telfer Mook, of Dartmouth, stressed the fact that there was arsenic in the flour in the form of rat poison, which was found in the defendant's warehouse. For the defense, Joseph Cornwall of Princeton, and Ernest Jennes, 1939, asserted that the arsenic could

Film Society Lists "Birth of a Nation" On Coming Program

Entering its second year, the Yale Film Society, an association of students and faculty interested in artistic and historical aspects of motion pictures, will open a drive for membership today. A membership fee of $1 entitles anyone to all privileges of the society, including admission to the six showings of important and historic movies scheduled so far for this year.

Morton Gottlieb, 1941, president, has emphasized that single admissions to the movies will not be sold, and thus the only way to see them is to join the society. Membership will be limited to 400 persons. Students wishing to join this organization should see their college representatives.

The list of pictures scheduled, is as follows: December 3, a program of comedies, including Harold Lloyd in

Anne Lindbergh with baby Anne, 1940

mission, the carrying on of what she believed in—Education for Women—she was magnificent. It was beyond her own personal feeling for college and beyond her feeling for us as children there. A kind of impersonal passion and devotion to something bigger than herself or anything connected with herself: "This thing I believe in must go on." And she burned so with this passionate belief that she fused that whole confused restless diverse body of people with it.

In that moment she had reached, I felt, a kind of peak in her life. She had reached that moment all scholars, scientists, saints, and artists strive for. I was terribly moved by it, happy for her and proud of her.

Then Miss Chase and I went for a walk around Paradise Pond. She talked to me about C. and his position, and did I mind the criticism. She talked very kindly, rather veiled; evidently there has been a lot of criticism here, at which I don't wonder. (The intellectuals turn to England as to Mecca.) I outline with some warmth and a good deal of bitterness my feeling about the war—that it should never have been, the price was too great, and some of my personal feelings about it. I tell her the college atmosphere is very heartening. The things that are still going on here, the young can be taught, one is living not for my generation now but the next. "And one lives for every day," put in Miss Chase (in a quiet Maine way), "for the here and now." Yes—I had forgotten that—for the moment.

Lloyd Neck, Friday, September 29th

C. is back. We walk to the beach. We discuss the embargo act and the points of view of various people in Washington he has talked to. I feel heartsick about it. I want them to get planes over there but I do not want them encouraged to go on with this war by any act of ours or any hint of our going in.

October 28th

It is almost a month and I have not written. Life has gone on too fast and I have gotten discouraged. A strange month, full of false hopes and suspense, like the weeks before the war. Full of inward struggles and outward arguments. I felt so passionately that our last chance was slipping by for peace. That the United States might act. That Roosevelt might act, that the people might urge him to.

A cessation of hostilities—what harm could it do, what good *might* it do? *Not* to yield to Hitler, *not* to disarm, but to stand fast behind the Maginot line and cease hostilities long enough to avert a suicidal conflict which will destroy everyone, winners and losers, with Russia there to eat up the remains. Russia has been encroaching all this month with threats into the Baltic states.

It has been a terribly tiring month, arguing, pressing this point of view which no one understands, no one sees. To buck the onslaught of press, radio, and opinion everywhere (even if you do it only in your heart or in personal arguments) is a constant struggle, like batting your head against concrete. I feel bitterly, bitterly. The chance is passed. The war is on again. But I am not resigned to it.

And I have talked and argued and written and prayed. How I have prayed. Prayed not only that those in power might see some way out of this but also that if there is no way out I may learn to understand it and accept it a little.

And I have not learned.

Then there have been C.'s speeches and the backwash of them. Bitter criticism, personal attacks. He has had two threatening letters: He is a "Nazi." He will be punished. Our other two children will be taken. We are thrown back again into that awful atmosphere. How can we live near New York and alone and in the country if there are people who feel like that, even if these people are cranks? One can't take a chance.

I feel angry and bitter and trapped again. Where can we live, where can we go? C. and I talk about Plans. C. thinks we might go out West, look for a ranch, have a healthy winter. Get some American roots. I think it is quite sound; we must get away from New York. We must get some roots—and there are certain things about the West that appeal to me. And yet to make our home there makes me gasp a little—like plunging into cold water. It is to cut off Europe, it seems to me, and yet at the moment one must—and perhaps forever.

C. is criminally misunderstood, misquoted, and misused. And I have fought this, too. I believe in him and in his absolute integrity and in what he is trying to do. But it has been so misunderstood. And that I beat against in my heart. There are problems coming that I do not quite understand and do not know how I can meet. This is true for everyone but I am more conscious of these problems than most people like me because I have seen them in C.'s mind—looming for years.

Yes, one lives in constant mental strife these days. Mental strife precedes physical strife and is more difficult to bear because it is indecision.

The house has been upset, too, these last weeks, perpetual indecision and change and temporariness—because we are not settled.

A week spent in Washington—unhealthy political narrow atmosphere, criticism rife around us, arguments and newspapers.

Hours I spent writing[1]—passionately, all I felt about the war —then seeing that it was bitter and realizing I must cut all the bitterness out of it and seeing that it was also not well founded enough or documented enough (the history part—no one would listen to a dreamer and a "poet" on the causes of the war) and then realizing bitterly that the opportunity was gone for it being used—if ever it could have been.

There has been the sense of pressure from all this mail piling up, the critical articles in the papers. The worst one being an article written by Harold Nicolson in England in "defense" of C.! By an "intimate friend." My breath was knocked out of me by this. If only he had *attacked* him fairly, intellectually, on issues (like Walter Lippmann). But no—he has to hit at him under guise of a "defense" with pseudo-psychological technique. It was such a temptation to write that little article, that clever little article, that biting little article. He could do it *so*

[1] An article for the *Reader's Digest,* "Prayer for Peace."

well. "The boy from Minnesota," all that. I try to remember that after all he is a disillusioned idealist and his two boys might be sent to the front.

But there have been nice things, too, to compensate. The children—mornings when they both tumbled into bed with me, Land on my lap. Beautiful fall days, maple trees that seem to *give* out a yellow light, like sun. Red dogwoods bending across the road.

Then nights when C. and I walked down to the beach and I lay on the raft, looking straight up at the vault of the stars, only it did not feel like that; it felt, rather, that they were looking down at me. The expanse of them, the magnitude of them, the beauty of them, ironing out all strife and anguish inside of me, all those petty desires and worries, filling me instead with an incredible peace.

The fun of seeing my article on *Wind, Sand and Stars* in the *Saturday Review* despite my feeling that it has not the vaguest connection with life as we are facing it today. The letters from the publisher about it. They want to use it as a foreword in new editions. That pleases me.

This last week has gone into plans, packing,[1] moving. It is now very cold. The winds are wild and the trees beginning to be beautifully bare. This I relish and welcome—fiercely. It is the way one feels—off with the trappings, let us see the bones, the beautiful bones of the trees. The hard inner core of spirit.

Sunday, October 29th

Cold—beautiful day. Gallup poll: large percentage of America for a Peace Conference. To the John Foster Dulles's[2] for supper with some trepidation. Will it be the usual Long Island conventionality? No—he is slow but a sound, objective, and quite profound thinker. Is *not* emotional on the war, though not in the

[1] The Lindberghs were moving to the Manor House on Lloyd Neck for the winter but had to return to Englewood for a short period until it was ready.

[2] John Foster Dulles, diplomat and lawyer who became Secretary of State (1953–59) under President Dwight D. Eisenhower.

slightest degree sympathetic with Hitler. Uses the philosophical-historical and humanist attitude on this and all wars. I feel in accord with most of what he says. And it is such a relief to breathe that sane cool air of tolerance, moderation, nonemotionalism. I go away feeling fed and strengthened.

Though of course an intellectual (and an old one at that) like him will never set the world on fire.

Tuesday, October 31st, Halloween

We leave in the afternoon for Englewood.

Englewood, Wednesday, November 1st

At night we argue over J. F. Dulles's speech,[1] because I still believe wars can be stopped—and still believe in some kind of world federation, which C. thinks impractical.

Wednesday, November 8th

Aubrey calls up in the middle of the evening and tells us that a bomb has gone off in Munich in the party building just ten minutes after Hitler left! He is very excited (revolution, etc.).

Tuesday, November 21st

Cable from Margot—coming tomorrow on (Pan American) Clipper!

Wednesday, November 22nd

Drive with Con and Mrs. Loines out to Port Washington to meet the Clipper. It is a beautiful day—clouds and sun, and ducks flying. The big Clipper is over us before we know it, American flags painted on the wings, then a big circle and it lands behind a point of land. I remember the end of our Atlantic trip—North Beach, gray December. How does Margot feel! From Europe—war. It pulls up to the dock, looking very clumsy and big. The passengers step out nonchalantly. Margot's stoop and arm. We wait in the businesslike waiting room, separated

[1] Given to the YMCA of Detroit on October 29th.

by counters from the passengers. Like a custom house abroad, which it is.

After a long wait Margot comes. She looks well and brown, full of excitement over the flight, getting home, the war, the blood-let exhaustion of Spain. She talks all the way in. She said she overheard some people talking of Saint-Exupéry. They said he was not in the front lines but behind somewhere, testing planes or training pilots. I am glad of that. I drive Margot to Englewood.

Saturday, November 25th

Type my article on peace all day—must get it done and then put it away. Get it off the desk. C. reads it; he is very enthusiastic about what seems to me a patched-up piece of writing—all my thoughts of this fall, especially at the period when C. was writing his speeches. I think I have cut most of the bitterness and anger out. I don't want it angry. But it lacks spontaneity and facts.

Monday, November 27th

Work all day at white heat on article. C. is making arrangements about its going into the *Reader's Digest* Christmas number. I want someone else to read it before it goes. I am filled with mistrust and misgivings about it. Although a plea for peace, it is, in a way, jumping into a world I *hate* from my whole heart to get into—I loathe, I shrink from, and I dread the arguments, discussions, ridicule, and criticism sure to come from my intruding, an amateur, into that world. And has not the time for it passed? How practical is it? Will it hurt C.? Or help him? Will it hurt the cause of peace? Will it destroy anything we might do later? All these and a thousand other doubts assail me in the moments when I am not working over words, phrases.

Tuesday, November 28th

C. stayed up all night to type copies of my article so we could work on it simultaneously! He got only three hours' sleep but he is very cheerful. I am still undecided about sending it. In indecision you are so weakened that you could rest on anyone or anything. That is why people get such satisfaction out of tossing a penny.

Work all morning on article, which is to leave at 1:30. (They are holding up the issue for it.) Their suggestions come, for a new ending. I work on that, finally decide—trying to get wisdom from the trees outside and from the wind on my cheek —to send it. It seemed to me that the reasons for *not* sending it were chiefly cowardly ones. I did not think it could do much harm except to me—bring criticism and ridicule on me perhaps— and there was a slight chance it might do some good, prepare the ground a little for a more tolerant reception of peace or peace plans when they might turn up.

We let it go. I telephone the editor. It is a strain; I *make* myself someone else and am calm and collected! I explain the new ending and what I was trying to do in the article. C. says I was *very good* on the telephone—couldn't have been better— which set me up.

We go out in the woods and walk. It is such a relief to have the article off that I feel all apprehension gone—for the moment.

Jo Davidson[1] for supper—also Con. He makes me feel Paris and the French and I feel light-hearted and warmed, also relieved we are still friends in spite of C.'s so-called pro-Nazi articles and speeches.

[1] American sculptor, who had done a head of C. A. L. in Paris.

1940

1940 started on the train coming back from Detroit with C. and Jon. We manage to slip on all right separately, though a group of people recognized us in the station. Jon in the top berth sings or chants gently to himself in the dark quite late. C. goes to sleep with his toes sticking out over the edge of the narrow couch. And I lie awake jiggled in the lower berth, thinking. It is hard to think about the new year, hard to see anything good in it, the war overshadowing everything and the grim feeling that the best of everything is over. The feeling that one does not know what one is facing. Perhaps war, the United States in it. Almost certainly the crashing of Europe and all we love there.

In the face of that one must think of fundamentals—what matters, what is your place. I feel at rock bottom, everything else having sloughed off—that I am simply a wife not nearly good enough for C. and a mother not nearly good enough for Jon and Land. Everything else is pretty much vanity. I must try to keep this picture clear and not live in the past, not live in Europe, not live in dreams—live in the present, in the children, in C. from day to day. There is joy and beauty there always, in spite of everything.

The first day of the new year is not an easy one. We drive out to Englewood. Jon is greeted by shouts from Mother, Soeur Lisi, Land. We hear that lots of people are coming for lunch. C. decides to escape to town. We go skiing first. It is beautiful and clear and skiing is satisfying—adventure and beauty (maybe I *do* love adventure a little)—and I feel: See, this is simple, living is simple, if you live like this, outside and well. But then lunch, company, all day. I am too conscious of all of them and of C. impatient upstairs, and want to help and can't.

Wednesday, January 3rd

Drive to Cambridge to see the Whiteheads.[1]

Mrs. Whitehead at the door of the apartment. She is a thin tall frail Englishwoman, *very* aware. She comes forward warmly. Then he comes in. He is bent over, a small man, baldish but still ruddy-faced, with keen eyes. Though very English and reserved, he comes forward kindly, beaming, and I warm to him. I take off my things and then we sit down. I next to *him*. Feeling I must take my courage in my hands, with both of us shy, I say that we drove up through New England and it was nice to feel how much of the New England quality was still there. And he (no longer shy) said how he felt perhaps it might keep a quality that would go out of the world elsewhere, now with the war. I felt relieved that the conversation had started and said, "I wish my husband could hear that" (leaning forward to catch C.'s eye), and C. turned to Whitehead and they started to talk. I felt great and deep satisfaction: "There, now it is done."

After that the evening went very easily, though I must say I felt rather breathless throughout. That wonderful old man. He spoke rather slowly, with precision, sometimes repeating, almost stuttering over a sentence which was, when it came, pellucid in its beauty. His very penetrating eye was a gentle one, too. In fact, perhaps the most impressive thing about him was his gentleness. A saintlike quality that made his humor and sometimes even sardonic wit rather a shock when it came.

She was surprising, too. I had not expected to find such a woman—frail, yes, old, gray, not beautiful, one hand crippled (with arthritis?), so that to help herself she had to hold one hand with the other, and yet she gave the impression of youth and of beauty, of lightness, of ease, and of intensity, "a sense, of life so lovely and intense."

[1] Alfred North Whitehead, English mathematician, philosopher, and writer, professor at Harvard University, and his wife, Evelyn.

I could hardly hear her voice at times, it was so frail, and yet what she said was "mordant." There was nothing soft about her; you did not want to be sentimental with her. You knew she would detect it unerringly. *"Elle est toujours tentée d'arracher les masques."* ("She is always tempted to tear off the masks.") She rather reminded me of Mme du Deffand—a bluestocking of the eighteenth century. That intellectual fervor, that passion for the truth, along with much gallantry, charm, beauty, and elegance. Yes—a kind of elegance. A Mme du Deffand without the bitterness, because she had discovered something she could worship: *"Le seul saint devant qui je brûle ma chandelle."* ("The only saint before whom I light my candle.") And no vanity—a brilliant woman with no intellectual vanity at all, content to parry for her husband, content to let him write the books, content to watch, guide, play to, understand, lend a hand to, in a casual taken-for-granted way.

She said that you didn't need money in old age. The young needed it, for opportunities. In age one needed very little: "One needs warmth—and I put warmth very high!—and books, and friends."

The little apartment was tiny but warm. It did not seem crowded, for it was furnished simply but with distinction, darkish walls against which daffodils and pictures and books glowed like jewels.

He and C. and she and I alone in the tiny dining room. I felt anxious all evening for it to go well for C. (Women are so conscious of the *artistry* of an evening that they cannot enter into it—they are trying to create it.) C. and he talked of America, its future problems. (Whitehead was much more cheerful than C. of our working out our problems here without undue suffering.) He was not discouraged about the "immediate future, the next two or three hundred years." He spoke of the dogmas he learned as a boy—all disproved. "Not true or false but relevant is what matters." He spoke of the idea of gentleness. The failure of the Church in not emphasizing the essential message of Christianity—gentleness. The North African and southern French culture was hard, ascetic. He said we are conscious of values before they are expressed. Christ was the first *expression* of gentleness but the ideal of gentleness was there in mothers, before Christ.

Next Day Hill, Englewood, New Jersey, January 7th
Dear Mrs. Curtiss,[1]
Your letter from the "wilderness" was such a joy and really brought me some of the confidence and peace that living in the wilderness gives you.

It interests me greatly what you feel about it [the desert] and its satisfying quality. I have been analyzing the places I have loved and lived in, lately—out of homesickness for them, I guess. One goes through stages. When we went to England I wanted only security and peace and for things to stay the same. Long Barn gave it to me. It was "the same," had been "the same," from time immemorial. And you could sit in the evening on those steps and count all things that did not change but were the same—the oaks and the walls of the house and fields— and therefore to me, at that moment, "security." But then on windy days or stormy days or even ordinary days when I felt restless, I began to feel, but *I* am not the same—*I* change. I cannot sit still in this perfect peaceful cow-like English world!

And then we went to Illiec. It was hard at first, it was so in-secure. Life did not even move by the security of clocks but by tides and moons and weather (the milk, the post, and provisions came across from the mainland according to *tide* not *time*). And there was always the roar of the sea and the howling of the wind. It made me restless at first and then I began to feel that it was like life and that in letting yourself go in it (as "letting go" to the bank of a plane) one found complete peace. It was adapted to the endless change in one's own life. It was like sleeping in a hammock on a boat. One no longer fought the essence of life itself.

And yet we are not *all* change. There is something changeless in us and perhaps if one could keep in touch with that, one

[1] Mina Curtiss, A. M. L.'s teacher of creative writing at Smith College, friend and author of books on Proust and Bizet.

would feel at home only in a place far less changeless than an English garden. Don't you think that is what the fascination of the desert is? The affinity between the changeless element in us and the changelessness of a desert.

This is already too long. But your life there sounded so exactly what I longed to do that I wondered if you had been drawn to it by the same reasons and what you were getting from it. I am glad you are writing in such a wonderfully timeless place. All writing should be done that way, it seems to me.

Besides, the cities are so full of urgencies and bitterness and passions. We, in the East, have caught it, a little, from Europe. It frightens me because I dread that the hate and suspicion and terror that is abroad in the world in general should come in particular to each individual's heart so that it becomes not war but an epidemic (as St.-Ex. says in *Wind, Sand and Stars,* of the war in Spain). The "front" is in each individual's mind, and families and friends are split wide open—or might be. Perhaps I have too gloomy a picture. We cannot predict the future, thank goodness, or know what forces may be at work, for the good.

At times like this I think it helps to feel that other people are living awarely in the mind and in the spirit—when so much mind and spirit is being destroyed—you sound as though you *were* living like that and it cheers me.

[*From January 29 to February 5 we were in Florida with Jim Newton and an Audubon Society game warden, Charlie Green, taking a cruise in a small motor launch into the Everglades, Shark River, and down the coast to the Keys. Guided by two conservationist friends, we made the first of our trips into the wilderness country (in 1940 the Everglades were untouched wilderness). We explored the many-threaded bayous and saw brown and white pelicans, American egrets, buzzards, white and wood ibis in their roosts in the mangrove swamps, and watched shark, turtle, and barracuda along the coast. I wrote of this experience: "One gets the sense here of life—life in the air, life in the water, life on the banks—all the teeming life of*

*a river. It is a kind of Forest Primeval. . . . It is wonderful to
enter into another world of life. All of life is precious and makes
you and your life richer and more understanding." Sometimes,
I was reluctant to leave the warm cabin (it was a cold season)
to go out in the small rowboat at night with my husband, but
was rewarded by the experience: "C. takes up the oars and we
drift soundless in the black night until we are part of that intense
stillness—only an occasional splash of a bird or a fish, and the
hoot of an owl in the distance. I should always go when C. calls
—break through my crust of inertia or fear—because life lies
behind it."*

*It was a rest and refreshment to be for two weeks away from
the conflicts and pressures of suburban Long Island. On our
return to civilization, I learned from the* Reader's Digest *that my
article "Prayer for Peace" in their December issue had rated first
in the poll of readers. Also, to my surprise, that the British
Ministry of Information had cabled for permission to reprint
the article in pamphlet form.*]

DIARY   *April 3rd, Lloyd Neck*

Ever since we got back from Florida I have been in bed—or
practically in bed. Nausea and vomiting and then just weakness
—all confirming what I hoped ecstatically was true in Florida,
that I am having another child. In Florida I was terribly happy
over it. When you are very sick, it is hard to be happy. One
is too intent on keeping down that little bit of broth. One can
only feel: I know it doesn't seem so now but I *will* get over this
and I *will* be happy again. At first I couldn't read at all or lift my
head from the pillow but gradually I could sit up a little and
read and finally go out and sit in the sun and delicious air.
It has meant sinking down deep deep into one's consciousness,
being very much alone. A lot of dreaming, a lot of thinking, a
lot of *mental* writing and a soaking up of old trains of thought.

April 8th

Spring is very late—the trees are still bare and wintry. But
yesterday was warm and the air very sweet—fragrant almost—

as though there were arbutus under the last year's oak leaves.

Yesterday I walked over the hill and sat on a stump in the woods. I sat so long and so still that the birds came back. Robins, a flock of field birds, and two woodpeckers.

Monday, April 16th

For a week now we have been absorbed in the war. Tuesday morning at about seven a call from Aubrey woke us out of sleep. Someone's died! I thought instinctively. But when C. said, "You've no idea how many there are. . . ." I said, "They've marched?" He nodded. "Where?" I asked.

At the news "Germany has taken over Denmark and invaded Norway" I felt that familiar sick-at-the-pit-of-the-stomach shock that all moves of Germany give instinctively to you. The ruthless speed, force, and efficiency with which they act take one's breath away. It takes me some time to get back to the premise which I keep forgetting—war is a thug's game. The thug strikes first and harder. He doesn't go by rules and he isn't afraid of hurting people.

April 23rd

The sun is out for the first time in twelve days. And it is warmer!

The morning was so delicious that I sat in the sun and basked in it. Everything wakes after a long rain. The line of daffodils has cracked yellow. The grass is that lovely golden green, and even the sky has blossomed—soft blue—and round comfortable white clouds that stay where they're put and don't tear off like winter ones. Also SMELLS! rich earth and drying bark of trees and sweet smells, too—from what? Budding trees?

Monday, April 29th

In the afternoon, C. telephones from the Long Island Aviation Country Club and I take over the children, Christine, and Soeur Lisi, and we all go up in the plane. Land (his first *conscious* ride) sits on my lap and is timid, though forgets at the sight of tiny cars running around on the roads below. But Jon is in an ecstasy all the time, goes up every time he can, eyes shining.

I go up alone with C. and fly over Lloyd Neck. It is sunset over water and intensely beautiful. It is still an ecstasy, I think, flying. Will it always be so for me, even when I am old? Does ecstasy go—ecstasy from the beauty of the earth? Or does one keep it all one's life?

M. Boël[1] for dinner. We greet him with some trepidation. All goes well, though C. and he are *poles* apart—generations, oceans, cultures, worlds! I am very nervous and make great efforts to bridge the worlds, for I love them both. Oh, how I love that world of charm, culture, intelligence, beauty, and tolerance—ideals represented by the truly civilized European. And how blind it is, how lost, how behind the times. It does not see the wave of the future that is even now suspended over it. It is looking back, perpetually, even when it thinks it is looking forward. Even the language is relative to another world, another day, that is gone.

I see the war as a "Revolution." He sees it as a "Crusade."

From this ultimate point of view it seems to me only an *expression* of one of those great mutations in the history of mankind and only one of many expressions.

Whitehead has given the best definition of it. "Human life is driven forward by its dim apprehension of notions too general for its existing language."

Something, one feels, is pushing up through the crust of custom. What was pushing under the "Great War"? What behind Communism? What behind Nazism? Is it nothing but a "return to barbarism" as the M. Boëls think, to be crushed at all costs by a "Crusade"? Or is some new and perhaps even ultimately good conception of humanity coming to birth—or *trying* to come to birth through these evil and horrible forms, these abortive attempts?

It has seemed to me that there is a common element hidden in these terrible things—an element perhaps social, perhaps economic, the same element that has shown itself in "the New Deal" and perhaps in the reforms of Blum. Hitler "taking in" the

[1] Baron René Boël, Belgian industrialist.

working classes, his deification of labor, "the dignity of labor," much of the "socialist" side of National Socialism, even though *forced* from the top, brutally.

But with it has gone so much that is terrible and barbaric. Why why *why* is it in the hands of these people? *Must* it always be so? Why do not the good and the wise see it and use it? Because only by suffering and terrible times is one forced to it? And violent times breed violent people?

I wish I could feel as almost everyone does that this war is all due to Hitler, that terrible scourge of humanity. A terrible and completely *accidental* scourge unconnected to other world events—alone responsible for all. And that if the scourge were only wiped out all would be finished. I cannot feel that he, as an individual, is that important. Nazism seems to me scum which happens to be on the wave of the future. I agree with people's condemnation of Nazi methods but I do not think they *are* the wave. They happen to be riding on it.

May 20th

Since M. Boël was here and I started writing, the world has taken another terrific lurch and people are still reeling from it: with incredible swiftness and all the horrors of war, Holland and then Belgium have been overrun, bombed, and taken. The French and English pushed back—first in Belgium and now through the French fortifications in northern France. These moves have come in successive stages but they have come so swiftly that one has not had time to catch one's breath.

When the Germans first moved into Holland and Belgium and I heard the news, I had, as always, that first terrible emotional shock that I always have with *all* acts of the Germans. "This is too horrible, they *must* be stopped. Oh, why can't we stop them?" My first reaction is always "French" or Allied, and it is the average reaction of normal people throughout America and, in fact, everywhere.

One becomes then only human and personal. You think of the suffering thousands of refugees, of the soldiers defending their inch of homeland, and you think of those few human beings, those minute morsels of humanity, whom you happen yourself to know in the vast conflagration. You think of them with a depth of misery and far and distant—*far* because they seem suddenly as removed as planets from your ken or your help—with hopelessness. What hope is there that *your* particular cinders will survive the conflagration? M. Boël, just now sitting at our dinner table, describing his bombproof cellar in Brussels. The Germans are now in Brussels—where are the Boëls?

The baffling statement of the French, after a week of this steam-rollering drive: "It has now become a war of movement." "My God! Has it ever been anything else?" one wanted to ask. (C. says this meant it was no longer a war of defense, behind fixed defenses. They were gone.) Talk of a "secret weapon" of the Germans. The baffling thing about all the reports, through papers and radio, being that though one gets only encouraging news of "Allied resistance, attacks, brilliance, and courage" it is always the Germans who get the points. With a sickening thud of realization each time, one finally comes to the ultimate fact that the Allies are steadily and appallingly losing ground, men, *everything*. The night C. got word from Truman [Smith] that the Germans were evidently massing troops (70 divisions!) for a gigantic attack on the Maginot line: "It is war—all out."

I *couldn't* believe it. But I thought it was impregnable? But I thought Hitler said he would never again have French and German blood shed over that same ground? But I thought the Germans considered *England* their real enemy, not *France*. He will pour the heart of Germany and France out on that line. Think of the cost! Why must he win the war *that* way—only to show he can beat the Allies where they beat him? German military pride? But the cost? I will not forgive it.

We went to bed very black. C. could not understand either. But he was thinking logically: Well, now, you can't tell yet what their objective is or what they know. Perhaps the line isn't invincible, perhaps it is the best military move—for *them*.

Then the cautious news creeping through that the French line was "dented." Belgium crumbling bit by bit. Disquieting rumors about advances into France. Then the shock that they had broken through—to Rethel, the "bulge," it was now called —toward Paris. Gamelin's[1] command that every Frenchman must hold his bit of land or die. The time has passed for retreating.

England at last realizes that she is fighting for her very life. The speeches of Churchill—some very stirring ones—and the English stiffening to them, show this. They have at last come to realize that people do great and even impossible things only when sacrifices are demanded of them. They do *not* do great things if patted on the back and treated with the bedside manner of a Chamberlain. No, they need to be told, "I have nothing to offer but blood, toil, tears and sweat."

C. calls me from Washington. "Brussels has fallen—Antwerp has gone—they are 60 miles from Paris."

But I can't *bear* it. Then I go to the window. It is a beautiful moonlit night, almost full. There will be fliers out tonight. I pray for them—but what to pray?

And here the apple tree by the window full out with big blossomy blooms, fresh as water, and the chestnut trees, magnificent, full, in the sky, their pattern of leaves and white candles repeated over and over, all pointing up—almost like voices in a song of unison. The chestnut trees which are so woven into my pictures of Paris. They were just like this a year ago when we left and I looked back on the big chestnut tree on the corner going into the Bois, "Oh, Jon, look back, look back, so you will remember the chestnut trees!" (And then felt I was being overemotional, inflicting my emotion and my premonitions—that I should never see Paris again, that it would never again be the same—on a child.)

Pain and Beauty are again woven together in my mind, unbearably, this spring.

Reports of the cracking of French morale behind the lines due to bombing, etc. One is aware of a kind of cracking from

[1] General Maurice G. Gamelin, Commander-in-Chief of the French army.

many points of a mighty edifice—the illusion of the invincible French army (just as we witnessed in Norway the cracking of the illusion of the invincible English fleet).

People here are terribly shocked. Nobody really believed they could be beaten. And the pro-Ally and pro-war people all thought they would at least have more warning of it—time enough to get us in. Just as they were getting ready to do this they suddenly wake up to find it is too late. In the typical way, we rush to extremes; from being sure Germany was really very weak we are now all hysterically fearing her strength. The President, in his speech launching a huge rearmament bill, hinted that we were vulnerable to air attack from Greenland. Fifth column, etc. People are organizing anti-parachute-attack units in Philadelphia.

C.'s speech over the radio—my slight gasp as he keeps on going after where I left him (before he went to Washington), like a train leaving the tracks and suddenly taking to the air! My! I think, he certainly has put teeth in it since I saw it. This will raise the roof! It will be taken as anti–New Deal and anti-intervention. They will quote his sentence "It is too late for us to participate successfully in this war" *out* of its context, which was that wars are won in the ten years of preparation that precede them. And it will be considered pitiless. The best things in it will be overlooked. And yet the strength, force, and sanity will somehow accidentally get through to people and sound a chord.

[*C. A. L. spoke for the third time in Washington. This subject was the "Air Defense of America." He insisted that the Western Hemisphere, if united, was secure against "foreign invasion." "Let us turn again to America's traditional role—that of building and guarding our own destiny." He urged greater defense preparedness. "To be successful in modern warfare a nation must prepare many years before the fighting starts. . . . We need a greater air force, a greater army, and a greater navy: they have been inadequate for many years. Let us cease the hysterical chatter of calamity and invasion."*]

DIARY

C. back—telegrams and letters (a *vast* majority favorable—surprisingly!). News of the war (inside news) confirming my worst fears. The French air force "completely destroyed" and the British only bombing at night.

C.'s speech carried in full in *Times* and *Tribune. Times* hits back with a short and lashing editorial: "Colonel Lindbergh remains a great aviator"!

Tuesday, May 21st

To town. Here the sense of the war seems much more terrible. I look at shop windows, cars, people in the streets, hats and flowers and jewels shining out of windows—like Paris. I read on a prosperous granite store façade: "Paris, New York, London." How familiar and solid it looks, from time immemorial. Will it be rubbed out now and read "New York, Berlin"? And people rushing about in taxis, in stores, on the streets, apparently completely unaware of the momentous changes overtaking the world, and them, too. For of course it will affect us. No one knows exactly when or how, but it will, I feel sure.

Lunch with Con. She says it is very bad and getting worse every moment but she doesn't seem as low as several weeks ago —only very weary and dazed. She thinks they will take over France and invade Britain. She says they hear that all the posts have been earmarked for various German officials, such as Police Commissioner in London, etc. Political plums for good soldiers. (It is just like Caesar!)

Con says she takes a grim satisfaction in thinking that the Germans will find that, like the Romans with Greece, the people they have conquered are still superior to them mentally, culturally, like the Greeks who became the teachers, philosophers, mentors of the Romans. In other words, they will not, even now, attain superiority.

At the same time she thinks we may come in—if they hold out long enough. Also that if the Allies *are* defeated it will be for us what Munich was to them, i.e., eventually we will have to fight Germany alone.

Black headlines on street corners announce Arras and Abbéville fallen and the northern armies trapped. Reynaud[1] admits rout of armies and "blames generals."

Home through flowering apple trees—very tired.

Wednesday, May 22nd

Go over wills with C. Mrs. Schuman here all day sewing on maternity dresses. Rain. News over radio indicates profound confusion about battle areas. The supreme dictatorial powers handed to the war council in England.

Hear Senator [James] Byrnes "answer" C. He uses all the old emotional gags (Göring medal, Munich, Lady Astor, Russian episodes) and a few new ones. Also he sets up straw men to knock down—implying that C. was not for preparedness.[2]

Friday, May 24th

Lunch with Mother at the Cosmopolitan Club. She is terribly worked up about the way the war has turned and at the appalling spectacle of suffering, which has only just begun. Everyone feels like her (only I felt that way last September—those first three days, when I cried so much). But not everyone feels her terrible sense of shame and even guilt for America not helping more. "How they will *hate* us—oh, how they will *hate* us." I have felt this, dreaded it, and known it for so long that it is no shock to me, though it will be difficult to bear when it comes practically in details.

Aubrey says that England will *never* give in; even if invaded, she will "go down fighting." Mother thinks this is wonderful (spirit) and right and all they can do—to hand on to their children the heritage of having fought and died for what they know is right. I think, as usual, that argued on *their* plane it is "right," only it does not seem right that this generation of young men should be slaughtered helplessly for the errors and blindness of their elders, that children be starved and homes ruined through

[1] Paul Reynaud, French Premier in 1940.

[2] Actually his speech had urged "greater defense preparedness."

no one's fault but those old statesmen now making speeches about holding out to the bitter end.

Mother sent cables off this morning to England, to the Miles', Morgans,[1] etc., begging them to send their children here "for the duration" (they've already written, at the beginning of the war). "That's all I can do," said Mother helplessly. "What *can* I do for them? I can give money, I can take those children."

I do not believe one *should* have such a guilty feeling about the *action* of America in staying out. I think she (America) has a perfect right to make her own decision on the basis of her own welfare. It is the attitude she took *while* staying out that makes me ashamed, urging the Allies to fight, blaming them for not fighting, criticizing their methods of fighting, while not going in herself.

"Isolationism" seems to me as puerile and feeble a doctrine for a nation as self-sufficiency for an individual. But one's *first*—not one's *only,* but one's *first*—duty is to one's own family or nation; only after that is looked at can one look further. Though my heart would feel lighter in many respects were we swept along in that maelstrom over there, my judgment tells me that it is *not* to the best welfare of America, or perhaps even of the world.

However, none of this is much help to one when you look at the vast misery that is going on over there. Nor does it help the despairing feeling of that abyss of separation forever—by their and your points of view—from friends.

Driving home at night I think how much more courageous C. is about all this than I am—more courageous morally as well as physically. Would I have the strength, knowing it meant criticism, scorn, losing of friends, hurting feelings of those who don't understand, being accused falsely, the giving up of old associations, places, and people and a life I loved, to go against my private emotions and desires and stand firm for my convictions—convictions which are for the good not of myself, perhaps

[1] Aubrey Morgan's family and close friends.

not even of my children, but the future of my country? I do not know—but he is a patriot.

C. calls Truman [Smith], who says that the Allied forces trapped in Belgium will have to break through tomorrow or it's over for them. They are squeezed into half the space they had before and *have* to fight. "The flower of the Allied armies!" C. walks up and down restless and disturbed. Finally he says, "I can't keep those troops out of my mind. I know what hell is going on there, what hell."

This is the man accused of "iciness" in the papers!

Lying awake very late at night, C. asleep, I come to the quite simple conclusion that perhaps my small and individual sacrifice or contribution to this war, or, rather, to this period, is the giving up of all contacts, associations, and friends in England and France or, rather, the having *them* give *me* up. It is giving up the European side of myself and all the strings that lead to it that I formed over there and that were dear. But I mind it so much for C. I mind what he has lost in France. It was something so beautiful, so pure, so fresh (perhaps too beautiful—like spring and youth—to last). *I* had no part in it. The feeling of the French for him was undiluted, clear, spontaneous. It never changed from that first burst of love and enthusiasm they gave the boy at Le Bourget. It came from their hearts and even after their own fliers had been killed and failed to get across. And he warmed to it as he never did to the enthusiasm in England or America. It was of a different quality. A first love.

Saturday, May 25th

Again bad weather, dark, cold, and damp. C. reads from the paper this morning—an article about Saint-Exupéry. It was so nice to think he was still alive. What a curious world one lives in that one can be glad that *today* a man is alive, sitting at a café in Paris, writing an article, seeing his wife, when you know that *yesterday* he barely escaped death and that *tomorrow* he goes back again to it. Of course he has always lived like that.

Jon and I went for a bird walk this afternoon in the rain across the fields. It was lovely. He got such joy out of discovering and looking at the birds and I really felt as though I were giving him something, some kind of armor, in teaching him *to see*.

Sunday, May 26th

The Germans claim Boulogne and Calais. The Allies admit Boulogne but not Calais. No conclusive word. The British prepare for an invasion of England.

It is a day of National Prayer in England. Crowds are kneeling to Ste. Geneviève in Paris. I pray, too—but not for victory, for peace, for patience, for understanding, for "Thy will be done," O God, and let us *see* and understand how.

The house is heavy with lilac.

May 27th, 11th Wedding Anniversary

Another dull, cold day—not like our wedding day—though the chestnut trees are flowering as they were then. A telegram from Elwes asking us to call him, saying he is going home. I call him, feeling timid as usual on the telephone. But as soon as he starts to talk I feel so overcome with sympathy for him that I forget everything but that, only it is *dreadful*. He has been called back, he knows what he is going to, he has seen it right along. He has no hope and is completely unfitted for war. He is a charming, sensitive, intelligent young artist. He talks to me as though I were his last friend—longs to see C. I am appalled. We are really *nothing* to him and yet he reaches like a drowning man. He is too intelligent to fool with false comfort. I promise to try to come in and say good-bye. I feel shaken by it.

In the evening C. and I drive up along Huntington Bay to find the spot we went to after our wedding. The lighthouse. It is a beautiful evening, clear and calm. Later we go over to the Colgate beach. I sit on the raft we sat on so often last summer and C. walks down the beach. I sit and think about the war—especially the doom threatening England. How is it possible?

And of Elwes, of all the Elweses—a whole generation of them —artistic, cultured, beautiful young men, doomed to be downed by fate, just fate.

I am depressed beyond words. But as I am thinking I catch sight of C.'s figure, dark, slight, small in the distance, coming up in silhouette over the rocks, toward me, and I instinctively feel hope. And I think, yes—*that* is what keeps one going in times like these, the thought, the realization that there are a few men in the world, here and there—one has met them—who are on top of fate. And I do not mean just that they always win, but they are not downed by their circumstances in spite of everything. There are men like that even on the losing side in Europe today, in spite of being beaten; they will survive, rise above it, superior to it—make something of it. And it is for this that one goes on living.

C. comes back and I tell him what I am thinking: "And there are people like that over there now who will be above it, will not be embittered, will get something from it, make something of it—if they are not killed." (I think of Saint-Exupéry.) He is quiet for a moment and then says, as though reading my thought, "I hope Saint-Exupéry survives." "Yes," I say, "but there is so little chance."

"There is so little chance, yes," says C., "but there are men who get through, even with so little chance, men who live a whole life like that and survive somehow—one doesn't know why—as though they were destined to."

Lloyd Neck, Huntington, Long Island, May 27th

Dear Mrs. Curtiss,

I wish I could come to Ashfield. But I'm afraid it's impossible at the moment. I have been laid up a good part of the winter (only very sick having a baby, which I hope to keep a secret as long as possible) and though I am very much better the most I can do at present is a trip to town and that not very often.

This is not in answer to your wonderful letter from the desert which came to me in the midst of flat-in-bed-nausea and was such a joy. It made even the war less terrible. I felt—while reading it—in a strange way much closer to the people I loved and was thinking about abroad. As though a survival of spirit anywhere in the world were a survival of them and the things they stand for. This sounds very odd and is difficult to explain. Perhaps I can do better when I see you. It set me to thinking about so many things that I wanted to discuss with you. But it is so difficult to write from bed or even from a chaise longue, I find.

About your second letter, again, in a way I find it difficult to answer, though I have waited and thought about it quite a lot. Perhaps you have already by now made your decision [she was facing a choice between teaching and writing]—in which case this will only be an academic discussion. But I should like to give it to you anyway, because I have thought about it, and hope you will not mind.

In general, I feel, or I have come to feel, that the richest writing comes not from the people who dedicate themselves to writing alone. I know this is contradicted again and again but I continue to feel it. They don't, of course, write as much, or as fast, but I think it is riper and more satisfying when it does come. One of the difficulties of writing or doing any kind of creative work in America seems to me to be that we put such stress on production and material results. We put a time pressure and a mass pressure on creative work which are meaningless and infantile in that field.

In Europe, of course, this is not true. The most wonderful experience I think I had abroad was the contact with Despiau and watching his slow painful patient work—completely oblivious of outside standards or of time. He said once that if one had three minutes of clear vision in a day it was enough, more than enough. And he talked of *"les séances blanches"*—the days in which nothing seemed to progress. He often works three years on a head, and seven years on an Apollo that is not yet done!

Over here the publishers expect you to write a book every two years at the least or you are not a writer. It is so awfully hard to withstand the production mentality that pervades everything. I am tortured by it myself. I look at the Book Sections and think—another book by so-and-so. He has written two to my one. How will I ever get a body of work done at this rate— how will I ever become a writer! It is hard to accept the fact that probably I will never have "a body of work" in that sense or "become a writer" just like that.

Perhaps *men* can specialize and dedicate themselves to writing better than women. But there seems to me a dreadful kind of infertility that grows like fungus from women writers who dedicate themselves to it alone. For instance, in spite of my admiration for their beautiful writing, I think there is a kind of fungus quality in the books of both Vita Sackville-West and V. Woolf. I know they are married, V. S.-W. has children, but it is a question of attitude. They think of themselves as *writers,* not as mothers or wives *ever* (what a statement!), so their point of view, it seems clear, is always the same.

On the other hand I do not know whether teaching can give one a different point of view or not. It is again *giving* of oneself, like writing, and perhaps it saps the very thing that should go into writing. Perhaps one cannot do both at the same time, but that teaching is only a help for those *"séances blanches,"* those times when one cannot be creative otherwise. I get comfort from pointing out birds to Jon, or clouds and wind to Land in the periods when I can't write and thereby get the feeling that I am giving or creating in a more elementary way, while waiting for the more specialized way of writing to come back to me.

But you don't seem to be in a "blank period." At least, the letter from the desert was so rich and full of things modern writing seems to lack, full, not of a sense of time, but of eternity. And it would seem a terrible mistake to cut yourself off, at least any more than temporarily, from such a source of nourishment.

This is all from the *writing* point of view. From the point of view of teaching I am again prejudiced because I am on the side of the recipient. You see I think you were a remarkable teacher. It is hard to go back to oneself in college, one was so different, but still I remember some things and I can tell you them.

In the first place your intellectual judgment forced us technically to sharpen our writing and in a sense formed it. This is a plain fact and you must realize it. A lot of your students did. No one had ever done that for me before and it was very

exciting. (I don't mean in a weak sense. I mean the *hard* excitement of learning to use a tool and not use it sloppily.) I don't
think I need elaborate this point as it is purely factual and
obvious. You have a gift for doing that. But that wasn't—in spite
of its great value—why people flocked to your classes or talked
about you. And this point is harder to explain. I think we went
because we felt in some kind of obscure way, or sensed, that you
had a vital connection with modern living that very few other
teachers seemed to have. It is hard to explain. If I were to try
to say it today I think I would say that we felt they on the
whole were sterile and you weren't. Or perhaps it is better put
in the words of a man whose speech I am sending you.

"To be modern is to be responsive to the mentality of the
present; or, to answer present spiritual needs; or, in creative
work, to express our thought and feeling in a form of our own,
as in a language of our own."[1]

And just here, it seems to me, your problem has an intimate
connection with the terrible tragedy of the world today. As you
sit and see your own generation slaughtered or embittered for life,
day by day over there, you feel more and more that the only
hope is in children and young people and therefore colleges
become more and more important. I don't mean simply as
reservoirs and preservers of the old cultures and traditions that
are being lost over there. At least *you* don't have to do that. There
are plenty of people in the colleges to do that. What seems to me
more important than that backward look is to give them something with which to adjust to the future, to the completely new
world which is going to face them. For the wave that is sweeping
over Europe will, it seems to me, surely sweep over us too. I
don't mean necessarily war or Nazi domination. But, rather,
something else which is trying to push up through the crust
of the world's habits and has thus far only found its expression
in such horrible and abortive forms as communism, nazism and
war. I wonder what it will be when it finally evolves, a new
form of communism or socialism, or world cooperation? At any

[1] From a speech by Josef Alber, German artist and refugee, who taught
at Black Mountain College.

rate the world will never never be the same again and we have all got to adjust to a different life. I hope with the minimum of suffering and the maximum of wisdom. And the burden of this will fall on the young, who ought to be prepared for this and can't be by people who are looking backwards or who aren't creative about teaching. . . .

I hope the writing is going well. I think it must be from the sound of your desert letter. I am quite envious as I do not seem able to add another stroke to mine. It isn't just the baby but the war, and the terrible struggle that goes on eternally between your heart which is in Europe and your mind which is trying to be American and determine what is the best course for this country.

DIARY   *Wednesday, May 29th*

Dreadful announcement of Göring that in retaliation for French treatment of Nazi air prisoners all French aviators will be thrown in chains. "For each German aviator shot, five French fliers will be shot in retaliation."

It is this kind of thing that makes one despair of the Germans having ever *ever* any sense of humanity. I know that the French are also cruel—in anger, in hate. But the Germans are cruel, are brutal, *in cold blood,* deliberately. I feel a kind of fierce anger at this announcement—a "this I will *never* forgive, *never,"* a feeling that all war brings and that I try not to fall into.

C. says we will probably never see Illiec again. The French will not forgive him. Of course I must face that—and I understand it—and so does he.

Thursday, May 30th, Decoration Day

A beautiful day—washed, clear, cool, fresh, like Maine.

Over the radio come again from Berlin terrible threats, warnings, accusations; citing of atrocities: French traditional cruelty, barbarism, sadistic tendencies, and degeneracy. The day of reckoning is coming, etc. Also (versus England) all civilian deaths being recorded so that they may be paid back many times over. All this makes me ill with a kind of blind rage against the Germans.

And all the time I and my family go on living peacefully in this hermetically sealed world. A world of love and peace and spring beauty in which we have given up the use of a deck chair because we do not want to hurt a wasp who has built her nest in the cretonne shade of it, and we have stopped using the front door for fear of frightening the mother robin who has built her nest above it.

C. goes off to have lunch with Carrel and Détroyat[1] (over here on a mission to get planes). It is a "bath of fire" ordeal because they are his friends, men of integrity and intelligence —on the other side. It is courageous of him to do it (and he *wants* to do it, takes the challenge). And I think it is superb of Détroyat to see him.

The war news is always this terrifying "rear-guard action."

The terrible hopeless suicidal last-ditch fight of the trapped armies in Flanders—apparently to let the British Expeditionary Force escape. The part of it that is not bombed, slaughtered, drowned is trying to embark from Dunkirk, under heavy bombardment. (The docks are destroyed; the men are going in small boats and even *swimming,* under terrible fire, to the boats, which are offshore.)

Friday, May 31st

Weather black, cold, and gloomy, but driving to New York I am filled with a strange kind of elation, due solely to C.'s report of yesterday's lunch with Carrel and Détroyat. Apparently they could talk freely and objectively and with complete trust and understanding. They understood—amazingly—C.'s point of view and agreed with him to a large extent! Only the French could do that! But—most touching of all—apparently Détroyat defended C. against attacks in the French Embassy. "You can't say that about him—he is my friend . . . he is right . . . it is

[1] Michel Détroyat, test and acrobatic pilot, one of the French aviators who rescued C. A. L. from the crowd at Le Bourget, Paris, in 1927.

useless." I had thought he was gay, charming, simple, open-hearted, and good in a boyish way, and knew he was fond of C. But I never dreamed he was as independent, as generous, as loyal, as courageous (morally) as that.

He has been there in the battle (pursuit), he knows what France faces, and he can still meet and treat C. as a friend. It is incredible. I do not believe, placed in the same position, I could do it.

To Sue and George [Vaillant] for lunch—very nice, stimulating. A relief to be with people with whom one is not fighting inwardly. They are almost the only people who *feel* the way I do but look beyond that feeling, with reasoned and unimpassioned thought.

They confirm what I already know, that this last speech of C.'s has made him far more unpopular than anything else—in a certain class. Not that it was more violent than the others but because *they* now feel more violently. They are so worked up themselves that to be dispassionate is to represent the Anti-Christ. I know the "class" well. It is "my" class. All the people I was brought up with. The East, the secure, the rich, the cultured, the sensitive, the academic, the good—those worthy intelligent people brought up in a hedged world so far from realities.

Sue says she wants "in her heart" the Allies to win because they represent her personal world but she is not at all sure it will be better for the little man in the street if they win. People are always saying to her: "Everything we care for will be gone." I feel this so often. She answers, "Everything *I* care for will *not* be gone. I do not want the pictures of the Louvre, the buildings, the books to be destroyed, but even if they *do* go, the things that inspired those people to make those things will still be here: the world, the skies, humanity."

I cannot be quite so magnanimous. The cost is not only in material things but in human spirit. The kind of human spirit I care about is going to go down in this war—so much of it.

The British Expeditionary Force is evacuating from Flanders

under terrific pounding, though they have had the good luck of two days of fog, which has prevented the worst bombing; I am relieved—as it seemed too horrible.

Sunday, June 2nd

The papers are full of war and there is no news. The British Expeditionary Force is still evacuating, the French still wondering what the Germans will do next, waiting for the drive on Paris. The Italians about to come in. . . .

A moment of terrible suspense before the crashing of the already blazing house.

Announced over the radio tonight from Washington, in connection with the government's great drive to get more help to the Allies, that two friends close to Colonel Lindbergh would speak against his point of view this week—Colonel Henry [Breckinridge][1] and Mother! Later Mother called to tell me that she was going to speak for the William Allen White Committee, which is working for immediate aid to the Allies (planes, munitions, and supplies).

It is a committee made up chiefly of high-minded idealists. These fine people are only following their deepest and highest convictions. Neither President Neilson nor President [James B.] Conant [of Harvard] wished Mother to strike back at Charles or see it that way (and Mother herself disclaims any such intention or interpretation) but of course it will be used and publicized in that light.

Mother said naïvely, "Of course I know it is only your father's name!" And that "Your father would have wanted me to do it." They used *that* on her, too. She is a big enough person on her own and a good enough speaker for them to want her for herself, but this time she is also being used for the superb publicity effect of her connection with Charles. I only say, "I know" (that it is not directed against C.) and that she must not worry if it is interpreted that way.

I wonder where Daddy would stand? Probably behind the

---

[1] Lawyer, Assistant Secretary of War (1913-16); for many years C. A. L.'s legal adviser.

committee *et al.* And yet he was, among those idealists, very practical, intensely practical—that was his great gift. The combination of vision and practicality.

He would surely have been shocked by C.'s *methods* but would he have been so shocked by the fundamental beliefs behind them? (I remember his arguing with me when I thought America should have joined the League.)

I realize more and more there is no one left in that world, no one among the "old gods" who can understand. We are alone and probably always will be from now on.

Monday, June 3rd

I am heavy with the apathy and lassitude that seems to come over me so often these days. Is it just having a baby?

In the evening I climb up the hill and in the breeze feel lifted a little and can breathe and think and believe and pray. Perhaps that is enough—a few moments of vision in a day. "If you have three moments of clear vision in a day it is enough!" Yes, M. Despiau, but what do you do with the *rest* of the day? I suppose he would answer, *"Travailler, toujours travailler!"* like Rodin.

One is never able to ask these questions of the great people one has met in one's life because it is only long afterwards, after much thought, that one begins to understand *really* what they said, and to think of questions to ask them in return. If only I could ask him *now,* one thinks, *now* I understand!

But one never gets a second chance.

Perhaps if you saw them again you would find them no longer heroes; you would find they did not have the answers to the questions you long to ask them now. You would find or guess that there is a divinity which places our heroes before us only for a short period that we may learn one special thing from them, and one only—at that special moment. They are not meant to be our oracles for life.

I come down calm and collected to the children going to bed and a report over the radio that the Germans have bombed Paris. It is not a big bombing and apparently they were chiefly after military objectives outside of Paris, but I feel sickened and ominous about it. It is the beginning of the end. I'm afraid if they bomb Paris I shall no longer be able to think in anything but a "French" way.

Tuesday, June 4th

Lunch with Con in a cool crowded dark Italian place. I say I don't want to go to a French restaurant as I can't bear to face French people. "Italy," as she says, "is still neutral!" Not very, though. We talk about Mother's speech, with some reserve. Though Con and I really *can* still talk—I am glad.

I listen to Mother's speech alone. I am glad C. is not there. Not that it hurts him—he is very objective about it and doesn't mind —but it is easier for me. It is a beautiful speech, a fighting speech, with much of her faith and spiritual force in it, but I cannot agree with its premises and I feel only sad at not being able to and very much alone and separated from all those good people.

Begun on Wednesday, June 5th

Mother darling,

I shall call you tonight but I want to write down all that cannot be said over the telephone, all the thoughts that came to me when I heard you speak last night, and later. It was a beautiful speech[1] and courageous and very much you, with some of that wisdom about living in it that is especially yours—the Miracles, etc. There was a fundamental spiritual truth in it that I agree with had I not agreed with a word of the text. And the text itself my heart and feelings go along with, though not my judgment. I wish so much they could pull together, but at the moment they are poles apart.

But you know that. You know I cannot agree with the application of your text when I personally feel that they should never have begun this war, that they should, once that mistake was made, have stopped it last fall; and that they should stop it now as quickly as possible. I personally believe, rightly or

[1] E. C. M.'s radio speech was entitled "Does America Deserve a Miracle?"

wrongly, that every day they go on fighting, they, their children, their grandchildren and ours will be worse off. This is not as strictly pacifist a view as it sounds. It is the conclusion in part I have come to, the bridge I have been forced to build between C.'s logic and factual judgment and my own philosophy or religion. (Though you know as well as I that C. is not all "logic" and "facts.") Nevertheless the "bridge" is built of those components.

Everything I love in the way of people, places, beliefs, dreams, and the general way of life over there, is going down before things and people that I personally hate. It seems to be such a fight against evil, sheer evil. And when people argue that way I cannot help but feel that they and my heart are right. Yes, we are right; there is no other way to look at it. And yet underneath there is something else that tells me: You are right, they are right, but only relative to the platform on which you are standing; but relative to the progress of humanity as a whole, I am not sure that we are right.

How I wish, oh how I wish, I could feel wholehearted about this war, in any way. Either that I could feel it were necessary for our self-preservation, or that the war simply and purely was a struggle between evil and good. To so many people— to so many *wonderful* people—it is clearly a case of the forces of Evil vanquishing the forces of Good. I cannot simplify it to that.

In the meantime Paris is bombed, London barricaded, hospital ships sunk, refugees machine-gunned—all those horrible threats of Göring about prisons, and into that cauldron are going all those beautiful and tolerant English minds—the kind of superb detached high-minded idealistic Englishmen one met at Lady Astor's. And Long Barn, and the peace of English fields in the evening, and children, and all of France, all over again, the dogged "little people," and all "our" people—down go the Carrels and the Monnets and the Boëls and men like Détroyat and Saint-Exupéry—and all the people in Brittany, the Savinas, the Pierres, the Keraudrens. The best people on earth.

Dear Mother, this is very long and not perhaps very clear. Inevitably it is not clear because in its essence it is a dilemma. I am glad, though, that you spoke because you spoke as you felt and it rang clear because of that. Perhaps in times like these everyone who feels deeply and surely and has a position of authority and—most important—whose integrity is not for a moment doubted should speak out. If it is the voice of integrity it rings clear and it helps to clarify other people and that is doing a great deal. I think it even clarifies the people who don't agree with you and therefore helps the truth to come more clearly one way or another. The issues crystallize. The problem must be stated, first, as Daddy and Chekhov said. And you have helped to do that.

I feel, too, pleased, grateful, rather, that—for the sake of people abroad—you have spoken. I want them to know that we are feeling what you said.

And whether or not it ultimately works out that war materials should be or are sent, or can be sent in practical amounts, a speech like yours will help people to feel their responsibility to Europe in other ways. When the time comes for us to build up a devastated Europe, people will be more ready to help in noncontroversial ways. No one, no matter what his beliefs, can hold much of a brief for withholding food, medical supplies, Red Cross aid—which we are going to have to pour out as never before in human history. This kind of succour is above all politics. "The quality of mercy," etc. And the more people's consciences are aroused to this terrific responsibility the better.

I hope you will send me the speech. C. did not hear it as he was out at a dinner with Carrel (probably getting the same thing from a different angle). Carrel feels it is a fight for Christianity. As so many people do.

DIARY   *Thursday, June 6th*

In late afternoon go in with C. to have supper with Sue and George [Vaillant].

I stop and see Mrs. Hand beforehand. She is about to move to Dublin, New Hampshire. But she is sitting quite calmly darning socks. What a comfort to go there.

But they, too, have moved miles away from me, or, rather, I

from them, on the war. Mrs. Hand I *could* get onto a common basis with, I feel, a broader, more philosophical one, but Mary[1] is white and tense and bitter and intellectual. She paints a picture of Hitler riding down the Champs-Elysées with French crowds forced by bayonets to cheer "Heil Hitler." I am chilled to the bone. Perhaps she is right. I had hoped *not* for a fair peace from the Allied point of view but still for more moderate treatment than that and some measure of integrity, autonomy, left to England and France. I walk away warmed by Mrs. Hand's kindly humanity but saddened, too. They are on "the other side."

On to Sue's for supper—meet C., George, and Quincy Howe[2] after his broadcast. C. was much impressed by it. We are all against U.S.A. going into this war and discuss the possibilities. Quincy sees the war very much as I do—on the "revolution" plane. It is a relief to be with these people. I realize, going home with C., that we have had a cheering taste of what we very rarely have, a feeling of working side by side with people of our own generation. We are always thinking and usually working alone.

Friday, June 7th

Today before I rush off to town I see Dorothy Thompson's column in the *Tribune*. It quotes a talk she has had with Saint-Exupéry. It is so beautiful that I am only conscious of a lump in my throat and tears.

"It seemed to me outrageous that he should be risking his life daily in the most dangerous of the services. . . .

"I told him so. After all, other men can fly planes, I said. But you can write . . . you see things, things ahead. France will need you. Europe will need you.

" 'You are absolutely wrong,' he answered. 'Nobody has the right to write a word today who does not participate to the fullest in the agony of his fellow human beings.

[1] Daughter of Judge and Mrs. Learned Hand.

[2] Writer, editor, and radio commentator for WQXR.

" 'If I did not resist with my life, I should be unable to write. And what holds true for this war has got to hold true for everything. The Christian idea has got to be served; that the Word is made Flesh. One must write with one's body.'

"He tried to elaborate this, rather hesitantly. 'The reason why we are in this war, why there is a Hitler, why our whole civilization is crumbling up is because this has not been so. Our words and our actions are not one. We say things and pretend to believe things, but what we say is not translated into the deed. And the deed is divorced from Faith, from the Word. And so, since we have not been all of a piece ourselves, personally, and in all our institutions, we have been divided souls and a divided society. To be free means to be trustworthy. Otherwise no one is safe in freedom. A democracy must be a brotherhood. Otherwise it is a lie.' "

What he says is so fundamentally true. It is true in its essence: the Word must be made Flesh.

I am melted even deep down into my personal life.

It is true, terribly true, of my own life—my dreams not translated into action, my ideals into deeds, marriage, the children, the spiritual life. How weakly do I carry out my beliefs.

But *how,* oh God, *how* to make the Word into Flesh in my own little day-to-day life? In C., in the children, in trying to live a really simple life, to think more about the people around me, to take more off their hands, to serve.

Going into town I was so full of it that it was hard not to cry.

June 7th [Continuation of letter to E. C. M. begun June 5th]
I have just read this over after seeing the beautiful editorial of Dorothy Thompson with the more beautiful words in it of Saint-Exupéry on why he is fighting. It is hard to seem to stand on the other side from such wonderful people (you, St.-Ex., and Carrel —I will not put D. T. in this galaxy!). The truth of what he says is so profound that I cannot but agree with it from the core of my heart. I do believe we should "resist" the evil, I do believe the evil will fall, I do believe that the good, the good as exemplified in all of you, will triumph. And that the word will be made flesh. Only

I am not sure that all this will happen in just the ways we are looking and praying for it to happen at this moment. One must pray anyway that it *will* happen and that we may have the wisdom and the strength to know *how* to make our word into flesh, to make our prayer join with the work of our bodies to bring the miracle. Your point and his are really the same.

DIARY   *Saturday, June 8th*

Mother comes down in the afternoon. C. goes over her new publisher's contract for her. That is nice. They can meet and talk without trouble.

Mother is rather upset by the number of letters she has had criticizing her speech. I tell her about some of the ones I have gotten and how you can't help getting, no matter *what* you say, a certain amount of the "Dear Sir, you cur" letters.

Altogether a successful visit though Mother is very nervous and tired.

C. working on his speech at night. Mother calls up quite worried about a call she has had from an unknown person.

"Aren't you worried about your daughter?"

"Which daughter?"

"The famous one."

It is only the kind of crank thing that one gets with any publicity but how it unsettles you—throwing you back into that terrible insane evil world of the Case. The hunted feeling, the problem of the children's safety, are we safe near New York, where to live?

I go down the hall to look at the children sleeping in peace. C. paces up and down though he belittles this incident. We pull down the blinds—that awful feeling: someone might be watching.

Sunday, June 9th. Damp and hot.

C. and I walk to the beach. He is tense and worried. The call last night, the war situation—a great wave of feeling is sweeping over the United States. Help to the Allies, even to going in. People are very stirred up (as well they might be). Anything may happen. Trouble is surely ahead. C. will be in the forefront of it, but the children—where to have them, where safe? And this eternal publicity, minus official protection, that we always have with us. "Like a cross," C. says, "that we have to take through life."

C. takes me to see a wild duck's nest he has discovered in a hollow stump in the woods. The duck is on the nest—still as a stone and beautifully blended into brownish shadows. She is frozen to alertness, her glass eye motionless upon us. She lets us get very near. (And I beg C. to go no farther. In a kind of mad reaction to the war I cannot bear to inflict fear on a single living creature or even to kill an insect. It is, of course, quite unreasoning. "Force is as inherent a part of the universe as harmony," Whitehead says.)

Aubrey and Con for supper—very nice evening. Aubrey and C. off for a walk and Con and I sit and talk. She looks pale and pathetically dark around the eyes but seems quite resigned and calm. I am happy we can still talk.

We talk, the four of us, plans for the future. Aubrey is, of course, grimly gloomy, but still not exactly depressed. They think the United States will come in and that England will hold out come what may. They expect the invasion of England. Perhaps even carrying the war on from the colonies. But we can still talk. It was a good evening, a cementing one, keeping the bridges open.

Monday, June 10th

Huge full-page advertisements in the [New York] papers: *Stop Hitler now.* America terribly worked up—letters to the paper. Speeches and editorials pretty openly demand we get into this war.

"Humanly speaking," the Pope says in a phrase that seems terribly moving to me, "peace is receding further and further away."

The Germans are reported near Rouen, Soissons, and Beauvais —within 35 miles of Paris—and to have crossed the Seine at some points. C. says, "That means a rout."

At lunch Mussolini speaks; we hear him on the radio. His voice rants ahead dramatically: "The hour has struck," etc. The French and British have already been given the declaration of war. (That means France is already beaten, C. says.) And as he rants, in the pauses you hear the bloodcurdling cheers of the crowd—roars of approval. (It is the cry for blood, C. says, over the wounded body of France.) "I know," I say, "I can't bear it." Soeur Lisi is crying. The world is being changed as we sit there. Is it always changed, I think, by such second-class men leading such blind and ignorant masses? That is the shock, somehow. I cannot call the man who is speaking a great man. He has played a lying and deceitful game and sold himself to the highest bidder. He comes in when the battle is won to strike at his old ally, who is stricken and down, close to him by race, taste, and culture. And he says it is a war that is forced upon him!

At night the radio announcer in Paris makes his last broadcast from Paris. It is quite moving. The French government is leaving Paris for Tours. Paris is being evacuated. The little iron chairs and tables on the sidewalks are empty. "The end of an era." "Good-bye from Paris."

Roosevelt speaks, accuses Italy. "The hand that held the dagger has struck it into the back of its neighbor." Wild cheers! We certainly aren't neutral any more!

Tuesday, June 11th

Down to law office to meet C. and sign our wills. The Germans have reached the Marne.

Headlines are black. One walks in a dream. The lawyer still doesn't think the French situation is desperate. He is caught fast in 1914–18, like so many people. C. says he thinks it's an utterly different picture, now. The lawyer implies that *that* is a matter of opinion. (How people hate to be told the truth! That is why C. is unpopular now; he is a Cassandra.)

Drive out with C. The Germans are 25 miles from Paris. C. leaves for Washington.

I take care of the children all day, clear out the cupboards, put away woolens. A humble way of putting the Word into Flesh, I think. End up washing a horribly dirty pair of trousers for Jon, at night. I will *not* ask Soeur Lisi to do it tomorrow. Very tired at night.

The hardest part of taking care of children is not physical but mental. One cannot *think through* one clear thought with them around. But they are a joy.

The Germans are 12 miles from Paris. They have Rouen, Rheims, Compiègne, and are on both sides of Senlis. Paris is evacuated and practically "a military city." Then it will be razed. It is unthinkable.

In the news at night it says that the French have authorized Bullitt[1] to tell the Germans that Paris is "an open city"—not fortified, not open to bombardment. The Germans, from Berlin, announce that they accept that and will treat it as "an open town." I am relieved beyond all words. More than I should be. I know many French would rather destroy Paris than have it go to German hands—but nevertheless I feel lightened of a great fear. All is not lost; Paris is not to be razed. I feel it is a symbol, that it will survive and someday return to its rightful rulers, the true French. I am grateful to the French for that much sacrifice of pride, and even to the Germans (or to fate if it is responsible) for that much discipline. Bullitt has stayed to hand it over. I respect him for that.

Reynaud appeals to the United States for aid—a last desperate appeal. The time has come for the other democracies to pay their debt to France. "I have claims on you." He demands planes, tanks, equipment, and that we speak out that we are against Hitler, i.e., to join the war and save France.

Every little man in France will look to us as the last hope, feeling that it is in our power to save them and our fault if they go down. It is only human but it is not fair and not true. "All

[1] William C. Bullitt, U.S. Ambassador to France, 1936–41.

is being done that can possibly be done" (Roosevelt). We have no planes, no tanks, and no army to send. We are more unprepared than France herself. But no Frenchman will *ever* believe this.

Friday, June 14th

The Germans are marching into Paris. The swastika will be put on the Eiffel Tower. It is harder to think of the Germans in Paris than in New York, in a strange way. Paris *is* France to me and it is gone.

Black headlines proclaim: "Paris Falls." Bullitt reported to be in German "protective custody." Will that involve us?

Dr. Carrel has been trying to get C. all day because of C.'s speech. To urge him *not* to speak? Or not to say something? It is useless and it is the old hurt: France—loyalty to friends, hurt feelings, misunderstanding.

I feel uneasy and unhappy about it though I respect C.'s integrity completely and understand him.

I buy the papers and am afraid to look at them. ("Who is *not* dead?" cried the Persian Queen after the battle.)

At night after supper—still dusk—I walk to the high point that looks down over the bay, the lighthouse with its bright eye, the beach far below, and the graying sunset on the dim far shore. It is still and quiet and I feel lifted up, stretched out by the clouds, those gray wings spreading up from the horizon, spreading wide over the sky, over the world. I can pray, and feel that I can hold *all* in my heart, under my wings, so to speak. I can hold C. and the other world, too—and love them both. And I go back serene.

Oh, if it would only be over *quickly!*

Saturday, June 15th

News from the war is cloudy. The Germans are advancing fast. But one has the feeling, from the increased vagueness in reports from France, the increased rumors of peace, the increased denials of any separate peace, that something is happening of far greater importance in the temporary seat of the French government in

Bordeaux. I do pray it is peace. Roosevelt answers Reynaud's plea with "our efforts will be redoubled . . . I can safely say . . . every week . . . more equipment. . . ." When it is physically impossible for us to send those clouds of planes, those swarms of tanks Reynaud demands. The President must know this. *Why* does he go on holding out false hope? (Or does he do it only to try to get us into the war, hoping the moral effect of our entry will be enough to turn the tide?)

I feel glad that C. is speaking tonight. Dreadful as his message is to them (we have nothing we *can* send) and bitterly as he will be hated for it, it is better that they know from a clear voice that Roosevelt is only leading them on.

C. gave his speech very well, better than any of the others. It is more of a piece than the others, too. I can tell that by the radio comments afterwards. They all pick out significant sentences; all point to the essence of his message. This will get across better than the other speeches.

[*C. A. L.'s speech was entitled "Our Drift Toward War." It warned that the course our government was taking would lead to war and that if we entered the war we must be prepared to invade a continent. It would take months to build up an adequate army for this purpose. He advocated strong hemispheric defense and an independent destiny for America.*]

Sunday, June 16th

The Germans have done "the impossible" again—crossed the Rhine in front of the Maginot line near Switzerland. They also claim to have broken through the line.

A clear cool bright day. It is "June" today. I am reading the papers at breakfast (C.'s speech) when C. blows in, smiling and energetic. He seems to enjoy a fight. He says he thinks the crisis is past and that we will not get into the war, but it was very close. The French will have to make peace in a day or two.

We walk to the beach, by the lovely bluff road. I feel happy and cheered to have him back, and full of life as I always am with him.

Various young people come up and speak to me—a first meeting of the summer. Greatly to my surprise many (in fact *all* in one way or another) compliment me on C.'s speech. It is more popular than any of the others. They all get the point about not encouraging the Allies to hope for aid we cannot send; most of these people are the New York–Long Island set, and violently and emotionally pro-Ally (and so am I, surely—only I look beyond that), so it is quite a coup to get them to see the facts. It corroborates what I felt last night—this speech is clearer and more directed to one end and is less liable to be misunderstood.

It is nice to see these young people, pretty, gay, occupied with their families, their summer sailing and swimming—the scene before me just like last summer—but, oh, I feel so separated from them. The war makes such a difference to me—I, who am supposed to be "isolationist" and therefore not pro-Ally, like all of them! How *can* they feel for France and England as I do?

In the afternoon, we work on books—sorting and marking all our books, which have just come from France. In some of them are little lists, marketing lists of what to get from Lannion: *"Pruneaux secs,"* etc. All my garden books, and a book given me by T. J.[1] the night of the Munich agreement, signed by all of us, underneath T. J.'s inscription: "In the moment of a great hope"!

At night we hear on the radio from Bordeaux that the Reynaud government has fallen. A new government, headed by [Marshal Henri] Pétain, is formed. The radio commentator tells us the history of its members: Pétain, friendly to Franco Spain; [Pierre] Laval, appeaser of Italy; two pacifists, and a man who circulated a pamphlet, "Why die for Danzig?" You can guess, he says, what the significance of this move is. "It means *peace*," says C. I leap inside at the word and go out and walk in the garden, hoping, praying. Though God knows "peace" means suffering, too, terrible suffering for France.

Senator Key Pittman answers C. on the radio. It is an *attack* of course and yet the tone of it is much more a *defense* of the

[1] Dr. Thomas Jones, Deputy Secretary to the British Cabinet in 1938.

Administration policies. No one has the *slightest intention* of going to war, etc. Which shows how much they have been forced to back down and shows C.'s success.

[*I was in fact mistaken. The Administration was actually in a very difficult position, not due to C. A. L., but because of the strong isolationist sentiment in the country and in Congress.*]

Monday, June 17th

Pétain asks for peace terms. It is very moving, that old man taking hold at such an hour. They can trust him; he is devoted to France, has known victory and defeat. I feel relieved that they have such a man at such a terrible hour.

I go about with a feeling of finality this morning. It is over for France, but at least the dying is over, too. Now perhaps we can start to help them.

At the 6:45 news we hear that France is still fighting: "For her honor." It is not an unconditional surrender. Pétain has asked for terms, so they have to go on fighting. The sick feeling comes back and sits in the pit of the stomach.

Over to the Foster Dulles's for dinner. As before, the evening starts out most casually. J. F. D. is the slowest, most deliberate talker in the world. Thoughts die and are buried in the silences between sentences. Therefore it is even more startling when he warms up and comes out with the most astoundingly unconventional ideas and theories.

To my question "How *can* we help them?" he answers with some warmth that we can *stop* encouraging them to go on fighting and *stop* pushing them on and *stop* leading them on with false hopes of aid we cannot give. We, of course, thoroughly agree on that.

He is, however, even more startling when he begins to outline a constructive, offensive policy for this country, to strengthen it. He does not believe mere defense will be enough. Hitler may not attack us, at least not right away, but he can easily make trouble for us and will unless we develop a more aggressive policy; we must unify our country and our hemisphere. What does this entail? An imperialist policy?

He says some nice things about *change*—it being a fundamental of life, for men, institutions, nations. When there is no provision for it the forces of nature get dammed up and finally break out in a conflagration (*flood* would be more consistent) as now. He also gives the picture of nations being like animals, the civilized ones having become domesticated for certain useful purposes, cows for milk, hens for eggs. When they become domesticated, we put a fence around them, make them abide by certain laws. For nations this works, too, and the laws are good and useful, but if you have no fence or a tiger has broken through, there is no use trying to abide by barnyard rules.

He feels Roosevelt never intended to get us into this war but felt he could bluff Hitler, also was playing on his passion for fine poses, dramatic acts, for popularity. This is too dreadful to believe. I give Roosevelt the benefit of the doubt and believe he earnestly intended and felt we should get into this war, otherwise his actions are unpardonable—urging them on to fight and die while *we* were not intending to fight ourselves, trying to get something for nothing, like Mussolini.

Tuesday, June 18th

Various public men, Willkie,[1] etc., have now come out strongly against war, against the Administration. Quite a wave, a change of opinion. C. says, "All they needed was someone to try out the water for them, to see if it wasn't too hot."

"And *you* always *have* to be that person," I say with some bitterness, thinking of other times when C. has broken the ice and borne the brunt of the criticism, taken the first missiles.

"That's where I'd rather be." He smiles.

Wednesday, June 19th

C. and I drive in to have lunch with Alexander Kirk[2] on his way back to Berlin.

[1] Wendell L. Willkie, Republican presidential candidate in 1940.

[2] Career diplomat, Chargé d'Affaires in the U.S.S.R. in 1938, in Germany in 1939, later American Ambassador in Egypt and Italy. See *The Flower and the Nettle.*

His sister is there and a young (*typical*) Embassy Secretary. Kirk seems genuinely glad to see us and we go up to have lunch in his rooms. This is just as well, because we are hurled immediately into a violent discussion about the war.

C.: "And some people are actually talking about our going into this war."

Sister (militantly): "Yes—and I'm one of them."

Kirk: "So am I!"

The good-looking Secretary says nothing but looks at C. with that weary "I-expected-as-much" expression on his face. We are "well in."

The sister is purely emotional. The Secretary is one of the vast conventional intelligentsia. Kirk, himself, highly intelligent and emotional, has here left the rails completely and gone off into the mystical. Of the three I can understand and respect his attitude the best. It is not undisciplined and it is not lazy. It is an honest and fervent attempt to find the answer.

But I don't agree with it. I might have if I had not married C., but now I see the practical side of life too clearly and not only that; the clash of the practical with my dreams has projected another and third point of view, a new child, which is a kind of new vision. Perhaps too planetary a one, but I cannot get back to the old one, any more.

Kirk feels, apparently, that Hitler is going to go on until he is stopped, that there is a strange mystical success psychology at work. A spiritual force (an evil one) behind Hitler, and therefore it is irrelevant whether or not we are prepared to go into the war now or not. All we have to do is to come out strongly —declare war, even if it is just a gesture at this moment. The moral or mystical force of the gesture will just blow Hitler right over—pouf!

I agree there is some (evil) mystical or spiritual force behind Hitler and I really agree that it will take some equally strong spiritual force to overthrow him. But I do *not* think that the empty gesture of our declaring war on him *is* that force.

C. argues very forthrightly and well with his terrible lightning directness and cool heat (lightning again).

In other words, we should do just what England and France did?

Kirk parries with a rather wild brilliance. He says England and France were "successful" and put Hitler "off his rhythm" for six months, by declaring war, which Hitler never expected.

C. says grimly that it is hard to see how Hitler could have been much *more* "successful" than he has been, militarily speaking.

I insert explanations and interpretations from time to time, somewhat tempering the fury of the blows as they fall. It allows the conversation to soar a little from the inexorable barn-door nailing that C. is doing. We all agree on the moral and spiritual apathy of this country, on its need for regeneration. On war being preferable to complete loss of moral and spiritual fiber. Only C. thinks if we go into this war the country *will* go to pieces, fast, and Kirk, that *unless* we do, we will.

When we reach this point the charming Secretary and I look at each other with wry smiles and say, "We're going to have revolution *anyway.*"

"We might as well choose our time."

In the meantime we have a delicious meal (Kirk always does), and it is a delight to see his mind play and to follow it sympathetically.

C. is not so happy with the sister. She is the kind of woman who says, as though this were the final slap-down argument to convince you, "I've always been a pacifist and an isolationist and I have two sons of war age, and yet I feel we *must* go in."

C. says, but not obviously in retaliation, that what seems unfair to him is that the people who disarmed their sons now tell them to go out and fight with their bare fists.

Well, finally the meal is over, everybody still arguing furiously, and, due to Kirk's gay detachment and the mutual respect of the two men for each other's minds, still very good friends and with no rancor at all (which rarely happens nowadays).

I think a little sadly, though, as we go down in the elevator, reviewing in my mind my part in the meeting—that feminine part of drawing off the fire, of not letting the "play" get to be "fight," of introducing charm, gaiety, distraction, of trying to lead the conversation into a vaguer and therefore more common basis—that undoubtedly they thought as we left that I was the more intelligent and saner of the two.

They do not analyze that I seemed more intelligent because I was more sympathetic to them and that I was more sympathetic to them because I am a woman and highly personal in my point of view—sympathetic to a certain degree (because more easily swayed, pulled off the track) to everyone I meet. Because I am fond of Kirk and do not want us to lose him as a friend. Because I am more compromising, more diplomatic and weaker than my husband.

And finally because all women (or most) in a discussion are less interested in making their point than in the sheer artistic delight of creating a whole and balanced composition. The Greek "nothing too much" is constantly their criterion. You must not spoil the picture or the occasion, you must not break the form.

The pudding must have *just* the right ingredients and be well mixed. Women are more interested in stirring the pudding than in anything else.

The Germans have bombed Bordeaux. *Why* did they have to? To force the government to unconditional surrender quickly? It seems unnecessarily cruel.

C. says the Germans have most of Brittany.

Jon is quite worried: "Have they got Illiec?"

I: "Well, they probably aren't on the island but they may have the mainland."

"Won't it still belong to us?"

"Well, I don't know, Jon. Perhaps you and Land will go back someday."

"And won't you? Why not?"

"We may not want to."

"Why not?"

"It won't be the same."

Jon: "The rocks will still be there and the trees"!

Thursday, June 20th

C. and I drive into town—way downtown to 39 Broadway for a meeting on "High Fields,"[1] to vote to turn over the place to New Jersey, who think they can use it for children. It is rather a gloomy meeting, full of ghosts—the ghosts of people we used to be, relationships we used to have.

Friday, June 21st

Go over some of the fan letters that have come in to C. The vast majority are favorable, 10 to 1. However it is the unfavorable *one* that I always think of and answer in my mind. Tonight it is onè from an "intelligent" high-minded Wall Street conservative. He says it is C.'s lack of distinction between aggression and defense which seems to him so "evil." ("Evil"! What a word to use of C.)

It seems to me that there are sins against man's morality and sins against nature's morality. The Nazis have certainly sinned against man's morality (so have the democracies, but not so much lately or so obviously). But the democracies, it seems to me, have committed the unpardonable sin against nature: *Resistance to change* (to *normal* change, one should add).

C. and I walk to the point and sit and watch the one-eyed lighthouse out in the bay, and the stars come out.

At night I say sentimentally to C., "Tomorrow I shall be thirty-five."

"You will *not*," says C. practically, from bed, "you will be *thirty-four*."

"But . . ."

We argue a bit but it seems he is right!

"I hope you feel a whole year younger," he says.

June 22nd, 34th birthday

The armistice has been signed between France and Germany. The peace emissaries are off to Italy. Technically war will not

[1] The Lindbergh home (1931–32) and property in the Sourland Mountains near Hopewell, N.J.

cease until six hours after an armistice has been concluded with Italy. But most of the fighting has ceased.

A French general [Charles De Gaulle] in London urges the French outside of France still to resist, in the colonies. He is urged on by Churchill and the English.

Sunday, June 23rd

C. and I walk to the point and down to the beach and back—a long walk! We sit on the rocks until it is almost dark, I staring out to sea with my own thoughts and C. with his. It strikes me, as often, how terribly Alone C. is. That first symbolic flight of his is still true. He was always, is now, and will be always out there alone over the ocean, alone seeing his destination, alone having faith that he can reach it, with people on the sidelines shouting, "Flying Fool!" And a few holding him blindly in their hearts—like me.

Monday, June 24th

Détroyat and his friend appear in the driveway. I come down later in my new rose-and-blue hostess gown–négligée. I *feel* very beautiful and sylphlike but both the men are so attentive, jumping up to shut doors lest I catch cold, rushing to pick up things I drop, that I fear I am not as well disguised as I hope!

It is, first of all, such a luxury, such a delight to slip back into that world of French talk, the deftness of speech, the hardness of mind, plus that disarming softness and warmth of sympathy.

Their objectivity amazed me, their acceptance of defeat, simply, sadly. They talked to us without bitterness, rancor, or irritation. The only bitterness is against Italy, which the friend says is going to be far greater than the feeling against Germany. I cannot blame them. *To still meet* them was such a joy, a luxury, and I was doubly, triply grateful for it, knowing how little of it is ahead of me, realizing suddenly tonight, with a rush of nostalgia, how much I missed it.

Détroyat and C. feel there is almost no chance of success for England and that the end will come fast. D.'s friend (a brilliant, quick Frenchman) was less sure and talked of the British bulldog qualities. We had a very good time analyzing the characteristics of the British (the friend and I being the more moderate, while C. and D. were outspokenly critical), until near the end of the evening when we learned that the friend's wife was British! *Tiens!*

Détroyat tells C. that he is planning to take the first Clipper back to France. His friend starts to argue with him, and the underlying tragedy of the evening is at last spread out. It is not that they are tragic about it or melodramatic. One *could not* pity them. They do not pity themselves. But the tragedy is there and they do not blink it. They only want to know, caught in it, what is best for a human being to do, quite practically.

The friend outlines the France he [Détroyat] is rushing back to—occupied by German troops, governed by a Gauleiter, Secret Police. What chance for a man, an independent man? "If you speak," says the friend, "you will be quickly disposed of and they know how to do it. Your profession will be killed. All aviation will be dead in France. Why do you go back?"

"I go back for my wife and my children," says Détroyat quite simply. "I have not been able to communicate with them for ten days. I must see if they are safe, if they have food. . . ."

The friend urges him to try to get them out, which he can do better from the outside—not to go back into France until the German occupation is over. One cannot start to rebuild France until then, when the French have some independence in no matter how small an area. And even then?

The friend comes over to me, gently, half apologetically, saying we should not have talked of such things all evening. I find myself strangely tongue-tied and try to explain my feelings. We cannot help thinking of these things constantly; why not talk?

"But human beings have always had the power to rise above them, to think of other things, to keep a culture . . ."

I say, yes, that *he,* that *they,* the French, have a *right* to talk of other things; they have suffered. They have a right to put war behind them, but I do not feel I have the *right* to forget, not to think of the suffering.

He says he is like me because he hasn't suffered or fought; he has been *here* (on the purchasing commission) with his wife and children.

And (to a question of C.'s) on what he considers his duty now that the commission is over, he answers it is to continue the resistance. He has not yet fought with his body and he must go to England, to the colonies, if they continue to resist. Is it hopeless? What should he do?

I go to bed touched by their dignity and their gallantry and their sweetness toward us, and a heart wrung.

Wednesday, June 26th. C. left yesterday for Detroit. Mrs. Curtiss arrives in time for tea and a thundershower—with a friend. Children, dogs, tea, and guests all crowd in at the same moment, with the storm bursting over us and Thor barking loudly.

Thursday
More rain but it clears up. The day goes in intense and finely pointed talk which is, of course, a great strain but also a great stimulus and joy. I have always felt with Mrs. Curtiss this intense intellectual joy in talking to her, about books, artists, life, personal relationships. On things of the hour, too, I find myself much more in accord with her than I could have expected. Her attitude on the war, our staying out, her part in it, the hysterical insincere attitude of most people—she is trying to stay an island of sanity in the middle of it all.

That it was possible to meet her above everyday issues, on a fundamental platform, was a great relief, giving me renewed faith.

Friday, June 28th
Willkie gets the Republican nomination![1] I don't know much about him but it seems wonderful that a man who is not a politician could get it, and also *not* a die-hard conservative. At least

[1] Wendell Willkie was nominated as presidential candidate by an isolationist-dominated Republican convention.

he knows we cannot turn backwards and has some conception of the forces of the future.

During supper Thelma comes over. It is so good to see her and yet I dread this first encounter. I know we have got to jump the hurdle of her violent political opinions, and mine. Once it is over it won't be so bad, I feel.

She starts right in, very intense, on Henry Ford. "Unspeakable," "immoral," "men like that ought to be forced . . ." All because Henry Ford has refused to turn over his American factories to the production of Rolls-Royce engines for British planes. (His factories in Canada and England *are* being used for the defense of those countries and he says he would not refuse to turn over his factories for the defense of *this* country.)

I am unfortunately drawn into his defense. I say that you may disagree with his judgment but you cannot call him immoral or wicked in his attitude. He is giving up orders and giving up making money because he does not believe it is to the best interest of this country or of England to continue pouring arms into England. He believes this passionately and he is *not* making money counter to his convictions. He is just as moral—maybe more so—than people on the other side. A pacifist is moral, though you may not agree with him.

"Anyway, he is a fool," says Thelma. We have to go through the whole pro-war, counter-war situation.

"I'm already in the war," says Thelma. "And Brooke is in the war—has been in the war for months!"

She has *all* the stories about German fifth columnists in Mexico, South America, etc. Menace of Japan. Also all the heartrending stories of individuals, refugees, etc.

I go to bed weary and sad and very alone.

Saturday, June 29th

C. back. As usual he is not in the house ten minutes before he is telling me gently to "quiet down." I know I am high strung and apt to be nervous but it is such a cold shower to be told to "quiet down" one's joy and excitement, which always spring up when he comes home, even from a short trip. But he does it only for my own good and health, so I should not mind. And he is also nervous himself when he comes back from a trip, but chiefly it is his concern for me.

We go for a walk in the woods, to the beach. It is delicious—cool sun and shade. I am happy.

Jon now has ten turtles! He has infected the other boys with the turtle fever and they are all collecting them. C. brings home a turtle (a small one) for Land and, opening his suitcase and taking the lid off a tie box, a garter snake for Jon! Jon somewhat stunned rallies to the occasion and soon has it around his wrist. We all handle it. I must say I don't enjoy it but the boys are much impressed.

The Smiths arrive. Truman tells us all about Washington. He was supposed to be writing C.'s speeches and Morgenthau *asked that he be removed!* T. offered to resign but the army [General Marshall] would not hear of it.[1] He is far too valuable to them. So he was shunted off temporarily, "till the storm blew over," to Fort Benning.

The most cheering thing he tells us is about the French—that the casualties were not nearly as high as first reported. He also tells us of the attitude of the French Embassy in Washington. A Frenchman went there asking what he should do.

"Go back to France and carry on your business."

"But my business is in Paris."

"Go back and start it up again."

"But suppose there is no business?"

"Then go back and work with your hands—for France."

That is the kind of spirit that makes one thrill. If that spirit is there, France will survive. It makes me feel happy deep down.

Monday, July 1st

C. to town.

I force myself to go over my files, requests, letters. How they oppress me, make me feel crowded, hunted, shackled! Try to clear them out a little. Must get some order into my papers and

---

[1] See C. A. L.'s *Wartime Journals*, p. 352.

my life. C. makes me feel this; he is eternally cleaning up the accumulations of our turbulent and scattered life. Will we *ever* get it done, deposited, stored away and forgotten? But we move and then do it all again. We *must* get a house.

Tuesday, July 2nd

Jon, at breakfast, asks me about St.-Ex. "How is he getting along?" He always says "Saint-Exupéry," not Monsieur de—as though Saint were a title. I say I don't know at all but that as he is rather well known he probably is still alive or we would have read of his death in the papers.

Jon, rather gravely: "Is he one of the saints of France?"

I start to laugh and then think, No, I mustn't laugh at him for admiring a good man or for believing in saints, so I finally answer: "Perhaps he is, Jon. In a sense, all the good and the brave people of a nation are its saints."

Wednesday, July 3rd

C. and I clean up boxes. C. does so much of this I am ashamed. He has our material possessions all in order and *in his head;* I *never* can remember where or what they are. It is the old story. He does it all because he does it better. He is not baffled or distracted by details. I think this is genius.

Thursday, July 4th

In the afternoon C. takes Jon and his friends, Roy, Werner, and Winnie, into town to buy firecrackers. They come home with paper bags full and Good Humor ice-cream sticks. Even Land gets one!

Then all hell breaks loose. Three excited boys hurling torpedoes on the brick porch, firecrackers on the lawn, noise, explosions, shouts. Thor cowers behind the sofa, Land shrieks with joy, Winnie holds her ears, and I sit calmly and sew up the hem on my cotton dress!

The biggest success is a firecracker in an empty tin. On top of the lid is a ball. Fuse is lighted, lid and ball fly high into the air, and each boy tries to catch it. There is a brief respite at supper.

But after supper when it is dark we go down on the pier and shoot off Roman candles, Jon, Roy, and Werner taking turns at lighting them under C.'s directions. They are all so happy. It is much better than last year, taking Jon to watch *other* people set off more and more marvelous fireworks. This time *he* did it.

Friday, July 5th

Mother for lunch. She is very tired and discouraged. I have never seen her quite like this—for it is disillusionment, like a child. She wanted so much to help and has been drawn into committees which she suspects are not sound. Also all the pro-war committees are fighting among themselves. Mother is shocked and wearied by it. Gone are the days when if you worked for "a charity" it was "good." I wish I could explain to her that it is a product of the times, not something accidental which has happened to her. Also people are plaguing her for help on a million things she cannot do—people who have never done one iota of the work she has for others. She has literally spilled her life out, given money, time, work for others ("But *they* don't think so, Anne," she says pathetically). I try to tell her that what she did for Smith College was far more important and necessary than all this. But it is hard. She has always before had a kind of invulnerable position, secure, good, sound, accepted by everyone.

But no one has that position now. It is the age. One has to hold one's own standards "and not lose too much time or too much courage in explaining your position to others" [Rilke].

C. and I flying in the afternoon from Long Island Aviation Country Club over Long Island. Its crowdedness bothers him. How he yearns for freedom—and how difficult it is for him to get.

Monday, July 8th

A bitter letter from Lady G. denouncing C. for his ingratitude to England. I can understand it. And yet it upsets me. The attitude seems to be that you should *sell* your country out of personal loyalty or gratitude to another country. It isn't as if we asked anything of England or *got* anything without paying for it (and *very* well) or received anything that any person living there or any ordinary tourist would not have. (C. even offered his services and advice to them, only to be laughed at and turned down.)

But everyone is moved by a personal vision. No one can understand the dispassionate conviction of a man like C. No one can believe it.

I, of course, am very personal, too.

Wednesday, July 10th

We are all packed up and ready to go[1]—and rested. When we leave, Land follows me and when he finds he is not going with me puckers down his lip. How hard it is, always, to leave children. I know he will stop in a second and forget, but it does not help me. The pang of the immediate is so real in one's relations to children. Jon and I understand each other closely and completely and take each other for granted.

We motor to Boston. It is very hot but we feel immediately the release of being off, eat sandwiches along the way, icecream bricks, and cherry cider! We get to the Wayside Inn about 7:30. They are not crowded for supper and there are nice people —they do not bother us. But after supper we start out to walk and are followed by tourists calling and running after us and cars coming by us. "Hey, Colonel!" *"There* they are!" "Hey, Lindy!" We try to walk away up by the church but they turn the headlights on us and follow. Finally we turn back to the inn, I feeling panicky, knowing I cannot hurry, wanting a cloak of invisibility to hide under. I don't like to think of them peering curiously at my figure and knowing about the baby. I cringe from it. Also I dread—even more—an incident; they will come up and be excruciatingly rude, and C. will flare back, and be misunderstood again.

Finally we get to the inn and go upstairs and pull down all the blinds. It is stifling hot. We are very depressed. An old sore place chafed again.

[1] The Lindberghs were starting a trip to North Haven, Maine, planning to explore the coast en route for a possible permanent home.

How can we live, *where* can we live? Again the endless round of problems.

Thursday, July 11th

The inn is quiet in the morning. We start off peaceful and happy again; back roads around Boston, farms. C. feels better just to see them. On the coast road it is dreadful again: hot-dog stands, road signs, cabins—all horribly painted—every few feet. One is suffocated by it.

After lunch we explore the Harpswell area on our way to Rockland [Maine]. It is tamer country than North Haven, not so beautiful or so wild. Also the points are terribly built up and touristy. We go down a point from Bath. Is it going to be possible to find great beauty, isolation from tourists, protection from crime, and accessibility to schools, doctors, etc. all in one place?

We are rather discouraged, and I, very tired. Meet Quinn[1] about 8:30 at Rockland. He is a young, lean, browned captain, quite trim and efficient. We come over on the *Mouette* in the fading light. Fading crimson behind the everlasting Camden hills. They are the same. It is soothing to look back at your life punctuated by this same view. Being young, part of a family, Elisabeth. And the Camden hills. Then C.—I brought him here in May—with violets. I wanted to see him here, test him against this place, before we were married. Against the Camden hills. Then those terrific trips, leaving the baby here. And the Camden hills. And all those years of sadness, of pits of horror—losing Daddy, the baby, Elisabeth. And coming back finally after it was all over, to find them the same—the Camden hills. Then without Elisabeth. The last summer. Little Jon. The Camden hills again.

Then the years abroad—what a gulf in my life; how different I feel. But the Camden hills are the same.

Margot is waiting on the dock at the Thoroughfare. It is all the same. The quiet streets with the light against the leaves. To the house. The smell, the wonderful smell of it—what is it? It is only tonight—tomorrow I shall smell it no longer—tonight I

---

[1] Captain Quinn, North Haven boatman, used by the Morrow family in the summers to run their boat, the *Mouette*.

smell the peculiar House smell and feel like a child, satisfied deep down.

I feel conscious of the child growing in me—the sense of life. One should keep oneself attuned to it and not lose it in the hustle and worry of daily life—as I have lately.

Saturday, July 13th

Wake up and look out at the Camden hills. One feels so rested here. Mother arrives, very tired, and *all* the maids! The house bustles into activity.

We decide to go tomorrow to Swan Island area to look for possible sites for a home. We think we probably can't get everything and we should try for beauty and a summer home that we *could* use in an emergency in winter.

Tuesday, July 16th

Today has been spent chiefly in a vague atmosphere of indecision. Is the trouble of moving up here going to be worth it? Will we be able to be independent of the life here? Social, family—or general tension? And underneath all these personal plans lie the great problems of the world today, C.'s unrest about them. His wanting to get at them and his wanting at the same time to get *some* kind of security for his family before the wave strikes.

Wednesday, July 17th

C. and I go out for a walk to the sunny point. We go over everything again. Out of the mist suddenly comes C.'s conviction that he would like to find out what's happening over there—technically, militarily, and every other way, and that this might be a good time for him to take his postponed Pan-Am trip.

I dread his going, both personally and also because I cannot see all the implications and I don't want him to get into anything that will hurt his future work or his position. But on the other hand it *sounds* right to me. It clicks. Yes, he must go, he must be in something positive, active, ahead of the times—not just marking time here in North Haven. The knowledge he may gain would help him enormously here, both technically and generally.

I have a long talk with Mother on the point. About plans and Jon and the war—chiefly the war—my attitude and hers. We talked it all out and it was a great relief. She says in tears that she feels that someone is dying, some old and dear friend is dying, and she cannot bear it.

It is true, of course; it is her world that is dying. It must die (I feel), but to die *that way* is horrible and that so much that is good and brave and true and *young* (that is the worst) should die with the old and worn out—*that* is the tragedy. There is no comfort for her generation.

What can one say? That one has hope for the *new* world? No, one cannot give that to them. It is a part of being old.

And yet to have met, to have talked it out so there is a deep basis of understanding between us is marvelous. She even understands my point of view—only she cannot *feel* it. How *could* she? It is a miracle that she can see it at all.

Leave on *Mouette* with Captain Quinn. As we drive down the coast, I try to figure out what we have had from this week. We are not any nearer the solution of a home. But we have come to some negative decisions.

Thursday, July 18th

Arrive home about 5:30. The children are in the garden. Land comes around the corner, golden and beautiful in a green-blue sunsuit. "Father's *venu*," he says, mildly pleased as C. steps out. Then, with a great smile and rising voice, "Mother's *venue!*"

Friday, July 19th

Terribly hot. I drive to town, see Dr. Hawks, who says he's never seen me looking so well, everything is going all right.

Home to meet C. and the children back from the beach. Jon's face is aglow. He says, "I swam to the lighthouse and back-" I couldn't believe it, but his father said it was true. It was a three-quarter-hour swim out against the tide, one-half hour back.

When they got around the base of the lighthouse, the light-house-keeper threw out a board on a rope and pulled Jon in. Then they climbed up an iron ladder, into the lighthouse. Jon was cold, so the lighthouse-keeper's wife rubbed him with a towel. They wanted to row Jon back but he wanted to swim. C. is very proud of him. And Jon will never forget it.

We walk to the point at night and look at the lighthouse. It looks miles away. I try to tell C. what an immeasurable thing he has given Jon in teaching him to swim and in giving him that rock of confidence in his own ability. And no one else could have—to do it with his father!

C. has done some dictating and gone again over the problems in his mind. He says it is a great help to him to talk them out with me, that once he couldn't but now he can (I understand more, I can see them now). And this makes me happy. Though I do not feel like much help or that I have any new ideas on my own initiative to deal with the problems of a world in chaos.

I try to think what I would do if I were alone. I tell him I don't know *what* I could do. He turns to me very seriously and says, "I want you to listen to me and I want you to remember my telling you this, now. If you are ever left alone without me and times are bad, you can always, always earn your living by writing. Your ability will be good under whatever regime you are living. *Don't* try to earn a living at something you can't do when you have an exceptional tool in your own hands."

I try to interrupt several times but he goes on. "*Please* let me finish." He says I could find a market either in my own country or in some other, that in times of great turmoil I "might have to scratch a bit" but that these times are comparatively short. He is so stern and grave about it that it frightens me and sounds prophetic. It gives me faith, of course, too.

Saturday, July 20th

A leaden day. I can do nothing all day, not think, not write, every motion is an effort, moving mountains. C. says he feels the same. I lay it to the weather on top of my extra weight and apathy. But he says it is because we are living in such uncertainty.

"I keep trying to put my foot down where it is not quicksand."

The Germans, Hitler's speech, offer a last chance of peace (vaguely and in the abstract; there is no real offer or terms) to England before the onslaught. "As a victor" wishing to spare lives. The English, of course, hardly notice the offer and do not consider it.

I dread the suffering and the terror and horror that is hanging over them.

Also it seems that famine is almost certain in France, if not revolution. There is criticism of the Pétain government, chiefly in Paris and chiefly, I gather, Communist. There is no sympathy for France here—and *no way to help*. This is the terrible burden that hangs over one, day and night.

Other people, on a day like this, get into their car, drive off to the movies, to the theater, have dinner out somewhere for a change of scene. But these distractions are not open to us—at least not in America.

Sunday, July 21st

C. talks to me in the morning about what I am going to do when he is away—if he goes. He does it because he worries about me, he wants me to be satisfied, he wants me to write, and he knows the burden of two unfinished books is a terrible blot on my conscience. He tries to encourage me: Couldn't I get the anthology[1] finished by the time the baby is born? To have something to show for this period. He says it is enough just to have the baby (enough for *him*) but that he knows it isn't enough for me.

He goes over the record—nine years, and only two books and wonders why it is. Has he not given me the right kind of environment? He analyzes very well our life here in the East with hundreds of people pressing on us, letters, demands, personal friends, charities, war obligations, duties (that drawer in the office that is *hung* around my neck even though I don't look at it). We turn these things off, we refuse them, we lead an isolated life—

---

[1] A. M. L. was collecting an anthology of her favorite poems and prose quotations, to be entitled *O to Whom*. It was never published.

why? In order to keep ourselves free to do "more important things."

And then, do we *do* these more important things? No, I don't, and why don't I? Because the very effort of pushing those million things off, the very weight of them on my conscience, keeps me restless, distracted, unable to write, makes me seek the anodyne of action, small errands, jobs, anything to fill up the hole in my conscience.

But you ask too much, I want to cry out. I cannot be having a baby and be a good housekeeper and keep thinking and writing on the present times (in my diary) and be always free to discuss anything with you and give to the children and keep an atmosphere of peace in the family (the bigger family which is so scattered and distraught now, all of us disagreeing) and keep my mind clear and open on the present-day things and write a book at the same time. I cannot be an efficient woman and house-manager *and* an artist at the same time.

Throw in a baby and it takes all your extra strength as well as all the creative urge in you. Once the baby starts to move and you are physically conscious of what you are creating you can no longer create in another line, at least *not* to your best capacity. I think I feel this so strongly that it is really what keeps me from writing. I know it will *not* be the best writing. The *best* writing is going into that child.

Also, I feel now this terrible conscience about the war and longing to help, to do something, to put back something into that wasted world. The worry about it puts off even longer any permanent writing.

But what *is* the permanent writing? The work I was doing before the war? There is a gulf there, a gap I cannot bridge. The world that I was brought up in was as far from present issues as the Victorian Era from that one—*further*—because that world was only a continuation of the Victorian one. And what value is there in presenting that world now?

I have the feeling I must begin again, as one has to begin life again now, with an utterly new conception, new ideals, new words even. But we are just learning them. The new age is just beginning. In fact, it is the transition stage. The old world is dying and a new one beginning, and this is the pain and uncertainty and anguish we all feel. How can I write in the new language before that world is born?

Monday, July 22nd

Letter from Con. She encloses a reprint of two letters from people in England on the present desperate situation. They are thrilling letters, infused with a kind of fire of sacrifice, gallantry, beauty of spirit, sureness of purpose, and courage heedless of danger, death, or discouragement. It is, as they say, truly Elizabethan. Heady excitement—wine of sacrifice. When I read it I think: "Oh, if they feel like that they can win!"

Tuesday, July 23rd (Train to Littleton)

Supper with Con at Cosmopolitan Club; Aubrey comes. It is nice and peaceful and quiet. I get the complete British point of view from him. It is like those letters—brave, beautiful, gallant. How *can* it not be right, I think. Dreadful stories of Dunkirk and the German treatment of the refugees. When you hear this side you feel the British are right to resist to the end, that there is no hope of dealing with the Germans. Though I keep feeling, yes, but is it *war* or is it *Germans?* I am not sure that it isn't just *war* one hates. They, of course, all feel it is just "Germans."

The pictures he drew of France hurt me the most. They didn't resist at all, just broke. Complete demoralization—not a good word to be said for the government. Pétain just a doddering old man, Laval a crook. According to Aubrey, all fine Frenchmen are in the English camp. Eve Curie, etc. St.-Ex. was last seen in Bordeaux walking about like one demented, so crushed by his disillusionment. Jean Monnet is in London. The men here are like people in a nervous breakdown.

I am depressed beyond words. I had so hoped something new was coming out of France. Is it a Crusade and not a Revolution?

What a nightmare—either way. Either to be disillusioned in my own faith or in "my own people." I am on the wrong side—for good.

Friday, July 26th

Back in New York. I find a note from C., who is having dinner with Roy Howard,[1] "who is taking me back by boat." C. took along (on Mr. Howard's swell yacht) bathing trunks, a raincoat, an aluminum container, sticking plaster, and a cord. Thinking they would have no dory small enough to get up to our little dock, he said to the astonished Mr. Howard that the yacht could just "drop him at the lighthouse" and he would swim home! He planned to wrap his clothes up in the raincoat, tie it fast, so it wouldn't leak, with the cord. Seal his watch in the aluminum container with sticking plaster, tie all around his neck and dive off the yacht. Roy Howard said, to this remarkable offer, "You take the all-time high on this boat for a considerate guest!"

The whole performance is so *typical* of C. (Down to the aluminum container and sticking plaster for his watch! Another man would have forgotten to think about his watch and then left it behind on the boat. Another man, in fact, would *never* have considered such a fantastic and unconventional act as at all practical. But C. considered it, *made* it practical, down to the last item, the watch!) So typical that I shook with laughter.

Sunday, July 28th. Very hot

C. working on his speech. I criticize it. It will bring down wrath, I fear, though his point is good and needed.

Tuesday, July 30th

Very hot again—though a slight breeze. I go up to my desk and try to think about C.'s speech. If it is going to be controversial it has got to be terribly good.

[1] President of Scripps-Howard newspapers. C. A. L. was having dinner on Howard's boat in Long Island Sound.

In the afternoon C. takes Jon to the club to fly.

At night in bed, just as I go out, Jon says: "I'll tell you something" (his eyes very big) "but you mustn't tell anyone—Father let me take the controls." I tell him about the first time his father let me do it (in the Moth over Long Island, before we were engaged; how long ago it seems) and we compare notes!

The sky is all gold tonight.

Thursday, August 1st

In the afternoon I work on C.'s speech. The boys have all become Indians, "Red Bear," "Spotted Fox," and "Chief Noki." No "Palefaces" are allowed near their tent. Land and Winnie are the "Palefaces" and have built a house of chairs for themselves on the porch in self-defense.

Jon—from a distance: "You can't win *all* the wars. . . ." And, "I've killed you several times already!"

Saturday, August 3rd

C. leaves for Chicago.

Con and Aubrey come for tea and walk. Lovely to see them. Aubrey thinks the English can win by the blockade; he admits they'll have to starve all Europe first, but the issue is so tremendous that they have no other choice.

I protest this point of view as mildly as I can. He says that even if we guarantee the food going only to the French, Belgians, and Dutch, the Germans will take correspondingly more of the supplies already there. He also says he knows our government is firmly against sending any food or doing anything to interfere with the British blockade. I am afraid this is true. He thinks we will be in [the war] if England lasts the summer.

Thelma and Brooke come just after they leave. Brooke also says we'll be in the war after the elections, no matter *who* wins. He thinks the British will allow us to send food to Europe if we guarantee that it gets to the right hands. But Germany will break such a guarantee and then we'll be in the war, which he is all for.

Supper alone on the porch. I walk to the point with Thor.

Think of C., look out over the water, the lighthouse, the sky, and try to adjust the conflicts in my mind from the day's haul of information.

> "He that seeketh after truth
> Shall in no-wise find peace of mind."

Sunday, August 4th

I sit on the porch in the afternoon and turn on the radio on chance of getting C.'s meeting in Chicago, though it is not listed. I get it! C.'s voice comes across wonderfully. It is very impressive and the crowd cheers him. I am moved when he says, "I prefer to say what I believe . . ." [or not to speak at all]. It is so HIM—pure fire of integrity—and the crowd feels it and cheers, a spontaneous burst.

Jon and Land are about, Jon awestruck, Land curious. Jon says: "Why does my father speak so loud? I could hear him all the way down in the cellar!" I said he was speaking to a big crowd of people.

[*C. A. L. spoke in Chicago on "Our Relationship with Europe." He reviewed events which led to the war and felt his view of the situation in Europe was vindicated by the course of the war to date. He noted with satisfaction that both political parties had declared against entry into the war and that steps were now being taken for a strong self-defense. He urged guarding the independence won by the soldiers of our revolution and ridiculed war proponents who claimed that only the British fleet protected us from invasion.*]

Wednesday, August 7th

[John] Cudahy, our Ambassador in Belgium, reports Europe faces starvation this winter unless we help feed them; says the conduct of the German troops in Belgium was exemplary, better than some Americans in World War I. He also defends [King] Leopold. He will certainly catch hell for saying this.

Friday, August 9th

Cudahy is being recalled and rebuked. The State Department says his views are not theirs and that there is no evidence that there will be starvation in Europe this winter and he had no right to say so. They are determined to let Europe starve.

Saturday, August 10th

Alan Valentine[1] arrives. We discuss the world situation. Great Britain—a world, a way of life that was doomed, even without a war. It was perfect, but only for a few, too few, and therefore it had to go.

Supper on the porch, talking about whether nationalism as an ideal is a good thing and if there is a "moral equivalent for war." Alan thinks war could be avoided if man were given sufficient outlets or sublimations for the fighting instinct. I don't know; C., I think, disagrees.

I watch a long-winged insect caught in a spider web on the porch during this discussion. I want so much to save the insect—vainly fluttering its helpless wings—before the spider gets there. But I can't interrupt Alan (it's just behind his head). But it is terrible to watch the death struggle. The spider gets it in the end and its wings stop fluttering. I feel horrible and as though there were some terrible connection between our talk and that little object lesson. Though I'm not sure what exactly.

Sunday, August 11th

[Herbert] Hoover comes out with a plan for giving relief to Belgium, Holland, Norway, and France. Guarantees of food going to the sufferers. He says Europe *will* definitely starve this winter unless something is done about it, and blames the government for its noncommittal attitude. I am relieved and hopeful. Perhaps something *can* be done if he leads it.

Alan, C., and I on the porch in the morning. Alan on C.'s speeches. He is all for him but criticizes and analyzes very well what it is that makes them unpopular with many people. We

[1] Old friend of the Morrow family, author, President of Rochester University.

discuss it a long time. Finally it comes down not just to his saying unpleasant truths or bucking the prevailing feeling and propaganda or that he doesn't "talk down" to his audience, not even that he doesn't give the whole picture—all of which are criticisms other friends give. Alan pursues it deeper and says the public senses that C. isn't giving *all* of himself, he isn't "selling" himself at all (because he despises doing it), he isn't using his "personality" on them, only his reason (for he feels he wants to win them on his *case* or not at all). They sense he is fighting with one hand behind his back. C. laughs and says maybe that is true and that he has something precious in that other hand that he doesn't want to give up!

Monday, August 12th

Much pro and con on food situation in papers; most people argue that to feed France or Europe is to help Germany. Cudahy says he knew coming home he would be crucified, but the truth must be told (on Europe's starvation). After supper C. calls Hoover on who to get in touch with in New York on the food relief situation. Hoover implies there is some chance that the British may agree, "after the battle for Britain is over." My heavens, he thinks they'll win, then!

Tuesday, August 13th

Has the Blitzkrieg on England started? Terrific number of planes over the Channel, the coast, ports. Both sides claim a vast majority downed on the other side.

Just before supper C. shows me two very angry telegrams from old friends. "You have let America down." "You stand for all the atrocities of Hitler." I am terribly shocked, hurt, and angry (I don't know why exactly, because I know hundreds of people are saying the same thing, but these people were friends). They had a right to criticize—but to throw mud, to leave issues and simply hurl names! It shocks me, for they supposedly are the intelligent, the moderate, the tolerant, the well informed, the people who have had advantages all their lives and therefore you would expect to be cool, quiet, unruffled. *Critical,* yes—

perhaps, completely opposed—but never intolerant, rude, and cruel.

It is so *easy* to hate and to feel one is being courageous in doing it.

C. says we knew it was happening and it should not shock me. The longer this war goes on and the fiercer it gets, the more of that we'll get. Besides, he says, he understands that kind of thing—he gets angry himself and knows what it is like.

But I feel deeply angry, as though I could not forgive it *for him,* not forgive them, ever. I say, "They will be sorry for those telegrams," fiercely.

And then later, when we walk to the point, I think, no, I mustn't feel like that, so bitter—it is just as bad.

Wednesday, August 14th
Terrible air fights and raids over the coast of Britain, terrific losses on each side. How long can this keep up?

Friday, August 16th
Jon's birthday. His father gives him his baseball bat [from E. C. M.] in the morning—Jon is quite impressed—also the ball, mitt, and catcher's mask, shield. As C. picks this up he says, "That *would* appeal to a grandmother, wouldn't it!" The children also have fun with the cardboard box that all this came in. C. slips it over Jon's head and he looks like a walking grandfather's clock.

I work on an article[1] all morning. I do not "write" it exactly, I am so full of it (the whole winter's travail of thought, anguish, doubt, arguments, defense—and affirmation). It flows out of me, unmindful of how it is "written."

Sunday, August 18th
Air war continues. There is an ominous tension underneath all this, a rising tension, the sense that we do not know the real state of things, combined with the feeling that interventionists

[1] A. M. L. was working on a long article that eventually was published as a small book, *The Wave of the Future.*

are all set for a big push to get us in. There is a boat of ours that has been warned by Germany not to take a certain route. Germans won't take the responsibility for it. It would take just that, I think, to break things wide open. I feel deeply pessimistic tonight, as though we would get into the war—yet it is not the war I dread but the chaos that will follow.

I tell C. tonight that we are exiles, exiles for good. For we are exiles in *time*—not in space. There is no place for us today and no people. He says he does not mind being an exile in time, even, with me.

Tuesday, August 20th

I go out and pick flowers in the early crisp morning sun. It is delicious, all the flowers are still wet and bowed and the earth dark and rich smelling. I love doing the flowers each morning, admiring them as I cut, watching the bees curled up asleep on a flower or the butterflies choosing deliberately which one to go to next. It is a kind of participation with the world's beauty before I enclose myself in my little house, to work. I rejoice in them and in the morning and it joins me to something fundamental and lasting and eternal. It is a kind of prayer, I suppose, a hymn of praise.

How fully one *lives* in such moments—and how much of life is unexpressed, always, *always!*

Go up to my desk and work on the article. One of those days that you look at what you have written and you hear it cracking all about you, even the strongest parts. How to mend it? What can be saved? What slashed? What rewritten? A disillusioning and wasted morning.

Friday, August 23rd

Thelma, Brooke (they both wear British emblems—"Bundles for Britain"—in buttonhole or as pin, and Thelma has "Bundles for Britain" ear studs on!), Con, and Aubrey for supper, which is good and goes well. And we are all gay and in good temper. I couldn't be more in "enemy camp," though; Brooke is more interventionist than Aubrey and says, "We're already in it,

Anne." He says we'll be in it *quicker* if Willkie gets in than if Roosevelt does. Aubrey is in good form and so are the Lees. They are all talking the same language, in the same fight. Con is a sympathetic observer. Only I am on the outside. I let them talk, pleased, as a hostess, that they are congenial and that each is getting hope and encouragement from the other. In the meantime I feel rather sunk—and terribly alone myself. Though I let them do most of the talking, I try not to be dishonest, and argue the points I feel strongly about. Besides, I want to know their answers.

Brooke doesn't consider the possibility of our not being successful in a war, nor does he think there is any chance of a revolution here. He is a completely honest interventionist, however, and I like him. None of this hypocrisy of "measures short of war." No, it is simply a case of: There is no living in a world with Hitler at large. And he is all for going in and stopping him, with his own two fists, too.

Aubrey quotes Jan Masaryk[1] as saying that the difference between Communism and Nazism is that if he were under the former he would be killed because he liked to have a manicure (i.e., class). But if he were under the latter he would be killed because he was a Czech (i.e., inferior race). Czechoslovakia, as a nation, would still go on under Communism but not under Nazism. He far preferred to be killed because he occasionally had a manicure. Class hatred not as terrible as race hatred, in other words.

I think he is wrong here. He would not be killed under Communism because he had a manicure but because he had a *better* manicure than someone else. Because he had a *better* mind, or because he was a *better* diplomat. It is not as simple as *class*. That is where people get confused. That is what the Russians *say*. But what actually happens is not that *class* but that *quality* is killed.

Con, Thelma, and I have a nice talk upstairs, ending up

[1] Foreign Minister of Czechoslovakia, 1940–48; Vice-Premier of provisional government in London, 1941–45.

with Thelma saying what is needed in the world is more *fear,* less cocksureness in all political leaders here and abroad.

It isn't *fear,* she means, but *awe,* or humility. The thing the Greek tragedies were written about: the gods never forgave hubris, or pride, or lack of reverence for the gods. And pride is the first sin on the Catholic list of sins.

It is, I think afterwards, *that* that I mind the most in Germans, even *nice* Germans. They completely lack humility ("We are so good at organization, *nicht wahr?*"). So, as a matter of fact, do the English—as a whole! The Scotch, the Irish (who will not "fly in the face of the Lord"), the French, the Welsh have it. The Americans, the old-fashioned kind, have reverence, humbleness, like Carl Sandburg. The Chinese have it and the Jews have it.

All these people I instinctively like.

Saturday, August 24th

I walk to the point alone at night with Thor. It is darkening fast, the wind has ruffled the bay a deep ominous purple, all the trees are stirred to their roots by this first wind of autumn. A roaring and a rustling sweeping from out at sea, up the cliff, and over me. A *Listen! the Wind* kind of wind. Autumn and the sudden turn of a season.

I feel somewhere the forces have changed, the gods have decided—we must go into this war, go through all that, war and disillusion and bad times. We must suffer and learn—there is no escape (I have felt it for a week, really) but this wind confirms it. I must accept it.

Sunday, August 25th

C. comes back in time to finish breakfast with us. He is very discouraged about the war picture. There is a terrific drive in the war direction.[1] And no one of real strength or force or spirit opposing it.

[1] Public pressure on Roosevelt was building up from the interventionist groups for the transfer of overage destroyers to the British. The trade of destroyers for a long lease on British naval bases was completed in September without being submitted to Congress.

The German drive seems to have slowed up; the chances for a swift Blitzkrieg are passing with the days. It looks as if it were going to be a long war of blockade and counter-blockade, with highly increased chances of our getting in. I have seldom seen C. as depressed—not just the war, but *after* the war, what?

I tell him about my dinner of interventionists. Strange that he and I came to the same conclusion and mood from different experiences—as though the same wind had touched us. We grow closer all the time. This hard winter has at least done that.

C. reads my article and comes up after, much moved and very enthusiastic. He says it is better than "Prayer for Peace" and worth the whole winter and must go into a book. I can't see it at all now. It has left me. There is no vision in it—only words.

Monday, August 26th

Sherwood[1] has given a radio speech in which he directly attacks C. and Ford. Ford is let off as a genius in certain lines but out of those lines "a very stupid man." But the burden of the attack falls on C., who has a "poisoned mind"—a traitor to America— and whose voice and utterances are detested by true Americans as much as those of Goebbels, Göring, and Hitler (for whom he speaks!).

Why can't the so-called intellectual attack on *issues?* He, of all people, should be able to, but in this crisis none of them can.

C. calls [Alfred] Harcourt [of Harcourt, Brace and Company] on my article. Harcourt is much interested and says he'd like to see it. C. takes it in. I work upstairs in the book room.

C. comes back from town cheered, with more fight in him than yesterday, or, rather, more *hope* of the fight being successful.

He has the "cat smile" all over his face, due to a talk with Mr. Harcourt, who evidently thought the article "beautiful" and is very anxious to take it as a little book. Can get it out very fast—a month or three weeks. C. is already thinking about set-ups and covers. I feel like the goose girl in the fairy tale, locked into the

[1] Robert Emmet Sherwood, American playwright, novelist, and speech-writer for Roosevelt.

room with a pile of flax: "Flax into Gold—Flax into Gold." (C. says maybe he's the gnome who can turn it for me!)

Tuesday, August 27th

London bombed. Apparently not much damage done. How one accepts it—now.

Sunny and warmer; pick flowers and do one bowl of autumn colors, but the garden is thinning and I cut carefully. I never take a zinnia with a bud next to it, they look too much like mother and child. And I feel so badly when sometimes I cut two flowers by accident instead of one. I wonder vaguely if Death sometimes takes an extra person—by accident—because the scissors are too large?

The bowl is a beautiful one; I am pleased. It satisfies me—a tangible creation before I start my intangible one.

Go over lots of little corrections with C. and work alone on the "big" changes—Mr. Harcourt's suggestions. How well I know this stage in writing. You keep feeling, "If *only* I could get *at* this I could remake it. I could really put something into it." But when one tries to one can't *get at* it. It slips through your fingers like sand. You can't see the wood for the trees. When you wrote it, of course, you couldn't see the trees for the wood.

Lloyd Neck, September 4th

Mother darling,

Lately I have woken up at night and written letters to you. Letters I could not write in the daytime because I have been working on an article—all the pent-up travail of the winter's mental strife. It now turns out to be too long for a magazine and Harcourt, Brace is printing it as a tiny book. The writing itself was so spontaneous that it has not been actually hard. I *had* to write it, all the arguments and counter arguments, all my own carving out of a conviction, building of a bridge between C.'s beliefs and my own, and not least, my deep sense of the injustice to him and to his side—all this has pushed the writing out. I couldn't help it.

But the decision as to whether or not to publish it has caused me a lot of sleepless nights and doubts and anguish. We took it in to Mr. H. yesterday and it has gone to press. Today is the first day I have had free—and I wanted to write you all about it.

I think the clearest definition of the article is that it attempts to give a *moral* argument for isolationism—which I think no one has yet presented. (The arguments of the isolationists are so often narrow, materialistic, short-sighted, and wholly selfish—I am repelled by them.) I have wanted to present these because I feel that the cause of staying out of this war has been so badly presented, so unjustly criticized and accused, and because I think it is vital to stay out.

I feel, of course, almost impelled to write it, because of my personal loyalty and desperate feeling of injustice to C. but I wouldn't do it on that alone. I wouldn't do it if I didn't feel convinced of his integrity and the integrity of his stand (whether or not I agree with the details and whether or not I agree with the presentation).

Although I have written it under great feeling it is not violent or immoderate or angry, or, I think, petty or defensive. But this will not prevent it from being violently or angrily criticized. Though I speak only for our staying out of this war it will be considered anti-British and "tainted" with German propaganda (though I don't defend—and *am* outspoken in my dislike of the horrors in Germany—also of my admiration for the English).

To be *dispassionate* today in a world of passion is a sin. It is to be complacent, immoral, stupid or blind. The most likely criticism will be that it is the statement of an impractical dreamer—and the charge of presumptuousness. To that charge, on my own score, I feel that the issue of war or peace is an issue that concerns not only experts on Foreign Affairs but every citizen of the United States. It is *my* husband who will fight—*my* generation who bears the brunt of the war—and *my* children who will suffer for it.

You may say that everyone agrees on keeping out of this war. But that is, sadly, not true. If all the "short-of-war" people were as sincere as you, I wouldn't worry. Brooke Lee says we're already in the war—and we'll be *openly* in quicker with Willkie than with Roosevelt. Their whole attitude (which shocks me profoundly) is that "We, the more intellectual, more idealistic, must guide the big dumb American people into this war—once they're in they'll see it's the only thing to do."

It is easy to be intolerant and angry. The war has been going on for a year. As I look back I feel it has been years—what I have learned—how much more I understand and forgive people! I never really understood before what it was to be a minority,[1] why they become narrow and intolerant and angry. One becomes so tired—it is easier to be hard.

The criticisms of C. since the last talk have been terrific, even from personal friends. I must say my admiration for a man like Walter Lippmann has gone up lately. He is almost the only intellectual who is profoundly opposed to C.'s arguments and who does *not* get angry (or hides it) and who argues back on principles and issues, who never resorts to personal attack on extraneous subjects, and who keeps his tongue or pen on the plane of reason. I always read his criticisms of C., study them, argue them out in my mind. Usually I don't agree—though it takes all my mettle—and there are great gaps I can't answer. But I always breathe more freely after reading them, as if we had all been sitting at a table with Daddy—arguing, yes, disagreeing, yes, but not in hate and bitterness and anger—in a world of tolerance.

Well—all this is only to say that there will undoubtedly be great criticism, but you will not, I think, be ashamed—however much you may disagree—of me in the article. You must think that *there* is where I stand, next to C., and where I always will probably, and that there is much satisfaction in standing there openly—especially if I might perhaps help him.

Also, by the time this comes out—early October—I shall be

[1] In this and other passages in the diary, A. M. L. speaks of "our side" (the noninterventionists) as being a "minority." It was true that they were a minority in New York intellectual circles and in the area of the Eastern seaboard; in the country as a whole, however, they were far from being a minority. See Introduction, pp. xvii–xix.

past all this worry and only thinking about the immediate future. I don't believe even the severest or most scornful criticism could pierce the immaculate blissful heaven of a maternity ward after your baby has arrived!

The title is *The Wave of the Future,* with the subtitle "A Confession of Faith."[1] I want to give the proceeds of it—*if any!*— to the Quakers, as they seem to be the only ones living up to the reality of the word *mercy.*

Lloyd Neck, Thursday, September 12th

Mother darling,

Your letter was such a joy and a comfort. You were good to write in the midst of all your life—to come so immediately to me. I only hope it will not be hard for you—the criticism, I mean. I had a dreadful night with Laura and George [Stevens]. I showed the essay to George and he wanted me to withdraw it, he felt so strongly about it. He gave me back all my own doubts and fears on it and on myself. That it was presumptuous—that I had no right to write it without more knowledge of history, economics, foreign affairs, etc. That it would be torn limb from limb. That it would be called—with some justification—"Fifth Column." That it would do C. no good and me, harm. After all this he said that it had an intuitive point that was valid (but that I had not sufficient evidence to back it up), that it was lucid, obviously sincere, and, "of course," beautifully written! And that he might, of course, be wrong about it!

It was hard to take—chiefly because I agreed with him. I think all those criticisms are valid. Only after I get through admitting them I still feel—even if it is badly said—even if it is not my place to say it—even if it is vulnerable—it *must* be said. I am sorry it must be said by me and I am sorry there is not time in my life or the world at the moment to say it better. And perhaps I am mistaken—still, it must be attempted.

How much faith one has got to have to do *anything* and how easily it melts away—how vulnerable it is! It is the worst torture,

[1] C. C. M. M. wittily corrected A. M. L. by calling it "A Confession of Doubt."

I think—or temptation—when people undermine your own inner faith. It is so much easier to have faith in other people's standards —so much safer.

Lloyd Neck, September 21st

Dear Mina [Curtiss],

This is not an answer to your lovely letter but more a letter that I have been wanting to write to you lately explaining what I have been doing. I have finally found myself—as a result of this long winter and summer of arguments, conflicts and doubts —forced to write out, no matter how badly or inadequately, my own moral defense of Charles's position.

I do not write you to urge or expect you to agree with me. I do not expect that any of my friends will agree with me. Nor am I apologizing or warning you—because I think you know, perhaps better than others, from our talks here, how I feel about the war. But I do hope that you will understand why I felt I must write it.

I think I know what to expect from the critics—I have already faced all their objections in my mind and many of them I accept as valid but there still remains an inner core of conviction that I must do it anyway. Perhaps it is only a stubborn personal loyalty. I know this has a great part in it but I would not do it for that alone. (I wouldn't do it alone for a cause and a man that I feel have been badly presented and misunderstood and unjustly distorted.)

I think I have less vanity about this than anything else I have ever done. I know so well that it could be better done. If only someone else would say it—but no one will. All the intellectuals are on the other side.[1] And I can so easily understand that too.

[1] This statement actually was not true. The long list of noninterventionist intellectuals included Charles A. Beard, historian; John Bassett Moore, Edwin Borchard, and Philip Jessup, professors of international law; college presidents Phillips Bradley of Amherst, Robert Hutchins of the University of Chicago, Henry Noble MacCracken of Vassar; liberal writer Oswald Garrison Villard; economist Stuart Chase; Socialist leader Norman Thomas; William Benton, publisher of the Encyclopaedia Britannica; Douglas Southall Freeman, editor and author of *R. E. Lee.*

My heart is there too. I am not on the side of evil. I want evil to be vanquished as much as they—only my mind tells me, perhaps wrongly, that it cannot be done the way they think it can.

I only hope that I do not add to the general confusion and I only mind being separated from "my own people." I do feel *that* now terribly—which was why your letter was such a joy. But I suppose one has got to discover sooner or later that one is alone. And as Rilke keeps saying, it is "at bottom not something that one can take or leave. We *are* solitary, we may delude ourselves and act as though this were not so. That is all. But how much better it is to realize that we are so, yes, even to begin by assuming it."

Sometimes it seems to me, too, that one should not write at all or try to see or think dispassionately when such things are going on as one reads each day in the papers. One should have another form of expression, like the cry of a child or the howl of an animal.

And yet I cannot believe that will help at the moment. What you said you were trying to do at your farm—the keeping of still pools of peace and calmness and thought somewhere in the world (difficult as it is)—seems to me the only solution.

In the meantime this last month of waiting for the baby goes quite well, though, of course, I am completely bogged down by my body. I keep feeling that it must be like this in old age and think with amazement of all the people who have managed to keep their minds and spirit unshackled by their bodies. How did Yeats remain to the end "a foolish passionate old man"?

DIARY   *Lloyd Neck, Sunday, October 27th*
I have been home from the hospital a week, with the new baby —Anne! With so many thoughts—life rushing by and no time to catch up. Life goes in the baby's routine—the delicious newness of it. The absorption of it, physically. Nursing, resting, lying in the sun, eating, drinking (for the milk!), nursing, and resting. Life itself is perilously precious—sitting in the sun watching golden wasps, a few left, and leaves falling one by one, and the sky, very blue against the last reds of the trees. I can

only sit and praise life and collect my thoughts that wander—still unattached to earth and life. The day is terribly cut up, no big chunk of it to spend on anything, except at night from 8–10, when I am so sleepy.

And in the afternoon when I should sleep my mind pounds out letters or arguments against some critical review or counterstand. In the midst of much criticism one loses faith in one's own vision. How can one be right against so many august, brilliant, experienced people? I find I am hurt, not by the reviews exactly, but by the growing rift I see between myself and those people I thought I belonged to. The artists, the writers, the intellectuals, the sensitive, the idealistic—I feel exiled from them. I have become exiled for good, accidentally, really. My marriage has stretched me out of my world, changed me so it is no longer possible to change back.

The daily accounts in the newspapers: "All writers who deserve the name" are fighting Fascism, Fifth Column, etc. And I am classed as the latter! Clare Luce is going to "answer" my book, which she considers "dangerous to Democracy."

In the midst of all this, one clings to certain very good things. Friends that reach across the rift—regardless—Mina Curtiss despite everything. Mary Hand's letter (how precious it is to be *loved* across differences—more precious than love from the people on one's "side"). The girl who did not agree but praised my tolerance and lack of hate. And that letter from Auden,[1] piercing through to the real pain of the moment.

Mother darling,

I meant to get a note off to you this A.M. after seeing that editorial in the *Times* on the stupid publicity of the W. A. White Committee [of disagreement in the family]. One of the hardest things to bear of this new life of opposite camps is finding that there are elements you don't like in your own "camp." It is part of this age I have dreaded where one must take "sides" and there is no place for the moderate—or, at least, the moderates are

[1] W. H. Auden, English-born poet who spent the war years in the U.S. and became an American citizen.

forced to join with extremists. There is no middle way. I suppose one has got to learn and bear that there are unworthy elements in any crusade. And that being so, the moderates are bound to be "used," so to speak. It is an awful feeling but there does not seem to be any defense against it and one has got to go ahead anyway on what one believes.

I have felt it strongly and bitterly this year and because of that I was terribly pleased—or, rather, helped—by a letter from Auden (W. H.—whom I don't know at all) on the book. He put it so well—this pain of not knowing whether or not one is being "used"—that I feel like handing it on to you. He said: "As a writer myself, I know that it is not neglect and scorn that is the hardest solitude to bear, but the knowledge that everything one writes goes out helpless into the world to be turned to evil as well as good, that every work of art is powerless against misuse; yet one has to take the risk, and pray that the good may outbalance the evil."

If only we could shake off the world and not be entangled. But we can't. I am upset by the Feeding of Europe problems and feel I must speak for it in some way or other—though it will not be popular to do so. I hope *something* may be worked out and think it may, in a small way, perhaps. Come soon again and we will only talk children and writing.

Lloyd Neck, Huntington, Long Island, October 28th

Dear Mr. Auden,

Thank you for your most generous-spirited letter on my book. What one dreads, as you say, is that one may help the "powers of evil" (taking this in a general and almost abstract sense) and, conversely, one's separation from the "powers of good" and the people one loves (again in a general and abstract sense). Today, more than ever, one wants desperately to "do right." But, it is difficult to know what is "right." And sometimes it seems necessary to go ahead almost blindly, knowing one may make a mistake.

I think of Despiau in his grimy studio in Paris, with his hands trembling over an infinitesimal point in a cheekbone, and saying, "I am afraid to touch it lest I make it worse." And then: "Now I *have* touched it and I have lost something. I have made a mistake." And then, finally, *"Mais il faut reculer—il faut reculer—pour avancer plus loin."* ("But you have to step back— to step back—in order to move forward.")

Thank you for saying something equally helpful to me.

DIARY   *November 12th*

I must write down some of the strange people we have been seeing these last months. It is part of our life, our new anti-war life.

There were the Quakers. I felt I could breathe with them— such a relief not to be fighting up the stream, as one is most of the time. At last here are some "good" people on our side. For it is this that has upset me the most this year, to find all the right people on the wrong side and—even more appalling—all the *wrong* people on the right side. The Quakers are both practical and "good." I can go almost "all the way" with them. But C. cannot.

Then Libby,[1] the head of all the peace organizations, a round-faced, scrubbed little man, full of vigor and zeal, shining with sureness, compact, tidy, and in order. How I envy people like that—but I do not warm to them. There is an enamel quality about them which is as hard as the enamel of a sophisticated worldly person. No crack to let you in. Bright and hard—like a button.

Then Armstrong,[2] dependable, earnest, hard-working, honest man, humble and yet undaunted—none of this disease of the soul, this pessimistic fatalism that attacks intellectual Easterners. He is Middle Western, American Legion, and *very* American. His mind is clear and undivided. He is not, or does not seem to be, besieged by conflicts. But goes right to work, writes a speech in an afternoon, has six all ready to be put out on records

[1] Frederick J. Libby, prominent pacifist, Executive Secretary of the National Council for Prevention of War.

[2] O. K. Armstrong, writer, journalist, and member of the American Legion's Committee on Foreign Relations.

and distributed throughout the Legion posts! He has done more work, C. says, than anyone else, without help or money, by himself, in a quiet dogged way. I suppose if we pull through it will be due to people like that and yet when he leaves I feel a terrible inexplicable longing for Europe and Europeans.

Then there is a Major K.—mystery man—a compact round little man in a snug double-breasted coat. Erect, he snaps his heels together and inclines his head as he takes your hand. He is very precise in his speech, purses his lips after he has told you something, as though to suggest he has much more to say were his lips not sealed! He is very decided as to his opinions and I think quite often wrong. But it doesn't seem to matter—he speaks with just as much conviction the next time. An evening with him and I feel as if I could be "with the Rover Boys in the Secret Service." Lots of his facts are authentic, though, and he is very keen and perceptive. He is an authority on the Spanish countries and very pro-Franco. I cannot believe it is quite as rosy as he paints ("The Moors committed *no* atrocities").

Lawrence Dennis[1] is by far the most interesting of this group we have met because of the war situation. (They are *not* a "group" but have only this one purpose in common: the anti-war stand. In fact, they are all as far apart as can be.) From his *Letter* and the things people say about him I had expected the devil incarnate ("Foremost Fascist of America," etc.)—a hard, brilliant, assertive man. But though very brilliant he did not seem hard, and I would say that, far from being assertive, he was rather reserved and extremely sensitive. He was very interesting and that first talk seemed sound and sensible. His brilliance carries you along "with the greatest of ease."

I only find myself disturbed by that curious downward pout of the mouth that is almost like the terrible mouths of the Greek masks for "tragedy." He has suffered, this man, and been badly hurt—why, I don't know, and it seems to have left him with that curious grimace (terribly revealing, changing a whole face in a flash) and with no love of mankind as such. Perhaps this

---

[1] Former Foreign Service officer who edited the right-wing *Weekly Foreign Service Letter*.

is not fair and I am judging too quickly. But I feel in what he says a profound bitterness—the ring of "the People is a great beast." This is where I leave him.

(Why is it that one tries—that one feels compelled—to find out immediately where one "leaves" a person? Perhaps in the hope, the chimerical hope in every human breast, of some-time finding someone one would never leave—never, anywhere.)

One night we had them all together, though not Dennis. It was terribly funny. Every once in a while I would look down the table at C. to make sure I was still on solid ground. [Ray-mond J.] Kelly[1] was on one side of me and Armstrong on the other. Kelly making remarks—precise bombshells about "You know his background, of course; he made all his money on the false armistice—oh yes. . . ." (Kelly always knows the "back-ground" of everyone.) Armstrong, quite shocked, made faces at me at this. I was beginning to feel hysterical. Could we all stay on the same road—with Kelly slipping off one side and Armstrong the other.

Armstrong is really the soundest, I think, and is also perhaps the most able and effective in the anti-war work.

I have left out of this chronicle of characters Kennedy,[2] whom C. and I went to see. There he was in his hotel suite, papers strewn around him, letters on a desk, telephones going, long-distance, Kennedy's voice blaring out: "Well, *I'll* tell them. . . ."

When we came in we sat opposite him while he sat in a great red damask grandfather chair, his leg over the arm (most curious posture), swinging his leg, talking in a great assertive free and easy voice that could be heard rooms away. We hardly talked at all. He just gave us his picture, loudly, boldly, slapdash. It was rather a relief to hear it in spite of its terribleness; in spite of its exaggeration (done in such bold strokes) it sounded true. One had the feeling that this great breezy, ambitious, healthy, and somehow nice man had more of the truth than any of the other overcultured, overcivilized diplomats. He said essentially

[1] National Commander of the American Legion.

[2] Joseph P. Kennedy, U.S. ambassador to Great Britain 1937–40.

what was in his interview—that England was finished, that the ports were smashed, the conditions bad. That it was hopeless for them to win on the basis they wanted to win on. That they only wanted us in in order to have someone else to share the blame, to keep the war going a little longer, in the wild hope that "something might happen in the meantime." That he was completely overridden. There was no American Embassy—only a British one.

He said that Bullitt was the most responsible for pushing war there and here. (I think a lot of this is personal jealousy—of B.'s influence on Roosevelt, so must to some extent be discounted.) He is evidently very irritated at the President, but maintains a kind of personal loyalty because the President appointed him (an Irish Roman Catholic) to the Court of St. James's. He said he was going to put everything he had into keeping us out of the war. I felt he was sincere in this and had great power. (It almost gave you confidence to be with a man with so much sheer sense of power even though you know some of it—maybe most of it?—was self-inflated.) I felt he was the most powerful person in the United States at this moment (could swing the country to war or peace). He, very evidently, also thought so.

He spoke of C.'s position in England, how he is hated. And with rough American humor commented on the reason they give for hating him. The worst thing they could say of him was: "And I *had* him to my house for *dinner!*"

"As if you could be *bought*," I said quickly.

"Yes," shouted Kennedy, "and for a *dinner*—for a *dinner!*"

He said the Queen did not feel this way. "I can quite understand . . ." Can she? She is a tremendous person.

I should like also to write about Auden, who came out one afternoon. I shall not see any more Audens for a long time, so I should like to describe him.

He is pure, as Mrs. Curtiss said, and good, and clear. He is, I think, perhaps the most unworldly person I have ever met. There is no dross about him—or very little. He is loose from the world and alone, suspended in space, and yet intuitively at the heart of its trouble.

Intellectually I am not educated enough to talk to him and emotionally I am too disturbed. I wanted to be completely honest with him—pure myself—but I cannot be, not at this moment, because I am confused and too tied to concrete problems.

I felt frustrated and humble and felt I had nothing to give him.

Charles has been working on the war, on keeping us out, new committees, where to get backing, how to join the groups together, who to lead, etc. And he the only one able to work with them all. He is, though, exhilarated at working at a cause— the "we few" feeling.

One morning, astonished at unexpected help from some-where—an ordinary person—he leaned across the table at me and said, "It's amazing—S——, S—— did this! That is what it is like—you never know where it is going to come from, the real stuff. It is like the Flight. Byrd with all his equipment and organization . . . and I alone with that plane made the flight. It is like a bulb pushing up from under the old growth."

The war seems more terrible every day, the bombing of England that has gone on for months, the pictures of smoking Coventry, boarded-up London, the stories of hospitals, amputations, children's terror. One wants to suffer oneself and feels it would be easier than this watching and not knowing what to do.

Monday, December 16th

Christmas is coming and I have done nothing and there is no time or strength to shop and the big rich glittering shops seem so appalling in the face of the war and the suffering abroad. I cannot bear to go into them. Even the catalogues are terrible. I looked over them last night in order to get things by mail, and each time I put down "Mary and Richard, Brandied Peaches," it seemed like a horrible travesty.

I have been trying to work on some article or speech on the Feeding of Europe for the Quakers. It is difficult. I want to have it terribly good, clear, appealing, and beautiful. It does not get there. Why not? Is there something unsure or unreal about the situation I am writing about? Am I cowardly about facing more criticism? It is true that it does haunt me and worry me and I get defensive about it. Deep down I have a vague premonition that it is going to be decided without me, without any of us struggling mortals here, by events moving outside us. Events abroad. This being so and perhaps for other reasons it has all been working against the stream.

I think one must do the thing—whatever it is (and it changes from time to time)—that unites you to the flowing stream of the world. At any price, one must do it first. Otherwise one can do nothing, nothing at all. One is out of touch, out of grace.

December 26th

I have not written in this since the morning C. came to me, while I was nursing the baby, and told me on his way to town that Pickett[1] had telephoned and *did* want me to speak after all (in spite of Hoover's plan being turned down by the British) on the Feeding of Europe and quite soon—just after I had written out and analyzed why it was I couldn't do it well. I knew C. could not help me because he is deep in the anti-war campaign and he has his hands full, keeping people at peace, working together. Because I felt this I could not ask for help or sympathy. I knew I must do it—and do it alone. So when he went off and I went up to the cabin to work, I felt, strangely enough, like him—some of him transmitted to me. It was a time to draw one's belt tighter. And the very hardness of it was a stimulus and a help, like those final moments in a plane when you have at last reached the danger point you have dreaded. You are no longer afraid, only tingling with something else— what is it? Not joy—you know how terrible it is. What, then? Courage? It can't be courage when one is so afraid. I don't know the name for it, a kind of *positive* acceptance.

[1] Clarence Pickett, Quaker.

And I worked, began all over again. And it began to come.

That afternoon I went and walked to the point. It was still and beautiful—just a light wind. The gulls out beyond the lighthouse were circling tranquilly far up in the sky, above the lighthouse and the waves and the shore—a slow poised spiral in the upper air. But my heart could not rise with them. It could not go like a beam over the sea as I feel it can sometimes. It was earthbound, tied like the boats with their old ropes. My heart could go out after C. going to town to his meeting, praying that he go in strength. As I felt his strength in me, something hard and firm and tough. But it could not rise with the birds.

That is marriage, I thought, those old twisted hemp ropes that hold the boats, gray and salt-drenched, and not beautiful at all, but tough and holding. And love is something else. It is that serene spiral of seagulls above the lighthouse, untouchable, untouched, unhurried, following its own laws in the upper reaches of Air. I wondered if I should ever touch it again.

Then working—giving up everything to work, the children, people, Christmas, everything except a walk every day to keep me clear. What writing means—*any* writing. It can *never* be taken lightly, never. Its cost is always in your lifeblood.

Saturday A.M., *December 28th*

Dear Sue,

I don't know how *you* feel after our excursion into the shellacked, unreal world of radio and Movietone[1] but I feel slightly prostituted (can one feel "slightly" that?). I feel most violently that I want to be purified of it (I realize that they are only agencies of this modern world and they must be used, and I feel convinced of the urgency and importance of the cause for which I used them—if not of the importance of my little move in it). But nevertheless I feel I want to be purified of them. Little Anne does it for me. *She,* at least, is still pure.

Thinking about it last night, I began to feel that it is this

---

[1] Sue Vaillant accompanied A. M. L. to the reading of her radio Christmas Eve speech for the Quakers, urging the feeding of Europe.

prostitution quality of the modern world, this c'
real things, this taking the heart out of what i;
sistence on the *form,* the *appearance,* the show and u.
that so sickens us both. (It runs all through the British Bund.
business, the smart women wearing British lions conspicuously
on their bosoms.) And makes one long for purity and to believe
in and touch pure people—like children and people who have
a childlike purity. (The poet Auden has this quality, too, and
perhaps St.-Ex. I have a feeling he is only coming to this
country in order to get back to England to fight.) Charles has
it, too, and has kept it in spite of his contact with the world.
You and George have always seen it.

Was it this desire for purity that made me want you to come
with me to those dreadful places, so that I could still believe
in something good beyond them? And was it your sensing of
this that made you give me that white flower? Certainly that
is what I felt unconsciously as I saw it on the table in the radio
station. Maybe C. sensed it, too, and that is why he wanted you
there and that is why—although he is rather Puritan about
flowers, thinks it silly of women to wear them and has always
objected to my doing so—he said, coming home in the car
that night, "You know, it was nice of Sue to give you that
flower."

1941

The speech is long past. All the pain and struggle of it—my terror of criticism. (There was no criticism because it was completely overlooked! "Smothered," C. said.)[1] I think it was good and well done. I gave it all right, too, though I had the dream feeling that I was giving it in a vacuum and no one heard me, a feeling accentuated by the lack of attention it got. Again this baffling pounding against a feather mattress that we have had all year.

St.-Ex. is in New York. I read about it in the paper eagerly. "Did you see?" I said to C. "Saint-Exupéry is here, but he is going back again!" (With joy I see this; I admire him more for going back to his country, like Détroyat.)

"Yes," said C., "I see, with jealousy."

"Why with *jealousy?*" (Do *all* men want to fight?)

"Because you seem to be so interested in him."

"I am, I am because he is a writer and because I admire him, and because I keep looking for someone to be left like that from *my* world, my world of writing. But there is no one left. I have lost them all this year."

"Yes," said C., "like a field after a bombardment."

St.-Ex. is being greatly fêted in New York, interviewed, etc. I read the interviews carefully, for I have always felt he had more "answers" to my problems than any other modern writer except Thornton Wilder and L. H. Myers. (They are both "on the other side," too.) But I feel a pang of disappointment that we shall not see him (since I am now the bubonic plague among writers and C. is the anti-Christ!). C. says to all this: "Now,

[1] In the newsreels it was captioned "Anne Lindbergh Suggests We Feed Hitler's Europe."

look here, if you want to see him you'd better try to—we could . . ."

"I couldn't, I just *couldn't*" (knock on the door where one isn't wanted).

"Well," says C., "don't blame him. Maybe *he* has the same attitude on life as *you* have!"

I feel, reading his comments on writing and living, in the papers, the way I used to feel in Miss Delpit's French poetry class, with all those girls who could talk French much better than I and who gabbled fluently while I had to sit tongue-tied in my chair because I couldn't talk fluently. And yet, and yet, I felt, silently rebellious, *I* understand the *poetry,* the heart of the poetry itself, better than any of them!

It is never right to force things, to "force" people. After all, we saw Whitehead and disagreed about the war and left in sadness, and my seeing Auden when I was too full of conflicts to talk freely to him.

It is not my "time" to see the St.-Ex.'s of the world.

Lloyd Neck, Huntington, Long Island, January 22nd

Dear Mrs. Neilson,

I feel I must answer you quickly—not to frighten you with such haste or intrude upon you, but only to let you know how much you have done for me by your letter—what a cloud you have lifted from my heart by reaching across that chasm which seems every day to get deeper with the—perhaps quite natural—distortions and misuse of my words in that book, which was, to begin with, chasm-making enough. It takes an effort to bridge chasms today, a positive effort of spirit—which is almost physical. And there is so little extra physical or spiritual strength. One has to hoard it for one's own life. But you spent some of it for me and I do thank you. It did more than I can tell you. It was as if the quotation, the beautiful quotation of Goethe[1] and your sending it united me again in one stroke, or made me feel united, not only to you but to all the people I love in the world who are now separated from me. One should, of course, never

[1] See p. 175.

feel separated from the good of this earth, even when one is alone. But one loses faith that this is so. And then one falls out of grace. It takes an act of intercession like yours to put one back "in grace" again.

But there have been good things, too, new things I never really felt before. I understand the feeling one has—a new kind of love—working with people with whom one has nothing in common but a cause. This is the "brother" feeling so often denied to women. It is "Love does not consist in looking at one another but in looking together in the same direction." This is, of course, a wonderful feeling and I have had it with my husband, perhaps more than ever before, and that is a great deal.

But there is another kind of love that is still more wonderful and that is the kind that is *not* between brothers, *not* between people who are looking in the same direction—a love which can leap over a difference in belief. And that love has a kind of divinity in it. I understand now why Christ spoke of it. "And if ye salute your brethren only, what do ye more than others?" It is only things like this that can really help today.

No, it is not true that individual suffering is diminished against the background of the war. On the contrary, it exaggerates it, as though the great blaze threw up gigantic shadows from the smallest flickering doubts dancing before it. I have noticed with everyone I know well that this is so. The general fever over the world only aggravates your fever. It is like atmospheric pressure. If you have a conflict, that conflict is doubly difficult, if you have a sorrow, that sorrow is doubled, if you have a problem, that problem is intensified. It is as though each person today is carrying in the seemingly small burden of his own trouble, the trouble of the world—unknowingly. Like the story of St. Christopher.

Perhaps this would not be so if one were actually in the war and actually suffering. Perhaps then one would feel that one was suffering in unison and for a purpose and it would be easier —while more terrible, of course. But now it is like Dante's Hell. Each person suffers his own punishment and suffers it alone.

That is why it is so difficult to help another person. Each person is isolated in his own trouble. (I wish I could help you as you have me.)

DIARY   *February 21st*

In the last weeks I have had chicken pox! And proceeded to pass it on to C. and little Anne. It is such an unlovely disease. You feel unloved and miserable and grouchy. And at night, not sleeping, the anguish becomes mental—I tossed and tossed in the conflict of the book, trying to explain and defend.

Then C. had it, up and downstairs with trays, food all wrong, orders not carried out. "I don't ask very much!" The baby crying and miserable and not eating and I getting tireder and tireder.

At the end of it I feel as if I had been living in a hair shirt for weeks. A hair shirt is not agony—not suffering really—just a hair shirt. In fact this whole year has been a hair shirt. The trouble with a hair shirt is that it makes you feel so awfully *good*—as though entitled to a little wickedness. You feel as though you had atoned for all your sins and even for a few you hadn't committed! It is a lucky thing there are no temptations in my path (Satan hasn't done right by me!). Although I am beginning to feel that I am so "good" that if I saw a temptation, I would turn and run the other way.

The first day in town I had my hair done and bought a wild "come-hither" hat with two Renoir full-blown roses burning off the front of it. It almost satisfied the urge for wickedness.

Though C. said it was dreadful—the hat.

March 6th. On the train to Florida

This winter has gone physically to little Anne, mentally to C., who is working, fighting constantly, writing articles, speeches, meeting people (with great force, with great fire and optimism and patience. How *can* he do it—he, a man of action, sit in that hair shirt), going over it all with him, watching for mistakes, pitfalls, little things in writing and in people. The people who want to use him. The people who are not essentially "good."

The people who are stupid. The people who are unbalanced, "off" a little here and there. All I can do is to watch, to think always alone. For I must not burden him with my fears and my doubts but only when I am sure say a word here or there or point here or there.

How much it is like those old flying trips, sitting in the back cockpit, silent, not wanting to touch him or ask a question for fear it may upset him, or, worse, shake his faith. Sitting there, silent and trusting, and now and then passing a note forward or a sandwich! Only that was easier—it was physical. It was a physical symbol of what was to come. How much of life is symbolic. Keats said: "A man's life of any worth is a continual Allegory, and very few eyes can see the Mystery of his life."

And again it is he who is enjoying it, enjoying the fight, and I who am apprehensive, seeing the fog, a long way off. That is not good. It is a denial of life itself. I am learning better.

This winter I have made a positive effort to do what Meredith says is the task of all true women and artists, to see a "divinity in what the world deems gross material substance." To live in and by "joy" in its Catholic sense. At times I can do it. In the morning at my window, singing at night to Land, and almost always with little Anne, nursing her, holding her in my arms, watching her uncurl, damp, warm, rosy from sleep—I taste real joy, real peace. Nothing exists but this, nothing matters. I am grounded.

And then those walks with C. The old path to the point, the lighthouse, the wind and gulls, down the steep bank, past the little beech tree that says "The crooked shall be made straight," past the dead tree that whistles, along the beach, up the long hill, across the fields, through our scrubby woods and down through the thick dead crusty (frozen) oak leaves to our lighted door and tea. We have always had a walk like this in our lives. At Long Barn, Englewood, Illiec, and even that queer circle we took through the Bois in Paris. A walk that becomes peopled with old thoughts, old problems, hung with the clothes of other days. But the thrill a new detail will make in it—a startled pheasant, a gull soaring, frozen foam on the rocks, a lovely wind in the face, or snow, or a smooth stone.

We have had joy on these walks. And then skating with the children. One moonlit night, too, C. and I went alone, down to the pond, striking out on the smooth black ice, shadows of the bare trees veining the ice ahead. The air cold, the stars, the cold blue light of the moon. And across up the hill the puny yellow lights of men, in houses.

I am learning better to catch joy on the wing, to use Blake's image. And if one does that, one can give it to other people, like Land and C.

And work? I think with envy of St.-Ex. sitting in his room in a hotel, just writing. He is not a politician; he feels he should exert what influence he can through his writings. *He can*—but I, I cannot. I am married—more than married—dedicated to marriage. And I care about the man I am married to, I care intensely about his life, our life together, his beliefs, our beliefs, his actions, our actions—everything must be worked at without ceasing, all the time. Because he *is* in it, C. In the midst of the fire and always will be. And I am so made that I cannot let him "go his way" and I go mine. No, our marriage is something else. And there is no room for an ivory tower in it.

I hope, I pray St.-Ex. can stay *free*, pure and untouched, in an age when everyone is being smeared black or white, forced to take sides. Oh, I hope he can stay above it and write. I can only write poetry—a little—and correct these dreadful diaries C. is having copied.

For six months this has gone on. It is, in a way, a strain, although I believe it should be done. Each day that I read the lies about us in the newspapers I think there must be some honest personal record to show what it really was like. And that record must be assured of permanence as C. is doing now. But it bothers me—especially the early adolescent diaries. We have had dreadful arguments about it. I wish I had got hold of them before C., and had them all burned. It is so painful to read them and see all my faults in exaggeration and recognize that I still have them. That adoration of an impossible he or she—what is that but the *"angoisse inguérissable"* that haunts me through life? Not always now for a person. No, it is rather the line of Yeats:

> "Bird sighs for the air,
> Thought for I know not where."

But the expression of it at 14, 15, 16, 17, 18 is just *sheer trash*.

Then one thinks: And *now,* am I writing what at fifty I shall think trash? No matter, one has to write, one writes not to be read but to breathe—I did even then. One writes to think, to pray, to analyze. One writes to clear one's mind, to dissipate one's fears, to face one's doubts, to look at one's mistakes—in order to retrieve them. One writes to capture and crystallize one's joy, but also to analyze and disperse one's gloom.

Like prayer—you go to it in sorrow more than in joy, for help, a road back to "grace." But that gives a false impression— to C. or to anyone else reading my diaries. My life is not that, or not that *alone.* My life is not gloom, but joy, joy in living all the time. But the diaries are thought, and thought is not "gay." Joy expends itself in action but thought in words. And the diaries are thought rather than life.

[*On March 7th we left on our second boat trip along the coast of Florida from Fort Myers Beach, through the Everglades and from there south to the Keys. Our boat was a sailboat with an engine and a small dory, obtained by Jim Newton. We had no guide since the boat was smaller than the one used on the 1940 trip and Jim knew the ins and outs of the coast from many fishing trips. The cabin was equipped with three bunks, a galley, and a table over the centerboard. "Sturdy, reliable, and a little perky," I described our craft. With this boat, which we named the* Aldebaran, *we had a number of adventures, bucking high winds, running on shoals, and poling into uncharted harbors by moonlight.*

The experience was very different from our 1940 trip, and we felt closer to the elements, wind, sea, and tide, using a sail, steering by compass and the stars. Occasionally we camped under twisted sea-grape trees on shore in a bugproof tent. We explored

Shark River again, silently this time, sailing before the wind with jib and jigger, into the timeless world of wilderness and wild life. Pushing through the maze of streams and rivers opening up before us, between bare ghostly arms of mangrove roots, we scarcely made a ripple, occasionally startling a great white heron, or a pink ibis, or water turkeys. Swallow-tailed kites circled slowly above our heads. At sunset we put the sails down and poled through small bayous under arching bushes.

The high point of our trip was setting out for Dry Tortugas, one of the southernmost of a chain of keys, inhabited only by an enormous deserted fort built in Civil War days. The twenty-four-hour sail across the Gulf to reach our destination was the hardest run of the trip but the most satisfying. C. and Jim had laid out the course, and C. planned the "watches" on deck—"two hours apiece until nightfall, then four on and eight below."

"The night watches," I wrote, "are the most beautiful. One is alone, out on the cold dark deck in souwester and gloves, steering the boat, watching the compass with a flashlight from time to time, one's head up in the stars, fastening on the stars; pulling the rudder against the wind, easing it back again, giving it its head, as the stars dance in and out of the rigging and from behind the mast. Under your hand, too, is the cabin below and its occupants, cooking supper in the warm lantern light, or perhaps asleep, like children trusting you."

Off the Keys we tried our first underwater exploration with a diving helmet, attached to a long air-line and pump on the boat. I found it a marvelous experience, "a strange world of motion, waving branches of seaweed and bright motes of fish drifting before you, yet soundless. You are strangely insulated from it, in spite of being immersed in it bodily. . . . Your timing is upset— you float down gently with no impact—you drift up unsteadily like a dream, or like the fairy story of the light princess who had no gravity. A new and beautiful world—purple sea fans, luminous blue fish, yellow, black-and-white striped, gliding in and out of ferns, coral branches, all moving to a rhythm we did not know or feel."

Once back up the coast and again on land, "I miss the com-

*fortable restriction of the boat, that all-enclosing world with
everything to one's hand—the compactness of it, the economy.
And yet one does not feel imprisoned in such a small space. One
wears a boat, like a plane, and outside of that shell one has the
whole sea, the whole sky for living space."*]

DIARY   *Friday, March 28th*

I tried to think out last night and this morning what I had
gained from this trip. What new approach I have coming back to
the old problems.

First, I seem to have climbed out, temporarily, from under
the persecution cloud that has weighed over me this year so
heavily. I do not believe that *everybody* hates me or that everybody is bitter and unfair and angry (I did not *believe* so before
I left but I *felt* it, in spite of myself). Many people feel that way,
especially around New York, especially a group of intellectuals,
writers, elite. But they are not everyone. I *feel* that it will pass.
And it matters less, at the moment.

I feel about the war much as I felt after the baby, coming
back from another world. A profound compassion for the
suffering but not a conviction of the black and white—the
complete wrongness or rightness of either side.

I feel about America that what is important is not ultimately
whether or not we get into this war or whether or not we can
avoid suffering (I do not believe we can). But that we pass
through our fire still keeping humility and compassion. At the
moment we are not headed that way.

Home again, to find Land and Jon tall boys with ruddy cheeks
and Anne a new baby—new, just as if I had wished one out of
air and there she was! Big, rosy, and *blonde!* A great surprise.
Her eyes look bigger and bluer and she is gay. I feel now she
should be called Elisabeth.

Land no longer goes to bed with "Teddy Bear and Rabbit."
He put them away in a trunk and said good-bye to them. "I'm
grown now," he said to me. Jon, singing "Onward Christian
Soldiers" and knowing the history of it.

Shells all over the floor, and Jon saying, "Is that all?"

Thursday, April 3rd. Soft and still—spring

Someone is writing an "answer" to my book. An advertisement says, "[So-and-So] believes that Democracy and not Totalitarianism is the Wave of the Future."

This kind of misuse is hard to bear. I never said Totalitarianism was the Wave of the Future; in fact, I said emphatically that it was *not*—and that I hoped *we* in America could be, in our way.

Sunday, April 6th

The Germans have started war on Yugoslavia. Yugoslavs say they are confident with such a powerful ally as England. It is sickening—more waste, more useless waste of lives.

Tuesday, April 8th

Delicious spring day. The top twigs of trees all golden with it. Go up to work on feminist essay. Read over old notes, including my "answer" to my critics. Wish now I had published it—and the thought disturbs my morning. How hard it is to remember "It is not our business to reply to this and that but to set up our love and our indignation against their pity and hate. . . ." [Yeats] But misuse—*misuse* is so hard to bear. Will it ever, I wonder, be washed away from my little book.

Do not write—only notes. Writing is slow and it is hard to live by what I preach and be content with "very little but pure gold." The problem of the woman and her "work" is still so unsolved. It eats at me perpetually. Soeur Lisi is a perfect person for my children, gives them all they should have. And I have the time to write (in the mornings). But it still is not right because I *should* be giving them what she does (and getting from them what she does!). There cannot be two women important to a child. Either you *are* that woman or you are *not*. I know, because I have been that person to Jon—for long periods—and now I am not. To Land I am important, now, still.

It should work but, as it is, it goes somewhat like this: Mornings for work after meals, plans, etc. Afternoons for

Husband and exercise and business. From teatime to 7 I see the children, put them to bed, etc. Evenings go to correcting diaries (the ones that are being copied), or writing in present diary. No letter-writing, no reading, people occasionally.

Then the week is interrupted by Soeur Lisi's day off and a day (or afternoon) in town. Can you write a book and have children at the same time? Yes, if you're content to do it very *very* slowly.

I feel pressed and frustrated, as though I were continually failing to get done what I should. This means I am trying to do too much.

I should like to be a full-time Mother and a full-time Artist and a full-time Wife-Companion and also a "Charming Woman" on the side! And to be aware and record it all. I cannot do it all. Something must go—several things probably. The "charming woman" first!

Flying this afternoon with C. at the Long Island Aviation Country Club. I practice landings and figure eights. I am creaky at it, but the discipline is fun and good. I think of Despiau (flying would be good for all artists) saying, "The problem in Art is that of extreme freedom encased in extreme discipline." This is flying, too.

Wednesday, April 9th

Mrs. Archibald Roosevelt calls up and asks us for dinner with the Marquands and the Nathans (Robert—poet-writer). I say, "Do you think the *Nathans* want to see us?!" She says, "Oh, don't feel like that—of course they do." And I feel encouraged. Perhaps I am wrong, perhaps people do not feel so bitterly, perhaps the two worlds can meet. Perhaps I myself have been raising a glass wall where one didn't exist. I feel released from fear.

Friday, April 11th

Mrs. Roosevelt calls up and I gather the Nathans *do* feel bitterly and it would be more tactful if we came for lunch instead of dinner. I do not blame him for bitterness but I feel sad and discouraged. After all, it is just as I thought. The two worlds are separate. That was just a backward look.

Monday, April 14th

C. says he thinks I *could* publish the "Answer to Critics." I work all morning and afternoon on it, with suppressed panic and excitement that separates me from life, the children, spring. This is what it is to write. That cloak thrown over the heart, that deep trembling concentration and terror (humility, really): *"Can* I do it? *Can* I hold it—can I?" And knowing it is, in the last analysis, out of your control.

And yet without the panic period nothing good, *really* good, is produced. Panic does not *produce* it but it shows there is something big there before which to be humble.

Ickes[1] strikes out again wildly, bitterly, completely unfairly at C. Also at me ("Fellow Travellers with Hitler"). Remember: "We must set up our love and our indignation against their pity and hate."

Friday, April 18th

Up early and work until 12:30—*well*. One of those days when everything shakes together—you can grasp it *all* and are not blinded by little bits. And you tidy up the ends one after another in regular order—always keeping the other ends in your mind but always under control. This is working. The morning flies. Oh—I should cut everything, everything, when the work flies like this. All the problems—each one of which might take a whole day—are washed along in the flood of good work. It is like going over the Alleghenies (that one struggles up and down sometimes in low weather or headwinds), high above them with a great roaring tailwind.

Cannot get C. on radio at night—his speech. C. calls up—I miss him. Evidently the Chicago speech was a great success—lots of people! He is being attacked again, of course; a minister

[1] Harold L. Ickes, Secretary of the Interior, 1933–46.

has denounced him as a pacifist, a defeatist, a coward, and a traitor. Undermining "all we hold dear."

[*C. A. L.'s speech at an America First rally in Chicago on April 17 urged an independent destiny for America. He stated that the mission of America First was "to clarify issues." He warned that the "groups whose prime objective is to get us into the war" were demanding the convoying of ships with the inevitable loss of American vessels and lives, which could not be called a "step short of war." He added, "Personally, I believe it will be a tragedy to the world—even to Germany—if the British Empire collapses." But he did not believe "that it is in our power today to win the war for England."*]

Dwight comes in and we talk alone for an hour. He is sweet and gay, too, and perceptive, on me and my problems. He says my book has been made the anvil for people to hammer out their opinions on. And that C. is like a fence post out in the field— just standing there undaunted in wind and rain and storm— nothing can hurt him.

There has been a dreadful air raid of London "in retaliation," the Germans say. Oh, why gloss over brutality with an excuse. War is just war. It is the falseness of everything that drives me crazy now. The false self-righteousness of the Germans, the false hopefulness and "morale" of the lying headlines here.

Tuesday, April 29th

Dear Laura [Stevens],

I was so terribly pleased to get your letter that I felt I must telephone you and I hope it works out, for it has been so long— so very long—since I've seen you. I was too tired all winter and too tied—to the baby by the nursing—and too depressed to see people, to make the effort. One puts up a kind of glass wall of defense of "They-don't-want-me's" to protect oneself and it is hard to leap it if one is tired.

And then after the chicken pox—which I got first and then gave to everyone—including Charles!—we went south on a boat, which was far away, like Illiec, and I saw how out of proportion I had let the glass wall get. Since we've been back I have been working on a rather bad "answer" or, rather, restatement of the "Wave," for the *Atlantic* [*Monthly*]. I think, fundamentally, it is always a mistake to "answer" or "deny." C. *never* does it. If you are strong maybe you don't have to. Anyway, I have and it is off today. I don't think it says it well or really answers much but it does put down awkwardly *some* of the things I *didn't* mean. Answers are not "news" and it will not be noticed or help—but it helps my conscience and is there for the record.

[*In the* Atlantic Monthly *article, "Reaffirmation," I redefined the thesis of my essay* The Wave of the Future. *I denied the interpretation put on it as an inevitable wave of Communism, Fascism, and Nazism to which we must bow down in submission. "To me, the wave of the future is none of these things. It is, as I see it, a movement of adjustment to a highly scientific, mechanized, and material era of civilization, with all its attendant complications, and as such it seems to me inevitable. I feel we must face this wave; that we must not be overwhelmed by it. . . .*

"I do not say we must meet it in the same way as the dictator-governed nations. I oppose that way from the depths of my conviction." I defined the evils of Fascism as "scum on the surface of the wave."]

I have thought often of what George said and of what you said. So many of the things he said were right—not alone about what people would *say* but that it would not help C. at all. (Isn't it strange—of the thousands of letters I have had, and the great majority pro (which is, I think, *always* the case), not one has said "Now I understand him better"?) I don't believe you can "help" other people that way. And how hard it is to help them at all.

But much of what *you* said is true in your letter. No, the

picture is not black and white. But only black and white ones can now be looked at. We are too near it and must *act*—and to act you must always see things black and white. In this, our men are right, it is the only way to see things when you are in them. My book was not black or white and therefore people— the most actively involved people—*forced* it to be black. It *had* to be, since it was about the present era, about action.

Yes, what I was trying to say is undoubtedly too big and too unripe to be seen or to be described. At least, too big to be described *directly*. It could perhaps be mirrored indirectly in novels or poetry (that was another wise thing George said—that I should have "said it in a poem"). For most of the war books or articles I try to read seem to me all words—floating on top somewhere—with the essence far down underneath untouched. I feel that way about the article I have just written and yet I could do nothing else. I must unsay a little of the wickedness. One does not like to have oneself used for evil.

But Auden was right when he said:

> "Art is not life and cannot be
> A midwife to society."

(Did you read that long poem in the *Atlantic?* It mirrored the times—I think it really got a lot of the facets, more than anything I've read in our time.)

Aside from all that it has perhaps been salutary personally for me to learn to get along without people—without people's love or praise. They have counted too much before always.

In the meantime C. is up to his neck in a bitter campaign. *He* is *not* bitter and there is no hate in him, which is a lesson for me. It is hard for me not to get bitter. And he says things better and clearer than I can. I help him where I can, but not as much as he helps me—with his great strength and purity.

Mrs. Neilson (they are of course violently against us politically) wrote me a beautiful letter. And in it she said: "Opinions divide, but the deeper attitudes of the heart unite." It is so lovely I feel I must send it on to you.

DIARY   *May 9th*

I have not written for two weeks. And they have been so full of emotions that it is difficult to go back over it. They have been full of increasing hatred for C. in the interventionist press, increasing bitterness, name-calling, propaganda—and a steady loud push toward war.

[*On March 11, after long arguments, the Lend-Lease Bill was enacted by Congress and the Senate "to enable the government to furnish aid to nations whose defense was deemed by the President to be vital to the defense of the United States." In F. D. R.'s words, "a plan for all-out aid to Britain short of war."*

The bill was passed with two amendments:

"Nothing in this Act shall be construed to authorize or permit the authorization of convoying by naval vessels of the United States."

"Nothing in this Act shall be construed to authorize or to permit the authorization of the entry of any American vessel into a combat area in violation of Section 3 of the Neutrality Act of 1939."

On May 6, however, Secretary Henry Stimson in a radio broadcast urged the adoption of measures to insure the delivery of supplies to Great Britain and said that the Lend-Lease Act was not enough.]

Charles is stronger and firmer and much less affected by criticism than I. He cares as little for blame as he once did for praise. He is true to his own convictions and that is all that matters.

One tries to work without hate but each morning's paper brings some mud, some dreadful lie or calumny that one must fight down in one's heart.

Like the [Alexander de] Seversky article—crying down Charles —which has been used by the *Times* and *Tribune* for editorial comment: "Comparisons are invidious, but," etc. I am angry as I see a second-rate man riding the wave of C.'s unpopularity, using it to advance himself. And it is always *the same* people,

I think in bitterness; the ones who rode on his popularity, now ride on his unpopularity.

The papers have done the best they can to smear the [New York] meeting before it starts, calling it the biggest meeting of Bundists and Anti-Semites in New York. The "Friends of Democracy" do this. They have sent C. a telegram saying all this and asking him to deny it. He gave a statement to the effect that America First did not want the support of Bundists, Communists, or any other un-American support, but of course it got no notice at all, wasn't even carried in the *Times* or *Tribune*. This kind of thing drives me wild.

Then the meeting, the crowds in the street—simple, plain people calling out: "Give it to them, Lindy, give us the truth"! The truth—that is what they want, desperately, and Charles is the only one who is giving it. Jammed in the crowd, the platform —my sense, first, despairing, of the second-rateness of the hall, the decorations, the people. *Not* the best hall, *not* done in the "best taste," *not* the "best people"—as the other side would have had.

And yet, these people have spirit. I had the feeling, as the meeting went on, that "they" (the interventionists) have the leaders of the past, but we have the leaders of the future.

Walsh[1] went on and on—a regular Senator's speech—full of sob stuff and sarcasm. I couldn't follow it but the crowd seemed to like it. Kathleen Norris[2] was gay and light and full of American humor and positiveness—very good (though one could pick holes in the arguments).

Flynn[3] was tolerant and managed the crowd well, disclaiming all literature distributed outside, saying he wanted the crowd to behave with politeness, as his guests—very good.

Then C. at 10, after a long evening (I was sitting back, to the left, on the platform, watching the crowd and the press in the

[1] David I. Walsh, Democratic Senator from Massachusetts.

[2] Writer and novelist.

[3] John T. Flynn, author, journalist, and lecturer in economics at New York's New School for Social Research; leader of the liberal wing of America First.

front rows). The crowd galvanized by him, silenced, turned to him. And when he started to read, slowly, with emphasis, I felt his great strength and power and I watched that crowd looking at him, with faith, with undivided attention, with trust—leaning on that strength (which was really unexpressed—not whipped up, not asked for. He was not using his strength or his power *intentionally*. This has always been so with him, always. No—it was simply there—*in him*). I kept thinking of Tennyson's Sir Galahad. "My strength is as the strength of ten because my heart is pure."

The crowd were so moved by it that they burst into applause whenever there was a chance, including two dreadful places unexpectedly, which made me curl inside with shock and distaste ("England is losing this war"). C. tried to read over it fast when he saw what was happening and raised his hand to stop the applause but the newspapermen in the front row had what they wanted, enough to "smear" the meeting. The applause, I think, was not so much from the anti-British sentiment (though there were lots of Irish there) as for C.'s courage in telling the truth and also simply because they were tired of the frustration of false news in the papers. "Right," the applause said. Still it was in very bad taste and I writhed over it.

The rest of the speech went well and they hung on every word. And at the end there were long and roof-raising cheers.

[*C. A. L.'s speech at an America First meeting May 28 in New York City included the following statement: "I have said before, and I will say again, that I believe it will be a tragedy to the entire world if the British Empire collapses. That is one of the main reasons why I opposed this war before it was declared, and why I have constantly advocated a negotiated peace."*]

We go back in elation through crowds and crowds, to Sue's house, where various people gather. The thing that pleased me the most, though, was the reaction of two Irish policemen talking about the crowd: "When you get people in a crowd saying 'excuse me' it's a different kind of crowd!" The same man also said to me, with devotion, "You know, he's right when he says that most of the people are working too hard to attend to politics, to go to meetings." Those are the people; they don't want war.

We get back very late, but thrilled with the success.

The next day out to dinner with the Marquands.[1] C. wanted to see [Frank] Aiken (Irish Free State Minister he had met over there and liked). It was a relief to be with people who feel the same politically and I like the Marquands and Flynn (who is healthily American—an old-fashioned liberal) but I felt very depressed by some of the others. The young on our side are good stuff, but the older generation are pretty seedy and washed out. All the good ones are on the other side.

Aiken's wit, good sense, solid understanding, and *wisdom—* old wisdom—made me ache with homesickness for Europe and Europeans. I feel so old, so much too old for America—and yet they are my people.

"Charles," I say, coming back in the car, "I could never marry another American." Home at 2!

The next morning, Friday, the interventionist forces have rallied. There is a great blast in the press: Knox, Stimson. England *can* win with our help, *must* send convoys.

In the afternoon we hear that President Roosevelt has called C. a "Copperhead" and compared him to a traitor in the Civil War—says this is probably why the army hasn't called him for service. It does not want officers who think the war can't be won.

C. says he will have to resign his commission. I feel rather sick about it.

C. off to Washington.

Sunday

C. back—says he has decided to resign; the President practically asked him to—and that there will be great criticism in the army if he stays on under those conditions. I say that it may have very bad effects (politically) but he says it doesn't matter, he

[1] John Marquand, novelist; Mrs. Marquand was the former Adelaide Hooker, friend of A. M. L.

has to do it. It is one of those things he is completely convinced of, *inwardly*.

Work all day on my article, C. helping and correcting.

I can't sleep. It is not only the article, which is not well done and a kind of desperate measure, but deeper still a kind of dumb misery over C. giving up his commission. The army meant so much to him. It was the open world, his first chance; he blossomed there. How he worked, what it meant to him, he has told me. C. scolds me for worrying.

Monday

The next day does not go as badly as one might think after a bad night. C. gives out his statement to the papers after the letters to Roosevelt and Stimson have gone.

At night we begin to get reactions on C.'s resignation. They are saying he has resigned his commission in the United States army but not returned his German medal. (I thought of this, but to have them use it as a serious argument is so incredible.) It puts me in the pit of misery.

Wednesday and Thursday work on C.'s speech. He has written it too fast and it is, I think, too long and too technical, although clear. I work on the ending, which, I feel, must have in it some of the idealism *implied* but never stated in C.'s practical talks. It angers me to have him labeled "defeatist" and "materialistic" when he is just the opposite. It is the idealism *implied* in him that moves people, not the facts he says.

Friday. C. goes off with Jim [Newton], who has come for the night. Jim says more and more people in the country feel that eventually we must fight Hitler but there is growing a feeling that perhaps we can fight him best here.

I feel spent after the last days. But I make a great effort to go in and have supper with Laura and George [Stevens]—to bridge the gap of our differing beliefs. It is easy to talk to Laura. Aubrey and Con are there. Also Miss [Amy] Loveman of the *Saturday Review,* who is a lovely person and comes up to me *positively* and bridges that gap so beautifully, speaking about my first books (the last one is, of course, anathema). Laura is sweet, Aubrey gay, but I am heavy and wingless with the work behind me and conscious of George's being tightly buttoned up in his self-control. Serious conversation is impossible—all roads lead to war. At the end of the evening we seem to rest heavily on the tragedy of the French—being the easiest subject to agree on. Miss Loveman tells of meeting Saint-Exupéry, who apparently feels so bitter about the war that no one is allowed to talk to him about it. He would like to go back and fight but he is too old. He is "separated" from his wife and sitting here in New York, just waiting—for what? He did card tricks for them all evening! The picture is so terrible that I could only pray—pray sincerely that he find his way out of it somewhere.

Altogether, a very difficult evening. It was like those evenings as a young girl when you smiled and put on a kind of carefree joy over a deep heartache.

Hear C. speak on the radio. It is very good. It *all* comes over. And they seem very enthusiastic—long and loud applause. I am relieved. Home late with Sue and George—tired, but happy for C.

[*C. A. L. spoke in Minneapolis on May 10, recalling his father's opposition to intervention in World War I. He pointed out that after our wartime victory we were unable to insure a successful peace in Europe. In the recent election he felt the American people did not have a genuine opportunity to vote on "the issue of foreign war." His speech included the statement: "I have never wanted Germany to win this war."*]

Sunday

Walk with Sue and George [Vaillant]. Sue disturbs me by telling me (re an editorial which says that C. is mechanical, hard, and unfeeling) that my books gave the most unfortunate picture of Charles, that I never opened up about him. If this is true it is because I respected his very strong feelings about privacy—

his passionate feeling of not wanting to be exposed, written about, journalized, interpreted. So strong is this feeling of his and so strong is my feeling that I must protect him from this kind of intrusion—that his wife, at least, should not journalize him, betray him—that I have, rather than give a *false* picture, given an incomplete one. And one equally false. It is very bitter to think so. But I hoped, oh I hoped so, that the truth would shine through, that my love itself would illuminate it. For some people it has.

Lloyd Neck, Tuesday, May 13th

Tonight Charles comes back and I feel I must write down before I get involved in life again what I have felt in these two weeks he has been away—what I have learned with the lid of life taken off me for a brief spell. For when he comes back and I again care passionately from day to day what happens, when I go up and down with the events, with the newspapers, with life itself—then I shall no longer see clearly. That is the trouble with life—the essential conflict between seeing and being, between vision and action, between art and life, between mortality and eternity. The two pull in opposite directions and one must try to harness them both. But it is difficult—almost impossible (like the two steeds of Plato that the soul is charioteer to).

Charles is life itself—pure life, force, like sunlight—and it is for this that I married him and this that holds me to him—caring always, caring desperately what happens to him and whatever he happens to be involved in. But for months now I have been steeped in life—fighting, angry, defensive, crusading, caring. But not *seeing*—at least not seeing from that level from which one sees when one doesn't "care," when one is free of life, when one looks from the point of view of eternity.

It has taken me days to reach that point. When the "lid" was first lifted—the article off and C.'s speech and C. gone— I was left completely undone, *"déséquilibrée"* by the lack of life. Astray without life I went "out" to see people, "do things."

But gradually I have regained a kind of vision and have let go my passionate bitter grip on life.

First I began to see a little why it was I had aroused such bitterness in people—that bitterness which hurt me so much and which aroused mine in return. It was, I think, because what I said and wrote was attempting to be a combination of my vision (which is essentially an artist's) and C.'s vision (which is of life itself). Not only that, my life and my art were inextricably mixed in it—my objective and subjective beliefs. I begin to sift a little what it is that I believe—pure—and where I am trying, because of personal reasons, personal devotion, personal hurt feelings or pride, to justify C. or C.'s belief.

And in the article I have just written they are still mixed and will arouse bitterness.

It is strange that vision only comes after action, after taking the step irrevocably. After I wrote the book my point of view on the war widened to another vision, some of which is in the article. And now after I have written and sent off the article my point of view has widened again. But it is too late—at least, too late for the *Atlantic!* Perhaps even too late for this fight of war-or-peace that is drawing to an end. (Is that why I am now just beginning to see clearly?)

I see for instance that the interventionists have on their side the fundamental truth of our era—the truth we have avoided for so long and for which we all hunger and to which we must come back—*One must lose one's life to save it.* This reaction to a materialistic age, this craving for something bigger than oneself to die for, is so true and so real that perhaps they will and must win on it. Churchill has seized on the same basic truth, Willkie sensed it dumbly, Roosevelt gropes for it.

Charles does not give in his talks an ideal to die for—at least he never gives it in words. He talks facts and he talks them very well—*why* it is impractical for us to enter this war, etc. But this, I am convinced, is *not* the appeal in his talks. The real appeal is the idealism *implied in him.* It is the dying-for-one's-belief *inherent in him*—though rarely expressed in words. I keep trying to get him to express it.

Sometimes I feel Charles and the interventionists both have part of the same truth—different arcs in a great wheel—separated from each other; we cannot see the whole rim and we do not know they are joined—one follows the other—as the wheel turns; whose truth will come up first?

This spring, which has been so beautiful and so swift, I have only felt in breathless snatches. I have wanted to share this spring with someone in fruitless, flowerlike joy. But there has been no one. C. away and occupied with his struggle and I myself down in it so much of the time.

But to let it go—one more spring—is a crime, I feel in some way. The days with the children I have it, and walking alone. Though so often one walks with one's own thoughts. (The day I heard C. attacked for not returning the medal, I saw an ugly branch, ugly and ungraceful sticking out unbending from a tree, and I recognized it as my own heart at that moment.)

And dogwood—white and pure—drifts of it at night in the gullies where I walk, almost making me cry. For there is such compassion, such gentleness, such love in the attitude of the branches.

Only today, walking in the woods, can I see and *feel* one with those pure open white blossoms lying flat—uplifted faces to the blue sky.

I know by the eagerness I look forward to seeing C. again: that very longing for him presages "life" and suffering—and temporary blindness in action—in life itself.

Wednesday, May 14th

I pick up Kay and Truman [Smith] at the Biltmore and we go out to Lloyd Neck. The evening is difficult because C., after telling me he was flying back in time for supper with them, does not turn up and telephones halfway through supper that he is in northern Michigan. Truman then tells me all the things he wanted to tell C.

Kay and Truman—like everyone else—give me ideas as to what C. should say in his next speech. They want him to reiterate all the points he has used. They think his speech from Minneapolis was the best yet. Though I didn't touch it, it had in it all the things I have prayed him to put in—a personal appeal, his father's stand, a dream of American life, his father's reforms, even, thank God, his saying at last, "I have never wanted Germany to win this war."

May 22nd and 23rd

Charles has been back almost a week. It has been living again and the tension has been very high—not only in our life but in the world. One gets the feeling that it *must* crack—it cannot go on like this long. It must be either war or a negotiated peace.

The sentiment for convoys is growing but apparently there is great reluctance in Washington to go to convoys because of the dangerous repercussions in the Pacific—Japan. Only the smart interventionists know this. It hasn't yet percolated through to the mass of the "faithful."

Roosevelt is evidently under a terrific strain, and ill from it. I can well understand it.

The next morning (after a bad night): C. and I go over and have breakfast with Norman Thomas[1] and Mrs. Thomas. He is very impressive. Good, full of a love of humanity, earnest, lucid, kind, idealist. Mrs. T. was forthright New England—dogged loyalty. She reminded me a little of Mother in her devotion to him. "You see—I always felt so *completely* sure that Norman was right." (*Always?* I wanted to ask. In *everything?* What wives those were!) While C. talked to him about the Jewish problem and the need for tolerance, she talked to me about being a minority. I felt full of admiration for this calm modest little woman, not bitter from a lifetime of being a minority (she is aware, too, and intelligent and sensitive). She told about the last war, about friends crossing the street to avoid meeting her. Then of gaining back to respectability in between wars, and now the whole thing to start over again. But she is not hard—gentle and kind and generous to people. But she has the convert's feeling of pity for the unconverted, the unenlightened. (This I cannot get myself. I cannot feel that superior—or that sure. I can

[1] American Socialist leader, reformer, and author.

only think: They have another truth, not mine; somewhere, sometime, they'll join.) She was so pleased when I spoke of N. T.'s last two speeches and how I liked them. Her face lit. Oh, these selfless wives—what a history they make.

I felt I could learn a great deal from her and that she liked us. The day, though, is full of bad news. My *Atlantic* article is out—notices on it are contradictory. "Mrs. L. against aid to Britain." I do not expect fairness any more from the *Times* or *Tribune*. Also a long passionate telegram to C. from Kirk denouncing his stand.

C. finishes his speech. It is *splendid!* Positive and tolerant— the best yet. I am so relieved and C. also.

Thursday

Hot and heavy. The *Tribune* prints in its book column edited by Lewis Gannett an editorial against me (calling me a coward) which appeared in a Western paper. L. G. says it (the editorial) should get a Pulitzer Prize. To be accused of cowardice is hard when I have done something that took more courage than all the flights. It is true I am timid—I am afraid of almost everything—but I do not remember *not doing anything* simply because I was afraid. Though about courage one never knows; one can never boast, one can only pray: when the test comes, *may I be courageous.*

Friday, May 23rd, C.'s speech

Going in in the car C. says he doesn't like my dress *at all* and can't I get another? (Not having noticed it all through lunch! It is a print and, I think, smart, conservative, and right for a meeting.) I try to argue that it doesn't matter, no one will notice my dress in Madison Square Garden! But since he feels very strongly I rush to Bontel—I have half an hour—and walk out in a navy coatdress with a very pretty white Irish lace collar, trim and simple, and it fits! Then I have to get a hat in three minutes. They are shutting up the store, but I get one and walk out—absolutely changed.

Taxi to the Waldorf, arrive a bit flustered but on time. C.

comes in. *Does* he like it? Yes—he does! He says quietly to me as we go in to supper, "I call that 110%!" I am so relieved—and immediately look ten times better, I am sure.

A long table, chiefly women: Mrs. Taft,[1] Mrs. Alice Longworth,[2] Adelaide Marquand, Mr. and Mrs. Flynn, Miss Flynn, Senator and Mrs. Wheeler,[3] Mrs. Kathleen Norris, Norman Thomas, Mrs. Thomas (little and all in black—such a nice woman), and Bob Stuart,[4] a nice open-faced young man—with a chin.

I sit between Wheeler and Mrs. Longworth. He talks the whole time—a nice slow drawl. He just radiates a healthy American confidence, courage, and taking-it-in-your-stride. I like him very much and trust him. He has integrity, like C.

He tells me I mustn't let it get under my skin (the criticism) and he tells about all the things they've said of him in the different campaigns—how he was slandered, chased out of town, defeated, smeared. And of his wife sticking by him, urging him on, never minding. "If you can stand it, I can." There was a wonderful pride in him about his wife.

American—American—American, I kept feeling as I talked to him.

Mrs. Longworth is the kind of person it is a shock to find in America First. Very English in her intelligence, education, bookishness, and just plain "air." She is the kind that naturally gravitates to the other side, except that she is highly independent, courageous, and not conventional at all (like an English bluestocking—that's it *exactly*). Such a relief to slip into that atmosphere, and talk the same language. Mrs. Taft—smart, efficient, alert, sensible (reminded me of Mother—I am sure she makes a good speech). Mrs. Wheeler—blonde, overdressed (a little), nice, honest, loyal, outspoken, "American." I liked her, too.

[1] Wife of Robert A. Taft, Republican Senator from Ohio.

[2] Mrs. Nicholas Longworth (Alice Roosevelt), daughter of President Theodore Roosevelt.

[3] Burton K. Wheeler, Democratic Senator from Montana.

[4] R. Douglas Stuart, Jr., a leading organizer and later national director of America First. See Introduction, pp. xix–xx.

Mrs. Norris—grand lady of charm and spunk and positive American quality.

Stuart, young, angular, lots of spunk and go, alert, combative, enthusiastic. I liked him.

Flynn, as usual, easy, open, gay, with that Irish sense of drama and tensity. (In a strange way he reminds me of Daddy. How shocked Mother would be! His gestures, friendliness, charm, positiveness, infectious humor. When he is gay he is like him— only his eyes are not. And in that lack is all the difference. There is no depth in Flynn's eyes, no vision, no real beauty, no dream. But I cannot help warming to him. He is a terribly nice man—and a *liberal* man—which is a relief.)

We drive down to the Garden behind wailing sirens—a whole procession—everyone stopping stock still in the streets as we pass. Medusa-like, eerie feeling. In the back door very quickly. Labyrinthine underground passages (shades of the circus and childhood). Into an office where we wait and meet other people. Feeling of pre-excitement panic. The house is full.

Then we start out (a procession down the passages), Mrs. Thomas and I together. She says, "I am so glad you are here. I don't know any of these *other* people."

Then suddenly out into the lights, the crowds, the people on the platform, people all around us, up to the dim balconies.

The roar of applause—and I knew C. and Senator Wheeler had come in behind us. I sat in the second row just behind C., Mrs. Norris, Thomas, and Flynn. Roars of applause and stray shouts, "Lindy" and "Our next President."

The press and cameras, poking up under C.'s nose; the committee members running back and forth. I notice a policeman in the front row, right in front of C. That's good, I think, then no one can get near enough to shoot him! (Nightmare panic.)

Flynn opens the meeting with a fine invocation by Cardinal O'Connell. Then—this has completely thrown into shade the rest of his speech—he lights out into the smearers of our meetings and the supporters we do not want (Communists, Fascists, Bundists, Christian Frontists, etc.). Raising his voice, and shaking his hand over the audience, he started out: "And there is a man here tonight not far from me—one Joe McWilliams[1] . . ."

The rest of the sentence was lost in boos and shouts, a wave of excitement sweeping over the house, people rising, men standing, and a kind of sullen murmur of disapproval from everywhere, like low growls of thunder. I had the feeling that a clap of lightning might burst at any moment. Flynn, now really excited and angry, shouted on against this uproar, his face flushed and his unruly shock of hair (amazingly like Daddy's) shaking down over his forehead: "I don't know *whose stooge he is* but I *do* know that the photographers of the interventionist newspapers always know where to find him!" The boos and roars and murmurs and shouts go on. "Put him out!" Hisses. People are standing up all over the house; the aisles are filling up, lines of police with their blue uniforms gathering.

I am frozen into a kind of highly controlled watchfulness. I can see from C.'s shoulders in front of me (how familiar) that he is the same. Miss Flynn on one side of me has beads of perspiration on her face, Mrs. Flynn (on the other side) is pleading with the people around her: "Please sit down, please, please *do* sit down—don't you see you only make it harder." But the meeting is well on the way to getting out of hand.

I try to spot McWilliams but can't see very well. My eye hits upon a tall, sullen-faced man, dark (one of his supporters evidently), who is slowly backing up the aisle, his eye fastened on the police walking up on him. Just like a dog beaten into a corner, I think. I could feel the suppressed anger in that man, his sullen "I'll-get-you-sometime" attitude. And the police following him slowly, controlled, rigid—like dogs, too. And all the time the ominous rumbles in the house, shouts, hisses, yes—but worst of all that rumble, like thunder about to break into a storm.

As I looked into the face of that sullen man and felt the animal quality of the crowd, I sensed for the first time in my life —vividly—the rumbles of revolution. Would it break now?

[1] Leader of the American Destiny Party, alleged to be a Nazi-oriented organization.

Or was this only one of those instants when a grain of the future has by accident fallen in among the grains of the present? But one knows in a flash of insight: of such will the future be.

It was only a few seconds. Flynn shouted into the microphone: "My friends, are you going to let five or six men break up this meeting?!"

This time it worked; the shouts died, the rumble subsided. The meeting was again under control. The pit closed up, but not before I had looked into it.

I don't know what Flynn went on to say.

Norman Thomas spoke. He is a powerful speaker, throwing himself into it—gesticulating and ranting in good old-fashioned oratorical style. It was a good clear speech, well thought out, and I agreed with it—the points were all ones I wanted said. The crowd liked it but I had a strange feeling while I listened to it that I knew why he was not a "great" man. There was a gap between his oratory and himself, his intellect and his passion. And into that gap he fell. His intellectual approach appealed to me; but his flaming passion—was it real? Was it rooted?

It seemed to me that he was inflamed about "Humanity" but not about men as individuals, only as workers, as sufferers, as classes. He was, in other words, a theorist. He does not really love *men,* only "Mankind." This sounds so fantastic for a man who has given up his whole life to socialism that it cannot be true. However, this is what I felt.

Then Flynn again, introducing Charles. Then C. The applause, long, shaking the house. His shoulders in front of me, slightly stooped, so familiar—his smile to the crowd. This is the "Colonel Lindbergh" I hero-worshipped as a girl. Can this be my husband?

He speaks slowly and deliberately. It sounded so calm and unemotional after N. T.'s oratory. Though the crowd hung on every word and cheered whenever they had a chance. I waited for all the bits I liked and thought of Jon hearing them, sitting up in bed at home.

But I had a curious feeling in the middle of the speech that though I liked this as well as or better than the other speeches,

Anne and Charles Lindbergh on the Aldebaran, *Florida, 1941*

Land with his pet lamb,
Sammy,
Lloyd Neck, 1941

America First Hollywood Bowl meeting, June 1941

The first house rented by the Lindberghs on Martha's Vineyard

The writing tent set up on Martha's Vineyard

Jon, Anne Lindbergh, little Anne, Land, Martha's Vineyard, 1941

Thor, Anne Lindbergh, Jon, Land, little Anne, Soeur Lisi,
Martha's Vineyard, 1941

Anne Lindbergh with little Anne, Martha's Vineyard, 1941

Little Anne and Land, Martha's Vineyard, 1941

Jon, Anne Lindbergh, little Anne, Land, Thor, Martha's Vineyard, 1942

Anne Lindbergh, Skean, little Anne, Land, Martha's Vineyard, 1942

Land and little Anne on boat to Maine

Charles Lindbergh at Willow Run, 1942

Antoine de Saint-Exupéry

the crowd didn't. It didn't *know* it didn't, but I knew. Perhaps the evening had been too exciting already. C.'s quiet thoughts of precision were imperceptibly beyond them. (Thomas, the intellectual, nodded at them.) They wanted a circus—Flynn's Irish temper and drama, Thomas's oratory—and (yet to come) Wheeler's inciting-to-revolt (almost) challenges.

In the end I forgot about this qualm of mine, for they cheered so madly (but they were cheering *him*—what *he* stood for—not the speech). The most spontaneous cheering during the speech was for the passages where he said the people were demanding to know how this situation in Washington had come about (the rumble again disturbs me).

Then Mrs. Norris—which upset me because it was almost pure sob stuff (mothers losing their boys), when she can be so much more positive. But the crowd likes her.

And then Wheeler. Wheeler's speech was not nearly as good as N. T.'s or as C.'s. His delivery was not particularly good, but I felt great confidence as he spoke. I felt he had the makings of a great leader in him. His intellect and his emotions are blended. And there is a cord between him and the people, a confidence. He is rooted in the people.

I felt better about America when he stopped speaking. The basic emotion in him is love and not hate. Although he exudes an American confidence he is, I think, without personal vanity.

Then "The Star-Spangled Banner" and quickly out to the car—the crowds, the streets, and, still tingling with heady excitement, to Webster's, where there were hundreds of people—everyone remotely connected with America First or anti-war. All the threads of my life crossing and recrossing and I frantically trying to remember in the split second where the threads led.

The Sikorskys—how hard to listen to a Russian in a crowded room! Selden Rodman,[1] dreamy-eyed, with a pipe. "I've been looking a long time for you—I'm Selden Rodman." Fleming Macleish,[2] of the *Common Sense* article; Cushman Reynolds of

[1] Selden Rodman, poet, coeditor of *Common Sense* magazine.

[2] Fleming Macleish, poet and writer for *Common Sense*.

Uncensored; Oswald Garrison Villard[1]—old war-horse of liberalism. I made an effort to get up and speak to him and he was touched and said, "Oh—do you remember me—from so long ago?" He is a lovely old man. The Pinchots—Amos Pinchot,[2] now a grand old man back of America First. Bill Thomas (Norman's son) getting me a seat. C., Flynn, and Webster are the centers of immovable groups. I talk too much, feel too much, feel what everyone needs, and most of them need praise.

Very late, and still soaring, we leave.

Wednesday, May 28th

Work on C.'s speech.[3] It looks better in the morning. I rewrite several paragraphs in the end. It goes well and C. is pleased and says he can use them as is. (How wonderful it is to give and have it of use.) C. puts in a new paragraph on the President, attacking points in his speech. I am against his attacking the President by name, also his calling for "new leadership" (a technical point—I say the phrase will be taken as a call to insurrection, which he doesn't mean).

He says he trusts my judgment very much but that I am "no good at all on attack"—which is probably true—and that the time has come to "attack." He says if the statement about the President isn't true or if it is said without dignity he will change it, but otherwise he will not change a word. I cannot answer him there, so I have to let it go.

Monday, June 2nd

Katrina McCormick for lunch. She is America First in Washington. She is intelligent, sensitive, civilized. There are very few people like her on our side. We have a good time talking and I feel could go further. She has, I think, had the opposite experience to mine in this work. It has opened up to her people of her

[1] Oswald Garrison Villard, author, journalist, and editor of *The Nation* from 1932 to 1935.

[2] A. R. Pinchot, member of the executive committee of America First.

[3] Given in Philadelphia in response to Roosevelt's declaration of "a full national emergency" in his fireside chat on May 27th.

kind, a new and exciting world—the *Uncensored* writers. (All slightly leftist and a bit hazy, but by far the most interesting people on our side.)

C. and I don't see them, partly because we have no time to see anyone who isn't right there and partly because he doesn't like "hazy" people. There is no doubt about it, the people on the "right" are more practical than those on the "left." Those on the "left" are more idealistic and *much* more sympathetic— to me. But the times demand action and not dreams.

Tuesday, June 3rd

I have a walk in the woods, sit a long time on the point and decide to stop staying at home, fussing and fuming and doubting. I shall—despite somewhat dreading it—go to California with C. on his speaking trip. Give up the eternal point of view and throw myself into his life, as I did when we started flying. I am happy after I make this decision and feel the apathy of last month drop off.

When C. comes home I tell him. But he is very much opposed! He wants me—unselfishly—to keep my own life, writing, not get into his, to work toward the future and not just in the present. To write—but always long-range things.

C. has taken such a generous wide-skied point of view. Can I live up to it?

Wednesday, June 4th

Kingman Brewster,[1] a senior at Yale, comes down to see us. He arrives early and finds C. teaching Jon to shoot with a rifle in the parlor (he has a metal box to catch the bullets!).[2]

He is sensitive, very intelligent, with a precise, searching mind. I feel on my toes again keeping up with it. He asks C. about the war and after-the-war conditions. In our own country and abroad. He is worried (as I am) about the reaction which may

---

[1] Organizer of a student group out of which grew the national America First Committee; later President of Yale University, 1963–77.

[2] He remembers C. A. L.'s commentary: "If only Dorothy Thompson could see me now!"

take place here against the present party in power and against the Jews.

He wishes we could do something to avert that bitterness and reaction—now. To plan for the future—for some kind of rapprochement of the opposing parties—with a constructive plan of reform for the United States.

I like him—*how* I like him—his sensitivity, his earnestness, his intellectual integrity (hard as steel), and something soft, too, in him, a gentleness, beside his hard thought. I think he gets from C. a kind of vigorous faith that grows outside academic life and is strengthened by it.

Friday, June 6th

I plan to go into town to see Adelaide Marquand for lunch (chiefly in order to explain to her why I *cannot* do more for America First).[1] C. gives me a lecture on being firmer and saying *no*—at which I am very bad. But, nevertheless, seems to understand my going.

Adelaide Marquand is dictating a speech to her secretary as I come in. She is also—in between things—packing and seeing her baby (to say nothing of the one she is having!). I am filled with admiration. We talk of C.'s last speech and the current misinterpretations and vilifications. (The call for new leadership is interpreted as a cry for impeachment or revolution.) Mrs. John Gunther comes in—a gay child of a woman with round eyes and blonde curls.

There sparkle off from her, however, hard splinters of gossip which Adelaide parries just as lightly and which give me, as always, the feeling that I am an innocent child in a strange world. So-and-so is supposed to be having an affair with a Hindu, so her anti-war attitude may be somewhat due to that. "Marianne is staying up near Red and Marianne's Mamma is there, too, so it's all quite proper." "Marianne," as Adelaide explains to me, "is the young nineteen-year-old actress Sinclair Lewis is amusing himself with at the moment." A lot of gossip about Willkie (after all those Sunday supplement pictures of

[1] A. M. L. never joined America First.

the perfect family life!), which for all I know is just gossip—poor man. Or even if it isn't, how can one judge another man's life?

It isn't the immorality which shocks me so much as the *levity* of it. I could imagine falling in love—unfaithfulness, even, in marriage—if one were swept by a great gust of loneliness and passion. But "amusing oneself" with love or talking over your divorced husband with his present wife—no, I cannot understand.

Saturday, June 7th

On the front page of the *Tribune* there is an account of a meeting in Chicago at which Willkie and Carl Sandburg attack Charles. Willkie's attack is angry and indignant but perfectly fair and decent—on *issues*. But Carl Sandburg says C. is proud that he has ice instead of blood in his veins.

I am shocked beyond words. Carl Sandburg, whom we met and talked to a year ago, whom we greeted and who greeted us with affection, warmth, who seemed to me to be so sound, so rooted, so American. As American as Charles. Carl Sandburg, who knew C.'s father, knew what he went through during the last war. A poet, a philosopher, a historian, a man who had studied Lincoln's life, who praised Lincoln for remaining true to his conscience, even if every friend left him. Who saw the bitter and unfair criticism of another era. A man of breadth and learning and life, of compassion, of understanding of people.

It is, of course, my own illusion—that the man who can recognize and write beauty and truth and wisdom must of necessity be beautiful and true and wise himself, when of course this is absurd. But I don't live up to my own words. Why should I be so intolerant of other people's imperfections? (As C. says so gently of this whole subject, "Why isn't it more wonderful that perfection *can* come out of imperfection? Why isn't it one of the most wonderful things in life? A deformed woman can bear a perfect child.")

Tuesday, June 10th

C. announces at breakfast that we should begin to think about moving away from the East. He "feels" the time has come for us to break. We are sick of it, have been for a long time. Let us move out, find life again.

It is a wave of feeling in him and a response in me that is seldom wrong or obstructed. I plan to go out West with him and look around.

Life swings again. Only (the backward look) I am disappointed to have to leave Jon and not go to camp with him. I have had so little of Jon lately because so much of the time I am occupied with C. or writing or war.

Thursday, June 12th

Dark and cold. The *Robin Moor,* a U.S. boat, has been sunk by the Germans. Is this the "incident" everyone has been waiting for? I wish I did not feel that everything is so tremblingly in the balance.

Monday, June 16th

Papers still gloomy—for our side. The President is closing all the German consulates to stop espionage, etc. Hanson Baldwin says we are taking the inevitable steps toward some kind of action.

I have read C.'s speech and think it very good, reasoned and clear. Not ballyhoo at all. Will the Hollywood Bowl like it?

Wednesday, June 18th

Up early—last details and off at 8:15 for La Guardia Airport [and Los Angeles]. Jon and Soeur Lisi waving us good-bye at the door.

It is so strange to leave this airport where we went off in the Sirius for the trip to the Orient and to Greenland (it was North Beach then—a converted dump heap), now in a silvered limousine of a plane, soft seats, small curtained windows, muffled noise, air conditioning, sky-hostesses. And I in a navy taffeta suit, straw hat, handbag, and high-heeled navy sandals instead of khaki trousers, helmet, and sneakers!

I cannot get used to it and it does not seem like flying to me. I push back the curtains and peer out of the tiny window and look down at the earth below the great silver wing. But it is separated from me. It is unreal, like a movie. I feel like pounding on the window to let me through—to life. It is so strange. Had I not married C., this comfortable, easy, safe world of a transport plane *would* be real. It might even be exciting. I would never have cracked outside of it, but now—because he has broken it for me—I am dissatisfied with it. I complained, of course, when he forced me out of it. On those trips, when we struggled with long hours, heat, dust, fear, storms, tired and windblown, cold and sleepy, afraid, often I complained. And yet it was real. And now I am satisfied with nothing less. It isn't a question of adventure; it is a question of *reality*.

I want life to be *real,* contacts with people to be *real;* unreality alone seems to me unbearable. (That is what is so dreadful about the newspapers and seeing oneself in them.)

We had delicious hot lunch served us on tiny pillows on our laps—jellied soup, steak, ice cream. A far cry from my sandwiches!

All the pilots come back and sit and talk with C. He is still one of them, greatly respected and loved. He knows their language. Their open trust and companionship is very real and nice. (The newspapers can't change this.)

We are met by Mr. Jeffrey[1] and Senator Worth Clark[2] and drive through unfamiliar blazing streets to the hotel, draped with "Lions" emblems. I feel the cheapness and glare of Los Angeles already.

The night's papers are full of rumors of German troops on the Russian border.

Thursday, June 19th

I have caught cold. Meet Mr. Jeffrey, crisp, efficient, intelligent, hard-boiled, managing the meetings. Also young John Wheeler (Senator's son).

After lunch with Mrs. Senator Clark we go out to a country

[1] Earl Jeffrey, America First organizer.

[2] D. Worth Clark, Democratic Senator from Idaho.

club to swim. It is full of well-groomed young women with beautiful figures, fingernails, and coiffures, who are reading fashion magazines in between dives. You would not think there was any war in Europe or any changes taking place in the world. I realize how much we live in the war and war issues when I see how unconscious they are of it.

Friday, June 20th

Miss Lillian Gish and Mrs. Wheeler for lunch. Miss Gish is charming—fragile and intelligent. How could she survive like that through the blare and blasts of Hollywood. She tells me that she realized when she took this stand (anti-war) that it might mean the end of her career. Alexander Woollcott told her no one would speak to her again.

As we go from the hotel to the car a woman runs out, well dressed but sharp-faced, and shouts out, laughing, "There he is! Lindbergh—Philip Nolan—the man without a country!" and "Kathleen Norris—thumbs down." Her bitter laughter and her bitter voice cut me. And yet, after all, it is not very much, only a kind of crack through to the bitterness of some people's thoughts.

Long drive to the [Hollywood] Bowl. We get there just in time, walk in the shell of the auditorium and see suddenly masses of faces, up to the sky. We sit on a lighted stage or shell enclosed on one side. A salty old Irishman, lots of punch and humor, leads the meeting. Mrs. Norris speaks first. We can hardly hear because the speech is thrown *out* onto the audience and is not clear to us. But it is her positive speech and she gets great applause. Then Senator Clark speaks—dramatic and a good speaker, although rather loose intellectually. He is cheered, too. Then Lillian Gish, who has a quiet and moving charm. It is personal and good. She quotes Scott Fitzgerald as saying, "France is a land, England is a people, and America is a willingness of heart." Her plea for a referendum of the people on war is cheered. Then C. His quiet thoughtful approach is listened to with an earnest attention, an eager hunger for truth. And the end cheered violently. I am pleased because it is the reasonable fair approach—no ballyhoo. And the whole Hollywood Bowl responds to it—that sea of faces up the side of the hill and cars beyond in the hills under the trees. I can see one star.

In the end individuals are shouting: "We want *you* for President" and "Our next President!" (Mrs. Norris says, I am told, "No, he is more like a Joan of Arc.")

Then out into the crowd and drive through faces and arms waving, people streaming away. The old Irishman says he has never seen such a spectacle in all the years he's been in California. We are all buoyed up by the success of the evening. (Adverse commentators said we couldn't fill the Bowl!—and it was overflowing.) I think, as always, now *this* must make a difference—to have the Hollywood Bowl jammed to overflowing, to have the crowds cheering for a negotiated peace and a referendum of the people before war entry. That *must* get back to Washington and make them see what the people feel.

Saturday, June 21st

In the afternoon C. decides to go and see Hearst because he has been so good on the war issue. Calls him up. He is in or near Oregon—we will fly up there tomorrow! (I rush out and buy a sweater.)

In the evening C. wants a letter mailed and I go out with it. The papers are full of headlines: "Germany declares war on Russia."

Apparently it is true. The next morning's papers give Hitler's speech exhorting his army to the "holy war," giving the Russian demands (which he refused to acquiesce in): a free hand in Finland, Romania, etc., the Dardanelles.

Hoover comes out with a good statement. "Now it is not necessary for us to enter the war." One's mind swims with the implications of this.

All the Communist propaganda in this country will now swing against us.

This seems to dwarf the war between England and Germany. Is the great split I have always dreaded coming—the split of the world into *left* and *right?* Two immoderate parties. And where will England stand? And America? I have a feeling that the issues are hardening and the age showing its true face.

Sunday, June 22nd (My Birthday)

Off to the "Lockheed Airport" to take the plane for Medford, Oregon.

Medford, green fields and orchards, a drizzling rain. Then we drive for three hours to Mr. Hearst's "ranch," through rain and mist, fruit orchards and farms first, and then up into the pine-treed mountains—like Bavaria, only the pines are so big.

I keep wondering what Hearst will be like. He is on the right side of this issue. Why? I don't know. Is he wise? Or just shrewd? Is it an accidental whim? Motives are so mixed in this situation.

We arrive finally, in the rain still, in a gully of great pines by a rushing river—a little Bavarian village around a lawn of green grass with a baroque gilt Madonna in the center. The little chalets (or small châteaux) are part wood and part plaster and painted with scenes from the fairy tales. We stop in front of one and a car draws up—Mr. Hearst. He gets out slowly and comes over to us. C. and I get out. He is a great figure in a tan raincoat, his head bent forward with age, at about the same angle to his coat as a turtle's head to its shell. His face is lined and rather flabby and it gives an impression of general kindliness, even benevolence. It is without emphasis except for the eye —a pale and even watery eye—but intensely aware, observant.

He takes us into the house. "A fairy-tale house!" I say. "Yes," he says, "we call it the Cinderella House." It has the story painted all over it—Cinderella tripping down the stairs without her slipper.

We pass by the hall where a medieval painting of the crucifixion hangs over the fireplace, into two big bedrooms beautifully furnished with old Bavarian furniture. The rooms are paneled and carved, quite elaborately. There are big Nuremberg stoves (tile) in each. A roaring fire is going and a maid already starting to unpack my clothes.

Miss Marion Davies comes in, looking incredibly young and pretty (very made-up) with long straw-gold hair around her pink face, beautifully dressed in coolie coat, full skirt, red shoes. She patters on and on like a child. But a very charming child. When most people exaggerate and flatter I generally mind. One doesn't with her. One feels she is talking nonsense like a child—but a *good* child. She says would I like some tea since they don't eat till 9? As we ate at 11:30 I say, yes, I would.

She takes C. into the other bedroom to show him a quilt she made. (An *enormous* old bed—big enough for six people!) The quilt is covered with little Kewpies that look like *Good House-keeping* and not Bavaria! and the rhyme "Wash on Monday," etc. It was exhibited at some fair! She says they generally wear a long skirt "and something" for supper.

The maid (very nice Swedish or German) asks me where my "make-up" is and says, when I ask her about dressing, that they usually wear "formal dress"—I am sure they do! I take out my black crepe with white lace on it and wonder if it will be formal enough. Another sweet-faced maid comes in with tea, from old and priceless cups.

I go out onto the balcony from our room. It is *right over* the river, rushing by with a wonderful roar. I lean out over it and feel like a princess—as if I and the village had been wished there. If one leaned there long enough a duck would swim by and in the duck would be a fish and in the fish would be a ring. . . .

I wish a wish.

At 9 a car calls for us. Miss Davies in a white-and-navy tea gown with a white turban on her head. We go down the road, over a bridge to another collection of houses, a big chalet where they eat. Perhaps fifteen people are in a big room, in front of a huge stone fireplace. The women are all beautifully dressed and porcelained with make-up. Two quite young girls, in the twenties. One with obviously dyed platinum-blonde hair (glamour-girl style, to the shoulders; they all are like this, including Miss Davies). The other is a brunette. Her dark hair down to her shoulders from a stiff pompadour. Beautiful eyes, wide apart, and small features. She is very beautiful in spite of the thickly caked lipstick mouth which bears no resemblance to any mouth I ever saw before—except on a magazine cover.

A rather florid-faced middle-aged man comes up to me and says he is so glad we are here because then they will have meals on time: "Usually we all sit around and eat nuts and make ourselves sick until 10 or 11." (Evidently, C. has found out, dinner is at 10 or 11. Movies start at 12. Breakfast is at 11. Lunch between 3 and 4!)

At this moment Mr. Hearst comes in. We go into a long dining hall, beautifully paneled and beams above held up by little carved gnomes. There are those elk-horn chandeliers one sees in Bavaria (a wooden hausfrau sailing on them, blessing the scene below). Also beautiful old German sideboards and chests —old steins, glass, etc. on shelves. A carved bust of a knight holding a scepter sits on the sideboard. But in front of it stands a cheap modern porcelain figure in a red coat. Cuckoo clocks on the walls. It is all done in excellent taste down to the details, and yet there is such mediocrity imposed on top, like the porcelain hunting figure (or the Kewpie bedspread in our room).

And the people—as I look around the table and study the faces (I know no one) I get the impression of blatant insensitivity. (C.'s fineness shines out like a diamond.) I feel that the people I see are on the whole good. It is not goodness they lack but fineness.

Perhaps even here I am wrong, for the man I am sitting next to has fineness. He is the young Conan Doyle—English—and over here on a lecture tour. He is sensitive and aware—finely chiseled face. He starts to tell me in his low modulated English voice that we have many "mutual friends" and mentions Harold Nicolson. He is no longer a friend of mine but I feel if he (Conan Doyle) can be broad-minded enough to speak to me I must try to be tolerant of Harold Nicolson and I say what I truthfully can of Harold Nicolson—that he must be very bitterly disillusioned (*Peacemaking,* etc.), all those ideals to crash in this war and his two sons fighting in it.

Mr. Hearst sits silent—sunken—on my left, like a Buddha.

Miss Davies opposite chatters on brightly and gaily, smiling with genuine kindness whenever you look at her. The man across the table from me (an editor) stares with an openly appraising light in his half-closed eyes at the beautiful brunette, two down from me.

I wonder how I can proceed with the Englishman. I feel Hearst is unapproachable, and my ground with the Englishman very insecure. I talk of Long Barn, Italy, and then we touch lightly—oh so gingerly—on the new Russian-German war. I say tentatively—a bridge—"If only it had happened *earlier!*" To which, to my surprise, Conan Doyle and the editor join in heartily: "Oh yes, two or three years ago."

However, we do not proceed on this subject. Obviously in the Hearst household the women are not expected (or wanted) to be intellectual. The florid-faced editor says with a beatific glance across the table, "No matter what happens, there will always be beauty and romance"!

We rise from the table and the ladies exit into a powder room to "make up" again. The hall of the make-up room is covered with a series of lush magazine-cover beauties of all over the world. Accent on the curves of breast and thigh. (The Javanese beauty, the Creole beauty, the Hawaiian beauty, etc.)

After I have put more lipstick on and powder (I still look pale and prim in my black-and-white dress next to these passion-flowers) I find myself talking to Mrs. Conan Doyle; a White Russian, anti-Communist. In talking we meet in another world. A world of ideas which doesn't exist for the beauties who sit around in a circle like children and listen to us.

But we soon are taken away for the movies. Mr. Hearst is waiting bent and polite at the door. "He wants to take you, dear Mrs. Lindbergh," Marion Davies purrs in my ear, coyly. "He looked around to see who the prettiest girl was and said he'd take you!"

This kind of obvious, completely whole-cloth-nonsense flattery is appalling to me. Not that one likes her the less for it. It is so completely overlaid—like the make-up—and a part of her life and therefore not intentional as much as habit.

We get into the car, Marion Davies throwing a fur stole over her shoulders, and drive to the big chalet where they have movies every night. Mr. Hearst sits hunched up, immobile, in the front seat while Marion Davies prattles on and on about their trip to Mexico and how she stormed at the front door of our house at Cuernavaca. Every once in a while Mr. Hearst would say in gentle amused remonstrance (like a fond father at the antics of his spoiled darling), *"Marion!"*

"Why!" (wide-eyed innocence) "I'm not lying, am I?"

"Oh no" (quiet amusement), "just *embroidering."*

The movie chalet is an old-fashioned nineteenth-century shooting lodge (belonged to Mr. Hearst's mother). We sit on sofas and chairs, facing a screen. Everyone pairs up with his or her respective mate, the florid-faced editor trailing the beautiful brunette. I am next to Marion Davies, in the very center, with C.—thank goodness—on my right. Mr. H. is on the other side of Marion Davies. I look at his profile in a kind of intrigued amazement. He does not look like a newspaper "tycoon" or a man of great power who had achieved everything he wanted. His face is not insensitive or imperceptive. It has no coarseness in it. On the other hand it has a lack of compactness that I find disturbing. I love the quality of hard compactness in a face, as in Dr. Carrel's. A seemingly impervious face, the startled eye gives it away. If I did not know who it was I should say it was the eye of a man who was frightened, always on guard, aware. The mouth is the best feature—kind, benevolent, sensitive. And yet the whole face does not give the impression of satisfaction, either physical or spiritual. It might be the face of a disappointed man. Nowhere does one see signs of the power, the control, the vision, and the courage of the editorials he is now writing on this war issue.

We sit and watch a movie about two cafeteria girls going to Miami and getting themselves rich husbands. The heroine, Marion Davies tells me, is Jackie Coogan's first wife, just divorced.

The whole thing is so cheap and vulgar and shows such a completely false set of values that I am reminded of my feeling of shock and shame at seeing the first American film after I had been abroad. ("Is this *really* America?")

It is about 1:30 when we get up to go to our cars. When C. and I finally get into our beautifully carved and beamed room and shut the heavy door, he says, "It's like touching earth to touch you again."

I feel the same way.

What an extraordinary shifting artificial world. As a matter of fact I think Marion Davies is one of the most stable characters in it. She and Hearst, I feel, are on a kind of rock-bottom relationship, strange and unconventional as it is.

But to arrest life at the moment when it is the most irrational —in the age of physical romance! The porcelain face of Marion Davies, the nineteen-year-old tricks. How much more interesting she would have been, allowed to develop beyond that. Age is exiled here—and children.

I lie in the enormous bed and think of the fairy tale of the Emperor and the jeweled nightingale.

June 23rd

We wake about 9:30 and, by exercise, long baths, eating fruit, stretch out dressing until 10:30 and then walk over to the dining hall, to arrive at 11. It is empty and silent as a tomb. Evidently we are too early. The cuckoo clocks chime out their charming nursery tunes. They sound pure and clear as the bells in some church in the Bavarian Alps. But curiously out of place here. How strange is the hunger for purity in people who have lost it. This whole place shows a hunger for purity and yet misses it.

Gradually people seep in. A young couple first—they are simple and nice. Then the Conan Doyles, and pretty soon the beautiful brunette and the editor, beaming with good will. They are obviously satisfied with the night they have spent with each other.

When breakfast is over, C. and I go for a walk up the mountain, among great pines, and look across at Mt. Shasta's snowy peaks between the pines. We sit and look at the bark of a tree that is near us and the distant peaks far away from us and feel for the first time in touch with the country.

We gather for lunch again at 3—but don't eat till about 4!

Then a group of seventy schoolchildren comes up from the village to see C. (Marion Davies arranged it. "They're *so* excited—deah Colonel Lindbergh!") C. is, I can see, turning over inside from the Public Hero role she is putting him into. But he holds himself in. The children are nice but the thing is whooped up by the teachers and Marion Davies (in all good will). They sing that dreadful song: "Amurrica I luv you . . . / Just like a little bebbie/ Climbing its Mother's knee. . . ." Then the chefs give them ice cream and cake by carloads.

The Conan Doyles go and I am disappointed since she is the only person I can talk to.

At dinner I try to tell Mr. Hearst—that gray and lifeless mask at my left—how good and how important I think his last editorial is. He simply looks at me with that expressionless face and shows no sign of being pleased. Someone else picks up the conversation and I lapse back into silence, chilled.

We see a very bad movie—a comedy—of a crazy man; C. says it is enough to drive one insane.

June 24th

Lunch goes better. C. gets a chance to talk to Mr. Hearst and he smiles at some of my stories about Illiec.

By dinnertime we are all very cordial. The cartoonist's wife says to me, "If you like *this* place you ought to see San Simeon —why, two rooms there cost a fortune!"

It is another set of values. I think they like us and are sorry to have us leave. But simply cannot make us out. Mr. Hearst told the story, with a kind of incredulous good humor, of C. turning down a fabulous amount of money for an acting contract. People at the table looked at us in a kind of dazed curiosity.

"But he didn't know how to *act*," I defended him, protesting. I think they are pleased that we came. Marion Davies especially so, in a pathetically childish way, perhaps because she has been snubbed for her unconventional position.

She gives me a huge bottle of perfume as a parting gift and Mr. Hearst gives C. a photograph of himself under the Madonna fountain.

The little Bavarian maid comes in to say good-bye and asks if she can take our picture. She has a gentle face and looks lovely to me with her gray hair. There is a peace and a beauty about her face that is missing from the rest of the faces there. She blesses C. for his work against the war and says, "God be with you wherever you go."

We go off in the rain to the station and take the night train to San Francisco.

Back to normalcy!

July

The last weeks have gone so fast and been so full that I can only sketch them.

The meeting in San Francisco—C.'s best speech, full of humor. The tolerance of the crowd—*no* boos at all, and the English were cheered! (when Senator Clark said, "I have nothing against the English—I greatly admire the English"). The crowds in the street outside, the enthusiasm.

But the smearing newspapers as usual the next morning, of course; also they play up what I was afraid they would of C.'s speech, and what I wanted him to omit, knowing its danger: "I would a thousand times rather see my country ally herself with Germany than with Soviet Russia." Only, of course, they omit C.'s saying, *"with England or even* with Germany, *with all of her faults"* (my phrase, only I wanted it to be an even stronger condemnation of Germany).

Then our swift flight back to Chicago—overnight. I liked all the people I met. There is certainly a bigger percentage of "nice people" in the Middle West who are isolationists. But the area itself is flat and inland—brackish to me. We could not live there.

Back to Long Island—hot and muggy and *full* of people. I

hate to go to the beach. Go out to see Conger Goodyear[1] in his beautiful house—a nice evening. Conger is on our side—surprisingly enough!—and says we are gaining even in the East. I am thrilled.

But a few mornings later the President without any warning says he is occupying Iceland, as a protective measure, that he intends to occupy other strategic bases and protect the sea lanes to all of these!

This is a move *into* war. If the Germans want to shoot we can be in war in a week.

But what depresses me is not so much *that* as that it is a complete denial of our system of representative government. The people's will does not count. The President does what he wants, regardless. There could not be a more compelling majority to stay out of this war. All the polls show an overwhelming mass of the people want to stay out. No movement could be more popular than our movement. No meetings more successful. And yet the President says he doesn't believe in polls. The interventionists pooh-pooh any talk of a referendum. They deceive the people and draw them along closer and closer into the war, *against their will*.

Even Charles, who has always been optimistic, says this move changes the whole situation.

Birkhead[2] says that for ten thousand dollars he will "do the same job" on Charles that has been done on Coughlin. In other words, any man, no matter what he is, can be smeared. It's just a question of money. Money can make things right or wrong.

We went one night to the Norman Thomases'. He is brilliant, able, and quick, and when he talks—which he does with precision, clarity, and force—he is very commanding. The room turns to him and listens. He himself is not inclined to listen to other people, especially members of his own family—his worshipful wife and sons. I like to listen to him but when I see

[1] Art patron, one of the early supporters of the Museum of Modern Art in New York.

[2] The Reverend Leon M. Birkhead, founder and director of Friends of Democracy, an antitotalitarian propaganda agency.

him interrupt his wife and laugh at his son I begin to feel resentfully feminist. He does not realize that he is the overbearing male—but he is, just the same. She is a woman of insight and a good mind and could have had opinions of her own but they have never been listened to; so now she doesn't expect it ("I never read those articles; Norman does . . ." "Of course I don't know about that; Norman says . . .").

And he has dedicated his life to the cause of oppressed people!

They are not oppressed, of course; that is ridiculous. They have an unusually happy and full family life and relationship that reminds me of my family in Englewood. It is not the individual I am holding up for examination but a general widespread tendency—in which Norman Thomas is no exception—of inequality between men and women, even in America. An unequal balance in the family, taken for granted.

C. is, of course, very rare in his attitude toward me. He is more of a feminist than I am! His always wanting me to share his life, his problems, his decisions, his wanting me to have my own career—writing. His letting me carry my own in the conversation even when there are only men there, and his constant generous giving me credit for the ideas of mine that he uses or quotes: "As my wife says . . ." or "I think my wife put that as well as anyone . . ." or "My wife is particularly good in picking up that kind of thing. . . ."

Mr. Johnson was there (on the Feeding of Europe), back from France and Spain (with Carrel). He says that C. is unpopular among the Germans because he said he didn't want Germany to win 😊 . I wish to goodness he would spread that around!

Also Dorothy Dunbar Bromley[1]—a bright woman *with a mind of her own!* She is a socialist and more worried about stopping anti-Semitism than stopping the war. She says *The Wave of the Future* is pure socialism!

[1] Liberal writer, sponsor of the New York chapter of the America First Committee. Her husband, James Wood Johnson, a friend of Dr. Carrel, was organizer and director of the American Volunteer Ambulance Corps (1939) in France.

One beautiful morning I came to breakfast all serene to find that Ickes had used the pretext of a July 14th meeting of the Free French to blast C. again, in a speech that was full of lies and calumny and false insinuations from beginning to end. Every single statement about C. or me was false, sentences mutilated, words twisted, from his speeches and my book.

C. however wrote a very dignified appeal to the President. There was no anger in it and no hate—as there isn't in him really.

[*In an open letter to President Roosevelt of July 16, C. A. L. refuted Ickes's repeated charges of his being connected with a foreign government and the criticism of "having accepted a German medal in 1938." He reminded the President that he had "received the decoration in the American Embassy, in the presence of your Ambassador and . . . was there at the American Embassy at his request in order to assist in creating a better relationship between the American Embassy and the German government, which your Ambassador desired at that time." He declared that he had "no connection with any foreign government" and had "had no communication, directly or indirectly, with anyone in Germany or Italy" since he left Europe in 1939. He offered to open his files for the President's investigation and to answer any questions that the President might have about his activities. The letter was not answered.*]

We meet the [Bernhard] Knollenbergs. He is librarian at Yale and a specialist in American history—very much on our side and intelligent and perceptive. His wife, Mary, is a sculptress and quite beautiful—a friend of Mina Curtiss and Helen Hooker. She is sensitive, aware, and very intelligent. I feel I can talk to her, and want to. It is an open door in my mind—a door *out*.

Also "Phil" La Follette,[1] whose mind is better than anyone's I have met in this struggle, at least it seems to me so (perhaps

[1] Lawyer and politician, twice Governor of Wisconsin.

General Wood's[1] is just as good and certainly *steadier*). It is keen, searching, tolerant, and forward looking. I only wish I had not just stepped off the sleeper and had read more thoroughly of the things he talked about. We all talked rather jumpily and C. felt there were many ends left unfinished. I *always* feel that with *everyone!*

C. has been getting great joy lately out of teaching Land to swim. He urged him at first when Land was timid. But Land, when he found he could swim alone, went absolutely drunk on it! Jumping off the raft and swimming around to the steps. And when he went to the raft on his father's shoulders he would push off and strike off alone and then come back when tired.

But I am sick of this place. We have no longer any privacy here; people telephone all day long—they know where we are. They even come out without calling up beforehand and look for us through the house and garden. The beach is so crowded with (chilly-to-us) people that I no longer can bear to go down there. I feel trapped—on weekends I don't want to walk for fear of meeting people and have to give excuses for not doing things and being around.

I go off to Martha's Vineyard in desperation and find a house, much too small for us and not nearly as convenient as this, but in a windy bare free place with a beach of its own, to escape to. Now we are moving, for good, from this area. I am caught in the burden of packing, moving, planning again. But I feel, desperately, that we *must* go.

A terrible article in *True Story:* "The secret thoughts of Anne Lindbergh," written by an "intimate friend" I never heard of. It claims I am completely dominated by my Nazi husband, and tells wholesale lies and twists phrases out of my books to prove this thesis, quoting from *North to the Orient,* C. saying of me (with infinite pride), "She's crew"! (Never have I been so proud as in that moment. He was treating me as an equal—in *his* world!)

---

[1] General Robert Wood, Chairman of the America First Committee.

Lloyd Neck, July 28th

Mother darling,

We have taken—for two months or three—a house near Margot on Martha's Vineyard, with the idea (very much a secret) of looking around and seeing whether we could stay there all winter, maybe. We would have to move again into a house with heat but there is one—in fact two—that would do. Of course it may not work out. But that is why we are trying it for late summer and autumn first, and trying it very lightly, too. That is, saying we are only there for a month or two, as a base for the children. So that the publicity won't get out that we're thinking about it as a semipermanent home. I thought we could make Lloyd Neck do for our base and it is perfect in the winter but we are getting awfully tired of the pressure of New York, which is getting worse all the time and increases with any work C. does.

The house we have taken is terribly small and means doubling up the children, the secretaries, etc. But it has lovely wild hills to walk over and miles of beach with practically no one on it.

DIARY   *Saturday, August 2nd*

Our last weekend. We shut all the doors and front windows and draw the shades and tell Mary that we are "away for the week-end" to *anyone* who calls. We stay in the house all day and manage, in spite of the cars going by our door, to feel quite private. It is very hot but we don't go to the beach, where we will see people.

The day also has a bitter taste because last night I went to Englewood and Mother showed me ("You *must* see it! I must say I think *I* come off better than you, my dear!") a dreadful article in *Who* magazine about her and me. I, the weak, sensitive, frightened, bewildered poet, caught between the strong personalities of my courageous mother and my nefarious husband. "Frightened by the Nazis," "immature philosophically," "will never find her way out." It is unpleasant to read it and even more unpleasant to have the family so placid about it.

Thursday, August 7th

The last days have gone into packing. C. and I went through all the barrels, furniture, etc. at Manhattan [Warehouse]; most of them I haven't seen since Hopewell. What a stack of memories, hopes, plans buried in those scraps of hook rugs, those bits of pewter we used on the table, those hunks of furniture crammed into a dark and airless room next to other dark and airless rooms. It was like visiting a mausoleum. I was torn with conflicting feelings—I wanted to rid myself of these and all other material possessions that weigh one down. And I looked at those dead clods of possessions and thought, incredulous: Out of these we once made a warm living home!

Another dreadful article in *Look:* "Why Lindbergh should be impeached."

Friday, August 8th, on board airliner [*to Cleveland*]

Mother darling,

In the midst of the packing and moving I jump on a plane to go to Cleveland with Charles! I did not plan to. I plan to step back from that life—chiefly because I cannot take it as C. does.

But here I am—chiefly because Cleveland is hostile to us. All the papers are antagonistic and I gather of the worst sort. And also because the Middle West is full of rumors that C. and I are separating on his America First work. There are lots of things (and people) I don't like in the work. There are lots of things I don't like about my side and about America First. Especially in Cleveland. They had an exhibit in a park of a lot of coffins marked *Bundles from Britain.*

But Charles stands for integrity. No matter who turns out to have been right in judgment of what is best for this country— war or peace—the issue of integrity in government remains the most important.

And Charles stands for it—almost more than any person I ever met. And so I stand behind him.

The smears on the meeting will be bad. I hope it won't upset Aunt Annie,[1] but she is away. How good she was to ask him to stay there anyway! How loyal and good. I was so touched.

I am only happy to be able to go to a difficult place with Charles. And then I will go with the children to Martha's Vineyard to rest and think and maybe write.

> "If thou canst get but thither,
> There grows the flower of Peace!"

Dear Mother, I am glad you are writing, think often of you. We will be nearer, even on two separated islands, than when I am upset and in New York. Though we are never separated.

DIARY   *August 14th, Martha's Vineyard*

Cleveland is already a confused dream. I took the midnight train back after a hot meeting. Although the house was full by the time C. started to speak I was worried about it when I came on the stage (introduced as "famous author"! What writhings inside to have to walk across the stage after that announcement). The crowd was an average Middle West crowd—only got steamed up for C.

Then a late Sunday arrival in New York. I went into St. Patrick's and to look at Picasso's "Saltimbanques" again at the Modern Museum. Then the nostalgic ride out on that crowded little train. Sunday very late C. arrives from Washington. Monday, last frantic packing. A lot left for C. and Christine to do. I hate to leave unfinished ends.

At the last moment when C. is hustling us into the car and saying that we can *just* make it, we discover that Land has no coat on. "Where is your coat?" "I packed it," says Land, firmly pointing to the minute suitcase in his hand I had given him to play with. We open it hastily—rags and empty toothbrush boxes, old twine, etc., fall out. "It is not possible!" says Soeur Lisi, leaping out of the car, going upstairs to look. But I delve below

---

[1] Annie Cutter, sister of E. C. M., who lived in Cleveland with her mother.

the rags and, sure enough, Land has folded it, all crushed, in the bottom! We leave with the bag, all rags and confusion, still open on the floor. No time for sentimental good-byes. And yet I have loved that house and the garden.

We make the boat with twenty minutes to spare but none of our baggage is labeled and I have left my keys (for the trunk and one suitcase) behind!

> *Seven Gates Farm, Vineyard Haven, Martha's Vineyard,*
> *August 15th*

Mother darling,

We have been here for two days and I expect C. this morning. I am so glad he did not come earlier for the first days were full of trying to make a bare summer cottage into a personal home. It is such fun to do it—for a woman. The joy of seeing a house get warmth and color under your eyes. Cover the dreadful pink chintz with some Japanese blue-and-white toweling (rescued from Manhattan [Warehouse]). Remove *half* the wicker chairs. Remove *all* the yellow tearoomy candles. Get out gay tablecloths and bedspreads. The big room is a marvel of transformation. It has been changed from milk-chocolate and pink to blue and white.

I wish you could have been here to do it with me, for you would understand the thrill. But I am glad C. was not. Men cannot understand putting all that effort into it. "You're only here for a few months!" Of course, but if one always acted that way about life one would never do anything. The very impermanence of life makes it even more necessary to give it some kind of security and continuity with one's possessions even if these are only cheap and gay ones.

I have not yet tackled the *next* house (though I find the big attractive warm one *is* available). Or the substitute for Soeur Lisi [who was going home to Switzerland]. Isn't it strange how there are periods in your life when it is just *all* business, house, family, and household business. And you know that the next weeks or months will have to go to that. Then it settles down for a while. It did at Long Barn and will again here.

I do not feel so overcome by them up here, for the other pressures are removed—no telephone calls, no people, no dates ahead. I feel deliciously lonely and hope I stay so!

This letter is full of business, but you will know the mood I am in—a dog going round and round in the grass making himself a nest to curl down into.

DIARY *August 15th*

C. arrives about noon with the car high with bags and bundles. We carry them all into the house and set them down in the beautiful living room, where they stay for two days until they are sorted out, slowly and precisely, by C.

We walk over the land finding a place for the tent. C. says it is beautiful and that he can work here.

Roosevelt and Churchill meet at sea and draft an eight-point peace plan.[1] As usual, beautiful words, ideals—*how* is it to be done?

Sunday, August 17th

Great wind blowing, all blinds flapping. C. and I look for new site for tent, more sheltered.

I walk up on the hill and lie on the ground. The security of it and the beauty make me able to think out all the things I am possessive about. The hanging-on feeling—about life itself and its passing by, of youth and romance, of time itself, of friends, of good repute.

It is easier here to "let go," not to put your heart "where moth and rust doth corrupt." And yet the complete ascetic denies life. "Between assertion and denial" there is a point one must find.

---

[1] The Atlantic Conference (August 9-12) of Roosevelt and Churchill produced a declaration called the Atlantic Charter. It included as its main peace aims: no territorial aggrandizement; no territorial changes without the free consent of the peoples; self-determination for all states in form of government; fullest economic collaboration between all nations; freedom from fear and want; freedom of the seas; universal disarmament.

I feel a new life is starting here but I am just now at sea and do not know where it begins.

Monday, August 18th

A lovely still day, with just enough of autumn to make one want to sit in the sun.

Also we go swimming. Anne sits on the sand in her pink kimono and pink sunbonnet, with me. Land paddles in a tiny blue boat with his father nearby.

But I am not yet sunk into myself enough to write—anything —still rootless and at loose ends.

Monday, August 25th [to North Haven][1]

Fields full of daisies, red barns, pine trees, white steeples, and little harbors. Get quite excited as we approach Alamoosook Lake. The motorboat comes quickly and takes us to the little island, tiny and completely covered with tall pines, a few roofs and tents hidden in the trees. In a group of children down at the water's edge and on the little pier, I can make Jon out in a gray suit with a white triangle of a sling. He is smiling and shy and eager with talk. "I caught a bass—even with my arm in a sling." —Mark and Quintus [Dreir, nephews of Margot] also in gray.

Load up the car. Boys in back, Jon in front, and start off. Jon volunteered, shyly, "What I *did* like were letters. I used to wait for them." (This was such a surprise to me and such a warming delight. I wrote every week, with the sinking feeling that he never read them.) "What day did you write?" I said, "I always wrote on Sunday." Jon, pleased, "I always wrote on Sunday, too."

We get to North Haven in time for lunch. Aunt Annie, Amey [Aldrich], gray and thin, Mrs. Rublee, Mr. Rublee,[2] the

---

[1] A. M. L. and Margot Morrow drove to Maine to pick up Jon, who was at camp, then proceeded to the Morrow home at North Haven.

[2] Friends of the Morrows. See *The Flower and the Nettle*.

[Learned] Hands and Mr. [Louis] Dow. It is almost too much to see them all at once. Amey and my beloved Mrs. Hand. And they seem glad to see us. I was feeling so shy about this weekend—into the camp of the interventionists!

North Haven, Saturday, August 30th

Dearest Con,

It does not seem quite right that you are not here to talk over the slightly stuffy atmosphere of too much excitement that North Haven weekends always had and still do—"too rich food," as you said. I am giving a wrong impression because it has been such joy to live in the excitement of the moment—in *people*—as I have not done for a long time. There has been lots of watching. The Hand-Rublee-Dow contingent setting the stage. The younger generation not being the center of the stage this weekend. And Margot and I observing.

Only you should have been there because the taste of other summers is on your tongue.

Mrs. Hand has been again "mother earth" to everyone. She is a "Mrs. Ramsay,"[1] isn't she? Winding her gray scarf around the elk horns to comfort the frightened children. Judge Hand has been the stormy, gay, and gallant troubadour, with his eye on Margot's laughing face. Mrs. Rublee flaunted her flaming red boa at us all. (She is incredible. All red—even to a bow on the elastic in her hair—or *all* yellow with yellow butterflies on a badly fitting hair net—perfect down to the last detail.) Mr. Dow sitting reading poetry on the point to Mrs. Hand. Mr. Rublee, sweet and mild and childlike, reading Wordsworth in the evenings. All was peace and harmony—except for the red-feather boa. Why is there always a red-feather boa in life?

Amey's little dog barking loudly, nipping at *every* pair of blue jeans running in and out of the house. All the boys running *in* to meals—or *out* to fish with Mr. Grant. They move in a tumbling shouting avalanche, calling out "Neat!" at intervals. Mark startles me by shouting out from time to time, "Where's Lindbergh?"

[1] The key figure in Virginia Woolf's novel *To the Lighthouse*.

Of outside visitors we have had Mr. and Mrs. Lamont (Père), Mrs. L. getting up to leave at 9:30—"I turn into an old witch at the stroke of ten." And the golden Valentines [Lucia and Alan]. Also Eve Curie.[1]

I have fallen in love with Eve Curie. So beautiful and so gallant and such a sensitive, proud, hurt face. I expected the beauty, the woman of the world, the charm, wit, chic. But somehow not that hurt child, not that slight awkwardness of body as she rises from a chair, pulling her thin shoulders together in a half-deferential way that betrays an ancient and not yet forgotten shyness of adolescence. And pain in the very bones of her face.

All this goes to make up a kind of purity I had not expected. It is so rare that one sees that monklike quality of dedication in a woman.

But you met her, so you must know. We saw her three times. The first time I saw all this she looked tired and sad. The second time she was simply the chic and perfectly poised Frenchwoman. The third time she was very gamine and beautiful and gay—in parchment-colored "long" shorts and parchment-colored bandeau, immaculate after a canoe trip around the island with Alan. Alan looked red and tired but she was sleek as a seal. Only she said with a charming insouciance: "I understand now why as a rule one walks without a canoe on one's shoulders!"

Conversation was very conventional except for the last time, when we got onto a very theoretical discussion of what is Left and Right. I felt afterwards rather ashamed of having talked so much. As though one were to discuss whether one would rather die of pernicious anemia or cancer while one's host's father lay upstairs under an oxygen tent. I didn't *think* Eve Curie minded.

At any rate it was extraordinarily heartening to me to be able to talk at all to them.

Frenchwomen just *never* look ungroomed, do they? And their noses never shine.

The boys have fished steadily for three days and have now

[1] Musician, writer, daughter of Pierre and Marie Curie.

just discovered golf (on the sheep pasture) is a good game, too! I think golf will last until Tuesday morning when we leave. The apple tree has been a help, too—green-apple fights have added to the excitement.

DIARY   *September 11th, Seven Gates Farm*
Back again—a week of household confusion—almost everyone in tears due to the fact that everything and everyone arrived at once. C. (unexpectedly) for five days to write his speech. Hilma, from her beau to this wilderness and more work than she expected; Christine from her vacation; and the new couple a little bewildered and doing nothing right. Unpack the boxes (the cook wants a potato basket). The two secretaries are busy fixing up their little house, which I got them because this house is too small for a house and an office.

It is still too small. Land slams the front door a hundred times a day. And C. is trying to write a speech and worrying about me. The tent, as he says, has been up a month—*especially* for me to write in—and what have I done?!

I try to pull the household together. If only I did not have to do it all before C.'s perfectionist eye—I feel, illogically, it would be easier. I wish I had got it all running smoothly before he arrived.

Then his speech—throwing me into black gloom. He names the "war agitators"—chiefly the British, the Jews, and the Administration. He does it truthfully, moderately, and with no bitterness or rancor—but I hate to have him touch the Jews at all. For I dread the reaction on him. No one else mentions this subject out loud (though many seethe bitterly and intolerantly underneath). C., as usual, must bear the brunt of being frank and open. What he is saying in public is not intolerant or inciting or bitter and it is just what he says in private, while the other soft-spoken cautious people who say terrible things in private would never dare be as frank in public as he. They do not want to pay the price. And the price will be terrible. Headlines will flame "Lindbergh attacks Jews." He will be branded anti-Semitic, Nazi, Führer-seeking, etc. *I can hardly bear it. For he is a moderate.*

I try to say some of this and tell him what it will mean, that the anti-Semitic forces will rally to him, exultant (then they will moderate their movement, he says). I am afraid of the effect of his speech—what it will start—and the effect on him and the cause. He says that the point is *not* what the "effect" will be on him, *not* in what they try to make him out to have said or be. But whether or not what he said is *true* and whether it will help to keep us out of war. (I doubt the latter and feel that the negative results will outweigh the positive.) When I say that it will be taken as Jew-baiting, he says that of course he does not mean to do that.

I then work over the Jewish paragraph, rewriting it and putting in some of the things he believes but never says—to avoid all trace of rancor or bitterness. He takes almost all the suggestions, but will people read down under the headlines?

I have a sinking of heart as he goes off. It is not doubt in him, but if only people could see him as he really is. If his true self could shine through—that is all I ask. If *he* could make himself clear and if *they* would listen. . . .

I listen to the President's speech saying our boats will now "shoot on sight"—an out-and-out declaration of naval war.[1] An amazing speech—what a wizard he is to make so plausible the thesis that we will continue to give all possible aid to the enemies of Hitler while being affronted if Hitler does not respect our rights as a "neutral"!

I hear C.'s speech, too—direct and honest as a clean knife. The frenzied applause of the crowd frightens me. Can he keep in

[1] The U.S. destroyer *Greer* was attacked September 4 near Iceland by a German submarine with torpedoes, which missed their mark. The destroyer was attacked while tracking the U-boat and relaying its position to British naval units for a period of more than three hours. On September 11, Roosevelt delivered his "shoot-on-sight" address over a worldwide radio hookup. He charged that the attack on the *Greer* was part of a German effort to "acquire absolute control and domination of the seas" as a prelude to domination of the U.S. and the Western Hemisphere.

control what he has in his hands? Especially since he does not really want that control, that power.

[*In C. A. L.'s Des Moines speech on September 11, he said: "The three most important groups who have been pressing this country toward war are the British, the Jewish, and the Roosevelt Administration. Behind these groups, but of lesser importance, are a number of capitalists, anglophiles, and intellectuals. . . ." He expanded on his statement in the following paragraphs, stating that Britain's hope was to make us "responsible for the war financially, as well as militarily. . . . If we were Englishmen, we would do the same. But our interest is first in America." In elaborating on the Jewish group, he continued: "It is not difficult to understand why Jewish people desire the overthrow of Nazi Germany. The persecution they suffered in Germany would be sufficient to make bitter enemies of any race. No person with a sense of the dignity of mankind can condone the persecution of the Jewish race in Germany. But no person of honesty and vision can look on their pro-war policy here today without seeing the dangers involved in such a policy both for us and for them."*]

Saturday, September 13th

I go out under the stars, which are very brilliant. I need to get calm again after the papers, which confirm my worst fears as to the reactions to C.'s speech. He is attacked on all sides—Administration, pressure groups, and Jews, as now openly a Nazi, following Nazi doctrine.

I lie down in the grass on the bluff and look at the brilliant spread of stars through the giant wavering grass tops which loom over my eyes. The difference between Jew and Gentile does not seem very great looking at the stars—nor do any earthly troubles. I cannot bear to leave, to go back to the house, to go back to tomorrow—to life.

For I realize dimly that the pull of the stars is the pull of eternity and of death. I long so deeply to keep that point of

view when I get up, but if I did I would no longer care—about
C., about the children and about life.

Lying there in bliss, I dread—like a Lazarus—tomorrow's
emotions with C.'s return. I will be so excited to see him, so
eager to know how it went, I will care passionately one way or
another. I will be filled with longings and frustrations.

His coming will fill the house with warmth, with fire, with
wind, with life.

And also with problems. How much time there is when one
is alone, away from one's husband. What *time* marriage takes
—but it is life. It would be death without it.

Around the house with a lantern to look at the sleeping
children and put on an extra cover. The miser's hour for a
mother—she looks at her gold and gloats over it!

Sunday, September 14th

C. comes about noon. We have already had a long discussion on
the Jewish question and his speech—and the implications of it
—which worry me profoundly. I cannot explain my revulsion
of feeling by logic. Is it my lack of courage to face the problem?
Is it my lack of vision and seeing the thing through? Or is my
intuition founded on something profound and valid?

I do not know and am only very disturbed, which is upsetting
for him. I have the greatest faith in him as a person—in his integrity, his courage, and his essential *goodness,* fairness, and kindness—his nobility, really. For he is incapable of being mean. How
then explain my profound feeling of grief about what he is doing?
If what he said is the truth (and I am inclined to think it is), why
was it wrong to state it? He was naming the groups that were
pro-war. No one minds his naming the British or the Administration. But to name "Jew" is un-American—even if it is done without hate or bitterness or even criticism. Why?

Because it is segregating them as a group, setting the ground
for anti-Semitism.

Because it is at best unconsciously a bid for anti-Semitism. It
is a match lit near a pile of excelsior. Of course he does not mean

or does not want to light that pile of excelsior, but his match, lit only to show the ground, may light the excelsior.

He spoke—if I analyze it right—not to create anti-Semitism, or even to use it as a weapon (which I first accused him of). But for two reasons.

1) To show the American people what the propaganda is that is leading them to war and where it originates—in order to insulate them from it. In order *not* to arouse their passions but to quell their (to him) falsely aroused passions. In fact, in order for them to be able to view the situation dispassionately. (I do not say this is going to be the case but this was his object.) In fact, I think just the opposite is happening—more passion is being aroused.

2) In order to warn the Jews that their action, if it succeeded in bringing on war, would be disastrous not only for us but for them.

Be that as it may, no matter what his intentions were, he has lit the match—and even if the excelsior does not catch fire at this moment, when or if it does, his match, innocent though it may have been, will be held responsible.

I say that I would prefer to see this country at war than shaken by violent anti-Semitism. (Because it seems to me that the kind of person the human being is turned into when the instinct of Jew-baiting is let loose is worse than the kind of person he becomes on the battlefield.) C. says that is not the choice. The choice is, I gather, whether or not you are going to let your country go into a completely disastrous war for lack of courage to name the groups leading that country to war—at the risk of being called "anti-Semitic" simply by *naming* them. (But it is more risk than that, I think. It is the risk of starting open anti-Semitism, even unintentionally.)

It is a difficult argument because I cannot analyze my feeling and therefore he has a right to lay my feeling to hypnosis, propaganda, or lack of courage or vision, lack of clear thinking; not that he says this, but he is baffled.

Poor C. I do not like to add another problem to his load when the whole world is fighting him. I have such deep faith in him as a person—in what he really is and stands for. My criticism and doubt is not like the criticism of the rest of the world. It is only at bottom a passionate desire that this true person underneath shine through, shine clear.

And he knows it, I think. We have—in spite of the long discussion—a beautiful day on the south shore's wide wind-swept beach, jumping the rollers with the children. C. and the boys.

To sleep in C.'s little tent, staked in a hollow on the hill, under the stars.

Monday, September 15th

The storm is beginning to blow up hard. America First is in a turmoil. Telegrams arrive. The Committee to Defend America by Aiding the Allies denounces C. He is universally condemned by all moderates (Lewis Douglas saying he transgressed the rights of free speech in naming the Jews). The Jews demand a retraction. Mrs. Curtiss has wired me asking to speak to me on the telephone. Quincy Howe in his broadcast (he is a moderate and noninterventionist) comes out and says all true Americans can unite in condemnation of C.'s disastrous speech.

I begin to feel bitter—not that I do not myself feel that the speech was disastrous but because I begin to see C. hated much as the Jews are hated—simply because he is Lindbergh. Hugh Johnson[1] can say the same thing in the *World Telegram*. But they are not crucified, because they are not Lindbergh.

I think how true was my vision of him as eternally that man in a plane alone out in the middle of the ocean, headed for an impossible destination, with all the world calling him a "flying fool" and only a few individuals—not understanding him, not able to follow him, left behind—looking after him with a kind of blind faith, holding him in their hearts.

I sense that this is the beginning of a fight and consequent loneliness and isolation that we have not known before.

I find—though I am sobered by it—that it is not so difficult to face. In a sense it is what I faced or thought I faced when I

[1] Former head of the National Recovery Administration; since 1934 newspaper and radio commentator.

married. (How strange it is that one makes the choice implied in marriage not once but over and over again. Are you or aren't you? Yes or no?)

I find it is again quite clearly *yes*. This is my life. And all the other dreams of literary people, literary aspirations, the joy and the gratification that come from that kind of contact and understanding, melt away as—in the end—inconsequential.

It would be of course a hard choice to make if it were for a man one did not have complete faith in. I cannot do otherwise than follow him and hope and pray and work to try to have his nobility shine through—to have it express itself truthfully.

I must remember this when it gets hard for me.

For I am really much more attached to the worldly things than he is, mind more giving up friends, popularity, etc., mind much more criticism and coldness and loneliness.

We sleep again in the little tent out on the hill, with the wind blowing. C. says he sleeps deeply and well, but I lie awake and think.

Tuesday, September 16th

C. calls General Wood and decides to go out to Chicago to talk to him and the Committee. He leaves at 4.

Wednesday, September 17th

Mother calls me up but we do not talk about the speech. She would not, of course. She would understand.

At 3:30 go with Margot to see a house we might take for the winter, with heat.

Write Mrs. Curtiss at night and Thelma.

Seven Gates Farm, Vineyard Haven, Massachusetts,
September 17th

Dear Mina [Curtiss],

I felt I could not call you on the subject of Charles' Des Moines speech. (In answer to your wire.) I have not spoken to anyone on the telephone about it—even my own mother, who called me last night. Because I felt I could not discuss my husband and his policy over practically a public telephone, especially since I do not agree with it.

I felt and I told him so before the speech was given that it would be disastrous from many points of view. I now feel however that it is going to be far more disastrous for him than for the Jews. In fact I think now it may even help the Jews and work against anti-Semitism.

It is very terrible for me to have him made the symbol of anti-Semitism in this country—to have him looked to as the leader of an anti-Semitic movement. (He does not wish to and he never will be this.)

I am not going to defend or apologize for him. I am not going to say what he meant or did not mean. I feel somehow that this would be beneath him and you and the situation. He must answer to all that himself in his own way.

But I feel impelled myself to write you—even before I know what you wanted to say to me. I want to say that if my husband were the man that the majority of the reading public of America today (as far as one can tell from the papers) thinks he is, I could not live with him. If he were what his words seem to many people to imply, I could not. For to most men who use them, words like that are only a façade for something evil and terrible underneath—which they hide but intend to bring up later.

My husband's words are not a façade. There is nothing hidden behind them. He says in private what he says in public. There is no hate in him, no desire to arouse hate. There is no plot or political scheming. (Unfortunately he is not enough of a politician or he would never be in the position he is now in.) It is bitter for me to see him unctuously condemned from the side lines by politicians who I know are anti-Semitic but who feel it is impolitic to say so—or by people who, if not anti-Semitic, at least fall into those obnoxious habits of speech and laughter which portray the hidden lines of superiority and inferiority in their own minds.

I have never heard my husband tell a Jewish joke. I have never heard him say anything derogatory about a Jew as such. I have never heard him say, "That is a Jewish trick." When he says that he admires the Jews, he means it, and when he says he feels he is taking the one course that will prevent anti-Semitism in this country, he means it.

This is not to say he has acted wisely—it is only to say that there is in him an integrity, a courage, and an essential nobility of spirit that I have never seen matched by any other human being. To have such a spirit in any way—even unintentionally—contribute to, or be used by, evil forces is terrible to me.

You will say that I am being unrealistic and no doubt I am. I am writing out of the urgency of my feelings and not weighing and considering the practical courses now open. I do not of course know what you wanted to say to me. If you want to urge my husband to some course of action I think it would be better if you wrote directly to him and not through me (though I should like to see you myself—if you felt like it). He likes and admires you and I think would listen to what you said.

I hope you will treat this letter with the discretion and privacy which you always have. I make no secret of my attitude on anti-Semitism but I do not want my husband to be the victim of both private and public scandal at the same time and it would be very easy for the story to get about that I was leaving him because we disagreed on what he said in his last speech.

We *do* disagree but I have the utmost faith in his essential goodness of spirit. . . . I hope this faith which stands like a rock in my life will not prevent me from seeing you, for if it does it will deprive me of a great deal that makes life rich for me.

Seven Gates Farm, Vineyard Haven, Massachusetts,
September 17th

Dear Thelma,

I opened your letter with some misgivings (the mail has been so dreadful lately), feeling to myself, "If she says '*Why* did you let him make that speech?' I cannot bear it."

You did not, of course. Why did I suspect you of not understanding? So few people do, I suppose that's why. You can't know what a relief it was. I felt—There—she's still there! It was

228

like hearing your name, your good pure child's name in a room full of strangers. Bless you for it.

Yes, I want to see you. I have moved from Long Island to Martha's Vineyard. It is far away, windblown, isolated and very quiet. It is better, for I was getting so upset and bitter and angry and hurt around New York. I could no longer think clearly or feel purely—and I was doing no one any good that way. Here it is much easier to keep my sense of balance. And heaven knows things are going from bad to worse!

I am here a good deal alone which is very restful, the nearest thing to a nunnery I've yet found—except for Illiec.

I would love to have you here but you must not come when C. is here. You could not help discussing politics and I must keep politics out of my relation to you. I cannot have it there. If he goes away again perhaps you might come. It is like Brittany.

I cannot write long tonight. My heart is heavy with the consequences of C.'s speech. Isn't it strange, there is no hate in him, no hate at all, and yet he rouses it and spreads it.

Did you ever read *Heaven Is My Destination* (Thornton Wilder)? In it there is a very good young man, uncompromisingly good. As a result of this goodness he finds himself three times in prison under charges of assault, kidnapping and contempt of court. When it is finally straightened out the judge says to him, "My boy, you are the only *completely logical* person I have ever met!"

Of course the boy was a fool. C. is not. But I sometimes feel it is his very goodness, his very purity which gets him into trouble.

I write lightly but I do not feel lightly.

DIARY   *Thursday, September 18th*

A still, warm, cloudless day, golden, suspended before autumn.

Land goes with Soeur Lisi to get shoes. And Christine to get blankets. I can never shop with my children because then they are no longer just ordinary children but become stared-at children. Now it will be even worse.

Will I be able to shop in New York at all now? I am always stared at—but now to be stared at with hate, to walk through aisles of hate!

Seven Gates Farm, Vineyard Haven, Massachusetts,
September 27th

Dear Mina,

Our letters crossed. Thank you so very much for yours which touched me more than I can tell you. I am planning on being in New York for about a week, probably arriving on the 3rd but possibly on the 2nd. I shall base at Englewood. Could you telephone me there and we could plan a meeting?

I am taking care of all three children this week and also trying to find another house to move into when it gets cold. My lovely Swiss nurse feels she must go home before the war breaks. So I am rather burdened with household cares at the moment and may even have to put off the trip to New York. But I hope not.

Did you see the Northern Lights? How is it possible that there can be differences, terrible differences, between honest people (honestly striving after right, I mean) under a sky like that?

I hope I shall be able to see you.

DIARY *Monday, September 29th*

A full week since C. came back. It has gone quickly, actively into the business of living, planning, settling down. We have finally taken the Webb House—old-fashioned, comfortable, but dark and Victorian. Covered with vines, porches, pine trees on the outside, and dark wallpaper, dark woodwork, pictures of the Colosseum, metal ornaments, gilt mirrors, etc. on the inside. It will be fairly compact and sheltered for winter. (Will we be here all winter? Will we move to California? Will we get into the war? Will C. continue with his America First work? None of these things can be answered now so this seems the best move for the present.) It now remains to be seen if it can be made warming to the eye—a home that shelters the spirit.

It means, though, a great deal of work and planning, for I cannot bear to live in a cold gloomy house. It must be brought alive. All my creative thoughts and strength will have to go into that for a while. (I wish it were being put into something more permanent. We seem to be always doing this—making a place livable, making it *ours*—only to move out and leave it to someone else. It isn't *moving* that one minds but leaving something that one has created—or, rather, having it go to nothing, though of course that isn't true really. One makes one's life warmer and more nourishing to those around you.)

There are other things, too. Soeur Lisi feels she must go home before we get actively into war (which seems imminent now). I think she is right. But it means a great change in our life. She was security to the children. She is simple, intuitive, warm, good—really good—full of a sense of joy about life and the natural things of earth. She was Mother Earth and yet she was aware, too, sensitive and alive to the true spirit of things (that is joy perhaps).

She must have her own life and home—marry, I hope. But it is going to be impossible to replace her.

Christine also must leave. She feels she must go back to her family. Until they leave (not because I *want* them to leave but because they are going to leave) the atmosphere of the house will be unsettled—nostalgic and somewhat tense with hidden emotions.

I am anxious for all these minor reefs to be crossed and our true new life safely launched.

Seven Gates Farm, Vineyard Haven, Massachusetts,
September 30th

Dear Mina,

Forgive me for a letter that must have sounded hard. It did not mean to be but it was written under tension of emotion and had the stiffness of withheld emotion in it. I did not mean really what you read into it. Although I *did* imagine that you might not feel you could see and talk to me (which I would understand), I do not doubt my friends but I lack faith, somehow, in their faith in me.

I am sceptical of life and at any moment expect it to fall about my ears. I do not expect much of life or count too much on it. On the whole I am surprised if I find that people want to see me again. And would not be surprised or even hurt if—on the slightest pretext—they disappeared from my life. This has always been so and is not due to the present unpopularity, but to some deep Puritan instinct in me. I expect all good things to go—and almost push them away from me in anticipation of the fatal moment. ("We seek too oft the thorn—alas, and find it.")

And now it is much exaggerated because of the present unpopularity and distrust I sense, as I go out, and because again I anticipate trouble. I cannot see far enough into the shadows, and expect the worst. ("So shall I taste at first the very worst of fortune's might.")

It is exaggerated now, also, because I see few people and meet the world chiefly through the newspapers, etc. Through those glasses the world is necessarily hostile and rather dark. And I find I have come to assume that most people—most people on the other side of the political picture—feel about me as, say, Dorothy Thompson does! Which is, of course, silly. And then I am simply astonished if I happen—as I do occasionally—to meet an interventionist who seems to enjoy talking to me!

Thank you and my love—please understand.

DIARY   *Monday, October 13th*

Back in Martha's Vineyard after a week in New York. The trip down on the train with C. The signs of war which creep even onto this faraway island but which are screamingly obvious as one goes off. Soldiers on the train, searchlights in the sky, planes maneuvering in threes. All the billboards have gone "Defense" mad, with pictures of soldiers and sailors on them. *Vogue* photographs its models in front of Bundles for Britain planes. Longchamps has V's done in vegetables in the windows. Elizabeth Arden gets out a V for Victory lipstick.

Remember: The trainman who jumped on the train on the

way down, stood shyly facing C. (he had seen us through the window), took off his beaked trainman's cap, smoothed his hair, put it on again, clapped his hand on C.'s shoulder and blurted out, "Boy, you've got a lot of good ideas—stick to 'em," and bolted out again, leaving me glowing inside.

Shopping, seeing friends, and interviewing nurses. This last has been the hardest work. It is so vital to get the right person, almost like marrying, and yet one must make the decision from one interview or two. One should work for months and see hundreds or try the best (but trying is hard on the children). For harmony in the house sometimes seems to me the one most important thing for children—harmony among the adults.

Mother shows me the terrible full-page reprinted editorial against C. (paid for, I suppose, by Fight for Freedom) from the New Bedford paper, put into the *Times*. It is long and well written, not just bombast. But it bases its accusations on false statements and inaccurate facts picked up from newspapers— things C. never said at all. It is reasonably and effectively done. It is full of pity and scorn and blame—not so much hate. I think it is the worst thing that has yet come out and it hurts me deeply—more than the Ickes blasts.

The real thrill of the visit came when Mrs. La Follette called me from Wisconsin on C.'s speech, saying that they were so moved they had to tell me so, that he burned through all the dross. That it rang clear. And Sue, too, calling me just as C. stopped speaking to say the same thing.

[*C. A. L.'s speech at Fort Wayne, October 3, dealt with the issue of representative government. He charged the Administration with throwing the country into an undeclared war without the consent of Congress. He accused Roosevelt and the Administration of "turning their backs on their campaign promises" and not consulting "the people's elected representatives in Congress." He warned that the country was being governed by a man "who is drawing more and more dictatorial powers into his own hands."*]

I felt happy, terribly happy—for him. (For it was a huge radio audience and no matter what the papers do to it, his sin-

cerity did shine through to those who listened.) And also justified as a wife, for I struggled over that speech—technically bind-
ing it together, smoothing it (this was only external and superficial), but most of all writing out what I wanted him to say
about himself—all that is so true about himself and that he
never says:

"I am not animated by hate . . ." etc.

It is so very rare that one can *really* help the people one
loves. And the morning in the tent I wrote out—in desperation,
feeling passionately it must be said—the paragraph on him and
he rejected it as playing to the crowd, as "letting your pen run
away with your mind"—I was profoundly discouraged, feeling
"I've done what I can and I *cannot* help him."

Tuesday, October 14th

At night Mother calls. Con has a little girl [Elisabeth Morgan]
and all is well. I suppose she wanted a boy for Aubrey. But two
sisters are lovely.

Friday, October 17th

This has been a rather unhappy day. Soeur Lisi's last with us.

At night after supper (which *was not* a great success—I had
tried to have pigs' knuckles and sauerkraut for Soeur Lisi, a
favorite dish; Helen couldn't get pigs' knuckles and had got
pickled pigs' feet instead, was going to serve *them* with the
sauerkraut). I go up and talk to Soeur Lisi, give her a present
and a pin of my own that I bought in Paris that happy winter,
for I knew Paris meant much to her, too. And I talked to her
about her going home and her rightness in following her intuition about things. And about her life and ours, how we might
meet again in Europe, and of all she had done for the children.
It was nice and close and I feel better now about her going and
she, too, I think, felt happier.

Saturday, October 18th

Soeur Lisi off early—her face swollen with tears, and an unbe-
coming hat on her smoothly parted lovely little head. Jon wants
her to see the tree he has cut down, so they run off together up

the road to the lake. My last sight of Soeur Lisi and so typical of her—joining Jon in what he is doing.

I will never find anyone else with that combination—so "old and gay." Like a child and yet with the wisdom and maturity of Europe. My last tie with Europe, with France, goes with her. She knew how I felt about it and felt the same.

Saturday, October 25th

Then followed a long week of having the children to myself. It was a wonderful week, though very hard work. This was partly because I was not used to it and partly because I had a bad cold. I found I was working very hard all day—a tight schedule—not only doing Soeur Lisi's work but also some of Hilma's: the diapers, the woolens, and the beds. It was peculiarly satisfying, not only being so close, so very close to the children, which is sheer joy—Land telling me every thought as he came back from school, running into my arms, Jon taking care of the two younger children with me. And the wordless communication of Anne on her hands and knees, bringing me with a smile a tiny leaf or shred of wool she had picked up off the ground, or sitting up straight saying "Da!?" mischievously before she put something in her mouth that she shouldn't!

But also the satisfaction of hard physical work—learning how to do it, learning how to make every minute count.

I found, oddly enough, now I was doing all the work every day, a complete lack of that frustration I used to find when I took the children for one day a week, when I was always trying to solve something else in my mind.

Now *all* my mind and strength went to this and it was like turning on a great current.

Webb House, Seven Gates Farm, Thursday, November 6th

The last two weeks have gone into an orgy of moving, planning, arranging. I cannot stop even to read in the evenings, much less write. It must be perfect first, not only in looks but in convenience. I want it to *run* well (I didn't think I had this much of my mother in me!).

The children and nurse have a separate wing. The nursery is really theirs, like the nursery of the old house in Englewood. In fact the whole house reminds me of the old house in Englewood—its comfort, workability, and homely Victorian substantialness. I feel like my mother in the days when we were growing up—matronly, and suddenly the center of a large family. I feel I am acting out the dream I might have had as a child of what I would be like grown up, with a house full of children. I am playing "Mother," playing "house," playing "married." But where is the real me? It is completely buried. I want to stop being a good housekeeper (it is a satisfaction to have done it). I want to go back again to being a *bad* housekeeper and a *good* writer!

C. sees what I have turned into and he wants to help me back. (Though he is sweet and full of astonishment at what I have done to the house.) He has set up the tent, banked it around with earth for warmth, cut branches for a view, carried out the stove. Now I am determined to come every morning to the tent, willy-nilly, and stay there, even if it brings no results.

C. himself is in the midst of his autobiography (*The Spirit of St. Louis*), which absorbs him passionately. He worked all through the moving in the bare living room at the big desk I had put down first of all—for him. (It, at least, is perfect!) I watch him, enviously remembering that fever of absorption with which one works when one has struck a vein of gold. But can you do it and be interrupted—even at lunch—by children and household problems? Wasn't this why I was always so frustrated on the nurse's day off at Lloyd Neck, because it was interruption? It demanded a different person. I had to put the writer and dreamer away and become the practical aware immediate mother-housekeeper. The transition from one to the other is terribly difficult, perhaps impossible. Can one be a good mother and write? Can one be a writer for half the day? I oscillate between the two. In Englewood (*North to the Orient*) I wrote but was a terrible mother-wife. At Lloyd Neck (*Wave of the Future*) I wrote and was a good wife, but not a good mother or housekeeper. At Illiec I was a good wife, an excellent mother and housekeeper, and not a writer at all.

The Colgate House [the first summer] was the best. The household was running smoothly for that brief period, I felt secure about the children with Soeur Lisi. It was beautiful—free, and lovely weather. I had a separate house to work in. It was only for a few months—then the war, the winter, moving, having a baby broke upon us.

Perhaps that summer will mark the high spot of my life. I feel now it had a certain freshness, innocence, youth, and ease that we will never recapture. The world has grown old.

We must not expect perfection any more but work in the teeth of the storm—in snatches of time and ease—in the twenty minutes's. It means disciplining my self—my two selves.

Margot comes over after lunch. We talk all afternoon in front of my fire. She is moving out West with the family. There is a lump in my throat to feel I shall no longer have the exquisite luxury of sharing day-to-day life with her. Oh, I shall miss her.

Wednesday, November 19th

Work rather uninspired on "Women and a Career." I feel like the cartoon in the *Saturday Review* of the woman sitting in the middle of terrible disorder—dishes piled up, unwashed floor littered, cat into the spilled milk, baby crawling underfoot, while she, serene in the center, is typing away at an article for *Good Housekeeping*.

Supper alone with C.! Wonderful! And a quiet evening in the big room which I begin to relax in and survey with satisfaction. The cheap curtains, the bedspread over the sofa—the Vlaminck on the mantel, C. at the desk, I on the chaise longue, writing letters to the music of WQXR. Very nice.

Thursday, November 20th

A letter from Sue which says she has heard from Galantière[1] that St.-Ex. is neither De Gaulle nor Vichy though he has been accused of both. Galantière "implied he was too great a man to

[1] Lewis Galantière, friend and translator of Saint-Exupéry.

be violently involved in either side," and that he was "not animous" toward anyone and still in the center. I am glad he is there and only pray he can stay there.

C. suddenly decides to pitch the tent out on the bluff. It is very windy and flaps too much for me to sleep, but is surprisingly snug and comfortable. C. says he sleeps very well after getting to sleep.

Saturday, November 22nd

It is lovely to wake in a tent and see it get incandescent with sunlight and then know from the inside what kind of a day it is!

Very tired in the evening. Write Mother and correct old letters, the kind of thing I have learned to do when depressed.

I am—this is at the bottom of my unhappiness—angry and hurt by two references in the paper to C. (in *Common Sense* and Irwin Edman's new book) "going around the country flaunting a martyr complex," and reference to his "hard-boiled insults to idealism." So utterly untrue of him. I mind deep within me. I think: How badly he has expressed himself, how inadequately I have helped him, and how basely (chiefly this) they have abused him that such a picture of him can be given to fair men.

He is so "idealistic," so far into the future, so far beyond these nose-on-their-face idealists that it will take a generation or two before the average run of "idealists" catch up with him.

And a martyr complex! It is *I* who have the martyr complex —for him—not he. There is no rancor in him and no self-pity.

Sunday, November 23rd

A hard driving rain all day. After lunch all take naps. I, too, but I discover that the puppy is gone. And all afternoon (we whistle, hunt) with the wind howling and the rain driving in great gray sheets across the bleak slopes outside, I fall again into that abyss of "something is lost." He is lost—where is he? It is lonely, it is cold and wet. He wants me—where is he—he is lost. It is the bottomless pit.

C. says he is probably asleep in some dry corner and goes off for oysters with Jon. Land and Anne and I sit in my room with a fire. Anne sits on my big bed, plays with balloons and little toys. I fix up a "jiffy tent" (painted muslin, on a card table) for Land. He is enchanted! Altogether a very successful afternoon. Especially as I go out before dark for a last look for Kelpie. I call and whistle around the house and look under the porch with a flashlight. At a hole near the porch steps a little black head sticks out. I tempt him out with raw meat and we all rejoice. C. comes back with oysters—which Jon has for supper—and says, "Well, who was worried about him?"

Monday, November 24th

C. and I get into an argument *à propos* of an article in the paper, a speech of a rabbi at a Jewish conference in which he said that the first thing that would have to be done at the peace table after the war was that a large indemnity would have to be paid to the Jews for their sufferings. Also speaks about having a piece of land of their own—which I am sympathetic with.

C. takes me up on "a land of their own" which I say *must* be set aside for them. He says it isn't as simple as all that. Whose land are you going to take? From whom? All the good land is taken. I agree it isn't an easy solution but even a partial solution, even a bad solution, is better than no solution at all. He says of course it is and must be worked at. But he is very pessimistic of its being solved without great suffering. It is this pessimism or realism, this unpleasant truth, perhaps, that I rebel so against. I can't bear it. And yet C. is more of an optimist than I, usually. He talks, however, absolutely the way I feel: that it isn't only what happens to the Jews but what happens to the people who Jew-bait. How it degrades a man or a nation. War is clean, but this other is disease. There are some good things in war but there is nothing good in this. I feel just this way and feel relieved that we are together on it.

Monday, December 8th

Back in the tent after a week in New York. A week that has completely vanished now in limbo—part of a world that is gone.

It was rather a gay week. New York in a pre-Christmas spirit, lovely weather, walking down the streets at misty lighted five o'clock with my Paris coat on and my Renoir hat and curls and no one recognizing me!

Seeing Con—in between her social Fight for Freedom teas. Mother is up to her neck in it and my beloved Mrs. Hand, too—whom I saw anyway and had a lovely afternoon with.

The shops, of course, were nauseating with the richness of material attractions. What appalled me was not so much the unawareness of people skating about on this thin surface of materialism as the insincere attempt to gild the materialism with patriotic motives, especially in advertising. "Be brave with Diamonds," "Defense of good taste—Buy So-and-so's Ale." "For the service of America . . ."

Some lovely pictures—Bernard Lamotte's Paris. So real, so damp, so gray—a sky ripe and pink with snow, soft whites and blacks of shabby buildings in Paris—that you could smell the pavements. And the "Journey of the Magi" by Sassetta. A ballet with Mother and Con.

And nurses—one after another until my mouth went dry—talking, liking them, trying to read them, endless conversations on the telephone and dreaming of them at night very tired, wondering if any of them would do to put my tired head on their shoulder.

I finally took an old Breton peasant woman very temporarily (while I am trying to get a young Finn). She had the earth quality and was gay and I hoped would do though not perfect at all.

On Sunday I drove up to Woods Hole—a beautiful day, clear and cold and a tearing wind.

Listening to the radio in the early afternoon I heard the news —that Japan had attacked Pearl Harbor, Manila, Guam Island, Wake Island. It is the knell of the old world. All army officers all over the U.S. ordered into uniform. Espionage Act invoked. (If C. speaks again they'll put him in prison, I think immediately.) I listen all afternoon to the radio. I am listening to the

Philharmonic, a beautiful concerto of Brahms. But it is interrupted every ten minutes with bulletins about the war. This
is what life is going to be from now on, I think.

Arrive at Woods Hole one and a half hours early. Sit in
front of the harbor and watch the sunset. Even our faraway
island will be touched.

The deck hand on the boat says to me, "Well, I suppose we
asked for it—but we've certainly got it."

Arrive home about 6:30. Jon and Land run out to me in
night clothes excitedly and C. Also Thor and Kelpie.

C. says, "Have you heard the news?"

"Yes."

It was a confused morning. I take the children to school. Land
telling me the Christmas story. "And the Angel said, 'Fear not,
New York City' "! How did he get that? ("New-born Prince"?)

When I get back C. is listening to the radio reports of what
has happened in the East, more and more places attacked.
Churchill's speech (anticipating less aid from U.S.). Rumors
there are two battleships sunk in the Pacific. That Germany
and Italy have declared war. That Pétain has handed the French
fleet over to the Germans.

C. and I go out for a walk in between long-distance calls from
Chicago, New York, etc. C. says it is the most important event
in our lives. I try to visualize just what it will mean. War—
revolution—poverty—suffering? Where will we be thrown
in the maelstrom—our private lives? Our last four months of
peace are over.

We listen to the President's declaration of a state of war over
the radio at lunch at the table. There is a lot of fanfare and excitement about the dramatic occasion and yet I feel chiefly a desperate
lack of dignity, lack of seriousness, lack of humility about the
whole scene. The President does say, "with God's help" we
will beat the enemy. But you feel he is pretty sure he can count
on it! All the blustering and cheers and excitement ("We'll
show them!" is the attitude) are to me inappropriate and un-

mindful of the significance of the colossal step we are taking. (It was like the cheers and speeches before a football game, as C. said.)

Anne, sitting rosy and fair-haired in her highchair, had to be kept quiet by being fed one grape after another! I looked at her and wondered if she would see the end of this. Land, whom I asked to keep quiet during the speech, tiptoed up to me afterwards, when the shouting (on the radio) had died, and whispered in my ear: "And more and more angels came and they said, 'Fear not' . . . !"

America First has decided to cancel all meetings. C.'s speech is brilliant and one of his very best. I am crushed it was not given but it is impossible now. He gives out a statement.[1] Very good, I think.

These four months have been close and happy family life even if I have accomplished little. That in itself is precious and may be rare in the future.

Tuesday, December 9th

C. and I listen to the President speak at 10. It is a very dramatic speech, well written and given (in spite of some bald contradictions. Why, if that long list of countries had been attacked "without warning," were we so appallingly ill-prepared in the East as we seem to have been by the damage done?). Evidently things have gone very badly in the Pacific. "Up to now *all* the news is bad." He implied that it would be a long hard war. He did it very well.

"The Star-Spangled Banner" is played after the speech. It is very moving. I feel as if all I believed *was* America, all memories of it, all history, all dreams of the future were marching gaily toward a precipice—and unaware, unaware.

Wednesday, December 10th

The British have lost a great battleship and a destroyer, the *Prince of Wales* and the *Repulse*. Our navy badly hit also.

[1] See Introduction, p. xxvi.

Japan still getting the best of it. Talk of investigation of navy. How were we caught so off guard? The interventionists are blaming it all on us. And Fight for Freedom has come out with a gloating exultant full-page ad, starting with a huge headline: "It's America First now"! This makes me sick.

Thursday, Friday, Saturday, and Sunday

Friday morning we discover at breakfast from Pat,[1] who heard it on the radio, that yesterday Germany and Italy declared war on us and Congress declared war back—with only one dissenting voice.[2] It is no shock. So now we are completely in it.

Saturday, in the evening, I at last have a chance to hear what C. has been thinking and arguing out in his mind. He wants terribly to get to work—constructive work—almost with his hands, work in his craft again, have his contribution count—his experience, his technique, his training. But in a kind of down-to-earth way. Nothing ballyhoo, no figurehead work. It must be *real*—a real help. We go over all the possibilities. I agree absolutely with him.

And I—what can I do? It looks as though it will all be cut out for me, for I think I am starting another child. I want another one, of course, but it seems just a little soon—physically and mentally. I feel as if I had just got over the last one. And I half dread going back under the lid pregnancy puts on me—three or four months ill, five months ugly and heavy and stupid and tired, and five months tied to the baby nursing it. The burden of the war, coming worries, conflicts, hates seem heavy enough. One should be in one's best health to carry them, to understand them and not be downed by them.

Monday, December 15th

Mlle Olivier arrives. She is genial, gay, comfortable, and thinks the place beautiful. She gets down on the floor immediately

[1] Patricia Troy, a new secretary.

[2] The "nay" vote was cast by Representative Jeannette Rankin, a Republican from Montana and long a pacifist.

with the children. I see her running out on the lawn with Jon and Land, a ragged old fur cap pulled over her gray hair. She is an old *"grandmère,"* and admits it. C. says she is as Breton as she could possibly be!

Monday, December 22nd

According to the papers the Germans are still in full flight from the Russians. Is it a strategic withdrawal to a winter line or is it a retreat? Despite Communism there is something very thrilling about it from a traditional Russian point of view. I think of *War and Peace*—Napoleon and Kutuzov.

1942

Seven Gates Farm, Vineyard Haven, Massachusetts, February 2nd
Dear Sue,

I should like to see you but I am underground myself. I cannot get up yet except for an hour or two in the morning and any extra excitement makes me ill. I feel I shall never write again nor do I wish to publish anything under my name. And I am discouraged about C. since it now looks as though he will not be able to do any real work in this period or be of any real use. The Administration were evidently much embarrassed by Arnold's having given out C.'s offer to help.[1] And they had to say *something*. I do not blame them too much for not wanting him in the army. That is perhaps only fair. But it looks as though the Administration were going to prevent him from taking *any* job with *any* commercial company connected with *any* part of the war effort. The companies are all anxious to get him but they come back with the same answer: The Administration frowns on it.

DIARY   *February 18th*
"If illness is not a repairing process I will make it so. . . ." I have been in bed almost two months. Very ill the first part of that time, unable to lift my head from the pillow; I could do nothing but lie flat and listen to WQXR all day and think, think out long conversations or just dream foolishly. This was the period when I felt so keenly the truth of the words of the old French letter—*"Le coeur plus ferme accepte les obstacles, les chagrins, les dégoûts même"*! ("A steadier heart accepts the

[1] After the start of the war, C. A. L. offered his services to General Henry H. Arnold, Chief of the Air Corps, 1938–40. Throughout World War II, Arnold was Chief of the U.S. Army Air Force.

hindrances, the sorrows, the disgusts even. . . .") How well he knew they are the hardest things to bear. As I said one day in protest to Mrs. Loines[1]: "In sorrow, or in pain even, the spirit is sharpened, more alive—but in sickness like this it just dies. I am just an inert mass of clay, imprisoned in a disagreeable body, with no hope of getting through to the spirit."

She said gently that I was confusing mind with spirit and that the body was also an instrument of the spirit and perhaps equally important, and that perhaps I was meant only to think then, "How nice and flat this bed is, how good it is to breathe— like taking a glass of water!"

Then getting better slowly. It has been very long and slow and so boring. There were, even so, lovely things in that time —C.'s happiness (at my having a child) and his help and strength to me. The children's love and gaiety, giving back to me, it seemed, everything I ever gave to them. Land, when I said I couldn't read to him, "Then *I'll* read to *you!*" Sitting out in the sunshine, a bird at my window, music—especially Bach. And an article like Saint-Exupéry's in the *Atlantic,* touching through to the spirit at last.

Seven Gates Farm, February 26th

Dearest Margot,

Your beautiful letter answered mine so acutely. I still feel terribly hurt when I see, as inevitably I do, my words "Wave of the Future" and my name taken as the synonym for passive acceptance of totalitarianism and all its evils. I flinch and build walls to keep from being hurt. There are times when the walls melt altogether, talking to you or your mother or hearing Bach, or reading a poem or a prayer—the words of a Father Zoshima or a Saint Francis, the words of Pascal—these things can put me in grace.

I have just read the last installment of Saint-Exupéry's book (*Flight to Arras*) in the *Atlantic*. It seems to me the expression of a wholly undivided man. It carries in it all the anguish of our age, personal and general, it cuts itself off from none of it,

[1] Mother of Margot Morrow, who lived on Martha's Vineyard.

it rejects nothing, not even sin. It carries it all, like a Saint Christopher. I was very moved, and felt—irrelevantly and suddenly, at the end of it—"I am forgiven."

I do not, of course, mean this in any personal way. The point is that somehow in the act of reading that beautiful credo of spirit I was forgiven. I was readmitted into a company from which I had been banned. I was no longer exiled.

This is, of course, only the old religious experience of being put "in grace." One should, I know, get it directly from God, from meditation or prayer, with no intermediary of poet, writer, or musician. But I find myself unable—except rarely—to do this. The language and forms of various religions so often put me off. My Sunday-school pictures of Christ have gotten in my way, the memories of the pews, the ugly and unmystical ethics of those Boy-Scout-leader ministers, prayers before horsehair sofas. And the more orthodox faiths, though they appeal to me with their mysticism, again put me off by the language—those capital letters, those blood and wine symbols, those rosaries and colored statues of the Madonna. They offend me and estrange me—just as the language of the modern revivalist groups does with its "quiet times," "been changed," "absolute purity" and "guidance." So also do the Eastern religions. I get confused and dizzy with those "shining ones" and "karmas," etc.

The trouble is really with translation in every sense, literal and otherwise. The spirit and the great spiritual masters and writings should only be translated in pure crystal. One keeps looking at them through cheap colored glass. The words of Christ are crystalline, of course.

After reading the St.-Ex. article and making C. read it, I said somewhat mistily, "It's wonderful, Charles, for the first time in weeks I feel that my tired, ugly and disagreeable body just doesn't matter at all!"

"But I think that's *dreadful!*" protested C. warmly. "And I think it was awful the way he talked about his body. After all, his body had taken him around faithfully all those years and in the end he just threw it away without a word of thanks, like an old shoe. If *I'd* been his body I'd have gotten chicken pox just to get even with him!" And I had to laugh with a kind of special delight at him and admit there was something to it and I had got rather far off the ground.

C. wants to know when this letter is going to be done?! Now. I guess I miss you so much. Last summer seems so far away and next summer too. I don't know where we'll be. C. has no job. That was just a pretend job on paper[1] to satisfy the talk. He is still looking for one but all doors so far are shut by the Administration. And I think it hypocritical, to say the least, to pretend they've given him a job and get credit for being generous when they have actually done just the opposite.

DIARY   *March 3rd*
Beginning to get out of bed again after two more weeks of sickness—flu this time.

Since Christmas—since I went to bed—the whole world seems to have changed. Manila has fallen and all of the Philippines except Bataan peninsula and Corregidor. Singapore has fallen (the British Empire). The British have again lost all they rewon in Libya. And now the Dutch East Indies are beginning to go. Submarine warfare has increased with astounding intensity. The shipping crisis for England is evidently very acute.

The dissatisfaction in England broke after the fall of Singapore and the escape of the German warships safe through the Channel, home. But Churchill blamed the loss of Singapore on Pearl Harbor.

March 5th
Yesterday I got from the bookshop St.-Ex.'s *Flight to Arras,* already read in the *Atlantic.* Looking carelessly at the back flap I see that they are advertising his other book, evidently with my preface now tactfully removed from it, my name and my praise carefully expunged, lest it hurt the sales of this book. I do not blame either the author or the publisher for this very

---

[1] The War Department had announced that C. A. L. was working on a "project" of "vital interest to the government," a statement C. A. L. describes in his *Wartime Journals,* p. 585, as both amazing and confusing.

natural reaction. I would do it myself were it in my power, and, in fact, did as much as I could in refusing to write a review of the new book lest it injure a writer still untouched by political controversy and smearing.

But this little item, absurd as it is, was a final pinprick added to my accumulated unhappiness about my book and its misuse. This man, too (quite naturally), believes I am bowing abjectly to an "inevitable" wave of totalitarianism. A coward and a defeatist—part of the world of "non-being" that he rejects. It is too much.

C. came upstairs and found me. He does not say I am absurd, he does not scold me for being weak. He did not try to argue with me. He looked at the book flap and said only, very gently, "I know—you have had so much—so much, Anne." He said it would change and I would only be the better for it. He spoke of my book and the final judgment he felt it would get. He spoke of his father's position—that was why he did not mind this so much, he had seen it all before. All these comforting things I did not very much believe, nor did I desire any comfort from them.

But I somehow got immense comfort simply from the fact of his accepting and understanding what I felt.

March 12th

C. is away—again looking around for work. I am hurt for him when he gets another telephone call from a company which wants him but cannot afford to take him because of Administration disapproval. And I feel that his exclusion from the world of Aviation is much more unfair than mine from the world of books. He is not bitter or discouraged, though, and it does not seem to affect his daily life or what he gives to others, for he radiates a kind of health and gaiety and steadiness. It is a constant marvel—and lesson—to me.

At night a letter from C. chiefly on business. I always forget how little of him gets across in a letter. All that warmth and charm and life that you feel when he walks into a room. All I can do is to try to squeeze it out of the last little phrase, "I wish you were here." I remember then the shy reserved pent-up-inside boy he was when I first met him.

When C. was last here he gave me the draft of his manuscript on the flight to Paris.[1] He said it was very rough and had to be entirely *rewritten* and a great deal filled out (not merely corrected) and he hesitated about letting me see it.

I read it all in one night, unable to put it down. It was so vivid and so moving that I had no words with which to tell him how I felt. I had *lived through* the intensely felt experience of another person, not merely read it. I was dazzled and unsteady after it —not on the earth. I felt humble, too, after reading, realizing, in my blood almost, what this man had been through. I had never been through anything like it myself (except the experience of having a child perhaps).

I told him it was the great book of a great exploit and would go down in time as that. Nothing that I can think of has ever been done like it before. I told him it was better than St.-Ex. Though what I mean by that it is difficult to say. It is not, of course, better "written." But it is almost better because of that. The glaze has been removed. And the glaze, no matter how beautiful, separates one from life. C.'s story *is* life—as much life as he is. Words do not seem to get between him and life. They are only there to translate life. I think of that time when I recognized him in the sky by the turn of a wing. There were no words between him and the wing. They were one—as his hand is his. And the writing is like this. It has the burning intensity, the integrity, the love of life that C. has.

I am terribly grateful he has written it. It is there for the future. The hoarded gold of what he really is.

Vineyard Haven, April 2nd

Dear Con,

Is Aubrey *still* away [on a wartime trip to England]? For weeks now I have imagined him back. It is really dreadful to

[1] This was a first draft of *The Spirit of St. Louis,* later published by Charles Scribner's.

wait, or to live in suspense, any kind of suspense. It just isn't living at all but a curious "timeout" period that doesn't seem to count.

Besides, living without one's husband is so curious. I am just beginning to feel it. I am reconciled to the Ford job[1] since it seems C. can really be vitally useful there and also since he got the army's permission to work there and can help them (the army) a good deal by keeping each in touch with the other. Altogether it seems a very good move all around, and I am happy about it. But I feel I shall *have* to move out there. Unattractive as Detroit is and difficult as it is to move in the middle of having a baby (*you* did it!) I don't think we can live this divided life (think of the women who are doing it!). If it were laid down as a necessity of course one could. But to sit in Martha's Vineyard (by choice) while C. works in Detroit— I don't think I can. I suppose that means having the baby there and leaving my beloved Dr. Hawks. Anyway, I shan't move immediately and it depends on what things are like there and how often he can get back.

But when you are separated, the short weekends in between are too precious, like those premarriage times together. The sense of urgency throws the whole thing out of kilter. The web is gone—is broken. It is no longer marriage. It is something else. Being a mistress, maybe. (An unenviable lot, I always thought!) I wonder if our lives are going to contain a lot of these separations from now on? It may be.

When C. was here for three days we talked madly of the old problems of where to get a home. I don't feel I can pick out our "little gray home in the West" at just this point either. But I look at you with pride and amazement (Con did it!). I think you lose faith in yourself while having a baby. At least, you lose faith in your ability to do anything except superbly to have babies! Maybe that is as it should be.

[1] C. A. L. had been asked by Henry Ford in March to come to Detroit and help with their aviation program. See Introduction, p. xxvii.

Today is the real Easter morning. Yesterday was overcast and chilly. This morning is still, warm, newly awakened. One walks out into it like a flower just opened.

The world *sounds* like spring, like summer, this morning. So still, so perfect, so whole is the morning that one can hear all the small sounds dropped into it. One hears superhumanly—like God. The birds, the peepers, the waves—but also a cart somewhere rumbling over a farm road, a steamer's whistle from miles away. One feels as if one could hear worms turning in the earth, and also guns across the sea.

When I was young I always felt a morning like this meant a promise of something wonderful—for me, perhaps. Good things happening I did not know of—love in someone's heart far away from me, or the success of some venture of my own. I thought —quite literally—it was a sign from heaven. The person who was ill would get well. He who was lost would be found. Or maybe something wonderful was happening for the world— some new spirit blooming. How could hate and cruelty and evil be "true" on a morning like this? The morning was a "sign."

I still believe it is a "sign," but not for anything good happening to me or the world, anything specific. The love is not blooming in someone's heart. The ventures fail. The one who is sick, dies, and the one who is lost is never found. Hate and cruelty and evil are still rampant, war goes on.

And yet it is a sign. It is a sign that in spite of these things beauty still exists and goes on side by side with horror. That there *is* love and goodness and beauty and spirit in the world— always. This is only one of the times when it is clothed in flesh —in the flesh of a spring morning. We doubt and we need the sign in order to believe. A morning like this is the morning of Resurrection—when we see and believe, "Lo, I am with you alway, even unto the end of the world."

April 8th

C. has come and gone again. The three days when he was here were so full and intense it seems they weighed more than the days before or after. And it is difficult to record them. They had that kind of premarriage intensity and preciousness that is difficult to capture. With the dull pain of departure—like a threatening thunderstorm—over an afternoon. The light is more beautiful on an afternoon like that, the green more green, the earth more vivid. But it is an unreal light.

Those days are not marriage. They are being in love, but not the casual give and take, the wonderful blending of silence and communication, sharing and solitariness, being bored and being stimulated, disputes and agreements, the everyday and the extraordinary, the near and the far—that wonderful blending that makes for the incredible richness, variety, harmoniousness, and toughness of marriage.

Marriage is tough, because it is woven of all these various elements, the weak and the strong. "In love-ness" is fragile for it is woven only with the gossamer threads of beauty. It seems to me absurd to talk about "happy" and "unhappy" marriages. Real marriages are both at the same time. But if they are *real* marriages they always have this incredible *richness* for which one is eternally joyful and grateful.

It is strange, I can conceive of "falling in love" over and over again. But "marriage," this richness of life itself, I cannot conceive of having again—or with anyone else. In this sense "marriage" seems to me indissoluble.

It would be impossible to cover all we talked of. I am sorry, as it seems to me so vital, and almost to carry the seeds of all our life and (real conversations do this) our problems. But I can only jot down to remember and think about.

Of C.'s job—working in Ford's new bomber plant. I get the sense that he feels it is new work and challenging and absorbing, and this is good.

But he is thinking of me, now his own war-future is temporarily settled. What will my war-future be? Shall I stay here with the children and write? Or shall I move to Detroit and join in his life there?

Another husband would assume that I would come with him

to Detroit, but he sees my side too clearly. He wants so much for me. He wants me to live my own life. He wants this so passionately that it angers him when he sees anything frustrating it. Household duties, cooks that can't cook, nurses that won't leave me alone. Friends and family obligations which take my time. Depressions which rob me of confidence. I think almost all our quarrels arise from this passionate desire of his to see me freed to fulfill what there is in me.

And to all these questions what do I say? I cannot give quick pat answers. The questions go too deep. I know I am naturally passive—or at least seem to be—am inclined to let life come, rather than go to meet it. C. is impatient for the answers. I can only work them out slowly—with much quiet and solitude and patience and no sense of urgency. How explain to a man that when a woman is expecting a child, that is the only question she sees clearly and the only answer she can give. One cannot see beyond the child—or only with great difficulty. One can force oneself to give *intellectual* answers—but the only answer one really FEELS is the child.

My intellectual answers are—No, that I cannot sit in an ivory tower during the war, that I want to share his life and home, if I can. That my present war-work is having a child. That I believe my writing must always be "marginal" in its attack. But that life itself should be participating. That one can "participate" in giving and caring for children, in feeding and nourishing and loving one's husband and home.

If I can build the right kind of nourishing home for him in Detroit I want to go there. If he can get more from escaping here to sea and beauty and peace and quiet, then I want to stay here, with perhaps occasional trips to Detroit on my part.

When it comes to writing, the questions go too deep for intellectual answers. I must, as Rilke said, "live the questions first" and then perhaps someday come to the answers. But this spiritual pilgrimage I cannot yet explain to anyone and it is not yet clear. I feel very isolated, very alone in it. But I find parallels to it in the thoughtful and the sensitive, the artists, everywhere. It is in Auden's long poem[1] and again in *Flight to Arras*.

I have not yet written out the afternoon with Sue—four hours of conversation after weeks and weeks of thought alone. It was a lovely day. We touched so much, deeply and lightly.

Sue and I talked about Americans and Romanticism, of books and of the war, of mysticism and of nurses, of wrinkles, of gardening and of marriage, of cooks and of eternity, of children. It was very satisfying. The thread that has spread out the most in my mind is Americans and Romanticism.

Almost every young person is a Romantic Idealist. Certainly I was—and am still, in a sense. There has always been a "dream figure" in my life—not always a person, of course. But some people learn to accept life and that it is better than "the dream." At least I got married and have had children.

I told C., speaking of this conversation (we were talking of idealizing people), and C. said, "You can't meet your heroes if you feel that way about them." And I said, "Well, I don't know —I didn't lose *my* dream by marrying it!" He said, "That's the nicest thing you ever said to me."

But I said it the wrong way round really. For I didn't marry my "dream." C. wasn't my "dream." I never idealized him before I met him. It wasn't the hero I loved in him. It was the man— the man who has never disappointed me. I had my "dreams," too, very different from C. That was what all the struggle was about, giving up my "dreams" for this flesh-and-blood man— whom I loved, God knew.

I sometimes feel it is the one thing I deserve credit for, the one thing I am intensely proud of, that I had the courage and the wisdom to give up my "dream" for real life, to realize that "life" was better than "dreams" and that C. was life.

TO C. A. L.   *April 8th*
I have put back the Chartres picture in the tent and go there every morning. There is a beautiful medieval Adam and Eve

[1] "New Year Letter (January 1, 1940)."

257

I have up and am anxious to show you. It is all marriage. Adam has lightly hold of Eve's wrist. And Eve has her face turned toward him. Her other hand, very lightly, rests on her body as if she were feeling a child move within her. I hardly noticed all this the first time I looked at it. It has all come out from looking at it. I thought this morning it was very symbolical. Woman *looks* at the present but she *touches* the future.

Is all this un-real-y far away from a Ford bomber plant? It must be. We miss you.

Sunday, April 12th. Train to New York

Dear C.,

I really hate your being away. How do apparently happily married people manage to live away from each other so much of the time? (And lots do.) There is no place to rest—not even to rest a hand. Though Anne's silky head will do.

I have seen more of Pat (whom I like better all the time), which has been nice for me—and her, too, I think. We have been talking about G., a regular Dostoevsky character. I keep realizing all the time that suffering isn't enough for true learning, for true understanding, for true vision. I used to think it was. "One learns by suffering." One doesn't, though. One learns through suffering *and* beauty. One *alone* won't do it. You've got to have both. It's hard to know just how to get suffering *and* beauty, because though suffering is there all the time, beauty is a gift and comes from the outside. You can't call it to you, or even seek it. It is an act of grace. All you can do is not to shut yourself away from it—not to close up. You must remain open—vulnerable.

You know, I wish you would drop me a postcard and let me know you are getting these letters, if you are. I hate dropping them into the well and never hearing the splash. I know you can't write, haven't time, and don't easily. But you could buy some penny postcards and have your secretary print on them, like the Smith College Registrar, "Letters 14 and 15 received OK," or even "I like your letters!" I don't know, you see, I've never written you before. I'm not really grieving about it. It's just a suggestion. And you don't have to bother for the next week or ten days as I'll be in New York and busy and won't miss you so much.

You don't want to fly to New York for a weekend with me? No, I suppose not. Englewood is not too much inducement.

Dearborn, Michigan, April 10th

Dear Anne:

Your letters both came in the mail yesterday afternoon. Reading them last night brought keenly to me the differences between the life we have been leading—our life, an independent life—and this conventional, artificial, and industrial life I have begun. It made me realize how far from this life I have travelled since I married you those long—those short—years ago. And it made me realize, too, how little desire I have to go back and to immerse myself again in the life I left at that time.

It is not that I find no interest in this work or that there is no opportunity or that my associates are not the kind of men I like. It is quite the contrary; there is unlimited interest and opportunity, and I have never seen a finer group of men in any organization. It is all too easy to lose oneself in the unlimited scope of war and a great industry. No, it is something else that I feel. It is the fact that largely through you I have touched and glimpsed something so much greater than this world of industrial power and whirring efficiency that all this fades to unimportance in comparison. Great four-engine bombers pouring out from the production lines of the largest aircraft factory in the world do not seem objects worthy of the effort put upon them—not that I am so greatly opposed to war—you know how I feel about that—but all this that I see done, for one reason or another, which I have no time to try to explain, even if I could, seems to me a sort of perversion of life and even of war itself. I feel that I am wasting time, that I want to get it over with and get into something that lies beyond—something quite vague and indefinite, but something I know is there.

When your letters came I had great happiness in reading them and the diary entry—and then this other feeling came over me for when I was thinking about what I would write in answer I suddenly realized that I hadn't time to answer them at all—at least to answer them as I wanted to, with no limiting clock hands to watch. I lacked the time to think and to write that is one of the things that mean most in life to me. I had had a full day and was scheduled out on the 7:28 American Airlines plane for California. The flight was cancelled on weather. I looked forward to writing today—filled again, but I have found a few minutes just before I must start for the airport. And now I haven't time to finish or even to read what I have written. Fortunately I have packed, and addressed the envelope to you in advance.

You know everything I send with this letter.

C. A. L.

Englewood, Friday evening, April 17th

Dear C.,

It was so strange tonight to get your letter—stuck together, the ink all run blurred, and be intensely moved by it—to lie on my bed resting after a day in town, thinking of you miles away in California, composing an answer in my mind—and then suddenly 20 minutes after reading it, to have them knock on the door to say "Detroit is calling." My first incredulous feeling was, "He *can't* be back," (then in panic) "They must be calling to say the plane has crashed!"

Now the warmth and reality of talking to you has knocked out of my mind what I was going to say in answer to your beautiful letter (beautiful, even if cramped for time, as you said). I have put it in my diary. I felt, after reading it—if my letters can mean that to you, if your letter can give that to me, then separation isn't so terrible. I had been minding—in a very feminine way—feeling you were in such an entirely different world that the things I wrote about and felt could no longer weigh anything in comparison with your world. And I should not understand yours, and we should be separated—spiritually. It is only spiritual separation that frightens me. But your letter answered all my fears. And all the other minor irritations—how shall I decide about the couple? the nurse? the house? etc. without him?—all melted away. It was only in the light of that spiritual separation that they mattered. I felt then, after your letter had joined us again: but of course I can decide about the couple, the nurse, the house, Dr. Hawks. . . . I may make a mistake but it won't matter—because we are not separated.

Good night.

Saturday A.M. I see no reason at the moment why Jon and I cannot go out Thursday or Friday night to Detroit. We'll have Saturday, Sunday, and Monday. Jon, of course, will be in a seventh heaven!

Dearborn, April 28th

Dear Anne:

I am back at my desk in the Inn, looking out over the green lawn and the spring blossoms, with an almost full moon about Bathurst take-off height[1] above the horizon. You are somewhere in Canada, almost exactly an hour out of the Detroit station. I feel as though you had not been here. The leaves are a little larger; there are a few petals from the blossoms on the ground; otherwise everything is exactly the same as it was four nights ago, before you came. What happened to the time between, I do not know—it was *last* night I was sitting here by my window; there could not have been four days between; the hours you were here have slipped through my fingers like water, and are gone. When you are gone, I feel your absence all around me and I am acutely conscious of the passage of time. When you *were* here, I was so surrounded by the warmth and satisfaction of your presence that time slipped by unnoticed behind my back. I was keenly aware of you before you came. I am keenly aware of you now that you are gone. But I cannot make myself aware that you *were here*. Possibly tomorrow, or even next week I may realize it; but now I can only think how little I have saved of your visit. Our search for a house, our discussions of the future,

[1] Reference is to take-off from Bathurst, Africa, on trans-oceanic flight to Brazil 1933 described in *Listen! the Wind*.

all those routine details remain clear and tangible enough. When I think of them, these last four days stand out like posts against the sky. But you—the essence of you—have not remained in that landscape. I think it is because you do not belong there, because the essence of you is not a part of these routine problems of life—it is something far above and far beyond, and when you touch life you leave a feeling of immortality behind, a feeling that is deeper and stronger than the memory of your presence. It is what I meant when I wrote you that you had a touch of divinity in your pen. It is what I have felt ever since I have known you. I feel it more strongly with every year that passes.

After leaving you and Jon at the station, I came back to the Inn planning on reading and studying through the evening; but I found that I had to write this letter, that I had to try to tell you in a letter what I have never been able to tell you quite adequately in words. Not that I have told it adequately here, but I have been able to say more, and say it in a different way, and in so doing to bring you more closely to me, for you seemed farther away in the hour after you left than you were in the days before you came.

With all the love I can send you,

C. A. L.

Seven Gates Farm, Sunday, May 3rd

Dear C.,

Jon and I arrived last night after a long but not too difficult day on the train. I wrote you from the train but now I feel days removed from it. Land and Anne and Mademoiselle met us at the door in the evening sunshine—Land red-cheeked, round-eyed, throwing his arms around me. Anne, sedate, reservedly pleased and *very* pretty in a stiff-starched blue dress and her golden hair curling like an inverted tulip on her shoulders. She ran around me with a kind of prim ladylike sense of form, realizing mildly that this was a stranger she knew and who had some attention due her. She tried her best to imitate Land's frank unconscious joy but succeeded only in being *exceedingly* feminine and coy!

When I saw her I missed you terribly—I mean I felt, Oh, Charles should see her! Charles should be here.

It has been your kind of a day—if only you had been here. Jon spent the morning building a fort out of driftwood on the beach. Land and I went for a "walk." We stopped in the long grass on the hill above the lake on the road to the Leavitts and "played house." Which consisted of my taking a nap in the warm grass while Land woke me up from time to time to feed me moss-salad and wild-rose-haw baked apples.

We had an early supper all together and then a little reading and then good nights and I have been sitting on the porch steps looking at the three pine trees against the sea and sky, looking at wisps of fog rolling in under a faintly pink sky, smelling with each gust of wind the narcissus in the field below me (getting whiter as the evening got darker) and thinking chiefly of you —wondering if you were at your mother's or in that room at Dearborn looking out at the new green of the trees, or in a car in hot traffic.

Now I shall eat an apple, take the dogs out, and go to sleep to the wind which is howling gently—wishing you were here to share the peace of the night's sleep, too.

P.S. I still have not answered your letter. It was a love letter. One does not say "thank you" for a love letter. One thinks only, "Why should I ever ask for anything else if I have this?"

DIARY   *May 13th*

Three weeks or more of what Huxley would call "God-eclipsing activities."

In Detroit with Jon. I spend Monday (Jon stays in Mrs. Lindbergh's garden—both very happy) looking at houses, planning how to fit a four-child family (what—*four!*) into a two-child house. Planning planning planning—with more and more restrictions clamping in on our already restricted lives. Will C. have any release here? Any privacy? Will the children be able to get to school from here? Will the nurse sleep with a child—two children—three children?!

It is *very* hot and tiring. C. says, "I wonder if we are making a mistake," trying to move in the heat of the summer and two months before the baby comes.

Go back finally, still uncertain. C. to see houses if any turn up. Plan to move—if possible—in mid-June. Give up house at Vineyard. Get new nurse. Send Jon to camp, etc.

Seven Gates, May 18th

Dear C.,

I feel always so alive after you have talked to me. It was lovely last night I went to bed happy and heartened.

This morning it is overcast again—it has been for weeks, it seems to me. I don't "count" it as spring when the sun isn't out. I think, it *will* be spring when the sun comes out; how lovely it will be! I thought this morning that it was exactly my attitude on life away from you. It isn't "life" without you, not *my* real life, anyhow. It is funny—I just don't "count" it in the same way: "life" will begin again when I am with Charles. It isn't lack of happiness either exactly. I am hungry without you, but I can be happy—I can be aware always. In fact I cannot turn off awareness.

I know and I face the fact that we may be separate a lot, maybe all summer (because I am not sure it would be wise to *move* to Detroit in mid-July or August. I think *I* could go out, maybe for long stretches, find a house, etc. But to *move* a whole household in the worst heat in the eighth or ninth month of pregnancy might be foolish. However, there are circumstances which could change this).

All this I want to talk over with you. In the meantime things are going well here. We have had delicious meals arranged with a kind of *care* that I didn't realize meant so much to me. I don't mean "fancy cooking." I mean the person who fixed them *cared* about her work and took a pride in it. It smoothed me out the first night to feel it and the household feels easier and happier with it.

I think we can manage all right on the gas, with one or two trips to town a week. And in some ways it is an advantage. I have an *enforced* solitude—that I have always had hitherto to *fight* to get! No old friends of the family or anyone else is going to use gas to come here to see me and I can say I am too restricted to go out—which is true.

Evening. I have just come back from a beautiful walk along the beach and back over the hills—to Mrs. Loines—with Land. It has been like summer—the wind, the sound of the sea, the earth smells. The goodness of the sea breeze which one is not so grateful for in winter and suddenly welcomes in summer. The apple blossoms are out by every gray wall, the oak leaves are only "as big as squirrels' ears," all pink and gold. Lilacs are beginning to bloom heavy and purple and gone wild in clumps through the fields. I have not walked so far since summer, and I thought of you and longed for you.

Seven Gates Farm, May 21st

Dear C.,

This is your day. I think of the first year I knew you—on a May 21st—before we were married. We were in Maine and we sat in front of the fire a long evening and you told me about it. I think, too, of your very wonderful book and when I think of it I feel a deep joy and satisfaction that it is there—like a child. (Yes, I know it is not done, it must be rewritten, but still it is there; even if you never touched it again, it is wonderful and gives something, in words, you have never given before—I am happy about it.) And since I read it I know more what you have been through. I am closer to it and to you.

I wish you were to come this weekend, but I rather doubt you will. It is so beautiful. The lilacs everywhere in great heavy fragrant masses so generous—with leaves and flowers, too. There is an abundance about them. The apple blossoms are full open, and a wisteria at the entrance and birds everywhere—goldfinches dancing on the lawn like winged dandelions. And the chestnut trees are out, the candles very white against the green.

It always reminds me of the night we were married, driving out to Huntington harbor. And of Paris, too.

The household is going smoothly—so smoothly I feel it will crack! I can't believe it. It is wonderful to have a quiet cheerful intelligent face in the kitchen and to find Hilma taking on extra things because "William has taken so much work off me I have a lot more time." I told her to spend it *outside,* not on polishing brasses.

Yesterday afternoon I went over to Mrs. Loines to talk to Miss Roser (the possible nurse) with Jon and Land. She was perceptive about both of them—both physically and mentally, and Land loved her. Mrs. Loines telephoned me this A.M. her reactions. She finds her tolerant, capable, pleasant, and vigorous.

I am taking Anne over this afternoon on her way to the doctor and on Miss Roser's way to the boat. She has not Soeur Lisi's grace and charm, but in many ways I feel she is the best combination of training, capability, calmness, perception, and intelligence we have ever had.

I expect to make the change next week and perhaps all will be sailing smoothly before you next come home—if you come next weekend.

At any rate I feel you *might* turn up in the near future and that makes me feel festive!

Seven Gates Farm, May 26th

Dear C.,

I felt so heartened and hopeful last night after talking to you. It has lasted all day—with a burst of energy.

I was, of course, torn with curiosity last night—hence all the questions. I am quite excited about the house and the Bloomfield Hills area—I asked about it first because it looked very beautiful from the pictures and also because I had a vague memory of hearing about the Cranbrook schools and it being a modern artistic center outside of Detroit. Carl Milles (Swedish sculptor) I think lives there. And there is a sculpture school there, too. I had thought of it however as a very isolated place with no town or facilities nearby—an isolated colony of interesting people. That was why I kept asking you last night about transportation, schools, doctors, etc. But if transportation can be worked out for you [to the Ford plant at Willow Run] and there is some sort of living center there, I really feel—I have a hunch, a hope—that you have found perhaps the most perfect place in the country for us during this war period where one can continue to breathe, maybe even to work, to contribute in one's own way to one's country and the world during this difficult period.

I am of course crazy to talk to you about it.

I wish you could have seen Anne today, running through the field by the tent, between high grass, her body all golden and her hair all flaxen. I met her unexpectedly and put out my arms and she ran—staggered a little uncertainly—laughing toward me. It was a Renoir scene and setting—deep sunny shimmering grass and that rosy figure.

Good night—tomorrow is our wedding day. (*Isn't* it?!!)

Seven Gates Farm, Wednesday, May 27th

Dear C.,

Wednesday has come and gone—Mademoiselle left this morning with tears and her jar of sugar [ration]. I spent the morning with Hilma taking care of the children and trying to clear out their room—toys, cupboards, drawers, clothes, etc. —all in the two hours between nurses. Miss Roser came on the 11:20 boat. "Why do nurses have to come to lunch?" asked Land plaintively to the orgy of cleaning up Hilma and I were doing!

But the afternoon was peaceful and sunny outdoors and by suppertime the children, washed, rosy, and serene, were all calmly eating their supper—no tears, no shouts, no whines, no *Noise,* I realized suddenly, no noise at all. The house had quieted down.

It is too soon to tell yet about Miss Roser. I only feel tonight profoundly grateful that she is calm, quiet, and has a low voice.

The children have all quieted down to it. Mademoiselle pitched the household too high, just her voice did it.

Poor Mademoiselle—I liked her, too. But the French bear transplanting badly. They lose their security, their peace, their wisdom, without their roots. *With* roots they are universal and superb, the greatness of all France pours into them, like sap.

But I am tired tonight. I shall listen to some Bach and go to sleep early.

It is our wedding day. I thought today during my nap, with a rush of emotion that brought tears, of how much I got when I married you. Had I ever told you—did you know—how could it be told? And then I thought as quickly, But he would not want you to cry, he would laugh at your tears—and I laughed a little myself.

Seven Gates Farm, June 1st

Dear Sue [Vaillant],

C. tells me he has found a house! Not in Ann Arbor, but in the Bloomfield Hills area (Cranbrook schools, etc.). I think this will be nice—as it is modern, good schools, and an artistic colony. It is *miles* from Willow Run and Detroit but apparently it was the only thing he could get. The children can evidently walk to school and I shall sit and nurse the baby!

Tonight's papers are gloating and triumphant over the frightful air raid on Cologne. I cannot rejoice in *any* bombing—even of Germans or Japanese. Did I tell you what C. said to me when someone suggested he bomb Tokyo? He said he wouldn't mind bombing a battleship—might get a kick out of it—but he wouldn't get any kick out of bombing civilians. He said, "I thought of the little poem you found of the mother who had lost her child:

> "How far in chase today
>   I wonder, has gone my hunter
> Of the dragonfly?"

Dear Charles,

"Isn't it sad Father had to go," volunteered Land, before we started reading Cinderella.

After supper I walked in the mist up to the Leavitt steps and sat watching the swallows—with the tune of Bach's you played last night running through my head—and asked myself what it suggested. I thought tonight maybe it was the flight of swallows and wanted to ask you what you thought.

Also if it were true that a dragonfly lives only one day?

And chiefly I asked myself how one could manage to combine the lovely and terrible dependence marriage gives you with the independence one must have for separation. I *shouldn't,* I kept feeling on the steps, be feeling "God-eclipsed" simply because you had gone. I shouldn't be feeling drained of my life's blood and confidence about living simply because you had gone. I shouldn't be feeling that I had chosen too perfectionist a nurse, that William would not cut the grass, that Miss Waddington[1] would be too expensive, that the summer was going to be hot. . . .

Simply because you had just left! It was silly. That was all so accidental. It wasn't real. My gloom bore no relation to the facts it was fastened on accidentally and was only due to your leaving. I do not like to be so dependent on you for my strength—my spiritual strength—and yet it is hard not to be pulled off balance by one's happiness at physical nearness and physical dependence and then resent it when it is taken away.

I know of course there is a spiritual nearness, I know there is a spiritual independence and that when I touch it I can get the spiritual nearness to you. In other words if I can stay in touch with the core of me then I can stay in touch with you, even better than by the physical crutch of leaning on you when you are there, beside me. Tonight I could not reach the core of me. A physical ache. I wonder if one does establish certain

[1] A trained nurse for care of the baby.

invisible physical bonds when you are near people and then sever them painfully when you leave. Spiritual nearness is something else, more direct, needs no intermediary, no physical closeness. It doesn't go over the wires but is more like a radio wave (comes in flashes).

I feel better now—I am refinding the spiritual nearness. Probably one is never further away than in that interim period when the physical bonds are being wrenched apart and the spiritual ones not yet recovered.

Good night.

DIARY   *Detroit, July 17th*

June was a wonderful month—only very much too short. One of those times when one is able to synthesize life and work and it shows in both. I did not write in my diary because all that went to C. every night in letters that distilled the day for him. The weather was not very good (except for a few beautiful days when C. came home). It was one of those springs that blossom under a conservatory roof of clouds and muggy weather and rain.

But still there was so much joy. Breakfast with the children, Anne running around the table afterwards, tulip-shaped golden head and blue smock. Doing the flowers with Land after breakfast, out with a basket to clip roses, lovely overgrown roses spilling down a wall. The yellow ones by the gray wall on the way to the tent, the white ones and red ones over the arbor by the back field, the reddish-pink ones—a great mass over the garage wall—forgotten and lavish and extravagantly gone to many, too many, blossoms. And some shell-pink ones (the loveliest of all—unreal, like milliners' roses!) on a broken-down vine by the orchard.

And then the morning of work. And back to the house just in time to see Anne—peas on the face and applesauce hands—sitting up in her highchair, sleepy and replete and satisfied, about to climb up the stairs to the nursery—saying " 'Bye" cheerfully but insistently through each bar of the bannisters on the way up.

And then a nap and outside again to prune the dead branches of the roses or clip off the dead ones—*so* satisfying to prune roses. It satisfies both the Puritan and the Aesthete in me. ("Charles," I say one evening when he is there, "when I am an old old lady—that is, if I'm not taking in washing—I shall have a rose garden and spend my time pruning them."

"Maybe," he said smiling, "we can manage to have a rose garden before you're quite that old!")

And then back to the house for tea and mail, sitting up on my bed waiting for the children to come in, reading the paper.

Anne came first, running uncertainly in her blue pajamas and little cream kimono on top—her pale hair all silky and soft and brushed, to pull out the scraps of paper streamers in her box or to set up Land's tin soldiers with delicate and precise hands or to turn around in the middle of the room to the music box.

Then Land with flapping arms and kimono, to jump on my bed and to be read to—*Grimm's Fairy Tales*—satisfied and stilled for once, sitting propped up against my arm while I read about the Fisherman and the Flounder or Lazy Heinz or Rapunzel. The only way I can get him to leave is to have him a kitten chasing a mouse down at the door of his room.

Then Jon last—rather austere and self-contained, jealous of his time and later bed-hour, proud and shy at the same time, eager and curious. "Can I see the war news?" and questions— always questions. Then supper on a tray sitting in bed and then a walk with the dogs to the beach or the empty Leavitt house, sitting on the porch watching the swallows and the sunset and the lake and the sea below. This is my hour—all mine— I have no house, no children, no husband, no work. There is only this landscape—the pines, the lake below, the stretch of coast line, the sea, the far shore—and the sky with swallows cutting it rhythmically and the stars coming out surprisingly soon in the still deep blue. Wish on a first star and go home, to write to C. about my "day's haul."

A lovely month. There will be no more life like this for five or six months—I must face it and not let myself get too discouraged or C. too impatient by any false illusions as to what I can do.

Two pounding days of packing, lists, arrangements, clearing out, good-byes.

And then one morning—surprisingly suddenly and with no fuss—good-bye to Mrs. Webb's climbing roses and the three pine trees that framed and placed the sea in front of the house.

Bloomfield Hills, July 18th

On June 27th I left the island for Englewood. It was so strange. As I got on the boat at Oak Bluffs and at Woods Hole, in all the little harbors down the Cape, boys and girls in slacks were rowing out to their knockabouts, unfurling the sails, getting ready for the summer season. Beach wagons and real-estate agents met the boats and trains at each country stop. "Yes, I have a house for you, but you don't want it till August, do you?"

The summer season was beginning. For me winter was beginning and the new life in Detroit, the war. That was why I was moving at this moment—to get a good start for my winter. I couldn't wait until after the baby came in September, because that would mean a late and bad start.

It was not really so strange after all—at least, not when I thought about my married life—only when I thought of my own life as a child, with regular "summers by the sea" stretching out interminably, peaceful like fields of daisies. Even the immutability of the seasons has gone—like other luxuries of the old life. C. and I have always been out of season, going to winter places in the summer and summer places in the winter, shopping for woolens in July and tropical equipment in February. Partly by choice and partly by accident.

The weeks in Englewood were as usual crowded with trying to fit too many things into too little time and space. But also people and the family, all pulled in different directions by their different lives, all wanting to be together. All trying to plan their lives, business, social engagements, duties, from one house and with dwindling means of transportation. Out of this medley, only scraps emerge as real. Dr. Hawks saying to me surprisingly and suddenly as I leave him (for he is such an uncommunicative man): "I don't know how you've stood it all—ever since the kidnapping—I don't know how you've taken it so well" (looking at me with a kind of curiosity and proud fatherly appraisal). "You've got a sense of humor—I know that."

Jon off to camp—shining-eyed, proud, self-contained, and very anxious that I get off the train lest I be left on by mistake!

Land and Anne toddling up the long cement ramp from the train in Grand Central Station with Miss R. very tall beside them. Anne, minute in pink piqué coat and sunbonnet. Land in a gray suit and Eton cap much too small for him. And then that mad rush to catch the train. We do—with seven minutes to spare—but the bags do not get on. And I am very ashamed and irritated at myself. Nothing but a raincoat and hatbox with me, no books, no pad of letter paper, no toothbrush.

C. met me at the train [in Detroit] but we missed, due to the double entrance. But I straighten out the baggage problem and taxi to 508,[1] where he is waiting with Mrs. Lindbergh. He looks beaming and in good spirits. We drive to Bloomfield Hills to see the house. It is quite nice looking and has lovely grounds, rather manicured by a gardener, a nice but too formal·hedged garden.

The walls are fairly light downstairs and conservative, though on the elegant side. Upstairs, I am somewhat appalled to find "our" bedroom varying tones of *green* (the one color I never wear). Gold satin on the beds, gold, green, and white satin curtains, a green rug, green plush chaise longue, and behind the beds great creamy white plumes of water lilies splashed on a green background. The other two upstairs rooms are papered in pink with white plumes and have elaborate modernistic cream and blue furniture and round chromium mirrors and fuchsia or mauve rugs! I try to imagine my children in them!

A positively indecent pink satin boudoir chair with fitted mirror on the back which turns automatically as you move! Very Hollywood!

---

[1] 508 Lakepointe Road, E. L. L. L.'s Detroit address.

The living room is large, heavily carpeted in brown, and the walls are a pale-apricot shade with deep-apricot curtains and imitation Renoirs and Millets, all in the same shades of apricot and brown.

The dining room has a pale-covered rug embossed (I want to say) with apricot-colored flowers—imitation Oriental—and apricot chair seats of velvet.

I feel rather depressed by all the ersatz elegance. I long for Illiec, bare as white driftwood or as those rocks on which the women of Brittany pound their wash. I long even for the shabbiness of Mrs. Webb's house—shabby Victorian—but it was decent, somehow, or the threadbare richness of Long Barn.

> "Down to the Puritan marrow of my bones
> There's something in this richness that I hate."
>   [ELINOR WYLIE]

It is more foreign to me than France. I feel desperately far away from Europe, and yet this place represents people just pushing up, just learning to appreciate culture and beauty. The striving in itself is hopeful and pathetic. The imitation Renoirs, the imitation formal garden, the overelaborate English silver, the sets of Harvard Classics, best works of the Russians, etc. I should not be snobbish, but understanding. It is the ersatz element that bothers me. What one wants is quality—any kind of quality—but a quality that is native and not forced.

Only in the kitchen—all shining Monel-metal sinks, gleaming icebox, and chromium tables—does one feel "quality" that is not forced. The man who did it knew how to make a good kitchen, the best possible kitchen, with all modern improvements.

The man—or woman—who did our bedroom didn't know about taste or even elegance. (The Paris apartment was real elegance. I didn't like it. It wasn't "mine," but it was real, modern elegance.)

Can I make this "mine," pound it into something real? Or shall I just have to let it go and live in it and get used to it?

But I don't *want* to get used to it!

The last week has gone the way all first weeks in a rented house go. I unpack a little every day. One wants to do it all at once. Chaos is so awful to live in, and to see order coming out of chaos such a triumph. C. says it is mental prostitution to spend my mind on this house—it is thrown away. It is only a lack of mental discipline that I can't turn it off.

I suppose he is right but it is so hard. A house must "work" and only the head of the house can plan that. One builds toward *later* ease of living, *later* liberty. One has no liberty if one's house doesn't "work." If the occupants are not happy in their rooms, if the children are not properly equipped, if the damageable objects are not put away. To say nothing of the aesthetic values. These I know I shall have to compromise on. It is not much hardship, since it is luxuriously furnished. But it is curiously disturbing. It is living with things that represent standards that are not mine.

If only it were bare—not all this false elegance!

Also it is crammed with gadgets, special systems that all require a specialist if something goes wrong (Pat has a long list of them). The sprinkler system for the garden, the water-softening system in the basement, the fan-cooling system in the attic. A special interhouse telephone system and a way to shut off all calls from the outer system. To say nothing of the lights on the porch which attract and then fry the insects (very disturbing!).

I find all this weight of mechanization very distressing. Is it just that I am unmechanical myself? But it makes me feel insecure—like the plush seats and tapestry curtains in the T.W.A. airliners last year.

The insecurity is deep, too, here. I feel I am sitting in a plush seat on top of a volcano. Cars go whizzing by the door and along the highways. There is no gas shortage, and the rubber shortage doesn't seem to worry them. Do they know about the war here? Life seems to go on just the same. Do they know about Lidice? Do they know that Egypt is threatened and the Germans still advancing in Russia?

It has been very hot here. So hot one is wet through at 10 A.M.

and still sticking to the chairs at 10 P.M. I shut up the house at 9 A.M. And then feel stifled. It is cool in the long-shut-up closets only.

Monday, July 20th

Kelpie was killed this morning, run over by a car in front of our house. Hilma told me. I went out to find C. by the enclosed porch with Kelpie stretched out on the grass, still in the convulsions of death. C. says he would give him morphine, but it is over.

He chased out after the car; it was not the man's fault. I feel terrible. I should have trained Kelpie while C. was away last winter. He wasn't used to cars and he had no chance to learn. He had been here barely twenty-four hours. Kelpie was so full of life. He chased everything—bees and robins and rabbits and swirls in the brook and butterflies and his own tail, running around in circles for pure joy as he did yesterday on the lawn. It seems wrong for so much life to be snuffed out, while Thor, old and crippled and sad, is left behind.

As C. and I went to find a place in the woods to bury him, I saw a man come into the garden. He walked briskly around the paths as though appraising the place, glancing here and there quickly. He did not see us, watching him from the cover of the woods in the back of the place. I hoped, in terror, that he would not turn the corner of the house and find little Kelpie, a small unknown dead dog stretched out on the grass. I could foresee his stopping his easy walk, breaking his rhythm, startled to find such an interruption in the perfect morning, the perfect lawn.

"Who is that?" said C., stiffening. "I don't know," I said. "I think it's probably the new gardener." But he looked so familiar, so very familiar, like a man in a dream. After he had passed the fatal corner—unseeing—and left the garden to Kelpie and to our privacy I realized who he was. He was "The Stranger." There is always a "stranger" on the outside of every tragedy.

We buried him in the woods, C. digging a deep grave and putting leaves in it to soften it. So terribly sweet of C. to stay home from work to do this. It shows a kind of sensitivity that I am deeply grateful for. He goes off to work late. I sit in the sun porch and get out my papers. It is a beautiful cool morning with a fresh wind—almost like Maine—but I can only think of death and the overabundance of life in Kelpie that killed him. It is unfair—but I instinctively lay Kelpie's death to the over-mechanization of this place. It could, of course, have happened anywhere, but it is somehow symbolic of this place.

Thor sniffs about sadly, looking constantly this way and that for the little black figure that was eyes and ears and feet to him, and then settles back into weary and melancholy old age and sleeps on his mat all afternoon.

Tuesday, July 21st

Couldn't get to sleep last night. It is foolish, of course, to be shaken by the death of a dog when the Russian front is so infinitely more horrible for suffering men and women. And yet, in young life snuffed out uselessly is all of death. Death is a kind of lowest common denominator—all deaths are included in it. Lidice *is all* the horrors of the war. It is all the cruelty and madness and evil of a war-drugged, a war-brutalized people. When one thinks of Lidice one feels it cannot be borne, it must not be borne. One feels one can never trust the German race. And yet other races have been as cruel, as brutal. Other atrocities have been done—by English, by Americans, in war. Must one accept it as possible in the human race? How can one?

C. home early—he has got a trailer as a permanent movable workroom for me!

Friday, July 24th

This morning C. talks about the furniture I have ordered. And says quite wisely that it is silly to buy furniture for such an unpermanent place (I'm glad he thinks it unpermanent!). He wants to keep things *light*—live in boxes, suitcases, etc., and takes all his things out of his bureau and puts them in a suitcase in the closet to show he can. I know he is right fundamentally. The burden of possessions is terrible and heaven knows I have learned to live in boxes and suitcases, too. I have two trunks (and two boxes) in my cupboard now that have never been wholly unpacked since I left Europe. They are portable bureaus I carry around with me.

But there are two things which tempt me in each new place to set up again—I like to live efficiently, or at least *fairly* so, with a sense of order and form. I like to have things run well. And I hate the ugliness of always living with the wrong things, other people's ugly things. He talks also about expense. But it isn't really the expense (these were three cheap unpainted things), it is the *bulk*. He doesn't want to accumulate bulk.

With three children *and* a baby, what a lot of bulk one has —the baby alone! C. says we must learn to live lightly, move lightly, but it is difficult with children. Children weren't really meant to move much.

Though the Gypsies do it.

Saturday, July 25th

I face now the last uncomfortable month of the baby and then the "tunnel" (nursing, drinking milk, recuperating, and the complete haze one dives into and goes under for months when nothing matters but the baby). But I am enough of an artist to resent life at times, to resent moving and babies and husbands and love. Enough of an artist to resent them but not enough of an artist to let them go.

I am reading the letters of George Sand and Flaubert. It is the eternal conflict of Art and Life. Flaubert rejected life for art. He let his life "grow overgrown like an old road," as Rilke said. G. Sand chose life, and her art is second-rate. She says to him: "The *sacrosanct literature,* as you call it, is only secondary in my life. I have always loved someone more than it and my family more than that someone."

This is me, only I have not the prodigious energy and talent of G. Sand to go on doing both nevertheless.

We listen to Bach chorales at night.

And he had twenty children!

Not he, though—his wife, I think with some cynicism—in fact, two wives!

Write on the porch in the morning. Over to 508 for lunch with Mrs. L. and her brother.

The drive to 508 is ugly and depressing—flat, untidy with trailer camps and rows of new "Defense Housing," most of it rather cheaply done and ugly (though I see one good design). I suppose Detroit is booming in one sense. Crowded with defense workers—a new, shifting, swiftly coming-and-going population, out to get what they can while they can. C. says there are enormous trailer cities around the factories. If the workers lose a job with Ford they move on to Chrysler.

This seems awful to me. No security, no home, and Ford is fighting a new federal housing project on the grounds of its being not necessary and wasteful! I suppose it _may_ be badly planned but the principle seems right.

Rest in apathy and heat after lunch. This baby is getting so heavy and painful and it is hard for me to rise above the heat, the weariness, and the ugliness of Detroit.

Monday, July 27th

Go down to see the doctor in Ford Hospital. It is as huge as a hotel—not a swell one, but more like a big railroad terminal.

I go up to a waiting room for outpatients. At least two pregnant women beside me. A Negro woman carrying her child a whole lot better than I mine.

Dr. Pratt struck me as perfectly reliable.

He thinks the baby will come a week earlier than Dr. Hawks did. He doesn't much approve of C. being in at the delivery or of my nursing, but I think both can be done.

Tuesday, July 28th

Mrs. B. (our landlady) calls me and wants to come and see if I'm comfortable! She is coming to tea tomorrow.

I put back those gold drapes on the piano, and put the fake Ingres back in place of our Vlaminck flowers in the dining room.

C. arrives home at night with the trailer attached to the back of the car and drives it over the lawn into the woods at the back of the house! He does a masterly job with that huge brown elephant—backing and turning. He takes the wheels off and props it up.

It is very nice inside—quiet, compact, and neat. A table and windows the right height at which to write.

We feel very private and far away in it and much more at home than in Mrs. B.'s house.

Wednesday, July 29th

Mrs. B. comes to call. She is immaculate in white and quite pretty. We sit on the sun porch and she tells me about the house —where to find things, etc. She wants, I think, genuinely to be helpful but I am appalled by the care the house takes (or took her). She gives me lists of all the special services: the "Faultless Cleaners" for the curtains, but Ridleys to clean rugs, and someone else to clean clothes. She tells me where to hang the satin curtains in winter and where in summer and what to do about moths (she had two men come once a week and spray the rugs!), and how a special awning company comes and takes up and puts down the awnings. She looks critically at the uncut hedges and asks if "her" George is still taking care of the garden. "And haven't we a lovely sprinkler system?" ("Mr. B. was a patent lawyer, you see.")

She thinks Bloomfield Hills is *just* like England and she just loves England.

She hopes I won't worry about the children hurting the house(!) and has taken an apartment near here and expects— as far as I can see—to pop in from time to time.

She says her daughter Kathleen is artistic and worked in ceramics. "Didn't I leave some of her things here? Wasn't there a black panther?"

I look vague. (There *was*—also two raspberry porcelain hounds. I put them in the basement on the fruit-cellar shelves.)

"And then—oh, there's the bust!"

"Oh yes—did *she* do the bust?" (Gilded bronze—stares at you as you come in the door.)

"Yes, she did it of someone of whom she was very fond . . . it's a *perfect* likeness."

When she leaves (I tell her that I expect to go back to New York for the baby and imply that I am not very strong, recline in a chaise longue, knowing it will travel far), I take down the fake Ingres ("A Southern Belle") and put it back in the "Vanitee Room" and put up my blazing Vlaminck flowers again—but I feel disquieted.

Finally sleep in the trailer—escape!

Thursday, July 30th

We go up to the house early. C. has to carry Thor out of the enclosed porch. He can't get up alone. It gets worse every morning. He is also eating very badly. He follows me to the trailer when I go to work and lies down in the grass at the foot of it. (The gardener says, "That dog sure is faithful to you.")

Friday, July 31st

Up early and go with William down to the station to meet the children. We are six minutes late and I see Miss R.'s tall form and Anne's tiny pink one, and Land in his gray suit. Land throws his arms about me but Anne looks at me from her pink sunbonnet with round wondering eyes and puckers up her lip when Miss R. leaves to find the baggage.

"She's your *Mother,* Anne!" explains Land impulsively.

C. comes home early from work. The place is full of joy. It is impossible to imagine what children will do to a place, how they will break down its formality and put everything in its proper proportion. Land is turning somersaults on the carpets, shinnying up the *Aïda*-chorus awning spears, sitting up on the piano stool drumming gaily and incoherently at the keys. Thor sniffs at the dining-room windows during meals or sits in the garden bed just outside them to be near us. Everything takes on new life for them.

I go to bed very happy, feeling infinitely better physically and mentally.

Sunday, August 2nd

C. has to lift Thor out again in the morning and he cannot stand up. He puts him on the grass. Later in the morning he tries to get up and slides down into the mud in the hedge. I lift him back. I cannot bear to see him like this. He is not in pain, apparently, but is losing the use of his back legs almost entirely—and so fast. We have talked of chloroforming him, since C. says he can get no better, only worse steadily—but I hated to unless he was in pain. Death seems to me—even in an animal—too big a thing to touch. And now he is making no effort to live, but sinking fast. He will not eat or move and only sits on the grass, his magnificent head still watching us as we walk back and forth across the lawn. Or sometimes just lying down panting with shallow breath. C. says he is dying and that it will not be very long. He is afraid he will not live until he comes back (he has to go to Pelley's trial[1]—he is subpoenaed by the defense, which irritates and worries me—I don't like his being touched by the Silver Shirts). He says he wants to dig Thor's grave himself, not leave it to any stranger. And so he goes and does it. It takes him all the late evening. I love C.'s tenderness in doing this—his sensibility. I stand with him a while but he sends me back to Thor, to make him happy during his last hours, so I go and scratch him behind his ears and smooth his fur and he seems happy. C. has to lift him onto his mat at night and we stroke him and leave him. But I feel so sad.

Monday, August 3rd

C. comes back for lunch, turns Thor over to change his position, strokes him—the last thing he does—and goes.

I watch over Thor in the afternoon. He is quite conscious and alert but cannot move and lies panting in shallow breaths. It seems to me he is waiting for death as I am waiting for birth—and the two seem so much alike. I look at him and know that there is very little I can do for him. I cannot follow where he is going; he must go through it alone. I stand on the outside

---

[1] William D. Pelley, organizer of the Silver Shirt storm troopers in 1933, brought to trial by the Justice Department in Indianapolis.

with my love and my hands. And that is like birth, too. No one can go with you. I wonder if it is different from birth—perhaps easier—since one is less aware.

At night we lift him on a canvas and lift the canvas onto the mat. Then I stay with him stroking him until he shuts his eyes, and leave a handkerchief (mine for scent) at his nose.

Tuesday, August 4th

The first thing in the morning I look out on the lawn—William has put Thor out. He is still alive. His head between his beautiful paws. I spend much of the morning washing and stroking him and pulling the canvas to a more comfortable position. I go to the trailer for an hour, to ease my conscience. I wish now I had stayed right with him, but one never knows—and life must go on. At lunchtime he is still alive but will not take water even when I lift his head; his eyes are clouded and his side trembles as he breathes. I put a wet hand against his nose. He is giving up life nobly—as he lived—not clinging to it. Animals show no fear of death (of pain, yes, but not of death), and so it is very moving. He makes no effort to live, his body accepts death, and with a kind of grace.

The children play on the steps near him, in the perfect sunshine. It is like an autumn day—clear, sunny, and a wind—all the zinnias out. They are so gay and full of life. Land wants to spray Thor continually for flies and Anne to pat the "wow-wow." But their golden beauty and gaiety is out of place beside him and I keep them off. It is the day of Thor's death.

After lunch before my nap I go out again to look at him. He has stopped breathing and the mouth is open, the pallid tongue out on the grass. He is dead. I go over to him and I have the impression of a great vessel out of which life has been poured, drained out. That is all.

I cover him so no one else shall find him, and then go to the woods to fill the grave with leaves, in the quiet of the early afternoon. I want to bury him before the children wake from their naps. I should like to bury him alone, before anyone knows.

For to others he is only a dead dog, while to me he is a life, a faithful friend, part of my life for so long. Jon and Land and Anne have been born since he came. Englewood, New York, Englewood, Long Barn, Illiec, Lloyd Neck, Martha's Vineyard—and then here. Elisabeth knew him when he was young and wolflike, galloping like a horse through the autumn leaves or winter snow, on the garden hill.

What he poured out to me always—with so little, it seems, in return (humanly speaking)—such devotion. I shall *never* meet it again in any living creature. But perhaps that is the true fulfillment of "dog"—a "dogly dog," as Chaucer would say, should be *pure* devotion perhaps.

I cannot find the rake and run into Anna [the cook], about to try to tempt Thor with some liver. (He has long been beyond that.) So I have to tell her. And I could not now lift him alone —even wasted he is too much for me. William and Anna bring him on a barrow and we lift him in. Then I send them off and cover him with leaves and shovel what dirt I can—about half the pile—resting in between. It is exhausting work for me—I did not realize. I think the baby dropped that afternoon. I had to go back and lie down, back aching and very tired, but satisfied that all had been done in the quiet of a still afternoon and no strangers around.

There is a stillness about the day on which even a dog dies. Life goes on around it but the stillness remains like these black holes in the Milky Way that drop one through to a further depth of the infinite.

At night C. comes back very late, by plane. I am still awake when I hear him drive in. He comes over to the bed without turning on the light. "Thor died." "Yes." And I find I am crying. "It's all right, I wanted him to die, he was so old but . . ." "It's hard to lose him."

It is lovely to have C. back and have him understand. I feel ashamed to cry over a dog in a world that contains the Russian Front and Lidice and France starving and Greeks dying in the gutters of lack of food and "saboteurs" shot in Holland. But Thor was a symbol of something—of devotion and love and family unity. A great unity of my life—the child-bearing years. His going ends a chapter.

Wednesday, August 5th

C. calls up and asks if I wouldn't like to go to "Harry Bennett's"[1] for a steak supper? I have been so much by myself that I think it would be fun. I put on my best slacks outfit and C. drives me over. We go to a kind of "bungalow" on an island in the woods, across the river from the Bennetts' real home (or *one* of them), a kind of stone castle we pass by on our way. The bungalow turns out to be made of simulated metal "logs," and simulated metal "tree" lamps light our way in. The big room is full of animal heads, trophies, guns, statuettes of boxers (Bennett was a lightweight champion!), gadgets, joke statuettes, animals, steins, and some paintings of the West, photographs of their ranch on the desert, etc.

Mrs. B. comes in in slacks. She is nice, young—35-ish—open and healthy looking—easy person. Bennett comes in in a Western riding outfit—a compact little man, gives the impression of youth and taut trigger health.

A lot of other people—women in slacks, all about my age, nonintellectual, easy, healthy. They ask me how I like Detroit and when the baby is coming. We drive down to a huge barbecue pit where there are a lot more men in riding clothes or very informal dress standing about a counter, drinking, eating sausages, and watching the horses in a race track over the fence. I find C. and Bennett are racing down the field on polo ponies. There's nothing sissy about these people. Most of the men take a shot at riding. The women talk to me—about their husbands' riding or their children away at camp or the housing problem. We sit in a big circular concrete basin with a grill in the center. I am next to a general whom I haven't the vaguest idea about. Bennett cooks the steaks over a fire and some "cowboys" sing songs. We eat enormously, helping ourselves from a big cafeterialike table piled with food on big metal traylike plates.

[1] Director of personnel, labor relations, and plant security at Ford Motor Company.

Bennett stands in the center and sings or plays a guitar—or maybe I just have this idea because he gives the impression, oddly enough for a high-powered executive, of having a hankering to be a troubadour.

I try to analyze the evening on the way home. This is wealth—Middle Western wealth. It has no taste as wealth in the East, but it has a lot more vitality. All those people are fairly fit and healthy emotionally, care about their husbands, their homes, and their children. The polo ponies are there to ride and not to talk about. They like to cook and sing and wait on themselves. Wealth hasn't deteriorated them, though they may not use it well and are rather dull.

I feel as usual aeons older than most of the people there. The general seemed a little older. He turns out to be General Short! (Admirals Kimmel and Short of Pearl Harbor were made the goats for the whole tragedy.) He is retired from the army pending court-martial. He is working for Ford. I break out in beads of perspiration trying to remember what I've said to him. Did I *mention* the Pacific?

Sunday, August 9th

A very bad night—pain—and up much of the night. I think I have just been doing too much. Taking care of the children is usually such joy but this time it has been painful and extremely exhausting. Lifting Anne, bending over cribs and bathtubs, going up and down stairs. Anne, though, is really easier than Land. Though what he is demanding is not physical, it seems like the last straw. C. says he won't go if the baby is started.

Monday, August 10th

Feel better and have no pain. Decide to go to Dr. Pratt and see if I'm all right. C. will telephone me from the factory in the afternoon to see if it's safe for him to go to Washington. Get the children up, through breakfast, and then go off with William to the hospital. Dr. Pratt says it's indigestion—though it might bring on the baby—to take it easy.

I go back relieved, stop at Woolworth's and buy a cheap tea

set (because I can't bear Mrs. B.'s gold luster teapot, which doesn't match *anything*); when I get the set bought I realize it is ugly, too, and second-rate and I am only buying it because I feel it is the last chance—must get one, better than nothing. This is the kind of useless activity typical of last days of pregnancy.

Another very bad night. The ugly tea set sits in my mind, an impassable obstruction to sleep, also some bad films back from the developers. Why do I mind these two details so terribly? How they depress me and weigh down on me! I suppose because they are indications of faults in myself. The tea set was a thoughtless stupid extravagence—not because it was expensive but because I don't like it. And the films show my fatal lack of precision. And it all shows exhaustion.

Tuesday, August 11th

C. calls from Washington; I say he can go on to New York. I cut flowers in the afternoon. Write Mother and Jon (this *must* be done before I go off!). I feel such a sense of pressure to get things done before I go to the hospital. Pack bag for hospital. Very bad night again. Thank goodness Miss R. has come back.

Wednesday, August 12th

Call Dr. Pratt, who orders me right down. Then I call C. at the Engineers Club in New York. Thank goodness he has arrived and has not yet gone out to his appointments. I say it is "like Long Barn" and he may have plenty of time. But he is going to try to get a plane. He calls back when I am dressing to say he has got reservations on a plane getting in at 4:45!

We get to the hospital in about thirty-five minutes, where I am promptly put to bed in one of those hospital gowns in a green room (*must* I suffer in a green room?) looking out on the front drive and lots of cars. (Is there a tree to look at from bed? Or a little piece of sky? I regret that I didn't go to the window at home before I left and look at the elm tree in the field next door. One gets strength from these things and I was too occupied with details to do it; now I am cooped in the city.)

I take a rest, all afternoon. It is delicious and I feel better and in less pain than I have for weeks!

C. arrives at 6, smiling and triumphant. I don't think I'm going to have the baby now and plan on going out again tomorrow to have my permanent. C. goes home for the night and tells me to call if anything starts.

I sit up after supper and write in my diary, feel I must write about Thor before this starts and tomorrow may be too late. They come in and turn my light off at 10. A blackout practice.

After they disappear I go to the window in the dark and pull up the shade. It is beautiful, with all the lights out and all the noise of cars stilled. The city has disappeared. The spirit of the country is here. I am very grateful for this half hour to look at the stars and feel I am having what I missed this morning. Now I can face the pain.

I go to sleep contented and wake at one. The pains have started. I wait for about half an hour to make sure and then ring for the nurse. They decide to take me down to a room next to the delivery room. The pains—although "good" ones—are not too bad. I am glad as I roll down the corridors on the stretcher, looking up at the chessboard noise-insulated ceiling and the lights. (One is always staring at ceiling lights with flies or bits of black dust caught in the bottoms of their bowls. They ought to make one of the nurses or doctors ride around on his back on a stretcher occasionally and see what the patient sees. Maybe they could decorate the ceilings!) They *have* put crosses on the ceiling here, red crosses. I take down with me C.'s old glasses case to hang on to and a postcard I had pinned to my bookbag to look at. It is of a deer's head—very old—carved by the Indians (Mother sent it once to Jon). It has the quality of restraint about it. All nonessentials carved away. The bones of the animal prominent and his great eyes staring out of this bare carved bony mask and the ears alert—alive—like fire. It would be good to look at.

They wheel me into a room next to the delivery room. (C. has got them so scared with telling them about the *speed* with which the last baby came!) It is a pink room and I feel better about it. But no, they only keep me here until Dr. Sill examines me and then wheel me into the *green* delivery room, where I am again looking at ceiling lights and plumbing pipes and cabinets full of instruments. But I look at the deer's head. I ask them to call C. after Dr. Sill has seen me. It is 3 A.M. He will be here then by 3:45 or 4. It is something to look ahead to. The pains are hard but not long and in between I look at the head of the deer.

The nurses sit around and talk, at my head and back. I feel I ought to be sociable, too—at least as long as I can—so I tell them about London and the doctor saying I had chloroform like Queen Victoria! And they sit around and laugh and I talk to the anaesthetist about her work and to the nurses about the shortage of nurses. Strange the feeling of social obligation one has —how far it takes you.

Dr. Pratt comes and I say I am sorry to be getting him up at night and he says very nicely, "*You're* the only one that's working." I keep looking at the clock over my head—3:30, 3:45— Charles should be here. The pains are quite hard. It is still easy to *give* to them—what I learned in London. Go *with* the pain, let it take you. It is easy at this stage. Relax, do not hold on to something hard, open your palms and your body to the pain. It comes in waves like a tide, and you must be open as a vessel lying on the beach, letting it fill you up and then, retreating, leaving you empty and clear.

There is a little stir and C. has come. They have put a green coat on him and a mask. I can only see his eyes. He has got a cold so I cannot touch him, and there are too many people around. It is 4 A.M.

I look at the card and C. asks what it is and I read off the back. "Wooden Maskette, Key Marco, Florida . . . the finest known creation of the fifteenth-century Calusa Indians. The eyes are of inlaid shell and the ears, on leather hinges, are movable." The nurses are not talking and the words sound strange in that room. They defy the room in some way, and the pain. This beauty exists apart from me in Key Marco (where C. and I had been). Yes—"the eyes are of inlaid shell and the ears, on leather hinges, are movable." Yes. Thank God.

C. nods his head silently and we go on to another pain. They are getting much harder and longer. Ten or eleven breaths long. And I feel my body stiffen with the pain. The body is frozen in the pain but somehow the breath is able to race it still, to keep itself intact from the pain. With a deep breath—it has to be as deep as the pain—one reaches a kind of inner freedom from pain, as though the pain were not yours but your body's. The spirit lays the body on the altar.

"You don't want any sedatives?" they say to me. "No," I say, but not from courage or stoicism, only because I know this is the only way I can deal with the pain and control it. Once I take sedatives I will have no control.

"Any time you want anything for the pain just tell us," says Dr. Pratt. "Yes, I will."

"The baby is making good progress," they say. Dr. Sill thinks it will be all over by 4:30 but I say it will be longer. I watch the clock over my head. And in between the pains I try to prepare myself for the next one. I wish there were something more beautiful to look at. I feel trapped and shut away from the things that give strength to me—the sky and stars and a tree.

"You don't want some gas?" says the anaesthetist. "Not to put you out, just to take off the edge of the pain?"

"No, not yet," I say. "I will tell you."

With the next bad pain I try to reach the stars. I try to break through those walls.

Dr. Pratt says something to the anaesthetist about gas. "But she doesn't *want* it," says the anaesthetist, almost in complaint. C. says to me in a monotone, "You can have gas any time you want it." "I know," I say. But I am waiting for the pains to get worse. "As long as I *can,* I want to go without." They do not understand, I think. I am not trying to be courageous. I know what this pain is and that it must get worse. I know the only strength there is for me. It doesn't lie in numbness or partial numbness. It lies in awareness, awareness and endurance of pain.

They want to give me gas. It will rob me of my strength. I feel like Samson that they want to cut my hair. If they give me gas I will be unable to separate body and spirit. I will be unable to pray, to touch the stars. I shall be afraid and scream. "No gas—not yet."

But how long would it be? How much longer . . . "sixteen . . . seventeen." "No, no gas . . . It's always worse after gas. . . ." I explain incoherently.

They are not talking now but all standing around in the room waiting. I am confused as to where they are, only able to concentrate on the pain and standing it. I no longer look at the clock.

"You'd better get her on the table," Dr. Pratt says to the nurses. They move me between pains. They have their masks on. The flickers of pain as they touch me are terrible. And I find I cannot now stop my knees from trembling. "You'd better give her gas for the next one," Dr. Pratt says authoritatively. "You will have to if you're going to examine me," I say weakly. They start to tie my hands to the table. *"Must* you tie my hands?" I protest, shocked. (Haven't I been controlled enough? I think in desperation.)

It seems they *always* do this but I had been unconscious the other times. The nurses hesitate a moment and one explains what I already know. But it is wasted words, for I have already realized it is useless to fight that. I have said "all right" and given up my precious glasses case to C. and my card. But I feel desperate.

Now I am trapped, I think. There is nothing to do—I am abandoned. It is the worst moment. And it is always the moment before the end. "It is beginning," I say (the pain). They put the mask on. "Breathe naturally." I breathe as deeply as I can, I start to fade out, I am beating the pain. Can it be that I am going to beat the pain?! It has not yet caught up with me—I am ahead—it is fading—it is far behind—it is gone!

I enter that whirling eternity of rhythms, pressures, sounds, and visions of going into gas. There is no pain but a kind of terrible intensity or pressure over everything. There seems to me memory of pain, awareness of its closeness and of closeness to

Death. But no fear—one is past fear. But one is still walking perilously through fire or as though on the bottom of the ocean, with leagues of water on top, and only a thin eggshell insulation protecting you.

Through this the dreams . . .

I am in a tomb—no, perhaps not a tomb, perhaps it is a hospital—but it is sinister like a tomb, a house of death. "They" say to me mournfully: "No one ever leaves Miss So-and-so's Home (where I am) with a smiling face." There is a kind of grim joke in this though I am not aware of it. I seem to see ages pass—ages and ages of time—like the leaves of a magazine, a dull one. The same picture turning up over and over again. I look out the window and there to my surprise I see Thor, very clearly. He sits alert, immobile, paws and head forward, ears up, nose pointed at the door, expectantly, as if about to leap. "But of course," I say, laughing to myself. It is all simple now—Thor is waiting for *me*. He will never move from that position until I come. "They" have been trying to coax him away from the front door, with meat, but he won't move. Through the ages (for cycles of time pound by) he waits. But they don't understand, I think, half humorously, half tenderly. "They" don't realize he won't move until I come. I'll just go out and get Thor to move, I'll go out the other door and when he sees me he'll get up. It will be all right. (I smiled at the ease with which this would be done.) It's rather unconventional, I admitted to myself. One doesn't usually *walk* out of this place (I have the feeling it is a house of death—I should at least be carried out, but I am all right—and extraordinarily light, free, on my feet). I will just carry my basket (what was in it? a baby?) and go out. I start to step out gaily but something happens. I never reach Thor—I fall, I drop. I am to be crushed or drowned. I have no fear, but I know instantly that it is death. And I feel only a little regret at my stupidity (like touching a third rail, or falling into a manhole, or getting crushed under a locomotive). It was unnecessary, I think, and no one will know what has happened to me—I am sorry about that. But still no fear. Yes, it is

Death coming instantaneously. I am curious, even adventurous, about it.

Where will I go next—be what? I drop into another world, a world in which I am less body than before. I am a bodiless entity whirling through space, to rhythm. It is a very familiar rhythm. As it pounds along and I with it I realize that it is vitally important that we reach a certain point in that rhythm. It is somehow connected with Charles and I realize—I, the unprecise, the inaccurate, the careless, the vague—that if we do not hit just that precise half-beat, that dot in time, that accidental count, I shall miss Charles—for good. He will be lost to me forever. I realize with a terrible urgency, a terrible poignancy, how it matters to me. All life balances on that second, all fate. I am aware strongly of his presence, like something I am journeying toward. I *feel* his face dimly through the space. I do not *see* it exactly—I *feel* it—his tenderness, his sureness, his eternally being there, and our quality of belonging together. But can I reach it? Will fate allow the incredible accident to happen of my meeting him? And I feel with sudden poignancy, "Oh, how Charles would understand, how he would understand the quality of this instant!"

The rhythm goes on—we are approaching the fatal "dot." Just before it comes there is a terrible pause—I am in an agony of suspense. Then it drops, the all-important "dot," falls into place, swings on nonchalantly just as if two lives were not balanced on it. Ah—I drop into another world with relief. It is all right. It is all assured. We will meet again; I shall get back to him.

I then find that I am back at some place where I have been before. I recognize it. It is a final test.

I am asked in some way—it is hardly a question in words—what is the secret of the universe, what is the point. I give answer after answer. And always it is shown to me (with such painful disillusioning) that my answer is only a vanity, an earthly illusion. I come finally to the point of protesting: But no, *no, all* is not vanity, when—this time I feel the dream speeded up, too fast for me to follow, too fast to learn—I am coming back. They are pulling me back before I have learned the answer. I do not want to be pulled back. But I recognize it as coming. Soon I will hear mortal voices. There is that curious familiarity and repetitiousness about this coming-to. C. says I said as I was coming out of gas: "I can't bear it." This must have been at this point. The only thing I can remember feeling is that "I could not bear" to accept that the point of the Universe was "Vanity."

"It is a boy," they say. "A *boy!?*" I say, incredulous. (Had I then so *firmly* been expecting a girl?) A boy! I see C.'s smiling eyes over the mask. They show me the child, who looks like all the others. "We'll never be able to name it," I say in an effort to be coherent. And with that I go off again to sleep.

"But it was marvelous—marvelous—you never brought me back at all—I never came back at all!!"

"Still pain—but it's all right, it doesn't matter." (Back in the room) "Can't I hold your hand *now?*"

September–October

Days in the hospital slipped by quickly, a timeless passage, with certain things only standing out from its peaceful routine monotony. Miss [Amy] Waddington's pince-nez twinkling over the top of her mask as she brought the baby in to nurse.

The presence of Miss Waddington filled the hospital for me. If I could describe her! Her sharp definite step down the corridors, her trim little figure in uniform. Her firm and definite clipped speech: "Now, Mrs. Lindbergh, if you want to nurse your baby . . .!" Her surprising and sudden softness with the baby—with me, too, at times. Her zeal over her work, even the ugly details. The gleam of a zealot in her eye over "a breast-fed baby" or "a good stool" or "four ounces" (of milk!). The extraordinarily gentle way she picked up the baby to put him over her shoulder. The soft way she said, "Good night, Mrs. Lindbergh" as she left me, as though she were shutting a box very softly that had a secret in it. The positive way she said, "That's fine, Mrs. Lindbergh, if you feel that way." Her prim humor with

C. Her rigid exactitude with the doctors—quiet, unassuming—but she knew her job! The way she opened the door in the morning, quietly but expectantly, as though there were something lovely to happen that day. Her extremely simple, flat, and quite sensible ideas on politics, life in general, her philosophy. The straight stick in her—unwavering and erect—to lean on.

I think she is the strongest person I have ever known. Strong as a monk or a Mother Superior, dedicated to something, to the service of Mother and Child. And though she seems and is, while she is with you, utterly devoted to you and your child, she moves on with a disconcerting equanimity to the next case, for it is service that matters and not the person. At least she is serving something timeless and abstract as well as something personal and immediate.

Dr. Pratt coming in and complimenting me on the way I acted in the delivery room. "It's easy with anyone as stoic as you," he said, looking at me seriously. And I laughed because I couldn't explain to him. "That isn't stoicism," I said. "What is it, then?" he asked. "It's having five children." But I'm not telling him the truth and he—vaguely—knows it. And goes on to pry me rather clumsily about my "good psychology" in taking the postcard down to "take your mind off the pain." But I cannot explain. It wasn't to take my mind off the pain; it was to concentrate it *on* pain. He says he'd like me to write a book about it sometime. And I laugh and say maybe I will.

Baffling days because no time with C. Waiting for him at 6, having just one precious hour with him, and being too tired to do and say much then. And having lots of practical details that must be decided in that hour.

Coming home

I feel I will *never* get home—we have to delay. The night before, I had a splitting headache and the baby a slight temperature.

Finally we leave—go out the back way. C. and I and then Miss Waddington and her pink bundle.

Lovely to be home—flowers and smiling faces and noise of children, doors slam, windows open, dishes being washed, and children.

Miss Waddington standing over me to protect me from the household, bringing in trays, bringing in glasses of milk: "Only *one* thing is necessary, Mrs. L."

The hum and warmth and glow and life of a house—a living house. And its complications and burdens, too . . .

I seem to hear babies crying *all over* the house! Which one is that?

Sitting out in the sun—perfect warm autumn sun and the golden wasps glinting in the crystal air. Joy to be alive and to be tasting that last precious bit of sun and color and beauty before winter. Wasps on a crushed grape on the arbor walk. I feel like a wasp, too—gathering while I can.

Land coming down my passage, sniffing in ecstasy: "I smell Baby just everywhere—don't you, Mother?!" Anne, shy and strange and very lovely with her pale-gold dancey hair and her wistful blue eyes and pouting mouth and her high little bird's voice. *She* is the miracle, now. It seems perfectly natural to have the boys and the little new baby, who seems like all of them over again. But Anne! Where did she come from? She is still a stranger to me. Ever since I stopped nursing her. There was the anti-war work and then that long period in bed. I have been having a baby or nursing one for so long. And she has grown up in the meantime.

Jon back from camp, stretched out, and brown and tousled and grinning through his brace. Asking how *long* the baby was and then saying with a slow grin: "As long as the biggest pickerel I caught this summer!"

But chiefly the routine of nursing, sleeping, eating, lying in the sun—all revolving around that one thing. And Miss Waddington the presiding spirit.

The "honeymoon period" of Miss W. is over. It was in the hospital, when one is pampered and coddled. Now at home, already she is weaning me, prodding me on, training me to take over "her baby." It is not so perfect either at home. In the hospital *only* the baby matters. At home there are other children, other relationships. I am oversensitive to them all—who is happy and who unhappy in the house, who overworked. The house arrangements are heavy on top of me, ridiculously so. I feel all the complaints. One is always oversensitive after a baby. I try to remember each time and be prepared, but I forget and have to learn again.

My only contact with the world is through the papers, full of cruelty, full of atrocity stories of "saboteurs" shot in France and hostages in Holland. Horrible stories of tortures inflicted on prisoners in Russia. The deportation of (and separation of) families of Jews from France. A woman flinging her baby out of a window and then jumping after. Soldiers standing around a delivery bed to hurry the mother (a Jew) out as soon as it is over. Polish prisons of young girls, prostitutes for German soldiers. I am obsessed by them—that such cruelty can exist in a world that holds the purity and innocence of a child like mine in the next room. How can I go on bathing him and feeding him when such terrible things exist in the same world? How reconcile the two?

I feel desperate now about France under Laval. No, I cannot accept their "revolution" if this is what it is. "Revolutions," as Sorokin says, "are initiated by idealists, carried through by brutal murderers, and profiteered upon by scoundrels." Laval, surely, is the latter—if not worse.

A week of colds, trays, and tension in the house, cold and wet outside.

Miss Waddington goes, running out the back door in the rain, not saying good-bye (because she can't bear good-byes). And I feel dreadful—not only because the prop is taken out from under me but because there is something not communicated between us.

And then the swift insistent weeks of intense care of the baby —I am in the midst of it now. Miss Waddington left me with her burning zeal to do all the details *just* right. At first I was only driven by it and the desire to do it efficiently and by the sound of her sharp voice at my elbow (like a ghost!) reminding me of what I'd forgotten. But soon it became a joy, much of it.

Only at night I am always too tired and the feeding is difficult and I am afraid there will not be enough milk and he will not sleep. I am discouraged at night, exhausted. But in the morning I sing again over his bath.

October 24th

The day—the night, rather—that C. and I went out for a walk. It was moonlight and suddenly we felt we must go out—escape this hedged-in house. For me it was a first escape. We walked out of the drive and down the road—and skirting the gate of the big park of the Girls' School we go in behind and find a path through the woods. It is so wonderful. I feel like a wild animal back in my own world. It might be anywhere—Martha's Vineyard! We climb over a fence into a field and walk back up the hill. This is what we have missed at this place, I tell C.

We have always had a *special* walk at each place we have lived in. The walk *belongs* to the place in some special way. And yet it belongs to us even more than to the place. It becomes irregular, arbitrary, taken in all weathers, colored with our conversations, our thoughts. It becomes part of the pattern of our minds. Sometimes I take these paths in my sleep. I wonder if in some strange way we form them after a pattern in our minds. Perhaps it is the same walk over and over again, the same pattern. And represents something fundamental in our lives, something symbolic.

The walk in Illiec—over the flats and rocky islands to the Carrels'—had a *Pilgrim's Progress,* allegorical quality to it. One had all sorts of difficulties to master before one got to one's destination. The mud, the sand, the briars, the rocks, the big pebbles, the hill, the fence. And even the one through the Bois in Paris seemed symbolical, and very lonely, even in the Bois. It seemed like a ghost path—we were alone on it, we followed it inexorably, it crossed other people's paths and sometimes accompanied them. But we never stopped or deviated, we went straight ahead, across sidewalks and beside streams—always the same walk, and always alone. The walk was *in us,* not in the Bois.

Only, I think, climbing up the field in the moonlight, my arm in C.'s in happiness, only we have no dog, no Thor.

"I almost feel as if Thor were with us," C. said, "heeling behind us" (waiting for the touch of my hand on his silky head and my "Go on ahead, Thor").

We came up on the house from a new angle. There it sat, lit up and long on the slight rise, beyond the hedges. "It looks perfectly unreal, Charles," I said. "Impermanent, as though it were floating on something."

"It *is* floating on something," said C. "It's floating on the war."

Lily Swann Saarinen[1] takes me one afternoon to see Cranbrook and the Milles's.[2] Cranbrook is beautifully done—too beautifully. As though it were wished there. The elaborate romantic-modern Egyptian of the Girls' School. The Gothic modern of the Boys'. The clean functional modern of the museum. The Swedish modern art buildings, all cloistered, all set apart, all precious—the Ivory Tower sitting on the outside of the volcano of Detroit.

We walk into Milles' house. He welcomes us at the door with a grave old-world dignity. I want to say he is in a frock coat. But this is not true. He just *acts* as though he were in a frock coat. I think he is going to kiss my hand. But he bows only and says gravely, with a slight accent, "We are honored." Mrs. Milles stands behind him in a long blue gown smooth under her prim folded hands (like Mrs. Noah in the Noah's Ark). The house is rather dark and you enter another world as you come in. There is a medieval carved wooden Madonna in the front hall.

"Where did she come from?" I asked quickly.

"Caen, in France."

"Oh, how I miss France!" I say without thinking.

"We all do," said Carl Milles quietly, gravely, as though he had known beforehand I would say it.

Then he showed me around his house—a museum it is—a tiny museum.

[1] Wife of Eero Saarinen, Finnish architect, whose father, Eliel Saarinen, built and directed Cranbrook Academy of Art.

[2] Carl Milles, Swedish sculptor.

He has a *forest* of statues and fragments (Graeco-Roman, Greek, and some medieval) in one room and he goes around with a flashlight and lights each piece up one by one, fondly, telling you its history as he goes. He seems grave, old, and rather weary. A miser who has kept these things above the flood of the years and the flood of America, too. He has not succumbed to the New World. And they are only waiting, two sad old people, for the war to end, so they can go back to Sweden. No, they are not really so old, but definitely exiled.

They are very anxious to see C. Feel he is one of them and feel an immense pride in him.

I tell them he wants to come and it will do him good because he is in a factory where everything is *production*—quantity and not quality.

"Yes," says Milles in his melancholy tone, "I have always known he was a man for *quality*."

We see his studio—full of mammoth figures—dancing figures he is doing for a cemetery in Washington. His things are lyrical, emotional, Romantic, and would be too soft (like the Graeco-Roman classics he loves so much) if it were not for the tartness of Swedish folk quality.

I hurry back to feed the baby, feeling I had been miles away and that it was something nice to tell C. and to go back to. As he helped me into the car he (Carl Milles) said, as an afterthought, or as if reading something in me: "We lived fifteen years in Paris so we too know what it is to miss France."

And I could not say to him what I was thinking, what I think so often: Yes, *you*—for you it is all right. *You* are European, but I am American. I have no right to miss Europe like that. But I do.

Monday, October 26th

Edna Millay's poem "Lidice." "We Refuse to Die"—written for the Office of War Information. Put over the radio. Is it great poetry? Can one write great *occasional* poetry? If I were asked to write on Lidice it would not be a poem about them—whom I know nothing about, whose suffering I cannot even comprehend, so horrible was it. No, it would have to be about how Lidice affected me, an ordinary person sitting at home far away from tragedy. It would have to say a worm has eaten into the apple of happiness—everyone's apple and forever—because it happened. And I cannot escape it. The most perfect morning is tinged with it—the freshest rose.

Wednesday, October 28th

Pat brings in the paper. The *Wasp* and a destroyer sunk in the Solomons and another carrier damaged and the atmosphere in Washington "tense." This means, I assume, worse news that they haven't told us. The *Wasp* was sunk over a month ago. They "save" the bad news to give out with good news but I guess sometimes it piles up on them. Pat's brother is on the *Hornet,* a carrier out there somewhere.

Sunday, November 8th

C. takes Anne to his mother's—"Bye! Bye!" she runs around shouting after breakfast. I am left with the baby—and the whole day. Go to the trailer at 11:30 to 1. Then eat outside in the sun. Back upstairs and fix and feed the baby. Then I take the radio and sit out on the terrace and listen to the Philharmonic in New York. Brahms Concerto No. 2 in B minor. I sit in complete peace in the sun and look through the haze at the apple trees with only a few yellowing leaves left on them. So still and so perfect is the day that not a leaf fell. Yes—that describes the day—not a leaf fell to break the spell. This exists—now, suspended, for an instant only. But in the truth of that instant I felt I could live and wanted to live despite everything. I wished I could give it to other people—suffering people.

Then in the last moments of the afternoon sun I picked the last of the chrysanthemums and some beautiful big round tropical-looking leaves, green tinged with red, from the rock garden, and I started to arrange them in a low copper dish. If I can do it just right, I think, and it is perfect I shall take it in to Pat, who feels bad. And it forms itself. The great darkish wine-tinged leaves stand up just right and I find chrysanthemums that bend just right and some red haws of roses. And I take it in. (The perfection of the whole afternoon has gone into it.) And she is pleased and I am happy. She says she is better. I hope so.

Then C. and the children come back. Land has a cold, and C. says, "Have you heard the news?" U.S. forces have attacked the French colonies in Africa. *We are at war with France.*

Monday, November 9th

Anne has a cold, too. The papers are full of excitement over the second front in Africa, Rommel's retreat in Libya. Vichy has broken off relations with us. De Gaulle calls on France and the colonies to join him. The President and the Commander-in-Chief broadcast to France that they are attacking her colonies only to forestall German occupation, to free her from the yoke of German domination, and plead with her not to resist. But evidently she is resisting. Frenchmen are fighting Frenchmen, then. I feel sick about it all day but America is rejoicing. We think we have won the war. It's all a big pushover from now on. The Axis has started to crumble. We have started our offensive. Roosevelt declares it is our effective second front to help our gallant allies in Russia. I wonder if Stalin will be satisfied with a "second front" in Africa.

Call Milles at night. I say, "This is Anne Lindbergh." He says, "Ach, my dear . . ." in his soft Swedish voice. We are going to see him on Wednesday evening. He says, "We will talk about Art—nothing but Art and beauty—and we will forget all the terrible things in the world." He lives in a world of his own. But he can afford to. He is old, he has lived his life and fought his battles and produced his great work. It is all before us.

But still, I felt happy to think he was there to see—"Ach, my dear. . . ."

Wednesday, November 11th. Armistice Day

This should teach the human race never to designate another "armistice day."

C. and I to Milles in the evening. He is alone and we walk through his forest of Graeco-Roman sculptures. He is a loving, lovely old man. He talks of Paris as though it still existed! He has seen other wars and he expects this to pass and things will go on. There is no hate in him and one can breathe and talk as if in the Old World.

He is evidently adored by all the art students who come in and look at his statues and his books and listen to his music and eat his Danish coffee bread and hear his anecdotes and ask his advice and cry on his shoulder. It would be a nice shoulder to cry on.

A windy night of stars and cold. When we come back, after looking at all those beautiful curves of sculpture, the gilded "businessman" that K. B. did in the niche in the hall literally hits me in the face as I walk in the door. Its crudeness, harshness, heaviness, and complete lack of spirit shout out to me as they did the first time I saw it, but haven't for weeks since I got used to it. This is the worst! *I got used to it!*

Thursday, November 12th

The Germans have occupied all of France. Rumors are wild. Darlan[1] has commanded the French to stop fighting, to give over the fleet. The American troops are successful all over Africa. The papers are soaring buoyantly. One doesn't know what's true or not. Pat says her art teacher said, "It'll all be over in three weeks!" and C. says a man at the factory said, "There'll be no need of these bombers now!"

Friday, November 13th

A wild wind, tearing all day, with snow flurries. The house is cold in spite of the storm windows. How I hate the wind— winter wind. It opens up all the black holes. I do the baby and go to the trailer—wind through the windows and my feet are cold.

C. comes home and I feel cheered. Ask him if he ever feels, "The flame is gone and it will never come again." He says yes,

---

[1] Admiral Jean Darlan, Vice-Premier and Minister of Defense of the Vichy regime, cooperated with General Eisenhower after the Allied invasion of North Africa.

he often feels the flame is gone, but *never* feels it will not come again. Tells me about his life and first gaining confidence—in army school.

Saturday, November 14th

Wind disappeared—almost—sunny and bright. Jon off early to his grandmother. I take a short walk before trailer work—work fast. Say all I want to say but not the way it should be said. The days fly in the routine—I rush from one to another.

After supper C. takes me to see the big iron foundry at the River Rouge factory. It is like a great city—a factory city with railroad, coal dumps, boats (ore boats come up the Rouge River), cranes, dumps, derricks, cars, and of course blocks and blocks of factory units. We go into the foundry, where they are melting the crude iron ore and pouring it out of the furnace. We climb up grimy stairs. It is black and not much lit and seems empty. We pass by one furnace—a great fortlike stack or tank that goes up into the darkness—and get to another that is pouring. Five or six men are standing about, grimy, tough looking, with smoke glasses on and great forks or iron poles. The heat is terrific, even standing back where we were, and a great roar from the furnace, and the streams so bright you could hardly look at them.

The darkness, lit only with the great mouth spitting out molten metal, gas, and sparks, and those roaring, tumbling, flaming streams of metal, the dark soot-covered figures with their poles glowing red on the end gave an infernal impression. And when you heard the foreman talk of "we used to do this [lift the gate] by hand but a man got burned so . . ." when you considered what those men were handling—liquid torture, liquid death, liquid fire—one false step would mean instant shriveled death, then you had the impression that it was hell—really hell.

I was afraid—full of fear before that terrible power and nearness of torture and death. And I had the feeling that one could not stay long there and believe in God or trees or sky or children. It was dreadful. A poster on one of the grimy walls showed a soldier flat on the ground with a machine gun asking for more—more production. To work in that furnace is war, too.

There were two men who did not seem to belong there. One a dark-eyed, soft-voiced Mexican whose face lit up quickly and sympathetically when you spoke to him. The other a Negro, bent and oldish, who at the orders of the foreman opened the small holes inside of the furnace and you could hear a great blast of air from it. When he had done this he made a slight gesture with his hands—a gesture you might make if you had set down a tray of food before someone or some flowers. It was an awkward gesture but a gesture of grace, just the same—an "I have given you what I could" gesture.

Those two men did not belong there. But then—who did? An inferno—the "creation of Faustian man," C. said. And "Blood out of Rocks."

Home to feed the baby—soft, clean, tender, and fragile, just waking damp from sleep—with the soot of the underworld still shining (its black metallic specks) on my clothes.

Sunday, November 15th

Rickenbacker is found![1] Down in Pacific; after three weeks on a raft. Think of his wife!

At night at the 10 P.M. feeding C. comes in and bends over the baby as he sucks. As I sit there with the baby sucking at the breast in even breaths and C.'s head touches mine over him I think: This is perfect Happiness.

Tuesday, November 17th

Go to trailer and work on "The Alps go up pretty high,"[2] notes only, read diary and think about it. It blooms as I think and I am excited by it—only, as always, in this stage I can't write fast enough and *there is no time*. If only I could just drop everything and concentrate on this, as a painter before the light goes. But I can't—I am nursing the baby. I must go back, I must eat, I

---

[1] Edward Rickenbacker, U.S. ace flier in World War I, back on active duty, had been on a special government flight when his plane went down. He described his experience in *Seven Came Through.*

[2] Chapter in a new book A. M. L. was writing, which was later published as *The Steep Ascent.*

must rest, I must feed the baby—and tomorrow Miss R. is off; there won't even be my hour.

To work at something like this, to summon up the past is very strange. One seems to have two kinds of memory. The first is just thought. I remember thus and so. It does not touch you. It is mental only, though quite accurate and cold. But the second is something else. There is an inner door to memory and when you open it, it is all right there. You *are* there. I am in Long Barn, I see it, I feel it, I smell it, I touch it. More important still I *am* the person I was then, with all the thoughts and feelings. Of course I am still myself *now*, looking on. I find it is quite painful to push open that inner door. It is not that the experiences then were painful nor yet that they were so happy that I look back with too much longing on them. It's just that I feel it—life—so vividly, almost more vividly than I did then, and its very vividness is a kind of anguish.

Thursday, November 19th

The papers are full of the advances in Africa. British, American, and French troops marching together. The *Marseillaise* played again. All the French under Giraud. I feel heartened for France and I should think all Frenchmen would take heart. I wonder if St.-Ex. will go to Africa?

Saturday, November 28th

Snow—real snow—soft and surprising, suddenly over the world. I never get over the surprise of snow. So gently changing the world. I must go out in it and see it. It is such a miracle—like conversion. Every neglected seed pod, every stray grapevine tendril, carries its burden of snow. Not one is forgotten. The change is complete. It makes me full of joy.

But later in the afternoon I am equally depressed by the terrible things in the newspapers. Especially the stories of the treatment of the Jews in Poland. Mass shootings, the planned extermination of all Jews in Europe by the Nazis. In moments like these I feel I cannot bear it. That it is best perhaps to be a Quaker and oppose all war. But the Quakers shut the door somewhere.

They refuse the responsibility of thinking beyond a certain point. I do not mind *supra*-rationalizing (i.e., the mystic) but the Quakers seem to me infra-rationalizing. They do not go beyond into mystic apprehension. Of course their purity—even their blind purity—is a great and useful force. But I wish it were not blind.

One feels everyone's happiness is smeared, sullied, robbed forever by such horrors, even though they are distant. There is a worm in the apple of happiness for all of us—forever.

C. says, There will be another crop of apples.

For another generation, yes. I look at the gay gurgling wide-eyed baby and wonder if he will have "another apple."

Monday, November 30th

C. and I to the Saarinens, late, for dinner. Eliel Saarinen, the old Finnish architect, is there. He is a sharp, dry, wise old man. We talk of cities of the future, city planning. He is for decentralization—homes around work areas, in not too large groups. Men to walk if possible to work—not more than 20,000 population in a group.

He says his first impression of America was the slums of Chicago in the slump—50 miles of slums! I ask if it is as bad in other cities, and he says you cannot judge it by *area*. It is a disease, like cancer, it spreads. He gives interesting parallels in physiology. Healthy tissue under a microscope gives an example of what good city planning should be—distribution of food, communication. Also that diseased cells are like cities.

Some interesting things come up as a defense of Cranbrook —what is lavished on it, its perfection, even if it influences only a small proportion of the population.

He is a quality rather than a quantity person and believes in other values than material ones. And has a ramrod of integrity under his stiff collar. I like him and felt he did not realize how close our points of view were.

An army officer came in—nice and bluff—but intelligent, a thinking person. The war comes up and he says he wonders if we are going to find out, before we get to the end, what we are really fighting for. There is a deep silence. The older Saarinen says he wonders if we have any idea *what winning is* (when we will consider to have won—the terms of winning).

The young [Eero] Saarinen sees it in stages: first period, when European war is over but Japanese war is still going on; second period, when Japanese war is over but reconstruction going on; third, possibilities of a terrible slump. People are at least beginning to *think* about the war as opposed to feeling vaguely.

Tuesday, December 8th

C. leaves very early for Wright Field to work on altitude flying. Two of the men have been killed on such flights, chiefly, they think, because his report on altitude-flying equipment was not read.[1]

In the evening I discover St.-Ex.'s appeal to all Frenchmen[2] to cease bickering and join in the fight in Africa—nonpolitically —for France. Wants only to join his "groupe" in Tunis. He is at peace again. He sees quite well that there is no position for the exile except that of the soldier, and even then they will always be in debt to the "Saints in France" who have stood there suffering. He knows that revival will come from the "cellars underneath tyranny," not from the exiles on the outside.

He is at peace. I am glad. But I can only feel humble in the face of that letter, and that suffering, and that course of action. What is the equivalent in our lives? in mine?

C. home late—I tell him about the letter. He says there is no "equivalent" because we are not in the position of France. But I feel there must be one, somewhere. I do not know where or how. It does not seem to me it can be in sitting in my trailer writing stories. It is more in the baby. But all my efforts seem trivial in comparison to the sacrifice of people like that.

Wednesday, December 9th

C. was home at night and we talk about St.-Ex.'s position and ours. C. says he is a wonderful man and, by *his* standards, "right,"

[1] See Introduction, p. xxvii.

[2] "To All Frenchmen Everywhere," *Time* magazine, November 29th.

though he does not know where his effort will lead. We go from here into another discussion of our whole position on the war. I feel rather ashamed of some of my arguments on the war stand —*not* of my thesis, which I believe in completely still, but of the arguments, logic, etc., I tried to use to enforce our stand. They seem to me nationalistic and somehow not to spring from my own ground—alien to it. I feel particularly so in front of the writings of people like St.-Ex. C. says St.-Ex.'s is the saint's point of view, but that the saint refuses certain earthly responsibility. He is all for the saints but feels they should (as far as I can see) be protected by the soldier. I do not like to see myself upon a hilltop all safe and saintly while I am "protected" by soldiers underneath me, using methods that revolt me.

Go to bed disturbed and wake very early unable to sleep.

I said, in my sleep almost, "But I want to be forgiven—oh, I want to be forgiven."

"For what?" C. asks. "And by whom?"

"I don't know," I say, "but I feel so strongly that I want to be forgiven."

"I know," he says, "one does feel that sometimes—for *all* one's mistakes. I don't know anyone who has less to be forgiven than you and I don't know any *way* to be forgiven except to want to. If you *want* to be forgiven, then you *are* forgiven."

St.-Ex. was a symbol for all the best people "on the other side." He was a kind of symbol to me. I wanted them to see we were not evil, but that is a private and worldly wish.

C. said, "I know what you're going through; I understand all those conflicts; I see what you see. You see that he'll go over there and he'll be killed, and he probably will if he gets over there."

I say, "Yes, but it will be worse for him if he eats his heart out over here."

C. agrees.

Yes, that is what I see. It seems to me very clear. The last battle he went to with bitterness. But this one he goes to with joy—with thirst even. What I feel so strongly in that letter is the pull to sacrifice, to death. He wants to pay his "debt" to those saints in France. Those hostages, those to whom he says the exiles will *always* be in debt, no matter what they do. So he goes to pay that final debt, to make the supreme sacrifice in joy. He was going to find his place "in some quiet bed in some cemetery in North Africa."

C. says if he is fated to die in Africa he will die and if he is fated to live he will somehow live. I wish I could feel this fatalistic. But I feel only practically; they will send him just where he wants to go—to death. He goes back to Africa that he loved. Where he once cheated death he now pays it back. There is a terrible fitness about it all.

C. says to my "Now he will never know"—"Do you cross them right off then, when they die?"

Saturday, December 12th

Call Miss Hamilton, an English economist who has written saying she wants to see me—why? To get the isolationist point of view? To lecture us? I am all prepared with formal statements of my (for she speaks only of me) nonparticipation in politics when she says over the telephone that it is only personal. "Mrs. Ames said to me 'Anne Lindbergh is . . . you ought to see her.'" Also because of my books. She is coming out Tuesday when C. is away.

It is so strange what a letup in the pressure there is from the smallest incident. To have a strange Englishwoman (a friend of the Whiteheads) want to see me relieves the pressure of rejection. I could breathe and walk and think more easily after that telephone conversation.

At night C. and I get into an argument about war atrocities, suffering, and their place on the earth. He feels, I think, that war, dreadful as it is, is better than decay. I can see that *theoretically,* but when I read of the atrocities in Poland, the shooting of hostages in France, I get to feeling: But surely *this is* decay, *this is* the loss of civilization.

C. says hostages are a horrible part of war—all war—and that atrocities are, too. He says *all* these things have occurred in *all* nations in varying degrees.

I am upset by the implication of these talks—though, or perhaps *because,* I know C. is a moderate, with a wealth of compassion, but scrupulously honest (so many compassionate people are not).

All my life I have prayed "that I may understand" the problem of evil. But perhaps one should not pray that, perhaps one should pray: Help me to live, to live right, *without* understanding.

Sunday, December 13th

Baby four months old. C. takes the children to 508. Lie down, listen to the Brahms Concerto in D and Symphony No. 1 on the Philharmonic. There is something in that music, in my window full of stars at night, in St.-Ex.'s philosophy and in myself in my most alive moments which I cannot reconcile to C.'s philosophy. Perhaps it is two irreconcilable pulls—Spirit and Body, Life and Death—which the heart cannot reconcile but must hold, even in strife, at the same time.

Monday, December 14th

Mrs. H. cannot come. She calls—her schedule has tightened. I am sorry now. I would like to have seen her. There was warmth even in our telephone contact.

Tuesday, December 15th

Trouble in the kitchen again. William and Anna are in a perpetual grouch about something. I feel I have perhaps taken away their pride in their work by trying to simplify it. They don't really want it simplified. I suppose it is a horribly dull and stultifying life: washing dishes and mopping floors, and naturally you prefer to fold napkins and roll butter balls and cut fancy grapefruit edges.

Agreement in Dakar with the English and Americans to work in a united effort for victory. This heartens me. I hate all the French squabbles—now if the Fighting French can just stop bickering.

Wednesday, December 16th

C. comes home late, after midnight, after going to Willow Run and up on a flight of 42,000 feet today! He seems in good spirits and says it was the best flight ever. He has a new job, with Pratt & Whitney in Hartford (part-time, of course, only) and is very happy over it. Kind of work he likes best. *Really* needed there, admires and likes the men. They could not take him a year ago, the political pressure was so high, but now, C. says, "Our stock is rising."

C. is pleased because I have put a red scarf around my neck. All I have to do to please him is to put on a blue dress and a red scarf!

Sunday, December 20th

I walk with Land to the service (all dressed up in my purple suit, which still fits. Yesterday I was not dressed up enough, so today I try not to disgrace my son!). We carry presents. There is a crèche in a corner of the church and at the end of the service we all march around and place the things before it.

It is such a nice idea but it was not—to me—moving at all as a service. Why not? It seemed just ritual, with no mysticism and not simple enough. And it was too much a neighborhood-house affair. That is all right, in its place. But its place is *not* in church. The church today, and the Protestant Church particularly, has become simply the Neighborhood House.

The service was simple and the old prayers lovely but I could not lose myself in it, especially with Mrs. C. chatting now and then in my ear. I like her. Yet it is *not* worship but neighborliness.

I felt more Christmas spirit walking home with Land in the cold bright snow with the Christmas bells ringing carols, and most of all at Land's "party" when the children sang "Gloooria in excelsis Deo" and Land's face lit up with joy.

Churches, I decide, reforming in my mind, should be dark; you should see *no* faces, no personalities. It should be impersonal, anonymous. One should be lost in nameless worship—an unknown soul.

The week has gone in pressure and weariness. Packages arriving. People going. Fights in the kitchen. I to the trailer every morning, feeling very tired working ahead on "Take-off."[1] Sensing the tension in the house. It is very unpleasant. Anne is in bed with a cold. The baby catches it. I am full of remorse. Put him in our bathroom all night. He fusses and sneezes. I get up and give him water. No sleep. But he is better in the morning—that is all that matters. That was Christmas Eve day. We get out some sleigh bells and let Land be a reindeer part of the evening. He gets so excited he jumps into his bath with his underwear on—still a reindeer!

Christmas was nice, though Anne was in bed and Scott still sniffly. C. takes the boys out while I nurse the baby, bringing them back in about 11, when we open presents.

But Christmas for me was in nursing Scott. I am nursing my baby. I shall never have another like it. The church bells were ringing carols through the window from a distance. I could hear them faintly.

Jon, Land, I sit by the fire at night and say the Bible verses of the Christmas story and look at the old pictures, play carols, and say the Lord's Prayer.

The day after Christmas William tells me they didn't want to spoil my Christmas by telling me but they are leaving in less than a week! I have to start all over again. The time, the time that goes into this!

Sunday

Anne opens a present from Jim—an enchanting pink corduroy Kate Greenaway wrapper. She looks very sweet in it. I feel so touched at Jim's thoughtfulness of all the children. Perhaps it was the thing that touched me the most deeply about this Christmas. Jim picking out presents in his rushed army routine, from that town in Georgia, for all the children—all beautifully suited to each child, each card chosen to fit.

[1] Chapter in *The Steep Ascent*.

C. says (in admiration) that to Jim personal relationships always come first. They always do to a woman, too!

Monday, December 28th

Darlan has been assassinated; Giraud takes command. Roosevelt condemns the act, but some Fighting French call it the arm of fate justly striking, and say the assassin should be spared as a patriot.

Sunday, January 3rd

C. leaves for Hartford. I finish George Sand's letters to Flaubert. I miss her generous humanity and kindly wisdom when I am through. It is not enough to copy down any one bit. But it is a quality in the whole collection of letters. I see why Flaubert leaned so on her.

Play Bach's B Minor Mass at night.

Wednesday, January 6th

It is strange how utterly mad one's thoughts are (Dostoevsky painted people as they really are) and yet one goes right on leading a normal life, hiding from people the depression or elation you happen to be in, hiding what you really are, playing as well as you can the role you must play. For this is the mark of maturity—the degree to which one can go on making the oblations, performing the rite when—as St.-Ex. says—the God has left the temple. There are always times when the God is hidden. But one must go on through the motions even when one sees no sense in it—clean out the drawers, bathe the baby, copy the last chapter, write the old nurse, comfort Jon in his gloom (so like mine. Can I teach him how to bridge these pits? For one *can* learn—in time).

Thursday, January 7th

Better sleep, though the baby cried at 4:15. And the cold is definitely trying to clear up. Do baby, work on notes for flying over France. Papers: oil and gas restrictions much worse in the East. All "pleasure driving" to be cut out, with a hint of strict checking up on this—examination of cars in lots near theaters, etc.

Land and Jon usually end up fighting; then I have to find reassurance for Land and occupation for Jon. But of *these,* the triumphs of the day are made. When I can make an aggrieved Land be policeman for the baby carriage—clear traffic, open doors, lock up the carriage, etc. (How Land *loves* to act!) "Yes, ma'am, I have a little girl of my own," says Land, "just two years old." This is the thrill of a Mother's creation. One gets an artistic pleasure from it. But Jon is harder. I finally get him to shovel all the snow away from the front of the garage because "Your father may come home tonight and he'd like to see it cleared" (for 25 cents an hour). Jon can't play-act. It has to be *real* to count. He did a good job and felt proud of it.

C. unexpectedly came home after supper. In leather coat and gray hat, smiling in the door. I am sitting up in bed. "How wonderful!" I say. "I didn't think you'd come!" He has to go off in the morning. But even one night is to touch base again. All is going well in Hartford. That is, all the men are pleased to have C. working there, and C. is in very good spirits. Apparently the Aviation people in Washington are pleased, too.

C. leaves early for the Coast. I hate so to have him go *anywhere* —*think* if it were to war! How do they bear it?

I go for a walk. It is snowing lightly. There is a dead possum in the snow, killed by dogs (I gather from the tracks). Gray fur and a smooth tail, a startling gash of red. And that small pink snout looking so peaceful, as though curled up in sleep. I stop for a moment in pity—death is always a shock—why, I don't know.

As I put the baby down at 3, C. comes back in the door! Bad weather (it is now snowing hard); I am so happy. After tea we go out for a beautiful long walk, the fine snow soft and constant in our faces, the lights of Cranbrook dim in the mist and the pines dark against the white hills. It is quiet and deserted—dusk and snow and no one about. We walk through Cranbrook Park up to the Art Museum, over to the Science

Belknap House, Bloomfield Hills

Trailer, Bloomfield Hills

Anne Lindbergh with Land, Jon, and little Anne, Bloomfield Hills, 1942

Little Anne,
Bloomfield Hills,
1942

Harry Bennett's picnic, August 1942

The two Annes, Bloomfield Hills, 1942

*Approach to Cranbrook Academy of Art Library and Museum,
with fountain group by Carl Milles
By permission of Cranbrook Academy of Art. Photo Harvey Croze*

*Carl Milles' house and private sculpture gallery
By permission of Cranbrook Academy of Art. Photo Richard Askew*

Jon at Teton Valley Ranch, Wyoming, 1943

*Anne Lindbergh
with Scott,
Bloomfield Hills, 1943*

Lillian Holm,
Svea Lindberg Kline,
Carl Milles,
in Milles' Greek room
at Cranbrook, 1944

Anne Lindbergh,
Bloomfield Hills, 1943

*Colonel Charles H. MacDonald, Commander of the 475th Fighter Group,
and Charles Lindbergh, Biak Island, July 1944*

Charles Lindbergh with First Lieutenant James H. Lynch, 1944

Charles Lindbergh, Emirau Island, May 1944

Institute and home. "It has been a lovely day," I say to C. as we climb back through the woods, "in spite of the possum." (The little furry mound of his body is sifted over with snow, now.)

"Yes," said C. "I know."

Supper with Jon in front of the fire.

Sunday, January 10th

C. off early again. I do the baby and go to the trailer.

After lunch, as I am doing my exercises to the Philharmonic, C. comes back again. Bad weather again. We go out for a walk. Up the hill outside Cranbrook, back through the woods and over fences.

At night I write letters in front of the fire while C. works at the card table on his *Spirit of St. Louis*. He says writing "takes the place of sociability." It is your form of giving to friends— *one* eliminates the *other*. I am always trying to do both.

Monday, January 11th

C. is off as I go to feed the baby. He pokes his head between the curtains, startles the baby, who looks at him with great round eyes not sure whether to smile or cry, then comes in, tickles him on his front and says in the most *incredible* tones: *"Oh, oui oui oui, c'est ton père qui parle, c'est ton père!"* (learned from the brief period when Land spoke and understood only French). Then the baby seems to know it is a joke and smiles.

He is very big now, almost leaps with delight when I come in to pick him up in the morning. It is hard to give up this close time with him. And it does not seem to be transferable to paper. The closeness of the weight of a baby in your arms, his cheek against yours (he smiles when I do this), his soft downy head under my chin as I sit him up. But no, it is not describable, because the understanding is all physical. In the way my hands work changing the diapers. In the way I turn him over— carefully, so both arms make a firm base. In knowing his laugh and his cry and his sociable talking, knowing how he feels. When he is about to fuss, to cry, to wriggle. The understanding is in my body and in his. He knows it as well and sometimes seems to smile—in answer to a smile of mine which has not yet come to the surface!

I speak in a special voice to him, too, because he always looks startled when I speak to anyone else.

Pack in afternoon and evening for two weeks in Englewood. C. comes home at 9! Locked out! (Bad weather again.) Jon hears him whistle outside the door.

While I do the packing and the baby (for the last evening), C. writes at his manuscripts. He has finished the first chapter (after three handwritten drafts!).

When I tell C. I am afraid of what his stands may lead to in the future he says, "No, you needn't be afraid" (gently) "because I don't like to hurt anyone." This last is true.

Tuesday, January 12th

To the trailer and for a walk. The wind has blown away the damp overcast and clouds—a clear whipping blue sky. I can almost feel C.'s exhilaration to be in the air again, setting out for the Coast in the plane. So many times I have gone with him.

Anne waves good-bye, still incredulous, and Land casually from the bathtub. He wants me to bring him bubble bath soap and a pot holder (because he is interested in cooking! Domestic Land). Jon wants gloves.

I can be happy to go now and to think of coming back, to my family. The baby has separated me from the other children. Jon needs me. I must find Anne again. To Charles—happy in his new work—and especially to the "Alps" story. I feel I have been given this dull winter in Michigan just to finish it. I *must* finish it. I may not have another chance.

Englewood, January 26th

Two weeks have gone by in New York. Now that it is almost over it is hard to sum up what has happened. It has gone very fast. I have seen a great many people, I have looked for a cook, I have shopped. Been to the dentist. I have walked all over New York and tramped up and down subways and in and out of buses. I have shared some of Con's life—up and down those interminable stairs, making a home for a lot of stray, gay young Englishmen, kissing Saran good night, remaining calm and objective, aware, amused, pounding out her hours at the office,[1] keeping the house going with too little help, entertaining, planning for Aubrey, etc.

Out dancing one night with Con and Aubrey and the two Englishmen. (How is it possible that anyone can be so young as those two young men? But they are forty! And have been through the Blitz. One learns through suffering? One doesn't, though, half the time.)

A great many people—so many that I talked too much, got too excited, couldn't sleep, got the people all mixed up in my mind afterwards. "Now *who* said that?" It was a kind of vivid flowering after the long dull months—and yet it was so full that I could hardly appreciate it. Killing a cat with cream! Certain things will remain, I hope, and sift out clearly in the memory during the long dull months ahead.

We saw Chekhov's *Three Sisters*—so rich, vivid, my kind of people and writing.

New York dimmed out, with the stars shining down between buildings and buses full of old Ladies of Quality asking the conductor how they can get to 57th Street. No bacon, tea, coffee, almonds, or cream at restaurants. Buses and subways jammed and *very* dirty and everyone in a dither over taxis. Should or should one not take them? What was "pleasure driving"? Ambrose taking Mother to the U.S.O. but *not* out to lunch. The taxi drivers all very talkative and grumbling about the confusion.

This visit to New York has been quick sharp contacts here and there, interrupted, passing, and quite deep. An intensity has lain over it all. I suppose the intensity is in me. I feel so on the brink of something. That everyone is scattering to the four corners of the earth. That all is in flux. That there is no time. That—as we pass for an instant on the road—we should

[1] In the Survey Department of the British Information Services in New York.

make our contacts real. "Speak quick and tell me—what have you on your heart!"

I suppose it is my long exile that has given me such a sense of the preciousness of human contacts. And also the sense of impending separation. The old life breaking up, new lines of enmity and of loyalty.

I am beginning to come out from under a cloud of guilt, of humility, before the war and all the suffering.

It is difficult to be balanced. For the sensitive, the dark side of life is so terrible that to accept it at all one must embrace it. But they are wrong, a little bit. It is a separation of life and death, and they must not be separated. I must see them together. I feel Charles is closer to this than I am and can show me, has shown me. But I see it more clearly suddenly away from him. I long to talk it over with him, to tell him what he has. What he is. Why I love him.

The pull to life is stronger in me than the pull to death. That is why I married C. That is what I want to live, to give my children, and to write. Will it be permitted?

February 2nd

I have been taking care of the children, plunged into it, pounding up and down stairs, carefully poking strained string beans back into Scott's pouting mouth. Collecting Land's scattered wet clothes and putting them on the radiator to dry. Coaxing Anne to eat some carrots. Stirring a formula, watching for it to boil, and washing—bottles, bottle brushes, nipples, pots, pans, orange-juice dishes, vegetable dishes, hemo glasses, all for the children. What has this to do with what I learned in New York? With what I hope to write in my story? Life is in such watertight compartments. One seems snowed under by one personality and then another. Yet it must not be divided. . . .

C. came back last night. It is unbelievable, like sunshine; I feel full of life and hope and happiness. I realize now, in the last days of bad weather, how I have been dreading something happening to him. It has been haunting me, insanely.

This morning, when the telephone rang, I thought suddenly

with relief: No reason to dread it—C. is back, he is safe, they are not ringing up to say he is lost!

It was Mother to say Margot has had a little girl [Faith Morrow]! Did she want a boy? I think so—and I a girl. But still it does not matter. Scott seems the embodiment of earthly joy in living, being, eating, stretching!

February 3rd

Land and I laugh and laugh tonight over a funny cartoon in a book of animal jokes. We both thought the same thing funny at the same instant! What joy to share humor.

In my one hour's "nap" I read the *Times*. I read not for news, but for trends. The *news* says we are winning on all fronts. The Russians driving back the Nazis from Stalingrad, from the oil fields, from the Caucasus, terrible casualties. That Churchill has won over Turkey (diplomatically). That Tunisia is at a standstill. That there is a new Solomon Islands battle on.

But I do not read for these; I read like a seismologist for tremors on the earth's surface, cracks in the crust, divisions. I read always for the same thing really—to find out where the lines are forming, what the real division, the real chasm, is. I want, I choose, of course, always *middle ground*. But in this schism there may be no middle ground. In every department of life— war, letters, etc. I am searching for it but I find only the faint lines, the cracks of division—presaging the great split!

It seems as though the German morale is cracking; the late speeches of Goebbels, Göring. The proclamation of Hitler. All harping on Russia, her strength, her resources, her power, her menace. The Germans must fight to the last drop to survive, to "escape enslavement," "to escape Bolshevism."

This is called by us propaganda for a peace offensive. But suppose it is true—meant *not* for us but for home consumption only? The German people are afraid, terribly afraid (that is the way it sounds to me), *not* of us, but of *Russia*.

If we win the war (and it now seems closer), then what? What will happen to Europe in the process? Where will the lines be drawn then? Does anyone really believe we can set down

our yardsticks and traffic lines and lights over Europe so neatly
and peacefully, as [Henry] Wallace and others propose?

Sunday, February 7th

C. has left for Hartford. A terrible wind has been blowing for
two days from the north and the house is cold. And how I hate
a crying wind. If only it would stop, just for a moment.

I said to C. last night that it was such a burden—being good.
I would like to put it down for a moment. He said not to try
to carry too much! He said, too, that we were both lonely for
our kind of people and we didn't know where to find them.

Monday, February 8th

The wind has stopped! And a beautiful crystal day stepped out
whole from the storm—not a breath. All stillness, whiteness,
and sparkle—crystalline. I take Land to school. The sun is just
coming up and a few thin wisps of pulled-out cloud—streaks in
the dazzling blue. Land and I kick a hunk of ice all the way
down the hill, wonderful game. I sing—the Doxology: "Praise
God from whom all blessings flow." Land sings, too—but not
the Doxology.

Back to the trailer for two hours and a half of work. It is
very cold. It does not go very well. I am not content to write
anything that has not in it *everything* that I know. Not quite
that—but I can't bear to write down half a truth, when I know
better.

C. says I have been limiting myself too much. "Choose something *Big* next time!" He has so much faith in me—*so* much—
it is unbelievable. When there is not a spider's thread of faith
in me there is always his—inexhaustible.

"O thou lord of life, send my roots rain."
[GERARD MANLEY HOPKINS]

Wednesday, February 10th

Shoes are rationed—three pairs a year! I am pretty well stocked
but the children grow out of them so fast! I will have to save

my points for them. (Nine a year Jon takes, I fear.) Meat is to be rationed on Friday. I tell Jon we will have to eat rabbits and he starts to make snares for them (as P'tit Louis taught him on Illiec) with wire and stakes.

Monday, February 15th

Russia demands—for the first time—Bessarabia, Latvia, Estonia, and Lithuania. This is not "aggression" but her rightful territory, she says!

The Germans are still doing very badly in Russia.

Arthur Koestler's article on what we are fighting this war for—a new order? No (he says), the old one patched up a little. Eighty per cent of people in Britain (Gallup poll) behind Churchill's "We mean to hold our own" speech.

Thursday, February 18th

A clear and lovely day. Over to light the trailer and take Land to school. But he is late so we are hurried, which spoils it. I usually love this quiet walk to school with the sun just coming up and all the trees white with frost and glistening in the sun.

Note from C. in mail—coming Friday or Saturday.

I try not to *waste* any of the day. By waste I don't mean exactly what other people do. Waste is being unaware. It is spending too much time—*unaware* time—on the newspapers, or reading an article only to be able to write a friend that you've read it. Or dreaming, or fiddling with pieces of paper worrying, or looking at catalogues, or making too many useless trips up and down stairs, or walking out of doors and not seeing it. And yet sometimes I feel I wear myself out being "aware." Is this why I am so tired at the end of the day?

Writing, of course, the sheer concentration, is exhausting. To write, I have decided, is to be possessed by the Demon Lover the ballads talk of. In ordinary life you look sane. You act sane. Just as sane as any mother of four children, any wife. But once you start to write—No. You are possessed. You think incredible things. You say incredible things. You are another person. You even love other people. You don't love your children and your husband at all. Maybe now I've written it out it won't worry me so. For it does. I want *not* to be separate but all of a piece.

Friday, February 19th

A beautiful day—Land and I get a good start and don't have to hurry to school. It is lovely. We see a cardinal on our way down. Jon is in bed with a cough. Anne is better.

The hot-water man comes and we have hot water again. Marie can do the laundry! Oh heavenly day!

It is a melting day. The trailer is warm. I open a window. Birds are singing.

The Russians are still advancing. The newspapers break the back of the day for me. Next to war, everything I am doing seems unimportant. Not the children, of course—but writing.

No Charles.

Saturday, February 20th

Another deliriously soft day. The snow melts from the sides of the hill. Before I finish with Scott, C. comes! The house is alive. "Father is here!" say Jon and Land, meeting him first. (They are all obedient and good as gold, too. Land going promptly outside.) C. and I go for a walk in the warm sunshine and down the melting roads. Comparing notes, talking too hard, C. on the changing sentiment in Washington and the East. C. says he is welcomed everywhere. He gives me the news on the war fronts.

We talk about moving and whether it is wise. Whether the complications of living—sheer living in New England, with all the difficulties of food, transportation, heating problems—may be so difficult that it may be better to stay here. Though C. says he will be half the time there and feels far more at home with all those people, their methods, minds, etc. than here, which means he will eventually, I imagine, be there more.

As usual I feel full of hope and energy with C. back.

Spring is here!

Sunday, February 21st

Another lovely clear melting day. C. takes all the children except Scott over to his mother's. I hate to have them go and feel left out, rather. And yet after they have gone I go out for a long walk alone, all over Cranbrook. As I turn toward home I realize that I don't want to go home. I feel conscious of how I hate the house—with an almost physical revulsion—that apricot living room, with the false bumpy walls, and the false beams and the shiny store furniture. Now, I say firmly to myself, it is just that room you hate—not Detroit, not Michigan.

I talk it over with C. at night. He says it isn't "just the room." I'm afraid perhaps the room typifies something that is more profound about this "Middle East," as Saarinen calls it.

Read Kafka's *Castle* at night. It is wonderful. How I understand his eternal search for some positive connection with, some sense of sanction from, "The Castle."

And also how I understand his everlasting sense of exclusion, of wanting to belong, to be accepted. The hopeless passion to be "ordinary," to be on the inside—which shows, alas, that one is still on the outside.

Tuesday, February 23rd

Dreadful headlines in the paper. Two transports lost—850 lost. And a Clipper crashed in Lisbon, with 20 killed. This dreadful news clouds the day and makes all the rest of the mail and news unreal. It makes writing unreal, too. How can one write when things like this are happening?

But I try to. I write some of the flying chapter and a swift preface, touched off by these tragedies, a kind of apologia it is, for writing this kind of thing at such a time.

By the time I get through with the papers, I feel tired and bitter. An accumulated bitterness—the terrible waste of life in those transports (and for what? If one knew). Starvation over Europe because of narrow-visioned fanatics. Russia bludgeoning her way over Europe—or intending to. (I am not talking about the common soldier defending Leningrad. One cannot help but be fired with deep admiration at the way they have thrown out the invaders. But Stalin's bullying threats.)

I go out onto the big green hill to try to blow it all away—to find the sky. I go up on the hill where the green is, where there is space. I stand a long time until I feel the wind has blown some of the bitterness away. I realize standing there that I have had three big things to fight against in my life. The first was just sorrow (the Case), the second was fear (the flights), and the third is bitterness (this whole war struggle). And the third is the hardest.

Wednesday, February 24th

A long hard day after a hard night. The baby eats almost nothing and cries at night. I get up twice and give him water—cannot get to sleep again. When I get up at 7 and go in to Land I find he has been sick all over the bed. "Darling," I say, "why didn't you call Mother?" "I did," he said pathetically. I was listening only to the baby.

Land is sick all morning. I am running up and down stairs with basins, hot cloths, hot water and soda, in between feeding and washing the baby, who is fretful and won't eat, and has a slight temperature.

When C. comes in the evening, I am completely dead—too dead to move. A hot bath and to bed. C. plays Bach for me and still seems to love me. I don't know why.

Friday, March 5th

The papers with their toll of tragedies as usual depress me. Over a hundred civilians killed—suffocated in a panic crush in a London subway—a woman falls with a baby and the people pile up behind her, crowding to get in from an air raid. The bits of news that come now from France are so horrible. Tightening of anti-Semitic legislation. Young men drafted for labor in Germany—no food—harvest from North Africa cut off—a month without bread (such bread as it was!).

They are all waiting for deliverance by us, a second front. At least the political news from Africa seems good. Giraud's relaxing of anti-Semitic restrictions.

The war news is thin—all fronts at a standstill.

Monday, March 8th

C. calls up; he is here, will be home for supper. I tell Jon his father is coming and his face lights up. "Gee, it's too bad he has to be away so much." Jon is the one who misses and needs C. the most.

C. gives me the war news. Bad in Tunisia though not serious or a large engagement. The Russian success was real—a real defeat for the Nazis but Germany shows no signs of cracking up. England has been going into her (large) reserves.

C. says—much to my surprise—that all doors are open to him everywhere (except the closest Administration circles). Arnold is saying he is glad C. is working at Pratt & Whitney since he felt he (Arnold) "let him down." Of course they have a guilty conscience about him, and *they should have,* I think. But C. doesn't. He doesn't bear a grudge against anyone.

C. says a French officer stopped him in the Carlton Hotel, pressed his hand, said he saw him in Paris on his first flight. "Now I am with General De Gaulle." They were both effusive with greetings. This pleases me very much. A De Gaulle man greeting C.!

I sleep—how I sleep—like a child, next to the security of C. I have not slept like this for nights.

Tuesday, March 9th

Harry Hopkins says "No more zippers" [as a wartime saving] in *Reader's Digest.* Oh, thank you, Brother Hopkins! I have ruined a slip, a pair of flannel trousers, and a zipper when the zipper gets caught in the slip. Thank God the zipper era is over! I always did hate them—cold, slippery, metallic things—never could trust them. They never hold when you want them to. They are rigid when you want them to ease a little. No resilience, no charm, no texture. Take a button, now, you know where you are. It holds till death, but it will give, too, humanly, if you gain a half an inch. Besides, the *feel* of a button—so friendly and comfortable, warm to touch.

C. comes back late and is cross because I say I won't be able to get to the trailer tomorrow. I have to make the formula. He says with three people in the house, can't one of them make the formula, wash the bottles, do the routine? He says I get caught up in routine, in which he is right. But I always feel it's cowardly of me, or lazy, shirking, to do only the nice part of taking care of the children. I have a kind of missionary zeal about doing all the dirty jobs, too. C. says he never knew anyone who made such symbolism out of picayune jobs.

Sunday, March 14th

C. is sad about his mother, whom he wants so much to help, and cannot. (She is ill and won't see a doctor or get anyone to help her. She is such a stoic.) I must go next time. I *might* be able to help—even though C. thinks not. I am a woman and she has no woman around her.

I read C. my "Anteroom"[1] at night. He says it is very good, especially the end. From which I infer that the beginning is *not* good, and that I have not quite pulled it off. I wanted it to be the struggle against fear, against the powers of darkness. How fear drags with it a host of other evils; turns one inward—self-pity, blame of others, deceit, and all the things one uses against it. Turns to dreams, anger, blame, escape into childhood, mirages—and finally the stoic escape, the last one. (But still *no* escape—no good.)

Monday, March 15th

Monday and a rainy sky and C. off again! It has turned warm and I wake up dizzy with a dream. An intense dream of young love that isn't really love at all, it is so young, so adoring, so idealistic—without a trace of the flesh in it. Here I am 36—old enough to stop falling in love for good, and I still dream of 16-

[1] Chapter in *The Steep Ascent*.

year-old love. An unsatisfied hunger—an *"angoisse inguéris-sable."*

And then of course I woke up and told C. about it. He looked chagrined. "It is a hunger in you." Yes, I say, but it isn't important. It will always be there. It can't be cured. It's what makes me write. It's what Kierkegaard calls "being unhappily in love with God." The Poet, he says, is unhappily in love with God.

"No," says C. "It *can* be fed—like hunger. Then you get hungry again. It's these green walls," he says, "and Michigan and the Middle West."

But I am rather cloudy all morning, still floating on the dim-remembered ecstasy of my dream. C. is irritated (mildly) and says I don't listen to him when he tells me about the ticket and the oil in the trailer and how gasoline differs from fuel oil, etc. I apologize for being so vague and impractical. "You're not impractical," says C., still looking at me ruefully. "What, then?" I ask. "Just far away from you?" "Yes," C. says with relief now, seeing I am no longer far away. "And that I can't bear."

Cranbrook, March 17th

Dear Sue [Vaillant],[1]

It is March—today a good .whipping wind, still little bits of dirty snow in the shadowed part of the garden, the ground still too hard to work. For a vegetable garden is going to be a *necessity* this year.

I am working hard. My story is almost done. I have put everything in it—everything I learned from that life in the past. It is a flight over the Alps but it could be anything. Childbirth or getting married, or the mental and moral struggles one has. There are those same peaks ("Is this all there is to the Alps?") and those same abysses ("I am abandoned—they have abandoned me!"). It is my whole life. But I still do not know if it is publishable—now or ever. I wish you could tell me.

[1] The letter was addressed to the U.S. Embassy in Lima, Peru, where George Vaillant was Cultural Attaché.

In the meantime I am happy because Giraud has made a moving speech calling all Frenchmen to unite in one army, one navy, etc., saying that all laws Vichy made are null and void in Africa, setting up a Republican regime, saying France when liberated will choose her own government, saying he has no ambitions except to free France—"I am the servant of the French people and not their master." Now I hope the others do fall in.

C. is away again. He is away so much that I think we might move East. We both long for the people of the East, though by the time we get there, all the people I want to see will be in Africa or England or Peru!

DIARY   *Tuesday, March 23rd*

It seems we are advancing in Tunisia. At least the British 8th Army is attacking and we are advancing without opposition. The Russian Front seems to be at a standstill. I read all Churchill's speech on the postwar world—*very* British. Very imperialist ("We mean to hold our own," etc.), very down to earth (written in "Pounds, Shillings and Pence," "no rosy promises," "no fairy tales"), but so completely honest. One cannot help but admire the man's integrity.

Wednesday, March 24th

Wake early. "Journey proud!" Already the excitement of going to New York has disturbed me down to the core. I don't like to get so out of touch—as I shall be now for two weeks—in the heady excitement of seeing People. ("Life is a feast or a famine.") Special delivery from Mother to say she has met Eden[1] at dinner—sat beside him and he praised my books! Mother *beams* so when her children are praised that a perceptive person always can see where he has hit a popular subject! Still I am pleased at his gallantry, praising me across the rift of politics. How much more generous English intellectuals have been than the American.

Anne and Land come in to watch me dress. Everyone (Hilma, the cook, the laundress!) thinks my violet hat is lovely. Land

[1] Anthony Eden, British Secretary of State for Foreign Affairs, 1940–45.

waves me good-bye at the door as I go off in the car. Calm down after I get started. Get to station one hour early! The dining car is full of hard-boiled Middle Western businessmen saying, "The old man's on the skids" [F.D.R.]. "I think there'll be less bureaucrats, not more." "The less the better." Etc.

Read Kafka's *Castle,* finish it at night. It is like a journey in a far country, strange and yet familiar at every turn, like a dream. How well I know it. I have plodded every step of the way to the Herrenhof and back, always to see Klamm, to find out from Klamm whether I am doing the right work, what my task is—is it acceptable to "The Castle"? Klamm, that one never gets any nearer to and whom one is bound to miss—whether you wait or whether you go. What a succession of Klamms there have been in my life—not important in themselves but as intermediaries to the Castle, as connections to the Castle, nearer the Castle than I. The anguish in the book is thick enough to cut.

Thursday, March 25th

To the Cosmopolitan Club, bath, breakfast, and over to Con's, where we talk furiously while she dresses and the children run over our feet. She is tired—overburdened with mothering three young Englishmen who fill up her house, sleep on sofas, and are in and out all day. All nice but she is never alone. Her staff is overworked and the cook leaving. And Aubrey is *never* there. She has not had enough sleep. I do not see how she does it—carry on a job, too—and give so much to her children and is so good-natured.

C. calls me, is coming down tomorrow night; we can spend Saturday and Sunday together in Englewood. It caps the day.

To bed very late and impossible to sleep. My mind spins, rests at last in peace and joy at the thought that tomorrow night I shall have with C.

Friday, March 26th

A delicious spring day. In spite of the bad night, I wake gay and free and go out and walk without a coat, down Madison, and do errands for the children. Back for lunch at the Cosmopolitan

Club with Freda [Utley][1] and Adelaide Marquand, about to have a child. Go back to Adelaide's for tea. Her husband, John, there. They are both such *good* people and she is so wise and courageous, struggling with the problem of a woman, a marriage, and a career. I hope we keep them as friends. Adelaide's delicious story of the woman attacking C. (after she had had three drinks!) and Adelaide's defense. The woman said C. mistreated me and all women, had no respect for women. Adelaide defended him and told the story of C.'s consideration for her—getting her out of a crowded meeting (when she was expecting a baby). The woman turned a jaundiced eye on her and said fiercely, "That *proves* it! *No one* but a Nazi would take so much interest in a pregnant woman!"

Supper at Con's with D'Arcy Edmondson and Isaiah Berlin.[2] The latter talks a flood of strange, fast, and brilliant conversation. I am sitting on the edge of my chair to understand. He is detached, brilliant, sensitive, and essentially kind. We get on Kafka, whom he thinks the most brilliant writer of this century. We race together in his country. I find out fairly quickly, though, where we part. I fundamentally disagree with K. I do not believe you get to the Castle by such frantic beating at the doors. I really believe in *Grace*. (Artistically, religiously, and in personal relationships.) Isaiah does not. Still, it is interesting to find someone with such a beautiful mind and I am exhilarated by it, and feel I have been a ballet dancer for an hour. Besides, I liked him and was flattered by his talking to me.

The Bach [at the concert] was something indescribable. And I felt, listening to it—to the Suite especially—how wrong Kafka was and Proust, especially Proust in his description of Swann, identifying Odette with the little phrase of music. Oh no, when

[1] Freda Utley, British socialist writer, originally in sympathy with the Russian Revolution. When her husband disappeared in Russia, she became militantly anti-Communist.

[2] G. D'Arcy Edmondson, Director of Research and Library of Information, later controller of the British Information Services. Isaiah Berlin (now Sir Isaiah), in charge of reports on the U.S.A. to the British government, scholar and author.

you get to the heart of music Odette falls away; all dross and anguish of unfulfilled love melts, dissolves, is no longer relevant. One reaches at last that point where "there is no giving or taking in marriage."

Afterwards we go with Isaiah—still talking feverishly—to the Gotham and drink milk and talk Tolstoi and Dostoevsky (whom he doesn't like), V. Woolf, E. M. Forster, Katherine Mansfield. And slowly progress to the door.

Suddenly, he whips around and is gone! We home to a party of tired Englishmen, John Wheeler-Bennett,[1] Aubrey, D'Arcy, and Ben[2] (still incredibly young, begging me to go out dancing with them!), and wait for C., whose train is late. Aubrey is deathly tired. Finally C. comes and all the men look small.

We drive out to Englewood and to bed, very tired, but delicious sense of rest. C. for two nights and a day!

Saturday, March 27th

Another delicious spring day. A late breakfast and a long walk with C. through those ugly, scrubby, second-growth oak woods. We talk politics, people, plans, and just simply walk hand in hand. A lovely walk getting back into the same country again. What does anything else matter, if one has this. It satisfies me like water after a long thirst.

Monday, March 29th

Quite cold and bright. Out for a run before going into town with Mother. In a taxi to Best's, where she shops for clothes for *all* her grandchildren and I for my children. Subway to Freda's "flat" on 11th Street. She has Sidney Hook there, a professor of philosophy at Columbia—a Socialist and a *real* liberal, and a young woman professor of economics at Holyoke, and Freda's son, Jon. Atmosphere very bohemian and fast furious arguments between Sidney Hook and Freda. He evidently believes in "the

---

[1] Sir John Wheeler-Bennett, British historian, scholar, and author, specializing in German and World War II history.

[2] Benjamin C. Thomas, the Establishment Officer of the British Information Services.

middle way" and defends his belief in it. He is brilliant, sanguine, unillusioned, nonmystical, and very kind and eminently just.

When the conversation gets around to me and Freda says, "I know you two would agree," Hook protests that he doesn't agree with me or the "Wave" (assuming it is a fatalistic philosophy). When I correct him,[1] he looks at me with astonishment, admits he never read the book, just took everyone's word for it, and exclaims, "They did that to it? They took it that way? They twisted it? Why didn't you deny it?" "I did, but I didn't shout loud enough." "She's too much of a lady," inserts Freda. I explain quite honestly, though, the faults of the book as I see them. The weakness of the image, the danger of its being taken as a political pamphlet, etc.

He agrees with me. Sees it all very clearly. Says I should go on and on, and not wait for "time to vindicate." (It never does—in his theory. You have to fight.)

I take a walk in Englewood. Supper alone with Mother. I feel again that old hurt that a good man should completely take it for granted that I actually said that totalitarianism was the wave of the future. It will never be washed away.

A lunch with Amey and Mother and a friend of Amey's, which I find depressing. I find myself trying to fit into old standards, old outworn ones, of feminism. Art for Art's sake, etc.

One does, unhappily, outgrow people. Not their hearts, ever, but their minds. And if one looked up to them in childhood it is difficult to make the distinction. One grows resentful and uncomfortable in the boxes they tend to try to fit you into. And one is embarrassed and uncomfortable for them. ("Oh, I am so sorry I cannot fit into your box. Maybe *part* of me can still fit into it—an arm or a leg.") Like Alice in the looking-glass

---

[1] The book never says totalitarianism is the wave of the future. In fact, it says: "It is not to claim that the things we dislike in Naziism are the forces of the future. But it is to say that somehow the leaders in Germany, Italy and Russia have discovered how to use new social and economic forces. . . . The evils we deplore in these systems are not in themselves the future; they are scum on the wave of the future."

house, one struggles. But no, it never works. One doesn't fit at all and one tosses about unconsciously and breaks the windows and chimneys.

On to Con's for a party. Dress with B. at the Cosmopolitan Club. She is desperately in love and blinded by it, impatient with it, blurred by it—the pool all stirred up. It is so long since I have felt that kind of love (haste gnawing at your heart) that it is hard for me to understand. Love for me was always—is always—waiting, watching, longing, a test of patience and endurance. A perpetual learning and humbling and something held in, that you had to learn how to give wisely and well. Carefully, in the right places. (One wanted always to squander it all—at the wrong place.) A whole science, loving is, an art. A dedication. One has to train oneself for it, discipline oneself to it, perhaps throughout a whole lifetime.

But I cannot talk to her about it. She is in too much of a hurry. And perhaps her kind of love is right for her.

Mother, Con, and I down to the station with bags and parcels. I feel (with a cold and not enough sleep) desperately as if I were going back to school. That sunken feeling—leaving the East, leaving all contacts and communications, leaving all roads to the Castle, all chances of meeting Klamm, of being forgiven. But I know in my adult mind I *am* wrong. The road to the Castle runs through Michigan. In my children, in C. And Klamm is probably waiting for me in the trailer, in my story.

Home again. (It is cold and snowing! Colder than when I left!) The heady excitement of it. Little Anne coming to find me—solemn, shy, tentative, yet seeking me out, as though to say "Here I am!"

Scott, big and rosy and suddenly beautiful, with beautiful eyes and a ready smile. Land—I go down to school to get him and he throws his arms around me impulsively ("He's been waiting all morning for this," his teacher says).

Jon, coming into the dining room at four, self-conscious, trying to hide his pleasure, his hands in his pockets, abruptly, "Hello, Mother!"

Feeding Scott at night (in mask and apron because of my cold). The weight of him in my arm. Surely this is enough, this is all.

And C. again—the comfort, the understanding, the peace, the strength of C. At rest, at last.

St.-Ex.'s fairy story [*The Little Prince*] comes and I read it with impatience at one sitting. But it is so terribly sad—sadder than the war book really. In spite of the fact that it is simply a very lightly painted, charming fable—fairy story for children. (No, not for children *at all*. He does not know what a child is. His Little Prince is a saint, not a child. He is an adult with the heart of a child. He is the really "pure in heart," like Dostoevsky's Idiot. But he is not a child. He has not "the hard heart of a child." He is more like a woman who has never grown up). But the sadness is not the sadness of war or tragedy. It is personal sadness—eternal sadness, eternal hunger, eternal searching. It is unbearably *"nostalgique,"* but a nostalgia for "the light that never was, on sea or land."

One wants to comfort him. (I feel he must have been miserable and sick and lonely when he wrote it.) And knows it is not possible.

There are beautiful things in it, too, all vulnerability, all tenderness, all hurt. And some answers.

But no, he has not the answers for personal life. He has not found them. And I am afraid he never will. He will throw himself into self-sacrifice—war and death. Thinking that is the answer, and it is not.

Monday, April 17th

Supper with C. We talk plans, business, and finally my story. That is a great mistake—especially since I am still tired with the trip, the cold, the children, and "my soul has not caught up with me." He says he does not believe the story can be published now or for a while. I realize that he is right and yet I am suddenly very disappointed. It is quite illogical. When I started to write it I decided that I should just write it anyway and decide afterwards about publishing. But now I realize abruptly that I have put everything into it and to "put it on ice" is not enough. C. says he is working on his manuscript and he knows it is not the time to publish it (in which he is right) and yet he feels happy in getting it done. It is like "money in the bank." He wants it published but he does not care when —even after his death.

I cannot feel like that, although I believe it is a nobler way to feel. It is not "money in the bank" to me, or food in the frigidaire. It is like milk in the breast. It won't keep, I feel. In two or three years I shall not want to publish it and I shall not be able to go on writing if it is not given. I shall not get past it. You learn nothing from a book until it goes to the publisher. And then, the moment it reaches the press, you know everything and can start out again.

C. says: Think of the writers who have kept on writing though they've had one failure after another, and that I've had "three very successful books," enough to satisfy any writer, enough to prove he is a writer.

It never gets *proved,* I say. It's like what Despiau said, "Each head is like the first one you ever did."

"Despiau has a studio *full* of heads," he answers. "Despiau may feel that way about starting a new head, but he *always starts,* he tries."

But I am stopped in my tracks and discouraged and say I cannot see ahead. I cannot think what I can do next. I don't feel as if I could write anything; I don't know that I even want to write.

At which, of course, he is angry. His anger always comes out of great love. He is angry because he sees me frustrated, and because it is beyond his control to free me. He is angry that I have been so hurt at the criticism of my book ("By a bunch of nincompoops . . ." "But it is *not* the bunch of nincompoops I mind" . . .), angry at my being unable to go ahead and give seriously and fully all that is damned up in me. He feels this is a time to plough and sow. (That's what he is doing.) He is content to be doing this for a long time. Why cannot I do it, too? He is angry at my being so temperamental—can't write on the flying trips, can't write at home when you're having a baby, can't write when people criticize you a little, can't write when we're moving, can't write during a war. It's always *something*.

All this is true, desperately true. Conditions are never right for writing and you've just got to write *anyway*. And I know things have really been pretty ideal for me—money, peace, ease. We haven't been through any hardships yet, we haven't suffered anything, I have no right to complain or be temperamental, and the time is passing.

I have no arguments to give. How can I say: But you do not know how difficult living is for me. Every step is a step on a tightrope. I must use everything—parasol, arms, head—just to keep on that tightrope.

How can one say *that* in a world at war, a world full of suffering, starving, wounded, exiled people? How can one say, but the struggle just to live the good life, just to be good and pure, takes all my heart and strength? There is nothing left over. How can one say, *"Il n'y a qu'une tristesse—c'est de n'être pas des saints"?* ("There is only one sadness—that of not being a saint") (Léon Bloy). Especially when one sees before one the visible proofs that one is *not* a saint. That one is *not* managing one's life right. That one's husband is irritated and angry (and rightfully so).

And all that anger is a great generous overpowering love, like a great torrent that only wants to free me—that alone. What a love—so few people are capable of it, so few people receive such a gift. I say, "I don't want to quarrel with you," and that it is true and perhaps will help me. I must think about it.

We laugh about it afterwards. My gloom and his anger. My gloom because I feel I have in some way fallen short of his ideal of me. His anger because he feels he has in some way failed to give me what I need, to free me.

Only I think perhaps the anger, in the end, helps me. (The first reaction is to destroy me completely.) In the end it makes me take stock of myself, stirs me up, burns away the trash on top.

I don't believe the gloom can help him like that.

Thursday, April 15th

Work with Jon in the garden in the afternoon, turning over the earth. Jon has a row of plants on his window sill. One beautiful bean in a flowerpot, which he tends as carefully as the Little Prince his rose. He puts it out in the hall each night so it won't be frostbitten. He has marked the flowerpot ("1 bean grew here in 1943").

Saturday, April 17th

I read in the paper that St.-Ex. has left the country to report for active service in the French air corps. He is then where he wants to be at last. The conflict's over. And I feel that the greatest personal happiness he has ever had in his adult life was in his relationship to his "groupe," in the war. He will go back to them. He will walk in shyly, stooping a little. They will shout, "Saint-Ex!" That will be his reward. And then . . .

But one shouldn't try to anticipate, to weigh or judge or try to understand the sacrifices of war. I feel so heavy-hearted with it that sometimes I cannot bear it. I, who stand on the outside, who have no husband, no son, no sweetheart in the conflict. I can do nothing. I feel a profound humility about politics and opinions and blueprints for a new world, and a profound distrust of words and wordiness. Then what? Writing? Writing what?

I wish there were someone I could talk this over with. But there is no one; Sue—or Jim perhaps—and Sue is away for two years and Jim is about to leave for Africa. Charles, too, perhaps —but I cannot talk to him until I am clearer.

I walk around the big hill and see all the birds, and around the lake. It is spring and yet it cannot lighten me. I must start again, I feel; the baby is big, the story is written. I must find my place in this period. I must do it alone.

Sunday, April 18th

I telephone Farmor [E. L. L. L.] and intend to take the children over to see her but she has had a bad night. (How bad? I wonder.) Her brother says it was just bad sleep and she says she feels only a little dizzy and tired. She did too much in the garden yesterday. But I worry. The children must not go and that is a blow to her. She misses them. It is all so touchy. She refuses to have a doctor or anyone to help her in the house. She refuses any help of any kind from anyone. And even to speak about it can cause her such worry as to be physically bad for her. I wish C. were here.

Sunday, April 25th, Easter

A very successful day—though Land wakes me at ten of six!

After breakfast we drive to Farmor's. Anne stands up by me and sings after me a strange conception of "Mary had a little lamb." We get there in an hour. The boys rush out. Jon disappears from view, Land, too, outside, in the basement—looking at a skull of a rat, finding a snake, etc. Anne runs to Farmor. She looks rather frail to me though not really worse; she has great difficulty getting up and sitting down. "Uncle" does all the work, the kitchen, etc. Anne plays happily around Farmor while I talk to her. She talks quite freely about her illness, her inability to do anything. Takes her hours to dress, to do her hair, only two chairs in the house she can sit down on. She is not complaining. She is just explaining for fear I may misunderstand. I feel torn with compassion, also feeling, practically, something must be done and can be done to help. I suggest various things. But she stiffens immediately—she doesn't want another chair, she is not complaining, she doesn't want anything. It is very difficult.

I tell her it may be unusual for *her* to be ill but it is normal for most people. This tack seems to help! For it is a psychological thing. The *illness* she faces squarely and even accepts; what she minds is something else—a kind of shame at being ill, at being dependent. This *can* be helped. Certain practical physical things —another chair, a spray shower, zipper dresses. And of course —if only it *could* be managed—someone to live in the house and help her.

At 4:30 we leave, picking up all our things, collecting Jon and Land from the back yard, where they have got a bag of dandelions. I have a few minutes' talk with Uncle. He is evidently very much worried, tells me in a few words that the attack the other week was much more serious than I thought, says nothing can be done, it is progressive. Says he daren't leave the house.

I go home feeling sad and also challenged by the problem; something can be done. I have got to do it, with C.'s help.

Read to the boys out of the *Great Story*—the Resurrection and the most beautiful words in the Bible. "Lo, I am with you alway, even unto the end of the world."

Mrs. L. calls up to say she has had a very happy day and I think that is true. I meant to call her but she did it first.

Leave the children at last to go out for a walk, with a feeling of great release. At last I am free to have my Easter. I will take a long walk. And then I see no lights in the kitchen or bedrooms. The maids have gone to the cottage. Miss R. and Christine have gone out.

I wonder if it would be all right to go anyway but decide against. Old memories, old pits—you never escape them, trapped.

I sit on the garden steps and watch the sunset, long ropes across the sky, banners. The first tulips have come out. The first hyacinth, the first daffodil. I wonder where C. is. I wait, but no one comes back. Then I go into the field, where I can still see the house and sit and look at the stars.

Monday, April 26th

Read the Sunday papers. Hanson Baldwin says we are at March 1918 in this war. Germany still is very strong, has one major offensive left in her (probably against Russia). After that, will be on the defensive or the downgrade. It gives me hope. Is the end in sight? It is spring in Tunisia, too. And it seems we have air superiority there. That is good.

In the afternoon the children are out in the sun. I take all the pine branches, bittersweet, cornstalks (winter bouquets) out of the house and pick forsythia and branches of little budding leaves—very small but that lovely green. Redecorate the living room—in case C. comes back.

He calls and says he'll be back for supper.

C. comes while I'm still fixing the big room and goes in to see Anne, already in bed. The boys crowd around.

We eat in front of the fire and C. tells me about his trip—a beautiful swift one in a new plane—evidently it has exhilarated him. The beauty, the swiftness, the sense of welcome he gets everywhere, the power he feels from being an expert in technical fields of air.

He has done this against every disadvantage, out of favor, stuck off in an unimportant position. Another man would have sulked in his tent but C. started out humbly over again, relearning a technical field, putting all past experience and present energy into it, working painstakingly and inconspicuously, quietly and determinedly until he has made himself an expert in two new fields—High Altitude and Fighter Performance. Also he says the attitude throughout the country is very different. People go out of their way to show him their friendship and understanding.

I talk to him about his mother and our visit. We go out for a walk in the dusk around the big hill.

Tuesday, April 27th. Rain

C. calls his mother, who says she had a wonderful day Sunday and that I did her a great deal of good. And that she has felt better ever since, better than she has for weeks. I did not of course help her physically but tried to take away her *shame of being ill.* C. is radiant and says: "If you can do that for someone that is the most important thing in life."

We go out and walk in the dusk. The ground is still wet and there is a strong wind blowing. We see the crows untidily blowing up and skidding down over the pine trees. "What does that remind you of? Florida and the flocks of ibis."

C. tells me about his flight from San Diego, right over the mountains, the desert, and flying through the night. "It was so beautiful. How I missed you!" We thought of the Easter flight we took so long ago, before little Charles was born. He said that technological worlds blind you to the real one. "When I see something very beautiful, then I think of you." Perhaps the loveliest thing that has ever been said to me. It is a rich and beautiful night and we go to bed happy and calm.

Saturday, May 1st

C. says he must leave again for the East on Wednesday night. About 4 Jon, Land, and I go with him to Ford Airport and fly in the little "Ercoupe," with *no rudder bars,* tricycle landing gear. It is a lovely sky—lots of little puffy clouds following the leader around the horizon. I have the strange sensation of being up in the air again, looking down on those ploughed fields, the line of the plough like thread on a web (one could stick one's finger through the loop at the edge where the plough turned around and pull and unravel it all). And the trees in a forest, growing straight up, bathed in air, free to the eye of God, each one alone—reaching, stretching, breathing toward the sky. And when I felt the puffs of air under the wing, the marble of a smooth bank, the stretch of the earth under you, the limitless horizon, the freedom, the expanse of lake spread out, cities dwarfed, the insignificance of factories and cars and man-made things—the beauty, power, richness, and life of the sky:

I felt again, as always: Yes, this is my country, my life, my vision. I am at home again in the air.

Jon goes up next, and then Land. Land and I stand and watch and talk to Mrs. Bennett. He [Harry Bennett] is flying the Fairchild, making landings. Jon is taciturn and proud after his trip, running off to see other planes and old engines in the hangars. But Land runs to me and hugs me and says, "Father let me fly it and I put the wing down!"

Sunday, May 2nd

Rainy and cold. C. takes the children to his mother. Sunday spreads out free before me—a wonderful feeling. I go for a walk. Stop by the pine trees, for I find they are full of birds, new ones I have never seen here before. The pine shadows are full of shifting quick flitting shapes—I can't keep them pinned down. And my heart stops when a new one comes. I see a kinglet and three different kinds of warblers. I watch with joy, keeping perfectly still, my back against a tree. And feel the sense of life as a gift. The beauty of life—in these swift delicate flitting shapes.

I go for a walk down the path and meet a squirrel coming up it. I stop before he sees me and stand very still, like a tree. He sees me, stops, and we stare at each other for a long time in frozen silence. He sits up on his haunches with his little paws folded across his breast, putting his head from side to side to take me in. I just stand still watching him and feel in this moment of frozen silent communication that I have somehow cracked the shell that separates me from his kingdom. He starts forward again up the path. (Will he really come up to me? I think wildly!) But he goes to a tree and proceeds to watch me from the root, waving his tail (in anger? or flirtatiousness?). Then I go on and he scurries away.

Monday, May 3rd

Read Sunday's and Saturday's papers. The thing that strikes me most is an article of Drew Middleton's on the American soldier— his immaturity, his lack of interest in politics, his lack of responsibility about the world (leave it to someone else—leave it to Roosevelt) as compared to the English and French soldiers, who know what they're fighting for. (According to Middleton the American soldier is dead set on winning the war, fights bravely, etc., but has no plan or interest for the future. He wants to go back to his old life, takes his privileges for granted.) Middleton lays this down to lack of experience and lack of education on the part of the American soldier, who hasn't suffered the pain of losing his privileges (like the French) or fearing he may lose them. He should be educated by discussion groups (like the English).

I wonder. Is it *just* immaturity, or lack of suffering and experience? Or do we really lack a sense of ourselves as a nation? It is so tenuous. We have no race feeling or soil feeling or language feeling. We pride ourselves on having none of these things, on being a nation of ideas alone. And we are supposed to be the best-educated country in the world. It is the basis of our democracy. Free, universal education—that is *why* America works, supposedly. And yet—the French and the English have a sense of nation that is not based on ideas alone. We seem to lack a solidarity that they have. What is America? Is it the idea in the head of Roosevelt, or Agar?[1] Or in the hearts of the idealistic New Dealers, or in the stomachs of the reactionary Republicans? It isn't in the heads of those soldiers, according to Middleton. This is what the intellectuals *want* America to be—but *is* it that?

I feel profoundly disturbed by this article. I envy the French in a way—I envy them something, even poor broken France. A Frenchman has a nation. And yet I could never be a French-woman. I want to be an American, to have my own nation. But America is still only a nation in the making. Thomas Wolfe was right. How long will it take?

C. comes home tired out from Ford Motor Company squabbles. We go out and walk in a dark stormy world and discuss Middleton's article and what is America? C. thinks it will take a long long time. The stars come out.

Tuesday, May 4th

Read paper. Giraud says he will be victorious in Tunisia in May and the war will be over (in Europe) in 1944. Could it be possible? He is asked what he is fighting for and says, "If I were an American I would say I was fighting for the freedom of the world, but as a modest Frenchman I say simply I am fighting for the liberation of France and French prisoners."

There you are—how simple for the Frenchman! It is only an American who is expected to fight for the world!

Wednesday, May 5th

Jon is miserable because he says his Bean ("1 bean grew here in 1943") is dying. He transplanted it several days ago and has covered it each night with a pot. He says it has got spots on the leaves and that "everything goes wrong for me" and threateningly and melodramatically says, with tears in his eyes, "If that

[1] Herbert Agar, American poet and writer, author of *Land of the Free, Pursuit of Happiness,* and *A Time for Greatness.*

bean dies . . . !" I feel quite attached to the bean myself now it has survived so much and feel it is symbolic, but this is a fatal attitude to give Jon. So I laugh at him and say, "Heavens, it isn't an animal, it isn't a dog or a horse you love, or a person. If you're going to be a gardener, lots of beans are going to die, and you've got to plant more."

I go out and look at it before supper. He has covered it carefully for the night. It is still erect, some of the first leaves yellowing (from mildew) but the new little ones green and nice. I go back and tell Jon. He also has some peas under glass that are doing well and his radishes are coming up in the garden. Jon seems more cheerful. I give him a talk about being a scientist. If you are a scientist you have to be very very patient. You have to make experiment after experiment and expect nine out of ten not to work. I tell him of the true scientist's rule that negative results are just as important as positive results. Jon says: "That's the same thing as saying failures are as good as successes." I say, "Failures aren't failures if you learn something from them, and anyway you have to expect some failures with any living things because life is uncertain. You can't predict it. You can't control it completely. You don't know what it is going to do."

We read *The Little Prince* (not the best tonic!). The part I love, about the Fox's secret: "It is only with the heart that one can see rightly; what is essential is invisible to the eye." And, "It is the time you have wasted for your rose that makes your rose so important" (this is hard to explain) and, "You become responsible, forever, for what you have tamed."

We talk about all this and whether it is true. "What is essential . . ." Jon is interested and says the Fox is pretty wise. We talk about the essence of life being invisible. We talk, too, of being responsible for what you tame—man's duty to nature and the things he takes out of natural surroundings.

At night I go out and sit a long time in the woods in the well of darkness and think why did Christ say that they that hunger and thirst after righteousness shall be filled? This gives me great hope and it seems to me one of the most beautiful of all his sayings, and yet those who hunger and thirst after righteousness are such a struggling unhappy lot—when will we be filled?

Thursday, May 6th

Papers after lunch. We seem to be driving ahead in Tunisia. The Germans say we are preparing to invade Europe or the European islands before we finish Tunisia. Since no one else speaks of it I think it might be true. They mention concentrations of troops, shipping at Gibraltar, etc. Russia says it is willing, anxious, to have a free Poland after the war. But what does it mean? An account comes out in the *Times* of what the "free" plebiscite in the Russian half of Poland was like in 1939. The voters were rounded up in armored cars, accompanied by guards to the polls, their votes looked at by the guards before put in the boxes. No wonder—as the Russians announced triumphantly—99 per cent of the Poles voted themselves into the U.S.S.R.

In the afternoon I walk over to the Milles's. She is frail but so alive and lovely and understanding. I wished she talked better or we could talk alone, for I feel she is more "alive" and understanding than he. He is so nostalgic and wrapped up in himself. The atmosphere was, as always, so European. It made me nostalgic, too.

Milles thinks men have just as many conflicts and difficulties to conquer as women in being artists. Perhaps—but they don't have children and they have more strength.

Friday, May 7th

Overcast, and some rain. Take Land to school and go in to talk to Miss Crofoot about his party, [a children's pantomime of] *Peter and the Wolf.*

To the trailer and write fast. A good day. During "nap time" I get Land to put six stars on his invitations for his party. He pastes and I follow after with a wet handkerchief to clear off the fingerprints. It is a real achievement, for he was not anxious to do it and I felt he should help for the arrangements for his party and would get a pride and feeling of participation in it if he did. (This, Mr. Milles, is where a mother's day goes!) Land is pleased and so am I. Back to trailer work until 4:30 (hack work only).

Go for a short walk in a soft rain—lovely—so many wild flowers startling me through the woods and a lawn sprinkled with dandelions, like a night with stars. And through it all the sound of soft rain like the sound of innumerable earthworms stirring in the ground.

Monday, Tuesday, Wednesday, Thursday [May 13th]
The week has gone in a swift trip to New York. Now I am back and it is all jumbled and I am not my aware self again, not yet. I am too tired perhaps and have tried to be too efficient—shutting out awareness. Papers all drunk with victory in Africa—end of war just around the corner—invasion of Europe practically begun—Germans surrendering, Europe revolting, etc. One feels delirious reading it, doesn't know what to believe. *Tuesday.* Arrive in New York. Go to the Cosmopolitan Club. C. calls—plan to meet after breakfast at St. Regis. C. in very good spirits—compliments me on my suit, hat, veil! See secretary for an hour; she will do, but I dread having her in the home always—a stranger.

Wednesday. Feel let down. *Must* I take that secretary? Decide to call Katie Gibbs [secretarial agency]. Yes, they have some I can see. C. leaves for Hartford, I move to the Cosmopolitan Club. See a Miss Brodie from Katie Gibbs. I am very drawn to her. Sensitive, aware, thoughtful, rather "lost." (Has just lost her husband.) I hope C. likes her. Feel cheered that I don't have to take the other girl. C. calls. I tell him about Miss Brodie.

Thursday. To Bloomingdale's for garden chairs for Mrs. L. and wraparound dresses (get four—*will* she like or wear them?).

To Cosmopolitan Club, tea, and write C. on secretaries. Taxi down to station.

The lovely freedom of a trip.

Friday, May 14th
Arrive at home at 10:30 to find the usual dustbin of worries. Land and Jon have both been exposed to measles (both sepa-

rately and both kinds!). The maid is not only quarreling with the cook but also with Miss Roser and Christine. I knew it was too good to last.

After supper I go out with Jon and see his garden. His peas are coming up and his bean is still alive! (Jon gets great pride from it all.) "My, it's nice to see something coming up you planted!"

C. called up in the early evening and said he liked Miss Brodie by far the best. And is going ahead with that. I am terribly pleased—for her, for me, and that he corroborated my judgment.

Sunday, May 16th

I go out in raincoat and boots and collect flowers for Mrs. L. after breakfast. C. comes from the train. We hardly have time to compare notes when he is off again to his mother's with three children, a basket of chicken, birthday cake, etc.

I have a wonderful sense of space—alone in the house, no children, no chores, free to go to the trailer—which I do. All afternoon work on a book review.

In the evening C. comes back with three messy children— Anne to bed, Land fussy—and we go out for a walk after supper and talk feverishly, dovetailing each other's remarks: on the new secretary, on Jon's camp, on houses in town, on the war news (he has been to Washington and talked to various people; it is all so different from the papers. Africa is a side show, an important one, but still a side show. War will probably be decided on the Eastern Front is his conclusion). We talk and talk until we get to the bottom. I can hardly see what we walk through because I am so anxious to share and find all we have together.

Monday, May 17th

Rain all day.

C. comes home for supper. We go out for a walk in the light rain. ("How I've missed these walks!" C. says.) We have always had them together after the day is over. One shares, and one walks openly, quiet and serene, letting the outside world and the occasional thoughts of another walking beside one drift into one, and the two become merged, in a still pool of perception. We walk all over Cranbrook. No one else is there, my hand in C.'s palm—both in his pocket!

Wednesday, May 19th

C. has given me, for our wedding anniversary, a big modern silver bowl! It is very beautiful, utterly simple. Very like him to choose such shape and lines. We keep it in our bedroom closet. I feel there is no place in this house it fits. It waits for "space" and our own home.

Friday, May 21st

Work in the trailer for an hour and then over with C. to his mother. C. has persuaded her to see a doctor and we are going to the Ford Hospital to see Dr. Maclure. C. thinks I might help.

Mrs. L. looks very well but is keyed up, nervous. They want her to come to the hospital for a three-day test. This is a great shock to her. She doesn't feel she can stand it. C. and I both talk to her. But it is so hard.

C. and I walk at night. Blow the hospital out of our bodies. I pray Mrs. L. can face it. The stars are out—after weeks. A window has been opened and I can pray through it.

Monday, May 24th

How I hate Monday. The pressure of all the petty decisions that have to be made. All the wheels must start going again. Information off to Jon's camp, his equipment, go over his clothes. Yes, it is true, Christine and Miss R. help, but the final decision is always mine. And the household's squabbles come up—after the peace of Sunday.

Wednesday, May 26th

Wednesdays are always a rush to be efficient *and* get something done as well. This is a mistake. I am getting more efficient. I *can* do the children *and* get to the trailer. But I am tired at the end of the day. I have to do it at a double-quick rhythm, a compressed rhythm. I can only do it with a heightened sense of time, which is wrong. True awareness is only when time is erased. By the time C. comes home I feel worn out and detail-minded; there is no peace in me. This is silly. I must be strong enough to try to do less and take Wednesdays at a different tempo—my own.

Why am I hurrying? To get the story done before I go to Englewood. Why? Because I don't want to break the mood. Why must you go to Englewood? Because Mother will be so disappointed. It is her 70th birthday. She wants us all there. She wanted all the grandchildren. But Jon and Land have both been exposed to measles, Anne is too delicate to upset by a short trip. It is terribly expensive. Upsetting for them. If I don't take the children the least I can do is to go myself on the date. I seem to be always saying this of Mother: "The least I can do," and yet, this "least" is always at a cost of my "right living."

Thursday, May 27th

A full day. To the kitchen to say that C.'s niece is coming for supper. Move Jon's camp equipment down to the guest room. Over to the trailer—work three hours straight. (Can I finish the story before I leave?) Back to late lunch. Intense writing at a sketch is really not good for one—I get irritable. Then when I'm interrupted, I go on thinking, drowned in it, and then I bark at Land, or feel frustrated when Christine brings up shopping problems.

Shall I go back to the trailer and try to get in another hour, or shall I do the flowers? Decide on latter. I pick, hastily, lilac and a whitish honeysuckle and tulips—white, pink and purple. And mix them. I work fast and it is a pleasure to see the bowls blooming with pinks and purples.

I am satisfied, like a painter. And feel rested, too, doing it with my hands. Seeing it come before my eyes. (What a crippling art writing is, no body to it, no *craft,* really. It's all in the mind and you never *see* it or *feel* it—only sometimes hear it. It uses only such a small part of man. I wish I were a sculptor.)

Friday, May 28th

Mrs. L. calls C. from the hospital. In very good spirits! It is like a miracle. Says she's been treated like a queen. Had a good physical exam yesterday. They gave her something that stopped her hand shaking and she had the best night in months!

C. and I are overcome. I am so thankful. Not only the physical end of it but the mental. She has got the best of something that was a bogey to her—doctors, hospitals, etc. Her confidence has been restored. A contact has been made, old resistances broken down. It has done her spirit so much good.

I am deeply grateful.

Pack, drive to station, onto train, and off [to Englewood].

Saturday, May 29th

Meet Con and go to Modern Museum for lunch. After lunch Con and I shop for a pin for Mother's 70th birthday. Finally choose a gold plume. Out to Englewood by subway and bus, carrying bags. Mother meets us. She looks so well and pretty in a pink dress just matching the color on her cheeks. She said she played golf yesterday. We have a children's tea party and presents outside, with caterpillars dropping from the trees. Saran and Elisabeth eating pink ice cream steadily through all the excitement. Birthday dinner very gay. Mother at head of table in pale-blue taffeta—like a child, so appreciative of presents. John [Wheeler-Bennett] does the honors beautifully with a toast to Mother.

Sunday, May 30th

A regular Englewood Sunday—too many people, the unexpected and unabsorbed guests (an English Admiral and an English war wife and a friend). Children, tennis, desultory conversation, too much to eat, and no chance to see the people one really wants to see alone except while dressing, in the bathtub, or while dressing and undressing the children.

In the middle of the afternoon they all play tennis (Admiral and lady, Betty[1] and D'Arcy). Mother says to Ben as the sets

[1] Betty Baird Murray, friend of the Morgans who lived in Englewood with her three children during the war.

heap up in the boiling sun: "Ben, what is the etiquette if a British Admiral drops dead in my home?"

I like talking to John Wheeler-Bennett. He has a subtle, quick, and sensitive mind and rich European education. But I think I really get on with him better than the others because he (though he disagrees with him) *really appreciates C.* I only get along *well* from this basis. In this soil I bloom!

Tuesday, June 1st

Into town to see C. at Hotel Chatham. After the first excitement of seeing him, talking to him, comparing notes, we feel as always when we are together in a city: cooped up, unable to do the things ordinary people do. We cannot go out together, shopping, seeing art galleries, dining out, dancing. And we discover suddenly that we have very few friends we can call up and see *together.* I have friends, literary or feminine, who either bore him or do not understand him. He has friends but they are one-sided, purely technical, and bore me. All our "general" social friends were cut off by our war stand. A neat break was made; one cannot cross over it again.

We sit down in gloom and make a list—like children. He does it for me, really. He does not miss people. He sees them anyway in his work, but he recognizes my need for them and worries about it.

We try to make a list of "our own people." The ones we both like. He puts down the Sikorskys, the Bixbys; I add John Wheeler-Bennett. C. puts down all kinds of impossibles, Jean Monnet and Saint-Exupéry ("We'll never see them again!" I protest bitterly). "Oh, you never can tell," says C. sanguinely. "We might as well put them down anyway." Jean Monnet is in the *heart* of the French Mystery Cabinet in Africa—one of Giraud's men.

I say I feel like bursting into a whole new world of people. There is something bursting in me anyway. What is it? A tension, as though some great change were about to happen in our lives or in the world. The German campaign in Russia, he says, maybe.

Thursday, June 3rd. Very hot

Catch the train to New Haven to meet C., coming from Bridgeport. How lovely to see C.'s sensitive face in the station. He takes my bag. Yes, I am married!

Friday, June 4th

In to Washington early. It is cooler than last night but still terribly hot. To the Carlton (C. has telephoned for a room). The bed is not yet made up. Washington streams with people. C. is worried about Phil Love,[1] who is missing on a bomber out of Colorado Springs. It is possible of course that he is down somewhere. It is desolate country. But C. can get no information. He is deeply troubled.

Back to hotel. C. has called out West, the field from which they are conducting the search for Phil. He has contacted the officer in charge, also talked to Cooky [Love]. There are some good and some bad things. He circled the house of an aunt (the weather was not too bad). But he was probably not flying the plane himself and it was a remodeled bomber not particularly good for forced landings. Some fisherman reported "a plane in distress" near the house he circled.

My mind kaleidoscopes back over my whole life—the first trip C. and I took out West in the Lockheed looking for a lost transport plane, the hours piling up ominously (24 hours overdue—48 hours overdue). The searching parties, the rumors (the plane was traced by false clues all the way up to Canada). The first word of the plane down. The rumor that there were five survivors. The faces of the father and mother in the airport— the helpless clinging to last words. "She wasn't a bit afraid. . . . She said . . ." All to end in that charred wreckage on the side of a mountain right on course. "No survivors." The long table of pilots talking it over at night. The subdued gloom over everyone. "He was a damned good pilot . . . but he didn't know when to turn back." ("It wouldn't have happened to me" hidden,

[1] Philip R. Love had been a cadet in Lindbergh's class at Brooks and Kelly fields in Texas, 1924–25, and was one of the two pilots who flew the mail with C. A. L. in 1926. He was an air force Colonel in World War II.

suppressed underneath.) Treason, it always seemed to me, treason to the lost pilot and cowardice in facing the chances of death in the profession. C. never did it. "It can happen to anyone," he always said.

Then there was Nelson's[1] death (Phil and C. went on the searching party). "He was one of the best," said C. And the Pan Am Clipper lost in the Pacific. And Amelia [Earhart] and so many more, one by one. Always the same sequence. Those fatal hours spinning out—"overdue"—and always the rumors, and always the same stark reality at the end. It is like the Case— the unreality of hope, how far one goes on it, but underneath one knows the stark reality.

Cooky has been through it a hundred times. All aviators' wives have. At times you forget the sentence you are living under and then something like this happens and all your life compresses into one thing, one tension. And you know you have been waiting all your life for this moment.

And then the minor comforts one strives to rescue from the tragedy. "He always knew." "He wanted it." "It was over quickly." "He was flying the plane himself and knew no fear." (This I should pray for—if it were Charles.)

We go back to Truman and Kay for supper. We put the tragedy down in our minds. (It's not yet true; perhaps they are down. "I wouldn't have said that Rickenbacker had a 10 per cent chance.")

Walk home. The flaw in the evening is a taut place in me somewhere, a trembling, anticipatory and fearful, to find, through a careless statement of Truman's ("He [C. A. L.] wants to take a bomber to Australia!"), that C. has been too long inactive, that something is brewing inside of him. He grins sheepishly at T.'s chance shot and says he hadn't quite prepared me for it yet. It suddenly makes visible to me what I have vaguely fretted against for weeks—the *why* of this indecisive life. *Why* does C. hesitate about moving to New England when he feels so much more at home with the men there? Because there is

[1] Thomas P. Nelson, fellow graduate of Army Air Service school and third pilot on St. Louis–Chicago mail run 1926–27.

something else brewing in him—it will boil over someday, into what? A bomber to Australia? A flight to Europe? I wait in apprehension. I think of Cooky. I feel so terribly on the brink—of what? It is the hour before the storm, but whether it is good or bad I cannot say—only that it is action, that it is violent change.

Saturday, June 5th

To the National Art Gallery in the morning to see the Chester Dale Collection and the modern French. Also Blake drawings. Blake has an understanding of the fluidity of life and time, "the deep river philosophy." Book of Job especially, and the Dante illustrations. I feel as though I had been in Europe and go away with my spirit strong. Lunch with C. at hotel. Bob La Follette[1] up after lunch. He talks about the general state of the nation. Is genuinely disturbed, grieved for the U.S. and tormented as to what he can do about it. He is alive to the danger of a long, outstretched war, danger of an all-powerful Russia, the accumulative strength of Japan while our back is turned. He sees us holding a small bridgehead in Europe, irretrievably committed to back it up. He fears also that the peace-hungry people of America will fall for a United States of Europe commitment after the war.

I feel he is a man of great integrity, courage—but limited vision. Perhaps because he is thinking only in terms of America.

Sunday, June 6th

Out to Englewood by bus, subway, and taxi, with my two bags.

At night a strange woman calls up to get C. I finally realize she is Helen Nelson (Herlikey), the widow of Charles' and Phil's third pilot on the early mail-flying route. He was killed in the Alleghenies five or six years ago. She is very upset and says they have found the plane and there are "no survivors." At first they said there were five survivors. She wants to get hold of C. I try, and finally do locate him in Bridgeport. C. says nothing except he doesn't feel he can call Cooky. I say I wouldn't

[1] Robert M. La Follette, Jr., Progressive Republican Senator from Wisconsin, 1925–47.

want to speak to anyone. He says, "Thank you for letting me know." And it is I who am crying.

I think of Cooky and of Charles. Phil was one of those who—like me, like Détroyat—held C. in his heart—not always understanding, not seeing where he was going—but held him always in his heart.

Monday, June 7th

It is rainy and gloomy. I pack, take my bags, and go gloomily to Grand Central. Nothing really settled. "Back to school," to Detroit, away from all the people I love to see, to share with, with whom I feel alive.

I feel rebellious at going back, as though life were here—and yet that is silly; it isn't. In fact, perhaps life is more, for me, in Detroit. I have written there, at least, this winter.

Read *The Birth of a Myth* by Koestler in the train. Brilliant study of this *mal du siècle*. And wince as always at a reference to my phrase the "Wave of the Future" as the inevitability of Fascism. Will I have to bear this lie through life?

Tuesday, June 8th

Back in Detroit. It is cool and overcast. They have had lots of rain, and the asparagus has gone to seed (could *no one* watch it but me?). Scott is covered with mosquito bites. The household is quarreling. Land has a great deal of dental work to be done. Christine about to leave. I am buried in details of the household.

Cut asparagus at night—in desperation. When one is very tired one always does one more thing.

Saturday, June 12th

Everyone in the papers is shouting that the fall of Pantelleria is the first conquest of territory purely by air (which, I gather, is true), that it ushers in a new era of warfare, an example of how Europe can be conquered by air. This last seems to me fantastic thinking.

It took us *weeks* and thousands of tons of bombs and I don't know how many men (and there was practically no resistance) to subdue that tiny island. What would it take to do all of Europe!

C. back late, for asparagus on the porch. He said he talked to Cooky. I must write but there has been no time—so much household!

Sunday, June 13th

The children go off after breakfast with C. and with an outdoor chair I bought for Mrs. L. I go for a short walk and to the trailer. What bliss. How I love Sunday. No sense of rush, noise, duties, children. I sink down and go over all that has happened in the last two weeks. Why is it so vital to do so? What justification have I in writing in my diary when I might be heaping up pages of a book, as C. is doing *in his spare time*. Why can I not write as much as he, when he is holding down a war job as well? It is four children and a household to run, I explain. But I have people to help. Yes, and they fight. I sometimes feel it would be better to do it all oneself. (I shall have to no doubt before long.) Why can't the secretary and the nurse take that off you? C. asks. Why can't you run your life like a business? Why can't you be professional? Why can't you work in the house at your writing? Four children—only an excuse? But if you walk away from them and leave them entirely to the nurse you don't know them and their problems. There are so many things only a mother can know or do. Writing comes out of life; life *must* come first.

And yet my life does not go well *without* writing. It is my flywheel, my cloister, my communication with myself and God. It is my eyes to the world, my window for awareness, without which I cannot see anything or walk straight. Writing in a diary is my tool for the development of awareness. It is the crucible through which the rough material of life must pass before I can use it in art. I am always complaining that there is no "craft" to writing, no brush technique, no finger exercises, no going back to the model in clay. But perhaps—for me—writing in a diary is my "craft," a warming-up process for writing. I must do it.

"I have had such a good day!" I say to C. when he comes back. "Oh, how I love Sundays!" "I can see it in you," he says, "but why can't other days be like Sunday—why not Wednesday, for instance?"

He has had a good day, too. The garden chair I bought was a great success! I am so pleased. And the children good.

A sunset walk—the angry crows cawing in a tattered cloud over us as we disturb their roosts. C. and I talk of whether I might take a course in ceramics. I feel a hunger in my hands, for a craft. But would I have time? There is so little now, for my own.

Monday, June 14th

The children's report comes from the school. It makes me (and C.) very happy to see one's children growing right, getting what they need and using what they get. This is everything—this star glows in a mundane day.

All my frustration at Michigan is symbolized in this house. It needs attention constantly, like an overgroomed woman. And unless it is pampered nothing works. All the beautiful modern gadgets bog down unless they have special care—screens tear, washing machines get out of order, pumps stop, windows jam and then won't stay open, screens don't fit, bugs get in anyway. And all the terrible business of storm windows on in autumn and off in spring, awnings on in summer, off in winter. All these things take men and there are none.

C. comes home very late.

Wednesday, June 16th

Miss [Marta] Brodie calls from the station and arrives hatless, with three bags, in a taxi. I take her around. She seems easy and natural, not at all appalled by family life and the children. She seems delighted with the unconventionality of the office, and the errands, shopping, don't seem dull at all. You feel she is hungry for family life and contacts after an office.

Friday, June 18th

Last details for Jon—his lunch, etc. We pick roses in the garden before he goes [to summer camp in Wyoming]. He is at my heels: "Only twenty-five minutes left, Mother!" Finally we are off, with gun, fish rod, landing net, suitcase, and lunch. Great coup: A boy calls up Jon to ask if it would be all right to wrap his gun up in a blanket since he has no gun case?

Jon says (with great authority!): Yes, it will be all right.

C. takes pictures of the whole family before he leaves.

On military fronts all is quiet but at home everything is splitting wide open. The antistrike bill has been passed by the Senate. (All labor protests it is reactionary, also liberals protest. Totalitarianism at home.) Chester Davis, food administrator, threatens to resign on bungled food program. New cuts in oil and gas for the East.

Saturday, June 19th

C. and I have supper on the porch and discuss what are our objectives for the future? I am always very bad at this, inclined to be too passive. C. believes in cutting out the future according to a preconceived pattern. I have no faith in the patterns, and although not completely a fatalist am inclined to think one cannot cut out a pattern in these times. That one must be more of an opportunist.

It seems to me—as so often in a woman's life—I am asked to think out an abstract problem when I am very tired out with a multitude of infinitesimal concrete and immediate problems.

What is my aim in life? (Ask me tomorrow; I am too tired tonight to think.) It is only to be put in the most general terms. I want to work toward a kind of pure (pure-in-heart) awareness of life and awareness of the true values of life. The meaning of life. I want to impart this awareness to my four children, I want to put what's left into books. I want to have it free my husband for whatever work in the world he is best suited to do. Writers have no "plan" of life. They feed on the lives of others. And women haven't much plan—they adapt to the experiences of husband and children.

We talk, too, of whether we should move—with four children—in the face of the rising difficulties in the East. But if we stay here are we any further along? It is only a stopgap.

Monday, June 21st

[Henry Cabot] Lodge [Jr.] of Massachusetts makes a speech saying that both England and Russia are fighting for their own interests as well as to defeat Hitler, and we should think of ours. Wide applause from both former isolationist and interventionist circles. Christine arrives from Detroit, where there are, she says, wide race riots. Trolley cars overturned, whites pulling Negroes out of the windows, Negroes overturning white men's cars. Miss R. back with same story. Land is fascinated and won't leave the subject. "Did you see any blood, Christine?"

Headlines in evening paper on race riots—nine killed. They have called in the militia.

C. and I walk late and discuss the ominousness of it. C. is afraid it is just the beginning of trouble.

Tuesday, June 22nd. 37 years old

Put on white piqué hostess coat with a black velvet sash and my new gold feather earrings (from Mother and Con) to celebrate; supper with C. on the porch.

The white hairs in my part are getting too many to pull out!

I take out and put on my dresser the golden heart C. gave me.

Cranbrook Road, Bloomfield Hills, Michigan, June 25th

Dear Cooky,

Although I have thought of you ever since Phil was reported missing I have hesitated to rush a letter to you, or a telephone call. Looking back at the losses in my own life and looking forward (as every aviator's wife does) to possible ones in the future, I have remembered with a kind of bitterness how shocked I was at the speed with which everyone else rushed to believe and accept a reality that I was still too dazed to grasp and understand. And looking forward I think—no, I would not want to talk to anyone at that time, if it were Charles. I would not want to be fussed over. I would not want to be condoled with. Perhaps the ideals of the men we married are too firmly ingrained in us to do otherwise—to take grief in any other way than the way they would want. (As I know from Charles' conversation with you

you are doing.) And the thought of that same reticence and courage and lack of fuss that characterized both of our husbands tends to make us inarticulate.

And yet, there is something in me which wants to try to write you, to express to you some of the inarticulate feelings. Even though I have not seen very much of you, still, from that first visit so long ago in St. Louis, I felt a kind of closeness that was not simply a reflection of what our husbands felt for each other. And as you said those few swift minutes in Detroit last winter, "We seem to have gone on just where we left off" in conversation. Perhaps it was because you reminded me of my sisters for whom I was homesick and perhaps because I recognized from the first that your marriage was a real one—like mine. Because it was a real one, what you feel now must be much more terrible than what many people feel. But perhaps it may be some comfort to know that an outsider like me saw and recognized that it was a real marriage and that you gave to Phil everything that he needed—that you made him happy. To have given all one could give—to make a man happy—is so very much in life.

Perhaps aviators' wives are more inclined to do this than other wives. They are like war wives—only the "war" has been always. We have always known they faced death—that they chose that profession with their eyes open. And we loved them for choosing it (I remember C. telling me of the early days and their saying that the average pilot's life was ten years and their deciding that it was worth it). Because of their honesty in facing the danger, we have had to take that attitude too, and laugh about it— as they did. (Did Phil counter your sentimentality as Charles always does mine with a glib "Oh, maybe I'll spin in before then!")

It is true that with that ten years' limit in one's mind one lives more richly. Every moment counts. Nothing is taken for granted. I think the men who have lived like that have a kind of richness and maturity about them—if they are thoughtful and deep-feeling people like Charles and Phil. And I think the women who are married to them have a maturity too and understanding above their years. And the marriages are richer and fuller and deeper—as though to make up for the threat one lives under, as though to make up for the shortness of life.

All of this will not help you. It is only to tell you that I am thinking with you, feeling with you.

I would like too to write through the inarticulateness for Charles. Perhaps it is not necessary. Perhaps you know what Charles felt for Phil. It was very deep, but he never tried to put it into words, even to me. It went back into some core of himself that was there long before me. And the way he spoke about Phil was different from the way he spoke about anyone else. When you see a feeling like that between men, you realize how useless little feminine words are. I remember in a letter Charles wrote to Phil, he put "You are always welcome," such ordinary words, and yet he gave himself freely in those words as he rarely does. They meant complete trust, complete understanding, complete loyalty. He showed me, too, the letter Phil wrote him the winter before this when Charles could get no job in army, government or commercial companies, because of Administration pressure. The loyalty in that letter of Phil's meant something to Charles that cannot be expressed. I know what it meant. Perhaps you know too.

These last weeks he has thought and spoken of you and Phil constantly. He has said over and over, "If only there were something I could do." Perhaps this letter is only saying that again. If we could do something we would welcome it. I seem to know that there is almost nothing that anyone can do to help in the great tragedies of life—and yet I have written this letter in the attempt.

Do not bother to answer this, letters are a burden at times and I do not want to burden you, even with sympathy. But if you ever should want to move from your home or to see people or to talk I wish you would feel that our house is open to you. "You are always welcome," in Charles' words. We lead a very quiet life. I am alone much of the time with the children. I would take you in as part of the family. Perhaps we should be able "to go on where we left off" except that I feel now you are way ahead of me in life. You have borne so much more and must know and understand more. You would be giving to me, not I to you.

DIARY   *Friday, June 25th*

Call Mrs. Milles on modeling course, ask to speak to Miss Kline.[1] She thinks they would accept me, even though an amateur, and that it is a question of which I'm most interested in, ceramics or modeling. Unquestionably the latter.

After supper C. and I walk over to the Milles's, I to see Miss Kline. Miss Kline encourages me to take the course. We go back and drink ginger ale on the Milles's screened porch in the dark and listen to music (Schubert Trio in B Flat, Mozart Concerto in C Major, Bach from St. John's Passion) looking out through arches dripping with ivy at their little Roman court, at the stars, and listen to the sound of a fountain gently underneath. At last I am back in the world of eternals again.

Walk home in bliss under shooting stars.

Saturday, June 26th. Very hot—humid

Letter from *Atlantic*. They like my book review and want to use bits for advertising. I am immediately set up. Why? If they want to use my name to advertise the book, then my name must have lost some of the stigma attached to it. I feel I should not be so pleased at such a straw, so at the mercy of people's regard.

And yet—it is the artist's desire for communication, too; without the answering voice you get so numb; you lose faith in your powers to communicate.

Monday, June 28th

Up early for Land (who leaves for camp). Land very excited in green shorts and striped shirt. Says good-bye to Anne and Scott: "Someday when you grow up, Scott, you'll go to camp." The bus is half an hour late. Finally they pile in. Land waves out the window. "Good-bye, Mother—see you again!" cheerily

[1] Svea Kline, sculptor and student of Carl Milles.

(the crowd laughs). But he looks like such a baby. I have a pang to see him rumble off in the huge bus. And once at home I miss him *terribly*. The house is dead—so still and so quiet—empty. No Land to catch first sight of me as I come back to lunch from the trailer. No Land to play on the piano at three under my room. No Land tearing the living room to pieces, pillows on the floor. No Land to get clean for supper or to come all shining-faced and brushed—like an angel—down to eat.

And then sitting up in bed, round-eyed, his red slippers cast wildly in two directions in the room, while I read to him. I miss him, I miss the everyday insistence—annoying insistence it was sometimes—of his life and his love.

Fortunately I go in the afternoon to talk to Miss de Coux[1] about a modeling course. She is young and sincere (looks like C., or Amelia Earhart), rather angular. She feels it is very much worth while my taking the course, just to look at a piece of sculpture differently, and sees why I am doing it. I can tell, too, that there are things we have alike—a point of view on Art. We both have—it is difficult to say but I think it is—a religious point of view about it. I am very excited by the thought of it, and interested in her.

Tuesday, Wednesday, Thursday, Friday, June 29th–July 2nd
Have gone on working in the studio on the modeling. I worked all day Tuesday. A beautiful day—clear, cool, and sunny. I walk to work across the lawns with a sense of utter freedom and youth. I felt "in love" setting out into a new sea. Then the hard work in the studio. The toughness of the clay, the weakness of one's fingers, the blindness of one's eyes—gradually learning to see, a little; "line" first—an entirely new vision—and then "planes," a second step, a second world one drops into; and then "masses," a third world and vision, as different from the ordinary one I live in as the vision of the earth from the air.

I work on tiptoe all morning, studying and building up a copy of a little terra-cotta cast of an Egyptian head. Then rush home in a daze for lunch and back again in the afternoon. There is a

[1] Janet de Coux, sculptor and teacher at Cranbrook.

model in the afternoon—a little Negro girl (23 or so). The students, two elderly ladies, strayed there from the ceramics department, and Svea Kline (Milles' friend, jolly, open, free, and kind), and a tall blonde who is quite good. We do line drawings of the model. I am slow and wooden and fearful. Then slowly build up her head. As usual I am behind, putting more and more clay on and not getting it even big enough by the time the hours are over, but feel the excitement of a new vision, a new beauty.

Wednesday. Leave right after lunch for the studio. More line drawing of the model and then proceed on the head. At last I have enough clay on—in fact it is getting too big.

Everyone else is ahead of me except one of the old ladies. But it is enthralling. One escapes entirely from oneself as one never can in writing—also from the war. For the first time I have forgotten it.

I enjoy, too, the sense of anonymity, of being a student, of having no aura, no reputation, no past or future. (They do not know who I am—except Svea, who doesn't care.) I am just "Anne"—Svea calls me "Anne," Miss de Coux calls me "Anne," I am "Anne" to the others—it is bliss! Hence I have no vanity and no fear, as I have in writing, no sense of pressure (I must get it done, I must get it published, nothing published for three years . . .). Perhaps this is also because I am immersed in technique, craft, materials, here—a relief from always working with concepts, as one does in one's own art, where one uses technique unconsciously.

To Carl Milles' seminar after, in his house, with all his beautiful Greek statues. They come alive. I can hardly listen to him for looking at the lines of the statues.

Friday, July 2nd

To trailer—write Isadore Smith.[1] To studio in afternoon and work (alone) on Egyptian head. Begin—in the end—to see

[1] Author, under the name Ann Leighton, of *While We Are Absent*. She knew E. R. M. M. in Smith College.

what is wrong and correct it (wonderful feeling). To Mr. Sepeshy's[1] seminar with Miss de Coux, whom I like more all the time—the sense that one has the same approach.

Cranbrook begins to come alive with such people.

Cranbrook Road, Bloomfield Hills, Michigan, July 2nd

Dear Isadore Smith,

To say "I knew Elisabeth" is to open a door in me. I do not remember the meeting (though I do remember Elisabeth speaking of Isadore Luce). But no doubt we were "a vision of solidarity." We always were—are still—too much so. My husband complains that though I wish to be international in politics I am intensely national as far as my family goes.

When I read your letter I realized that I did not really care much about having my review of your book published. And that, feminine-like, I had written from a personal motive to have it reach you. It sprang from the moment when I read the book in one gulp in the lovely isolation of a sleeper and felt joy not only at the artistry and lightness of touch which at the same time probes so deeply but also joy at finding what one conceitedly calls "one's own kind of person." Joy and definitely pain, too. For she will never know, I thought. She was on the other side from me, she probably feels bitterly. She probably believes all those lies about me. She will never know I am her kind of person. And so I wrote.

As for the criticism, it was not really criticism, it was recognition (I thought) of a characteristic in you that I know only too well in myself. I could not help smiling as I read the pre–Pearl Harbor chapters. In a strange reversed sense they might be mine. My friends looked coldly at me (or not at all) because I was an "isolationist"—not, as in your case, because you were an "interventionist." My children were harried in school because their father was fighting *against* the war—not, as in your case, because he was fighting *in* it. Your story revealed to me as in a mirror that it was really not (as much as I had thought)

---

[1] Zoltan Sepeshy, artist, teacher, head of painting department and later President of Cranbrook Academy of Art.

interventionist or isolationist stands (terrible words, which lie in their sledge-hammer rigidity) which separated me from people and made me feel an outsider, too.

It was something else that I have always felt to some degree but especially since returning from Europe. I feel—horrible confession—older than almost everyone I meet. I don't say this in conceit (I think "supercilious" was not quite the right word to use of this mood—I worried over putting it in the review. It is not quite right. But unfortunately writing is not like modeling. One cannot take one sixteenth of an inch off a word, as you can off clay). I realize that the people around me (in America—this is not true of Europeans. I mean, I do not feel "older" than Europeans) are often more intelligent, more brilliant, more studied, better read, more experienced or expert in their fields than I. But I persist in feeling stubbornly that they are younger than I am. They haven't lived as much.

Analyzing it I think perhaps they haven't felt as much. It is a fault, I suppose, to be afflicted with the habit of pulling everything you come across through some knot hole in the center of yourself (like the princess in the fairy tale who insisted that her voluminous wedding gown be fine enough to be drawn through a wedding ring!). I am afraid I do this and I suspect, from the book, you do also. To live that way naturally makes one grow up faster. Artists universally do this. Europeans have had such big things to pull through the knot hole, and for such generations, that they are born old. Born with the "having lived feeling" already strong in them. War and suffering accelerate the process.

I, too, felt in those early years completely out of patience with all the people around me, because they did not *care,* one way or the other. They did not realize what was happening. They did not see the importance of what was going on. Above all they did not *care.* And it was bitter to me to be accused lightly of wishing Europe to "stew in her own juice" when it was Europe I cared about—had cared about for years (it was my home). It was for *Europe* that I wanted the war to cease, not for America First. And I found myself incredibly separated from both sides. Cut off from the America Firsters because I simply could not feel as they did about Europe. And cut off from the interventionists because they would have none of me.

This is not completely true, of course. I am eternally grateful for all those who reached across the gap—my sister, my brother-in-law (who is British), and many of their English friends, who were so much nicer to me than my own friends and to whom I felt so much closer despite our differences of opinion. I remember one English girl saying to me—when I had remarked how good of her it was to keep on seeing me: But it's only people like you I can see. The only people I can't bear to see are those who don't care deeply about this war, who don't see its importance.

All this is now in the past. Certainly my "opinions" no longer seem important. I feel humble about them and only sure about other things—feelings, I suppose. Do you know George Sand's letter to Flaubert in ripe old age in 1871?

"What do I care for this or that group of men, these names which have become standards, these personalities which have become catchwords? I know only wise and foolish, innocent and guilty. I do not have to ask myself where are my friends or my enemies. They are where torment has thrown them. Those who have deserved my love, and who do not see through my eyes, are none the less dear to me. The thoughtless blame of those who leave me does not make me consider them as enemies. All friendship unjustly withdrawn remains intact in the heart that has not merited the outrage. That heart is above self-love, it knows how to wait for the awakening of justice and affection."

This is already overlong (like the review) but there is still something to answer in your letter—the missionary in China who would not read Conrad. Yes, I understand her. Humanly I know from my own life that there are times when one will barter anything for self-control, when one is grateful, as my puritan grandmother said, for a long life of self-discipline.

Artistically and spiritually, however, I reject the escape from life that unawareness implies. Actually, I don't believe one has much choice in cutting oneself off from feeling. Nature conveniently knocks one over the head with a crowbar of insensibility after one has felt too aware for too long. I always resent this but probably one should accept it gratefully. It is an impossible ideal but I do believe the artist, to live and grow and stay alive as an artist, must remain vulnerable. The saint must never carry a shield. (Shields are really not much good anyway. I've never found an adequate one and am coming to the conclusion that it is better to throw those cardboard ones away and make of one's vulnerability a shield.) One learns not to be as hurt—as you seemed to me to show in your book. "Only the ultimates" can hurt you, you say in the end of your story. After all, the shield doesn't protect you against the ultimates. And to protect oneself against the pin-pricks—like Conrad—seems to me like hoarding small change when you are about to lose a fortune.

This would make another review if I should go on. I have spent my precious morning writing you when I should be correcting and rewriting a story of my own I wrote last winter and put too much of myself into (spiderweb-like) and which perhaps cannot be published now and, even if it is, very few people will understand or like. Though I hope you will.

DIARY   *Saturday, July 3rd*

Lunch—C. is home. He teases Anne by holding a cherry before her eyes and then while she is looking up at it popping vegetable in her mouth. Anne realizes it is not the desired cherry she is eating but is slightly confused as to how the trick is done. It is some strange game her father likes to play and she acquiesces—patiently for a while, femininelike. But in the end howls for her cherry and gets it!

Sunday, July 4th

C. calls up from 508 [his mother's house] where he has seen in the last *Progressive* an advertisement of my article[1] in next week's issue! Evidently they have taken it.

Over to the studio after lunch. I work in peace and joy on

---

[1] A. M. L.'s review of Ann Leighton's book *While We Are Absent* was published by the La Follettes' magazine, *The Progressive*, July 12, 1943.

the Egyptian head. It begins to look right and I can work on the detail. *"Les points sont fixés"*—I think of Despiau so much as I work. Later Svea, Barbara (the blonde girl), and a new student (whose head is in the stage mine was two days ago) come in. They all remark on the progress of my head. The new student remarks apologetically that she has never done anything before but drawing and painting. I do not say—as I think—I have never done anything before *at all!*

Tuesday, July 6th

C. leaves [for East Coast]. Work in trailer in the morning, 1:30–4 on head of model in studio. Four back to the house and the children. No Charles to come at five. Supper alone on the porch, do flowers after. Some shell-pink roses in the gray-pearly Chinese jar, hollyhocks in the big green vases, and some yellow buds in Jon's bowl. Then up to bed, lost without C. How hard it is to have the beautiful interdependence of marriage and yet be strong in oneself alone.

> "I went in tears up to my lonely bed
> Oh, would it be like this if you were dead?"

The German drive in Russia has started. The Russians emphasize the terrific cost and sacrifice of the German losses. That means the Germans are advancing.

Thursday, July 8th

The model all day—the morning is wonderful. The light good and I feel I can work well and fast. I see the planes, the shadows; my hands seem to do instinctively what I do not even tell them to do. They "find" the mouth, the droop of the upper lip, the fullness under the nose, the planes of cheek and brow. I do not look or talk to anyone but work anonymously and excited. It becomes smooth and firm. Miss de Coux says, catching me outside, on my way to wash up, that it is coming along *very* well. "It is strange," she says; "it has a look of Despiau about it."

How funny it is. How influenced one is subconsciously by what one admires. I have been amused to watch Svea working on her head. Does she not realize, I think, how much she is influenced by Carl? While I have gone along happily unconscious that I was being influenced by Despiau!

It is a bad morning. The exertion of the last two weeks accumulates, my eyes ache, and I am too tired to see—see mistakes and don't know how to fix them.

Also a Mrs. G. talks to me. "Mrs. Lindbergh, did you really like England?" My beautiful anonymity of the last two weeks is gone. I feel no longer free, young, and a girl; I have to be on my guard. "Yes, very much."

Sicily is being invaded! The "invasion of Europe" has started. It leaves me rather sick at the pit of my stomach—I can only think of the cost.

And then I think: You must not feel that way. It may liberate millions of people. It may liberate France. You must look at it that way. And I cannot. I do not know what France they are liberating. (Starved, embittered, torn. Why don't we *feed* France if we care for her.) And I am unhappy that I cannot look at it with the eyes of a patriotic Frenchman.

Dearest Con,

Before the light goes, on this blessed porch, I have just time to write you. You sound so much more peaceful and rested—I am so glad about the short story! You have worked and lived under such pressure. Perhaps it does teach one to use the fifteen minutes better—so when one gets a free Sunday one *can* write the short story.

My plans: I will be here now until August 9th because I am taking the six weeks' course at Cranbrook summer school. It is vaguely art appreciation—with practice in line drawing and modeling. I go only in the afternoons. I work in the trailer in the mornings.

But the modeling is the most exciting—teaching me to see—

in lines and planes and masses. And the joy of working with one's hands in an anonymous art (one is never anonymous in writing) is something indescribable. Of course I am clumsy and it would never be my art. And I cannot really justify it except as vacation and education. At the moment, it works very well since it clears my mind for the rather dull work of correcting and rewriting I happen to be on now.

If I never take more than this six weeks it will be worth it and if we stay next winter I shall try to keep up one or two afternoons a week. I suppose now that the place has come alive we will move. Life keeps doing that to you—dealing you a series of bridge hands, as Elisabeth once said, and none of them alike. As soon as you learn one and know how to do it and it is easy, you are dealt another completely new one.

I feel so strongly that I—perhaps all of us—are on the edge of a complete change in our lives—that I do not worry about the flowers I am picking up at the edge of the chasm. Maybe they will help one through it.

Cranbrook, of course, is floating on or in a bubble, I feel. I could not stay here long. No one but myself and Mr. Saarinen knows there is a war going on. Yes, and one girl I like whose husband is in New Zealand. Mr. Milles lives entirely in a dream world of the past.

The house is quiet and peaceful without Jon and Land— and so much less work! You wait till you have boys. But I miss them terribly, too.

I shall probably be in New York from the 9th–16th of August. Maybe house-hunting—who knows. New clients come every day to see this house.

DIARY   *Tuesday, July 13th–Monday, July 19th*
A whole week has gone by. In that week Charles has come home, on Tuesday morning, while I am washing my hair. I am full of joy, even though he says he must go off again on a longer trip of three weeks. I do some better drawings—Miss de Coux says I should feel proud of them! But I am behind the others as usual on the figure.

Thursday, July 15th

A long day at the studio working on the figure. I am behind and awkward. (What shape is a human torso? Is it a pear? an apple? It is an entirely new shape.) I don't know where to begin and the proportions are all wrong; just as I leave I see they are wrong. At night I am very tired—too tired to do anything but listen to Bach.

The only nice thing today was the gesture of a French boy—a new student—in opening a door for me.

"Are you coming?"

"Yes, but really, I can open a door by myself," laughing gently.

"It is not necessary." He smiled back. And I knew he was French and warmed to his gesture.

Friday, July 16th

Casting lesson all day. It is quite exciting to see the plaster head emerge smooth and perfect from the mold as it is chipped off, like a chestnut from its prickly shell. In between I draw from the model upstairs.

Janet de Coux for supper. We talk of sculpture. I say it appeals to me because it seems to me purer than the other arts—the pen lies, the brush lies, music lies, but bone doesn't lie.

And today one wants not to lie. There are so many lies—one wants not to separate the word from the deed. In children and in sculpture this seems to me possible.

It is strange that she has been all winter feeling stifled in Cranbrook, not interested in her pupils. And I was so gloomy here. It is fun to talk and meet and understand. She is unliterary but understands much—through her hands, somehow.

Saturday, July 17th

Work all afternoon on the Alps chapters with C. In the evening we sit on the porch. At least I lie on the sofa and look up at the sky. C. sits just inside the door and reads my ms. When I play Bach he comes out and sits beside me and suddenly I *see* him—really *see* him. It is painful really to see the person you love, to see his eternal self. It is too much to bear, too sharp, too vivid. He sees me, too, he says. "This afternoon was earth," he says, "but this is spirit."

Monday, July 19th

All the chores of Monday, and C. leaving as well. We sign checks, go over letters, etc., C. sitting at the desk with papers in neat piles on the floor around him. He spends the early morning dictating, I in the trailer. He comes to say good-bye. It is only a trip of three weeks around the country and yet I feel lost. It is like a physical hollow in you. Life drops from under you and then slowly you build it back.

Cranbrook, Monday night, July 19th

Dear C.

I arranged flowers tonight, so I should not miss you so much —two vases! The first night is dreadful. Tomorrow I shall start again to build up my life alone, brick by brick. It goes all right, it always does. I shall dictate letters and go to the trailer and then to the studio—and enjoy it—and to see the houses with Mr. Snyder in the afternoon. [The house the Lindberghs were in was being sold.]

But tonight, no—I only feel like that poem in *O to Whom:*

> "Dear Love, it was so hard to say good-bye today!
> You turned to go, yet going turned to stay!
> Till suddenly at last you went away.
> Then all at last I found my love unsaid
> And bowed my head;
> And went in tears up to my lonely bed—
> Oh, would it be like this if you were dead?"

Scott is fed. The stars are out. You are on the train. Good night.

DIARY   *Thursday, July 22nd*

To studio and work absorbed all day on the torso, different planes and making the torso, abdominal cavity and diaphragm

—a whole. When the day is over we lay all the figures together on the platform and look at them. I suddenly see that mine is ugly, out of proportion, not beautiful as design—as a whole. It is also rather wooden and cramped. Parts are very well done, the torso. But I am disappointed that I did not see it *whole*. The other students did, though they did not get the torso as finished as mine.

How like oneself one always is, in every action no matter how slight. I look at all the figures and read the person in each. Svea: generous and big. Barbara: full of grace but not quite put together. Mrs. P.: facile and finished and completely meaningless, loveless, without emphasis. Miss H.: half a conception and unfinished, incapable of being finished. (And yet a better conception than the other two schoolteachers.) And finally Mrs. G.: small and hard and finished, down to the toenails and fingernails! It was hideous to look at. I felt I knew all about her from seeing it. What her life had been like. How she treated her husband. The kind of woman who nails a man to a barn door, and not from cruelty—from fear, from insecurity, from wanting to possess, to have something to show. To think she is an art teacher! It makes me ill to think of her freezing her pupils into molds, nailing them into boxes. Her figure haunts me. It was a corpse. "The Letter Killeth."

Cranbrook Road, Bloomfield Hills, July 23rd

Dear Sue [Vaillant],

Your letter and picture have come—this morning.

Oh why are you not here. There is no one else who feels as intensely as you do, who is as honest about it, but who has at the same time as rooted a sense of life, of the things that count, in an earthy way, in life—and yet of the mad unreal things too that grow inside one.

I am still writing in the morning—correcting and recorrecting ms. I am hoping to send it for perusal and advice—in two weeks —to Mr. Harcourt of the publishing firm.

I had one exciting trip to New York and Washington with C. We talked hard to lots of people. I found myself sitting on the edge of my chair listening to a round bald military man expound a philosophical and historical approach to the war and military strategy. It made me think of my father's mind and also of something you once said. If I had not married C. I would never have appreciated this hard-boiled military man's beautiful mind. There was nothing aesthetic about it, and yet —yes, it was a beautiful mind and I warmed to it.

How strange it is—as you said, "You turn down A. and marry B., and then meet C., whom you could not possibly have even listened to had you married A.!" Listening to him I understood how men look at war (women, of course, do not look at war at all—or else through sentimental patterns). Men don't look straight at war either. They look at it through the patterns of a game or a science—an art (like this man) of logistics, etc. (It was fun, too, since C. was as much thrilled as I. We saw and appreciated the same thing—only to me it was a shock of surprise—I was coming into *his* world.) No one looks at war stark naked except a few saints and artists like Hillary, Koestler, and St.-Ex.

This house has been sold and we are moving, but not to Connecticut, since C. feels it would be "flying in the face of the Lord" with conditions so perfect here and so uncertain there (food, fuel, school, transportation, etc.). We are moving to a new house on the other side of Cranbrook which by some miracle is bigger, simpler, made for a family with five children, and altogether nicer (though I am again in a green room!). We will move the first week in September before school opens but I must plan *now* since I am taking Anne to Maine for two weeks— August 9th.

DIARY   *Monday, July 26th*

Mussolini has abdicated. What does it mean? Could it be the beginning of the end? Martial law in Italy. [Marshal Pietro] Badoglio in charge.

Supper on porch, read papers. Most important thing that has happened lately is the Russian propaganda for the Germans. They are setting up a Free German association in Russia, laying out plans for Germany after the war. They do not talk about "unconditional surrender." They do not talk about trials and revenge. They do not talk about an Allied government, or splitting up Germany. They are working *through Germans,* planning for *German rule.* (While we train Americans to rule Germany—only provisionally of course!) It is Russia's bid to the German people for a peaceful understanding. More than that, it is Russia's bid for control of Europe. It is a most important move. And it passes almost unnoticed in the fanfare about Mussolini's abdication (obviously much more spectacular).

July 28th–August 18th

The last two weeks of summer school, a week in Englewood, and half a week in Maine have gone too fast to write. So much has happened and it has been rather intense.

It was partly just the excitement of what has happened to me at Cranbrook. All kinds of things have begun to flower around me. Friends, all kinds—all at once. After feeling alone and dreary for so long suddenly to find that I am not alone, that people love me, that there are people who talk the same language. It is almost too much. There is Saarinen, who pulls and stretches my mind (the place my father used to hold). And Janet [de Coux], on my own level, who understands creatively everything, from a different angle. And neighborly Mrs. Bromley (satisfying one's need for a mother). And that strange boy of eighteen—perhaps closer to me than any of the others, like my own adolescence walking around in the slight hungry-eyed body of a boy.

But there were casual touches, too, just as nice—almost. The lanky boy, also eighteen, and the most talented person in the school, lean, with a wonderful dry American humor. That touch of earthiness that Americans have—aware, sensitive, and *earthy*—I thrill to it. I am proud of Americans when I see it, I am proud to be an American. I was so pleased that he treated me as someone his own age, "razzed" me, like a brother. He was the only one there who was aware enough to see what is wrong with Cranbrook—that it lacks ugliness, strife. "And life isn't like that," I said to him, throwing out a rope to see if he would catch it. "No," he said, with a quick understanding glance at me, "that's why I like Wayne" (Wayne County Art School). He is going into naval air after summer school. The last day, he came with his father. I was so pleased that he should introduce his father to me but shocked to think of him pouring his lovely youth and gallantry and talent into the Pacific. I could say nothing but "Well, my husband's testing a plane for you now," sweeping up the floor vigorously after casting all day. "Hope it's a good one!" He laughed and went out.

[August]

Dear Mr. Harcourt,

I miss my visits to your office even though these were not very frequent in the past. I do not like to think that if I should walk into Harcourt, Brace & Co. now you would not be there to give me—as you always did—the sense that there was plenty of time and many excuses for a good talk. And I miss not having your judgment to rely upon. That is really why I am writing you.

For last winter, lying in bed recuperating after my last child, I dug up the outline of a flying episode I had written before the war, and, reading it over, decided that it should be finished before it was forgotten. I thought it would be a short story but it turned out to be an awkward length, a long short story, about half as long as *Listen! the Wind*. ("How long is a string?" you asked me when I said my book *North to the Orient* was not long enough, the first time I walked into your office.)

I wrote this story simply because I had the chance to write it, because I felt very strongly it ought to be written, because I did not want to lose it. I tried to put into it—a kind of final record—everything that a life of flying taught me, as though it were a final testament. And I have in fact dedicated it to this. I had no thought at the time of publishing it. But now that it is written I would rather like to have it published. Until a book is published one learns nothing from it, one does not grow beyond it, one cannot get on the next step.

However I have some doubts as to the wisdom of publishing it at this time. Can one publish a book of prewar vintage in a passionate war period? Can one publish a story of peacetime flying against the flaming background of wartime flying? What adventure, what risk seems real against the risks aviators are now taking every day of their lives? Just what is valid today in the way of literature? Is one even justified in writing in the face of so much suffering?

These are the questions that pursue me. I feel there is no one who can answer them for me as well as you—no one whose judgment I would value as much on this matter.

North Haven, Maine, August 18th

Dear C.,

I wired you tonight to the Engineers Club, after getting Harcourt's letter. (I can't be parted from it yet.) He says:

"Mrs. H. and I have just finished reading your ms.[1] It most certainly should be published. Both of us were completely absorbed in it while we were reading it and for hours afterward. Anything so beautiful is without a date-line; it is about a flight of the spirit as well as about the flight of a plane. The plane is merely the vehicle for conveying the heightened sense of awareness. The last two or three chapters are, I'd guess, the best writing you have done so far."

He suggests tightening the Preface and taking out "an apologetic phrase or two," with an amusing paragraph on prefaces, which he says are apt to be either apologetic or belligerent.

He has a few other suggestions and I think I could see him in New York on Monday the 30th on the way through.

I am afraid I have no time to work on it here because I am with Anne every moment. It is wonderful to have her to myself. And we are in the sun all day—a quiet lovely existence. She eats twice as much as she did at home and we both sleep like logs.

---

[1] The manuscript was published in 1944 by Harcourt, Brace and Company, titled *The Steep Ascent*.

She is a joy—she is like something I dreamed, so sensitive, so aware, so responsive. I feel very close to her here.

You were right that it was best for me to take her alone. I do not read or write, just sit and sink into the earth—sun and sea air and sounds. I feel washed and filled up by it—and somewhat numbed—as though all the scribbled nothings on the blackboard were being gently erased.

If only you were here. I miss you much more than I did when I was working hard at Cranbrook. If only we could sink into this together.

The time with the children is peaceful and healing. But I feel strange at night with the Cutter sisters listening to Cecil Brown on the radio or playing bridge (I play music—they bridge!). In the evenings I miss you terribly. But I go to bed early.

I wish I could talk to you tonight. I hate not sharing things with you. And it has been so long. Forgive me.

North Haven, Maine, August 23rd

Dear Mary [Knollenberg],

I had such a beautiful day in New York with you.

I have now sunk into a life of children and sun and swimming and endless trudges up and down the long meadow looking for gulls' feathers. I feel stupid and lazy but quite happy.

I have read two articles on Henry James—one in the *Partisan Review* (by Rahv) and one in *Horizon*. The British one slightly aggrieved at the ever sinful view of old Europe he takes.

After reading them I longed to talk to you and to read at least the last three novels of Henry James. Why did I stop reading him at 20? Perhaps because he is just what I should read precisely now. We have touched on it in conversations and both they and the articles have illuminated something for me. About my story. I realize now that the story is a kind of coming-out of the spell of Europe. It is a protest against the spell, in a strange way. A positive assertion against that negative thing in Europe and Europeans that draws one so and is so fatal for Americans (not, of course, fatal for Europeans). It has the seeds of death in it for us because it is not grown in our orchard. It is not our apple. But it's all right for them. Did Henry James realize this? Do you agree with me? My story, I think, is a kind of protest against this. But have I quite got out from under the cloud? Am I still under the spell? Is this story *mine*—or is it not? I don't know.

Well, perhaps you can tell me. At any rate, no one else can.

(Both Harcourt and Charles think the Preface is too apologetic and it will have to be shortened and sharpened. No one will believe that humility is true. Unhappily, it *is* true!—but I see it must be changed, since no one will believe it.)

DIARY   *August 30th* (*Written on sleeper to Detroit*)
Then two weeks in Maine with Anne. It has been a lovely two weeks, having her to myself. Waking and going to sleep with her, learning all her little words and gestures, all her curiosities. And seeing her the first time she really *looked* at a sunset. ("What color is the sky, Mother, what color is it?"—quite excited. She wants to know what color everything is.) It was lovely sinking into Maine again, on a child's level. Pine cones and feathers, smooth stones, and climbing up the long green meadow after a swim.

One golden afternoon with Con. All summer was blended into that afternoon, all dreams and memories of summer. We were children, tasting those joys again, and mothers, with a child pulling at the hand, up the boathouse road—and sisters, sharing our joy, our talk, our appreciation. Why should one ask for any more than that? A whole summer should not be asked to yield more than one afternoon of that water. And we knew it.

Now it is all gone and a crowded day in New York, talking to Harcourt about my story, and [Donald] Brace, too. It seems it *can* be published! The exhilaration of it—the doubts later.

Tomorrow home, in a new house (they have moved!). Jon and Charles—for whom I'm hungry—Scott, too, and then probably all the excitement of fitting into the new house and

Land coming home. And then art school. And people. I look with pleasure to this—the Saarinens and Janet. I wonder if I will be allowed to enjoy it—or will something else happen?

Tuesday, August 31st

Anne and I arrive in Detroit. We go straight to the new house. It is in horrible confusion—bundles and bags and mops and brooms, pots and pans, all over the floor everywhere you look, just where anyone happened to leave them. I take Anne up to her room, which is in the same state, but she is pleased to see her own bed. And she goes up to a little sofa covered in blue-and-white check (just like Mother's dresses) and says with an exclamation of joy, "Grandma Bee's chair!"

I gather the house is not only in terrible confusion but boiling over in relationships, too, quarrels and complaints.

At night C. comes home. It is unbelievably good to see him. At last I touch base and am at peace.

Wednesday, September 1st. Four years ago, war

Again the whole day goes to rearranging furniture, carrying loads of debris upstairs, moving chairs, finding slipcovers, appeasing each member of the household. The rooms begin to take form. At last one room emerges perfect and ours—the little paneled library. The Vlaminck flowers, the French water color, the Mexican gourds, some red needlework chairs, a desk, a lamp, a low table, our books, the Victrola, our records. Yes—this will be our room.

C. and I eat in it at night. Then walk in Cranbrook and watch shooting stars and feel at peace after the fuss of the day.

Patterson House, Bloomfield Hills, Friday, September 3rd

I work on the office today, take down the yellow curtains, which killed the eggshell-blue walls.

Miss Brodie is a great help, nothing downs her, she feels "Do it *now!*" as I do about a house. I feel I must work at a frenzy fixing up a house when I first get into it because a moment comes (as in writing) when the house simply "jells," as is, and then I cannot do a thing more. It is with the greatest effort that I straighten a picture or move a chair and the sloppy sofa throw stays as I carelessly pinned it, for months.

I cannot pull all my selves together yet: the one I was last summer at art school, and the one I was in Maine, Anne's mother, and C.'s wife, and the writer I am to Harcourt and Brace. And the real me I am with friends, and this house-tidier. The image is blurred. It is like an astigmatism of the soul.

Saturday, September 4th

C. home all day. We rearrange furniture, closet space, fix up the hall. C. is using the table I put in the window in the big room. I am pleased he finds a place to work. Though I thought he would prefer the study, where he can shut the door. I must put up curtains to give him privacy in the big room.

In the P.M. I read the papers. The Germans have been retreating steadily toward the Dnieper.

Yesterday we (or Anglo-Canadian troops) started invading the toe of Italy. The most important news seems to me political. The propaganda campaign in Russia for a second front—accusing us of bad faith—broken promises.

What does this propaganda drive mean? Is it their preliminary move for control of Europe? ("No fight, no say" is their warning to us about the control of postwar Europe.)

Sunday, September 5th

Storm in evening. I have been waiting for Land's return all day. At 10:30 I give up and go to bed, only to be rung by Mrs. W. saying she has arrived and is at her sister's. C. and I drive over and find Land golden and gay on a sofa drinking milk with a brown-eyed little girl. I shall never forget how beautiful he looked. (They had washed him and put him in a clean white sweater suit!) Skin golden brown and hair bleached light with the sun, close-cropped. His language was strange to me (how quickly they change!), full of set phrases ("good citizenship stars" and "hill-topper," "Did I ever"). But his eyes twinkled as before. He is electric as a wire, very excited about the new house. To bed with many hugs.

Sunday, September 19th

A long strange week—and very full. I feel definitely that I have taken on too much and am getting too tired, but perhaps the second week will be better.

Terrible war news—Battle of Salerno. We are really running up against the Germans and our losses are high.

Thursday Miss Brodie and I go to a faculty tea where I hope to introduce her to some people, and where we end up in rather an exciting argument with Sepeshy—a philosophical discussion of the justification of art in wartime. We get quite far afield and forget all about the rows of schoolgirls sitting primly with eyes starting out of their heads as we went on about the pull to death, "the point of intersection of the timeless with time,"[1] "procreation," etc. ("Are there any babies around here?" said Sepeshy, hastily looking around—at one point.) I do not feel I understand all he is driving at but I find his corrosive honesty very challenging and it is a relief to talk to an adult, a European.

The next night we go out to dinner with the Saarinens. Milles told long stories, and Saarinen dry jokes, and I interjected questions and links between C. and the men. But nothing took. Milles looked bored and C. shy and Saarinen rather stiff and expectant and Sepeshy hid his face in the shadow of his hand and I was aware of something eating at him inside—what, I wonder?

One cannot have a conversation with Milles exactly. One can only love him and bask in his sunshine and give some of one's own.

With Saarinen it is different; one can talk. There are in general two kinds of men for me: the kind one feeds, flirts with, or flatters, and the kind one talks to, exchanges something with. I really prefer the latter. I feel too old to flatter and flirt. And though I enjoy feeding people, it is the *young* I enjoy feeding and not the old. The young who are going to do some-

[1] T. S. Eliot, *Four Quartets* (The Dry Salvages).

thing with that nourishment, the young who are not just taking it to warm their bones but in order to give it back in some other way.

Milles, of course, feeds people, too. He has heart-wisdom, but I feel I know a lot about that already and don't need it. It's my mind that is hungry and not my heart.

Wednesday, September 23rd

The French are in Corsica again—the first reconquest of French soil! How they must feel. The terse little communiqué of Giraud, "Things are taking a better turn," is very moving to me.

Friday, September 24th

Read a stack of papers. I am way behind, trying to figure out the news. Churchill's long speech—on the top of the wave, success reported in every field, air, land, sea, and production. It is a wonderful speech, full of his marvelous phrases. The only clue I can get out of it to what is really happening politically underneath is his complete lack of mention of what is happening on the Russian Front *now*. Does he not know? Or is this enormous build-up of the U.S.-British successes given as a counter-thrust to Stalin's persistent call for a second front (Churchill is slightly defensive on this, also bitter about the English Communists who urge it).

Stalin has also made a speech, obviously implying that North Africa and the Mediterranean are not a second front and are in no way comparable to what the Russians are doing. The headlines are: "Stalin urges us to buy War Bonds!" Which I must say makes my hair rise. What kind of a nation are we anyway and what opinion must other states have of us if they feel they can tell us what to do, sneer at our efforts, belittle our claims, criticize our conduct of the war? (Constant criticism in Russia in the government-inspired press of our administration of the conquered territories. They say Amgot[1] is Fascist, Hull is Fascist, etc.)

[1] The Anglo-American government of occupation in North Africa and Sicily.

Saturday, September 25th

C. has passed all his exams for flying ratings,[1] now has every rating in existence and can fly *any* type of plane. Blind flying, too. He always makes good a slack time.

Friday, October 15th

I have not written for days because life has been too full. And now there are only scraps left—nice ones and disagreeable ones. I don't like living too fast to savor it, too fast to be conscious. Conscious only that one is wasting it on trivialities for the most part and not putting it into anything that counts.

There was the Wednesday when I came to wake Land and he said, "I'm so happy the day you take care of me!" Goodness—one could slave for that.

The day with Charles and the children at Dearborn, watching the ceremony for the helicopter, the first helicopter being put into a museum—already a museum piece.

It was a thrilling moment when Sikorsky[2] took it up for the last time. Little and bald, with his out-of-the-world face, he looked so intense you felt he was holding it together by his very spirit. Such an awkward homemade-looking piece of machinery, with its two rotating vanes, exposed cockpit, and bicycle basket out in front. They spiked a ring off a pole and did a landing on a handkerchief to show its precision. The most thrilling thing to me was to see it go backwards, hover, and waltz around in one spot.

We went afterwards to see C. fly his Chance Vought Corsair. C. looked gay as a boy and took it over the field at 450 miles an hour (half the speed of a bullet, as Mr. Sikorsky said!). You did not hear the snarl of the engine until the plane was past. And it literally dissolved in the air like tablets in water, just got smaller and smaller. One was hardly conscious of speed.

[1] After starting work at Willow Run, C. A. L. took basic training in the current war planes in order to be able to test and advise on all types in use.

[2] Igor Sikorsky, Russian-born scientist, aviation pioneer, and aeronautical engineer; developed the first successful helicopter in the Western Hemisphere.

Then C. took the Sikorsky party and Land and Jon and me and Deac Lyman[1] (how wonderful to see him again!) through Willow Run. We went on a little train with the guide-announcer speaking through radio amplifiers. One noticed chiefly the size, and the number of women working (they all looked like housewives —quite nice ordinary Middle Western housewives—not a new breed of "modern woman," as I had expected; quite a number of elderly women with gray hair; they wore navy slacks and *everything* on top). The noise (Land with his hands clapped over his ears) in the riveting section. The depression of working in artificial light and air in the center of the building. The relief to get to the end of it, where there were hangar doors open and real light and air. The number of people who seemed to be just sitting around. The flags hung everywhere. The notices on absenteeism, the general cleanliness, order, and good conditions.

Then back to the unreal adolescent world of Cranbrook—even more unreal after my excursion into the grown-up world of aviation.

C. comes back unexpectedly for Saturday and Sunday. Two wonderful days after the rush of the week. Golden Indian summer days—we work over the ms. and play in the garden with the children, in the leaves. Scott in my arms, Land with a cowboy hat on burying red-overalled Anne in the leaves, C. with a rake making the pile grow. Jon has got walnut stain on the rugs and Land let Jon's garter snake loose in the house. I found it one evening while undressing. "There!" I said quietly to C. "There is the snake!" Curled up on the rug under the dressing table. "Oh," said C., "what kind of a snake?! Are you sure. . . ." He took it out far away from the house.

Then walks together, C. and I, in the soft warmth of Indian summer. ("This is the last day, the very last." And there was always another.) Walks over fields of blue asters and the elms dropping golden leaves and the maples, a shock of flame here and there.

And music at night—C. lying on the floor, his head on a pillow

[1] Lauren D. Lyman, friend of C. A. L. who covered the 1927 New York-to-Paris flight for the New York *Times*.

and his hand in mine, I curled up on the sofa, and "Now let every tongue adore thee."

Then Monday he went off again and I have had a long week, tired out from it, angry at myself, realizing I am doing too much and none of it well. I must try not to see so many people and get back again to the writing person, the person I really am.

I ran away from it in Cranbrook but I am not a sculptor and I am too interested in the people. I take a writer's interest in all those people. I know when they are happy or unhappy and I feel I must do something about it and all my creative energy goes into that. Everyone who comes into a room sets me vibrating.

Feeling very low the other night I read Katherine Mansfield's letters again and felt with a pang: Oh, how far away from myself I have gone—so far away from the person I mean to be!

Monday, October 18th

The ms. goes off but there is no one to celebrate with, and anyway I don't feel much like celebrating. A flying story—what place has it today? Sixty [Flying] Fortresses were lost in the last raid on Germany; that means *600 men*, in one night. Why does the loss of aviators seem so terrible? It does to me.

Tuesday, Wednesday, Thursday, Friday

Another rather discouraging week, getting too tired, not sleeping, and being uncreative in every way and very cross with the children—which I am really ashamed of. Tuesday night, flaring out in exasperation at Land, who was following me about on all fours into the nursery and waking up Scott, already asleep, I realized: Why do you do that? There is nothing wrong with your children, there is something wrong with you. I have been giving away to other people what is their right. It is stupid and wrong to get so tired that you are unable to give to your children.

Friday, October 22nd

Jon and I go to an educational movie at the Science Institute— Jon with six frogs in a jar, to give to Gilbert, his friend who has snakes. They croak through the glass jar at his feet all through the meeting and I make him go out with them when the lights go off. Fortunately he finds Gilbert in the hall and can hand over the bottle. I am relieved.

Frogs in the bathtub, snakes in the bedroom, caterpillars on the window sill, walnuts on the rug! Chestnuts *everywhere*— what it is to have boys!

Monday, November 1st. Train New York–Detroit

Six almost completely unreal days in New York. Seeing Mr. Brace about my book (strangely enough, this was real). C.'s voice over the long distance (this was real!). Supper at Le Bistro (French!) and to *Oklahoma!* with Barbara. (The Duke and Duchess of Windsor brushed by us in the dark aisle.)

Mother sitting up in bed talking about how Wallace and Henderson[1] led her out on the platform! Life burning in her—like a young girl.

Go into the Erich Remarque collection, stilled at last, looking at the Redon intense flowers, the Renoir woods, the blue-and-white mountains of Cézanne (lovely water colors). "Forgive me," I find myself saying to them.

The papers say "a new League of Nations" agreed on in Moscow. I long for C. and home.

Thursday, November 11th

I have been home over a week. The joy of being with the children again, of bathing Scott, of having Land's arms around me, of watching Anne's precise little fingers arrange her animals, Jon drawing my head down to his at night. Walking to school in the morning with Land skipping down the gutter. Singing to Anne at night in her bed, and Scott's weight in my arms.

This is where I belong. Tuesday was an exhausting day but it was worth while—frantically building up my figure (one day lost). Home to problems. Anne still (or again) in bed with a cold.

My pleasure to see Janet and Eliza [sculptor friend] again.

[1] Vice President Henry Wallace and Leon Henderson, administrator of the Office of Price Administration.

Thursday, a peaceful day at home, the last work on *The Steep Ascent*—and it is off!

Saturday to Carl's [Milles] for tea. I have a chance to talk to Olga—which I never have—on the eternal problem of being a wife *and* an artist. I feel she has poured out her life to him and it makes me feel rebellious and feminist. She says it is only worth while struggling at her painting if she can someday do a portrait of Him.

Monday and Tuesday are long days in the studio, working under pressure and very badly. The feeling of pressure is my great temptation—and sin. It always wrecks me. I have written a book about it and still I am unable to conquer it, not to care, to work at my own pace, "in the groove." To let time and the sense of competition harry me—it is so wrong. When will I learn to work quietly, impersonally, alone?

C. comes home for the night, two nights. It is this I have been hungry for. For this reason I have been so unable to rest anywhere. C. frees me of the pressure-feeling, gives me a sense of infinite space and time.

He is off again on Wednesday morning. I see him two short evenings only—and one of those is with people.

Thursday, November 11th

Armistice Day—unreal armistice day. What is happening out there? I have no idea. I am separated from it by my safe life here in the Ivory Tower of Cranbrook.

I go to the trailer in the morning. I feel steadied after being alone, and writing, even though bad writing, in my diary. After all, writing is my flywheel and I have not written at all lately. One is lost without a book, without something one is working on. And I do not know what to do next. One writes from the past, but the past is too far behind—separated from one by an unbridgeable chasm.

Friday, November 19th

Another week has gone by. Monday I start on a head of a girl. It comes up much quicker than the other one. Tuesday I get ahead fast. Janet says it is a good start. I begin to get a thrill out of it again. Can it be I am beginning to see again? Beginning to get out of the arid period I have been in, in everything? Or is it just that a head is easier for everyone?

Wednesday. Over to the lecture and back to find C. home. I touch life again and feel steadied. We walk to the studio. He is very pleased with my head and Barbara comes in and says Janet and Eliza are excited over it. Back to a really good sleep.

Friday. I do Christmas lists in the morning. I hate Christmas. It was not meant to be like this, but simple and unmaterialistic. And I have not the guts to cut it out. I do less and less each year, but still I do not break the habit completely.

I go over to Cranbrook, see Janet, and she talks to me about the head. She says that it has everything in it she has tried to teach, to say, a sense of pure form, pure design, all the fundamentals—and it seems to have come so easily.

It is true it came easily—I don't know why. Because I did not try too hard?

It is only a beginning, of course, but even if it goes badly from here on at least *once* I got the fundamentals, saw it *whole,* did not get bogged down in details. Let it grow inevitably from a strong true inner core.

I tell Janet what sculpture has given me, even in the blackest hours: a sense of pure form, pure design, pure beauty, so different from the wordy beauty all mixed up with emotions that writing has.

We talk, too, of the difficulty of working here, how one is drawn from work to help people, and that one drains oneself that way. What a temptation it is because the result is immediate —the smile, the friendship, the gratitude. But that artists must not save souls that way. As Margot said to me about answering all my letters: "You must not try to answer them. You must bless them in your heart and someday write a book that is a kind of long answer to them."

I say all this to her but also to myself.

It is a nice talk—one of those unexpected snatched ones—but it helps us both. That is the best kind of relationship, the kind in which one is both giver and receiver. Not the kind in which one tries unsuccessfully to fill up a bottomless pit.

Saturday, November 20th

Carl says he has seen my head and is "astonished." . . . "It is so simple—so good."

C. bursts with pride—"What did I tell you!"

Sunday, November 21st

Mother arrives in the morning by taxi from Detroit; Land runs to the door to greet her. We have a quiet day at home. She has been going for two weeks, speaking [for the U.S.O.] and traveling, sometimes one-night stands. She does not seem tired, only a little wound up nervously.

Monday, November 22nd

I to studio to work on head. Mother off to Detroit. She comes back between meetings for one hour with the children at bedtime and then off again to Detroit by two taxis. In this hour she has supper, reads to the children, changes her dress, hat, has half a glass of sherry, and is off again. She is incredible. She says, "I could give this speech in my sleep!" Home late at night.

Thursday, November 25th

Three children in bed with a cold (Jon, Anne, and Scott). C. stays home in the morning and works on a cover for *The Steep Ascent*. The children make such a mess of their rooms—even in bed! Jon throws spitballs around, Anne's bed is full of potato, Jon burns toilet paper on the tin wastebasket catching the sun with a magnifying glass. I am perpetually cleaning up or blowing Anne's nose.

C. is altitude testing, leaving vapor trails in the sky! I shout to all the children, who stick their heads out of the windows at the white streak down the sky like a comet.

C. and I go over galleys at night and walk to the studio. I am very tired. But the walk means so much to him and to me. We walk in the cold, under the stars, in silence, and sleep well after.

Sunday, November 28th–December 10th

Almost two weeks have gone by. I have been too busy to write. Extra work at the studio. Anatomy classes on Wednesday (all day long). The galleys every spare moment at home. C. has painstakingly gone over them all and marked repetitions, commas, and "oh gods."

Sunday the children and C. go off to Mrs. Lindbergh and I go out for a walk. I stand a long time on the top of a hill and look down over the orchard, to a willow on the sky line and lovely feather clouds raying out behind it. The orchard, the willow, and the sky are suddenly beautiful and significant. Not beautiful only—for I almost always see beauty. It is another vision. They are significant, they mean something. It is not ordinary any more. I see it as significant—of what? I don't know— of itself perhaps. I see the archetypal orchard, the archetypal willow tree, I see—"A tree, of many, one."

And then suddenly there is a flicker, a breeze blows, some undistinguishable thing has changed, like those kaleidoscopic boxes full of bits of colored glass. You shift it just slightly and the pattern falls—suddenly it is gone. It is no longer a pattern, no longer the archetypal orchard, no longer "a tree, of many, one." I am standing on an ordinary hill, looking at an ordinary orchard I have seen a great many times. It is accidental—no longer significant. And I am getting cold in the wind. I turn and go home, still happy with my vision.

One lovely afternoon at Dr. Scheyer's.[1] He asked the class for "primitive music and tea."

It was a lovely room. Small and in an old house, but the walls covered with things that spoke to me and I felt happy as I walked in. It was as if all the things he hides or apologizes for in his lectures (the things I always like best) were here visibly on the walls—drawings and paintings and bits of sculpture—and a piano.

[1] Ernest Scheyer, art historian and author of *Baroque Painting*.

At first we were the class: angular, unabsorbed, uncomfortable, not fitting together. I tried desperately to throw out paper chains of conversation. Dr. Scheyer also, but it was difficult. Then Mrs. Scheyer came down. She is lovely, direct, simple, and sensitive. Yes, I could talk to them. Yes, I like them. And two children about two and six who were quite unawed by guests, but simple and natural, too. And then, after tea and primitive music, she played the piano, flawlessly, with that same clarity and sensitivity that one sees on her face. She is simple and good, one feels (like Bach). Bach and more Bach and Debussy and Chopin and Schumann. And I who had felt so conscious, so overconscious of all those personalities, their raw edges—I had the feeling that the music washed over us like a tide and covered up our awkwardnesses. We were blended into one group of listeners, and yet not conscious of sacrificing any of one's solitude.

I felt, in fact, at last, alone. Not for weeks had I been so freed, so still, as in listening to that music. I could reach that inner place one can sometimes reach at the heart of the music, where "all losses are restor'd and sorrows end," where the things one believes in are true, in some world of eternal values. If this exists, one feels, what else matters; each person, one felt, entered alone into his own "Kingdom of Heaven." And yet not selfishly, for one knew they were entering, too; no one was left outside, not even the awkward, the fat, the strange, the aging. One could be happy about them. Now I could accept them all; my heart expanded to take them in, to bless them, to feel "Our Father which art in heaven."

This, I realize, is what church should do for one but doesn't for me.

I felt warmed—expansive, full of joy. I tried to communicate some of it to the Scheyers. I feel I must see them again. And there is a nice ember of happiness in me at the thought, as if I had found a bit of Europe here. It isn't Europe of course really, it is a sense of values, and one finds it more often in Europe perhaps —that is all.

They chose a piano over a limousine; one must choose. We

think here that one can have *everything*. One can't. There is always choice, always.

I came home that evening to find Scott with a temperature of over 103, and Anne about the same. Thank goodness C. was here last night and the doctor came.

There followed a long ten days of illness—flu—Scott and Anne and Land in bed at the same time with temperatures going over 105. It was one of those times when one pours oneself out for the children. Up and down stairs with trays, making beds, cleaning floors, washing and sterilizing dishes, taking temperatures, giving pills, wiping noses—a constant round and constantly cleaning the rooms (since Hilma was ill, too). Making my bed every morning and thinking only how good it would be to get into it again but how *long* it would be before I could.

There was a kind of wonderful satisfaction about it, too, though—when the worst was over and I was not afraid.

I have no idea what is happening in the outside world, or what the weather is like even. How the urgency of illness isolates one.

Christmas Eve day it lets up a little. Jon makes a stand for the Christmas tree. And C. and Jon set it up in the window of the big room. It is a lovely bushy tree with pine cones still all over it. I bring down Mother's crèche, the carved Madonna, the angel, and baby in cradle, and the little figure of a girl with a lamb in her arms. I put the "hay" on the ground and group the figures on it. Then erect a little "stable" with four log-cabin blocks of Land's, a cardboard roof, with grass on top for thatch.

"Now we must have a star," I say. "I'll get a star," says eager Land and runs to the Christmas tree and finds a silver foil star. The afternoon sun shines full on the star and on the angel below and the grass (Land put some grass in the crib under the baby!). And it looks for that instant beautiful beyond words—a miracle of creation. Jon comes in full of admiration. "That's my idea of something pretty much perfect." C. comes home at five. Anne comes down in nightgown and wrapper. We light the fire and all the candles and we have our little service. The children are fresh with excitement and a Christmas wonder. They all sit together on the sofa, facing the crèche, with C. We play carols on the

Victrola first. All the old familiar ones. Anne's face lights up at "Silent Night" and she turns to me in recognition (I have sung it so often with Land this week). Land says, "We are singing to them," looking at the crèche. Then I read the verses of the Bible. "There went out a decree. . . ."

And then we blew out the candles and they went up to bed.

It was lovely and quiet; the children were hushed and expectant and happy, as though they had shared something secret, and something holy, too.

Jon said, "That's the nicest Christmas Eve we ever had!" And Charles said so, too. I was happy. Yes, this was Christmas, a touch of it, as I want them to remember it. C. says the service was "like Illiec," that one summer at Illiec was enough for a lifetime, and that the memory of a night like this would last a whole life, too. I quote Dostoevsky, "And even one good memory may be the means of saving us."

1944

Three weeks have gone by—one at home and two on a visit to Washington and New York.

I have two mornings when I work at the head and then C. and I take the train to Washington. Feeling very dowdy in a hat, coat, dress, shoes, and permanent very much too old. We have Truman and K. [Smith] for supper. Truman is, for him it seems to me, rather low-spirited. He talks about the increasing horror and cruelty he sees coming in the war. The frightful bombings can only result, he feels, in unspeakable savagery on both sides—no prisoners, shooting or torturing of pilots, retaliation. He sees nothing but "chaos." Stalin has tried, and succeeded somewhat, in driving a wedge between the British and the Americans—played up to Roosevelt at Teheran and Cairo, and snubbed Churchill at every opportunity.

The men also talk a good deal technically about rockets and rocket-propelled planes. How much damage can rockets do? All military people, I gather, are doubtful as to how, when, and at what cost the invasion can be accomplished.

I see Mary Knollenberg and we discuss art, work, life, at a wonderful level we always seem to reach. She is so very honest and perceptive. I also go to see some of her things at the Washington Artists' Show. She has done a very good head of her stepson, blooming and pulsing with a kind of life that is very American—an earthy quality, with tenderness and idealism in it. The thing that makes Americans—good Americans—so touching to foreigners, and to me.

I spend the second afternoon with Thelma, who seems to me as vibrant and alive as ever, in spite of sickness and the general atmosphere of disillusion and cynicism of Washington, which is prevalent *everywhere*. No one seems to feel a crusade any more, on any side. Americans are fighting the war, someone here said, in order to take the car out of the garage and continue the drive that was interrupted on December 7.

When I repeated this to Deac Lyman, he said, "And a darned good reason, too."

To New York. New York is bursting, jammed, full of servicemen in uniform on leave and girls giving them a good time. There is no more blackout or restrictions on taxis and pleasure-driving.

My hunger for "real life" is getting very bad, *"inguérissable."* Where is it? It is not in Detroit, not in Washington, not in New York. It is in seeing Con, sometimes, in between her work, in little glimpses, real life is always with her.

We went to a concert on Sunday at the Frick Collection—the Budapest String Quartet—a free concert. We sat in the court behind pillars and listened to the music coming from another room and looked at the crisscrossing of palm leaves. Real life has *always* been in music for me. The concert was real, too, because of the people. Poor people and rich people, but no one came for false reasons, only for the music—no snobbery.

Real, too, were the moments I spent in St. Patrick's that morning, streaming with people, young and old, rich and poor, fashionable and plain, and so many soldiers with their girls, people with bags, off the train—a never-ending stream of life passing through that church, making the church part of their life. People thronging in to buy candles in a corner next to me. People bending over the last row of seats, crossing themselves, kneeling for a moment. People standing, like me, out of the stream in the back, waiting perhaps for someone, praying perhaps, unnoticed in the dark. There is something to a church that can take in so many different people.

One evening Mother gave a small dinner in Englewood for Mr. and Mrs. Merz of the *Times*. Mr. Merz once wrote a fair editorial on C. and knew his father (when he was a cub reporter). And Mother, with the flame of loyalty burning in her, has always liked him since and has tried to get us to meet. Con, in her "little seal" satin dress, D'Arcy and Betty, C. and I, John Wheeler-Bennett and Mr. and Mrs. Merz.

Mrs. Merz, the smart, intelligent, well-informed American woman, quick, curious, competent, frank, and nice, *plied* C. with questions, discussed current events with J. Wheeler-Bennett, and U.S.O. and Travelers Aid with Mother. Mr. Merz was polite, urbane, eminently just, sane, and cautious with C. and me. He was like the New York *Times* in human dress. It is pleasant, of course, to feel oneself in such a safe, sane, just world but I keep wanting to knock on it to see if it is real. Mr. Merz was pro-war (thinks we went into the war with our eyes open this time; C. disagrees), is still, I gather, pro-Willkie. Neither he nor the *Times* give any opinion on the now raging dispute on the Polish-Russian border (Russia intends to keep that part of Poland which she won as a result of the Nazi-Russian pact). They—the *Times*—say that far more important than *who* gets *what* territory is *how* the dispute is settled. Which seems to me to be passing the buck, because one knows that legal means can be found to excuse what Russia certainly has the force to take.

The accepted formula now seems to be the Curzon Line— decided by a commission in 1919 to be a just ethnological line. J. Wheeler-Bennett assures us that this is ethnologically correct. Not many Poles to the east of that line. But whether or not it is just, the joke is that the ethnological argument so well upheld on one side of the border is completely overlooked on the other. Russia generously offers to recompense Poland for the Ukraine territory by giving up to her land on the other side. (What?! Russian land? No—*German!*) This land, the Russians point out, will mean much more to the Poles, since it has a seaport! J. Wheeler-Bennett, however, who is very honest, admits that ethnologically the grounds are thin here. This land is populated chiefly by Germans.

Believe it or not—as W. H. Chamberlin said somewhere—this war was started over the boundaries of Poland!

One afternoon I see Janey[1] at Con's. I tell her how when you

[1] Jane Bannard Greene, classmate of C. C. M. M. and co-translator of Rilke's *Letters*.

are in Bloomfield Hills you feel that real life is in Washington or New York. And the people in Washington and New York feel real life is somewhere else—in the army perhaps, and people in the army feel real life is abroad, in Africa perhaps. And the people back of the line in Africa feel real life is in the front line of fighting. And the soldiers in the front line feel that real life is back at home, in places like New Canaan or Bloomfield Hills.

Janey said quickly and surely, "Real life is in work."

Of course she is right. But where and what is my "work" now? C. says it is in writing a novel of our times. But, I protest, I can't, I haven't lived it yet. I don't know enough to write it.

He says I can and must.

I realize that it is wonderful that he has that much faith in me, but I feel it at the moment—at sea, not knowing where to turn —only as a burden, a terrible responsibility, a pressure.

I feel as though I were inhabiting two worlds, one my own— a world where one can live by Father Zoshima's words, where one can love and trust and have faith. And then another world, as C. sees it—a realer world. And I cannot adjust the two, I cannot bridge them. What bridge is there, what ladder to throw across? "Thy Kingdom come" one throws across, and yet . . .

I try to explain some of this to C.—though it is not very clear —as we walk through the bleak scrubby woods over thin snow. Yes, he says, there are ladders. *That* was one (Thy Kingdom come). You must try to throw one.

Thursday, January 27th

I have been back with the children for over a week. Scott has learned to walk alone and is staggering around the house drunk with power. He is not timid in the least or tentative and he is not a bit upset by falling. His big feet now suddenly look too small for his big body and head, which he holds up proudly, smiling and gurgling. Land is in bed with a cold. I realize all the time what a privilege it is to live with Land. The morning we go to school and the world is all frosted, every weed by the side of the road, every curling vine silvered, "Oh, Mother—how beautiful it is!" And one other morning when we were late and

I went out the door with him but couldn't walk to school, "Well, anyway, I'm glad I'm your little boy!" "Are you, Land? I'm *so* glad you are, too." "Yes, aren't you proud of your children, Mother?" "Yes, Land, I am." "Yes," said Land, skipping along happily, "I can't wait to have children!" (with enthusiasm).

Jon goes on a science walk with two teachers and one boy, to collect cocoons. He is also interested in sociological problems such as the overpopulation of the world. I mention birth control. It seems Jon has read two articles on it in *Reader's Digest* (pro and con). "The Catholic Church seems to be against it. But the General Public is for it. I think I'm on the side of the General Public!"

The terrible bombing of Germany continues; the papers boast: Brunswick is "killed." Also headlines of tons and tons dropped on Berlin.

Have been reading [C. S. Lewis's] *The Screwtape Letters*—brilliant satire, especially good on petty sins, dullnesses, smugness, and hypocrisy.

The rest of the week has gone to class. A new world. I am drawing better, the old excitement back.

"Real life is in work."

Thursday, February 3rd

Another week has gone by. I have been taking care of the children—Scott and Anne in bed. Anne with a ceaselessly runny nose and Scott with a temperature. Also having a terrible cold myself.

We are beginning to get fierce fighting in Italy. The huge raids on Germany continue—more cities "killed." In the East, a new Pacific push. Terrible stories have been released about the torture and deliberate starvation and maltreatment of the prisoners left on Bataan. The war becomes more horrible every day.

Friday, February 4th

C. is back. "Take off your coat—are you going to stay?" asked Anne. Scott walked for him. Land on all fours was a monkey around his feet. And Jon tripping him up, wrestling with him, which developed into an evening's struggle. Jon pretending to pass out, C. reviving him with smelling salts. When he is finally into bed ("What *was* that stuff, anyway?!"), C. and I walk over to Cranbrook and see my figure, meet Janet, and walk back in the damp and dark.

C. has seen Harcourt, Brace, who report that the Book-of-the-Month Club has turned down my book—apparently because they have received a number of fanatical letters saying that if the club took my book they'd resign. (All this simply on the *announcement* of my book—on my name—a flag being raised.) The *Reader's Digest* has also turned it down, supposedly because "it is too exquisite to be cut and unfortunately there are no incidents that stand alone." Harcourt, Brace has planned a 25,000 first edition (half of what the first edition of *Listen! the Wind* was). Harcourt also tells me that *Under Cover*,[1] a book purporting to expose spy rings in the U.S. and full of lies about C., is a best seller, going like wildfire. "Why do the wicked prosper?" I cannot believe, like C., that it will all change, that integrity will come out on top in the end.

I must face the fact that this book, too, may be killed before it is even started. Yes, I have been living in a dream world at Cranbrook, where people take me on faith.

Saturday, February 5th

In the evening C. and I go over to Janet's and Eliza's. The Scheyers come and we listen to music. My Corelli, their Prokofiev, a violin concerto (strange and thin, like a new country—beautiful as the moon). And Schoenberg's "Transfigured Night"— very beautiful and moving. In between we talk—Kafka, V. Woolf, Rilke. Dr. Scheyer and I chiefly, since we are the most alike mentally, psychologically. Even though we do not go very far in words, I can tell by the scraps, the snippets that fall, that we are made of the same material. Mrs. Scheyer, no— she is not of the same material—some finer, smoother silk, unruffled, clear. She is like those beautiful women unexpectedly

[1] Widely publicized book attacking America First, by John Roy Carlson.

found in the blacksmith's shop in Kafka, who are "of the Castle," nearer to the Castle, effortlessly, shine with the aura of the Castle. She, alone, sits under the light and sews on a smock for Annabel. How typical, I think, looking at her bent head. All the rest of us were playing host to the music, sitting like marble statues outside of it. But for her, no, the music was no guest. There is no duality here. She and the music are one—it is inside of her, part of her life. *"Ils sont dans le vrai."*

Saturday goes into taking care of the children. Though I do nothing else, I feel it goes well. Everything runs smoothly and I don't lose my temper and get exasperated. The children are happy and calm. Yes—a good day.

Sunday, February 20th

Sunday morning C. and I drove over to the American Gothic frame church on Orchard Lake where his great-grandfather preached years ago. In the middle of white snow, facing the frozen lake, oak trees around it. It must have looked much the same then.

Inside, bare plank floors, golden-oak pews, plain glass Gothic windows (except for one hideous blue-and-red window in the form of a trefoil in the back above the altar on which was printed a Bible motto). There was also a Bible motto on the walls behind the altar. The church was steamy, with its congregation of about thirty. (There were almost as many choir members as congregation, mostly women in tight curls and black robes, faintly rouged cheeks and lipsticked mouths.) Heated by a big stove in the back, with a long black pipe suspended over the heads of the congregation by wires, across the church, to its outlet. The back of the church had a big table covered with children's scarves, coats, Sunday-school pictures, and collection envelopes. In fact, the back of the church was crowded with coats on hooks, galoshes, etc.

A wheezy organ up in front on the slightly raised pulpit-stage led the singing. The preacher in black robes sat on a large undulating black horsehair-and-mahogany sofa of the massive

Victorian style. The rest of the pieces were cheap Victorian—lighter wood, more decorated, flimsy. A marble-topped offertory stand, a pulpit draped with worn brown velvet.

The people were none of them very well dressed—comfortably, but not smart. Dark coats, with worn light-colored fur, around their dumpy figures. "Best hats" of several seasons back, shapeless, with a veil somewhere on top to blur the outline. Middle-class, healthy, rather dull, respectable, and good people. They did not stare or turn around except for the children, who squirmed a lot and played with the collection envelopes.

The sermon, read for the most part, was an explanation of baptism, given by a young rather shy, stiff preacher.

The hymns, Doxology, the Lord's Prayer.

It was all quite simple and sincere—rather New England except for the laxness of children playing in the pews and the disorderly galoshes in the back of the church. Two of the children had red-painted nails! They were girls about two or three.

After the service C., never out of place, went and talked to the preacher—blushing and shy—about his great-grandfather and said the sermon was interesting to him since his great-grandfather, he had been told, baptized by total immersion in the lake!

The minister changed his coat and we went out into the sunshine and cold clear air, I feeling closer to Michigan than I had any time since coming here.

Read Koestler's *Arrival and Departure*. A study of the essential "nostalgia of our time," conflicts of our time, seen through war and torture, love and (chiefly) modern psychiatry. The terrible guilt of not suffering enough (I know it so well).

Monday, February 21st

Monday was a cocoon day—dull, damp, and lifeless and cold. Interview a nurse at noon.

Janet and some of the Cranbrook people go to the blood donors and give blood. I determine to do it, too, get Marta [Brodie] to find out when is the least rushed time.

Thursday I go down to the Community House to give blood to the Red Cross. (Feeling very wicked and rebellious, since C. has always been against my doing it. "You're not the kind of person to give blood. You haven't got enough extra.") There is a long line of sitting people, all kinds, but mostly simple people, dumpy housewives, working men in shirt sleeves, young girls in sweaters. No one has a hat on (neither have I). I sit with dark glasses on, so as not to be recognized. I want to give the pint of blood but I want to give it as Mrs. John Jones, not as Mrs. Lindbergh—as a personal act of participation, not as a publicity gag, not to be photographed as a decoy duck to get more people to give. The pictures of people doing this make me ill and I should think they'd make the soldiers ill.

I find it very moving, going up the line after the housewife, the man in shirt sleeves following me. The people were the same type of people we had in the America First meetings—not smart, not rich, not intellectual, dowdy, hard-working good people, housewives, shopkeepers, etc. I suppose it is the heart of America, those people who protest against war and then give their sons and their blood and their money without grudging or making a great fuss over it, taking their generosity just as a matter of fact.

Not that these people were unfeeling. You sensed they all felt quite deeply and personally; their sons or their fathers or husbands were "over there in it." ("In it" is this war's phrase, rather than "over there.") And so they wanted to give their pint. It might go to *him,* everyone was thinking, silently and secretly, with a constriction around the heart, stiffening and stimulating one, with a kind of hidden joy and pride.

I answered all the questions, wrote down my name (my heart pounding—now suppose I faint and it gets into the papers—I *mustn't* faint). But when I bare my arm to have the blood pressure test, the nurse says suspiciously to me: "How much do you weigh?" "About 105." "I'm sorry, but we can't take you. It's a rule of the Red Cross; we can't take anyone under 110. You see, you haven't a pint to give."

The man in shirt sleeves moves up in my place and I go out into the sunshine, feeling very let down.

"Thank you just the same," they call after me.

To the studio to work on the head. I work all afternoon on the nose, which has got squashed in being moved around. C. comes in late and looks at it and at my figure—the last one—which he likes *very much*. I like it, too. So I am pleased. It is the first time I have got into a figure the beauty I saw there. It is strange with me—if I *see* the beauty, really *see* it and have a kind of excitement over it, then I can usually make something of it. It is the moment of vision that counts. Even though one loses it while working. If one has *ever* had it, it is enough. It is a quickening seed and seems to work by itself, independent of one's conscious effort. Without that quickening seed, nothing beautiful ever comes, no matter how hard and long one works.

At night I read C.'s take-off chapter.[1] It is *very* good, compact, all-of-a-piece, unconscious taut writing. Very moving. The style is adapted (unconsciously) to the tempo and story. And so the whole is a clear integrated perfect piece. One is not conscious of the writer, or, rather, the aviator trying to be a writer, as one sometimes is. It is not overwritten or suppressed. No, it is true—"on the beam."

He is very pleased at what I say, touchingly pleased.

I also confess to him that I tried to give blood. He is at first upset: "You shouldn't do that. You can't stand it. . . . You shouldn't run off and do things like that. . . ." And then rather pleased, almost proud of my "running off" and wanting to. But relieved that they didn't take it.

"This has been a good day," he says, elated, going to bed. "You like my chapter and I liked your figure."

Thursday, February 24th

Another week has passed. Thursday is my day for summing up —weighing the week.

Saturday C. and I went skiing. It is wonderful and I am taught how to control the turn by stemming and throwing my

---

[1] C. A. L. was writing chapters of *The Spirit of St. Louis.*

weight. It is like a magic key, like suddenly getting your balance on a bicycle or finding that you can keep yourself up in the water.

Sunday we go for more skiing, from 6 to 7 A.M. The hill is empty and frozen again. The sky clear and pale—fading light. We climb way up through the pine trees to the top of the hill and start out one after the other in turns down the hill. It is wonderful—like two birds in the air following each other or dolphins playing with a wave. Inhabiting a different element. For the first time I feel a kind of joy as I see the next curve coming. I go to meet it, give to it, bend and follow it, like jumping to a wave. The hill, the skis, and I are not separate elements to be juggled but all one. A thrilling feeling—almost I reach the state of those careless, happy-go-lucky little boys completely at home on the hill. C. is exhilarated: "This makes up for everything." I am happy I made the effort to go out with him, though I was tired. It was worth it.

Monday is a beautiful warm day. All the snow is melting. Scheyer's class is in the Museum. He shows us lovely things— Mexican, Mayan, Aztec, and Peruvian. "Do you want to touch it?" (I always do.) And Peruvian textiles.

It is too bad. I feel quite close to Dr. Scheyer. We like the same things, talk the same language. But we never talk about the real things, only hint at them. We play with the little snippets of cloth that fall from the tailor's scissors—never unroll the great bolts of uncut material that are there stored on the shelves. Because we are both shy, I suppose, and reticent before the shelves. But it is too bad—when communication is so rare in life—to let it slip by, out of shyness, and good taste. I should like to talk to him about Art and Life, maybe even war, of the miracle of grace, and one's feeling of guilt at nonparticipation. Would he understand? Perhaps not.

All the people in Cranbrook seem to inhabit such a safe world, so far from the wickedness and the terror, the sins, the mistakes, the responsibilities, the problems, the conflicts out there, where I have been and must go back before long. How immune they seem from these troubles. (Of course they *have* troubles—

troubles I have never had—of money, security, personal troubles, too.) Their troubles, though, seem so small. They do not affect other people. Their mistakes will never be so great, or their responsibility, or their guilt as in that outside world. And who is out there that understands? St.-Ex., whom I shall never see again; Koestler, whom I shall never meet, who I suppose would despise me, for the *Wave*.

Tuesday is dark and misty; I work all day at my figure of Myrtle, which is very bad (after doing a good one, too). I feel I am back at the beginning—very discouraged.

Also I am too tired at night to go walk with C. But I read his chapters each night and go over them. Correct them, analyze them (if I can't write I have certainly done enough writing to analyze and comment well). The chapters are improving—almost always well written, though not well *composed,* but getting *much better.*

Scott cries at night. He is stuffed up again. I sleep fitfully.

Wednesday. C. home early. He has invented a wonderful game for the children called "Vild-Cats" (after Anne's dreams!). He drapes the big blue blanket over two armchairs. Jon, Land, Anne, and C. crawl in the dark cave, C. distributes Vild-Cat food (malted milk tablets). I also crawled in. C. has got all the children primed to get me for "a little sister." They get on all fours and recite, "Please, Mother, may we have another little sister!" I have not even said "maybe" yet. Four children are enough, especially on the nurse's day off!

Land goes on a strike and says he will stay in the Vild-Cat den until I promise I will give him one!

I say to C., "It's *your* game and *your* idea, and your responsibility to get him to bed!"

Thursday. Trailer in P.M., and then for a walk late. It is warmish and the roads are soft and running streams from melting snow but it is wonderful to be out. I go up over the Apple Orchard Hill (where I saw the archetypal Orchard) and break some

branches off a fallen apple tree to force in the house. The bare
black branches of the apple tree look alive and vibrant on the
wall, even without a sprig of green. You sense the spring hidden,
explosive in them.

After supper I read Churchill's long speech reviewing the
progress of the war and analyze it. In the first part he analyzes
the military situation, apologizes for and explains the slow
progress in Italy. Admits air war is the only big offensive of
Britain and U.S. Indicates that this is the prelude to invasion but
that invasion won't come until air invasion has gone to much
further lengths.

The second half of the speech is on political ground. And
here he certainly is treading on eggs. Italy, Yugoslavia, Greece,
Poland. He takes up each in turn. What one gathers is that
there is civil war in every country and Britain is trying to support
both parties. The King, Badoglio, *and* the anti-Fascists. Tito
(and Mikhailovitch) *and* King Peter and his exiled government.
The Polish government in exile in London *and* the Russians. In
Greece he admits that two parties are fighting each other with
arms given them to fight the Germans. He feels great sympathy
for the Poles. England went to war over her boundaries, he
reminds any ungrateful Poles who might be in the audience.
He seems willing to agree that the Russians may advance into
Poland as far as the Curzon Line. (He reminds his listeners
that though England went to war over the boundaries of Poland
they have never guaranteed her *any particular boundary!!*) He
wants a strong and independent Poland. (Hah!) Poland, he
agrees, can be compensated by German territory. The Atlantic
Charter, he hastens to explain, does not apply to Germany. We
are not going to have the Atlantic Charter thrown in our teeth
at the peace table the way Wilson's Fourteen Points were, he
says, in more diplomatic words. Unconditional surrender is unconditional surrender.

The speech is one sensitive to heckling and criticism. He does
not want to be prodded further on such delicate matters, he says
in so many words.

None of this is brought out by the press. What is brought out and headlined is the opening of Churchill's speech, in which he says he has never expected the war to be over in 1944 (predicts hard fighting, perhaps a long war, etc.).

This is so accepted by me that I hardly notice it but it is picked up by the press as the "news" in the speech for the American people. Some say that this will come as a shock to most Americans, who expect the war to be over this year. Eisenhower and Mark Clark have both predicted victory in 1944!

C. comes home very late after testing bombers all day and we sit and talk in the kitchen as he makes himself supper. I go over the high points of Churchill's speech.

Saturday, February 26th

I read the papers—Churchill has had much criticism in Parliament on his speech, especially backing down to Russia, abandoning the Atlantic Charter regarding Poland, and setting the stage for another war in granting Poland large parts of Germany.

Thursday, March 2nd

The week has gone fast as usual. I always feel it is "gone" by Thursday. Sunday, C. did not take the children to his mother but stayed and worked on the tax report and on his ms. I go to the trailer, rather down. I am unable to start any new writing or take up the old.

A "marking-time period"—that is what the war seems to me, to C. More to him than to me, I think, for I do not look forward to a time of action after the war. What I miss is not so much *action* as *participation*. It is hard for me to participate in this war—because I stood against it believing it would only destroy the things we were fighting for. Even though we are or seem to be slowly winning. The destroying, the complete nullification of the values we went to war for, seems to be happening even faster than we feared, both here and abroad. Russia's deals in Eastern Europe, Poland, the Baltic States, have made a farce of the Atlantic Charter and the beautiful statements of complete accord given at Moscow, Teheran.

Saturday, March 4th

At night C. and I talk and I read his ms., analyze, correct, suggest. And then to bed—with the complete uncertainty of the future and the cut-off-ness of the past. I try to break myself of the long habit of daydreams as I go to sleep. "No one in his dreams ever seriously thinks of himself as empty-handed." They used to be dreams of personal popularity. And I shall have on a beautiful ball dress and I shall waltz into the room, and I shall be the most beautiful person there . . . and *He* (there was always a He) will see me.

But now it is no longer that. I know that never will I be the most beautiful and never *was*. The dreams are of praise in connection with my work, or talk, or wisdom. *They* will say, "What, *you* did that—that beautiful head!"

They haven't changed much. Such adolescent dreams. I realize at moments how absurd they are. I am a woman approaching 40, with a young figure, the intensity of a girl, lines on the forehead, an occasional gray hair, and eyes that still glow suddenly and unexpectedly. I have written four books, have four nice children, and an absorbing, alive, loving, growing, and happy husband. Isn't that enough? Why not turn my thoughts to life as it is. Isn't that exciting enough? Happy enough? Yes, of course, and my days are full of joy, too. I determine each night instead of daydreaming to think about some pure immediate joy I have had during the day with my children or husband or friends. Every day has moments of pure joy—even the dullest and saddest day.

Saturday, March 4th–Saturday, March 18th

Two weeks have gone by. I have been to New York and back, looking for a nurse. C. is again away. The book has come out, the reviews started. The political stage of the war is still going on—very little else.

The things that stand out from the last two weeks are: the Ferry Command supper with C. at the Officers' Club. A most disillusioning experience. I went humble ("these men are in the war, facing death; I will find real life here") and I found—just the opposite. The conversation was entirely about the stag party the night before, which was one of those parties, the Colonel admitted, where you just sat and saw how much liquor you could take without bursting. Or else they discussed at length the new clubhouse of which the C.O. was inordinately proud: "Going to cost so many thousand dollars . . . have showers . . . good cellar . . . dance hall." Also all about the other clubhouses he had organized on various other posts! How he got So-and-so of the Ritz and So-and-so of the Plaza. Best wine cellar in the country! The officers' wives were all dressed up fit to kill (or capture someone else's husband). I should have worn a hat. Some of the officers had sensitive faces and looked as if they might talk but the tone was set by the convivial Colonel, who called every junior officer's wife "Sweetie," got drunk with the rest of them. Most of the officers I talked to were ground officers and had not been flying much. They talked about what an awful place Detroit was and how they liked *Oklahoma!* and their C.O. The atmosphere was that of a Hotchkiss prom (not even a Yale prom!). And for the first time I felt I really forgot the war. No one discussed it or thought about it and they all seemed to be having a wonderful time. Juicy steaks, gobs of butter on top, lemon pies, plenty of liquor, a jazz band and dancing—and *no responsibility at all.* We danced in the old administration building of the airport; the back halls were lined with those gambling slot machines, men sticking their nickels in—hoping against hope (and every law of statistics) to break the bank.

One boy I danced with looked as though he thought about other things but I couldn't get through to them. The Colonel spoke with evident praise of the Russians he had seen in Montana ferrying our planes back to Russia, especially of their discipline, which he said he admired; told the story of a plane about to be delivered to a Russian pilot at Newark airport. It was rammed by accident by an incoming commercial plane. When the Russian was told about it he said, "They shot the pilot of course?"

"A little of that wouldn't do us any harm," commented the Colonel. "Why, if I so much as slap a sergeant's wrist I have the whole of Congress writing me!" "The Nazis would certainly have shot the pilot, too," I comment acidly—but no one gets it.

I go back with relief to my own "real" life. But there must be real people in the army—even in Detroit. Where are they? In the ranks, perhaps.

Wednesday I go off with C. to New York on the chance of being with him to the last moment. (He says he may go West —even to the Pacific.)

The first reviews come. C. calls me the day they came out from New York saying they are "on the whole" good. I realize how much, how perilously much, I have been counting on their reception of this book for an answer, for a steer—too much. Hanson's review hurts me. Am I really that selfish, that much of a snob, that supercilious about my husband? No—he is unfair, but why? The Marshall Field papers carry a terrible review—so nasty that it is funny. "Unimportant finger exercise," "dangerous position the romantic gets into," "egotistical escapism," etc. "Because Saint-Exupéry was relatively unknown in this country her writing seemed good."

"It is no accident that these two fliers dangerously lost in the Alps found safety on Mussolini's soil." One very perceptive review in the *Sun,* surprisingly enough written by a man. The rest are safe and good, if unperceptive.

I think them out at night, weighing Hanson's accusations. After all, I feel in the end, the book is me—completely me— what is wrong in it is wrong in me. What is lacking in it is lacking in me. But at least I have followed the law of the date tree. I gave only dates—and only because it was my nature to give dates.

Monday morning in art history class Scheyer says for me please not to run away after class since he has something for me. He then presents me with two of their books "as a token." He says more about my book, but I feel rather shy. I cannot talk about my book, neither can I apologize for it. I say something about the criticisms and what it is like to have a name that is no longer a name but a problem in semantics. And then suddenly for no reason he is saying, perfectly naturally, as if released: "I feel we must sometime have a really good talk; we have never had a really good talk; we have talked—but still . . ."

"Yes," I say with relief, "it has only been the snippets of cloth and there are great bolts. . . ." He then goes on to say, "As I told you before, it means so much, so very much to me to have you in my class. . . . If you were not there . . ." He lifts his arms in a little gesture of despair.

"And I think," he goes on quite naturally and quite openly, like a child appealing for understanding and beaming with a kind of trustful goodness, "I think one should say these things. . . ."

"Of course," I say, myself warmly and openly, "obviously we talk the same language," and then I go back (crossing off old scores) and explain to him what I meant when I said on visiting their house that it was European (for he had protested so poignantly—now I understand why—"but we want to be *American"*). "I only meant," I explain at last, "that I felt you were my kind of people and I was so hungry for something I had had abroad. . . ."

"Thank you," he says quite humbly and simply.

He says he will come sometime in the spring, when the weather is better and he has less work.

And I laugh and say, "Don't wait for the spring—the spring is a long way off!" And go off finally to class mulling over the strangeness of life, the strangeness of understanding which strikes unexpectedly as lightning, here, there, everywhere, in the most unheard-of spots.

It is very rare. I put it high on my shelf with other isolated jewels. (Not a hunk of gold—they never weigh much, these moments. They do not bulk at all in one's life. They are only rather light, precious, and perfect instants outside the main stream of one's life.)

The night before C. comes home I read all the papers and catch up.

Some intellectuals (including William Agar[1] of Freedom

[1] Editor of the Louisville *Courier Gazette*.

House) protest the unilateral actions of Russia in Poland, Czechoslovakia, etc.

The London *Times* publishes a leading editorial saying that perhaps the Atlantic Charter will have to be modified, that in some cases self-determination of small nations and "security" are incompatible!

Russia is advancing in Bessarabia, planning to reimburse Rumania with part of Hungary.

The Germans are also advancing into the Balkans.

The Italian campaign has bogged down and it is frankly admitted by Hanson Baldwin here and in a column from England that the results of preinvasion leveling by bombing, as tried out in Cassino, are of doubtful value, did *not* wipe out all ground resistance and perhaps provided better cover. (The results of the wholesale bombing of German cities are also being questioned —55 per cent of Berlin has been destroyed, more bombs dropped on it in one night than in the whole of the Blitz on London! Most of it is blind bombing from above clouds, no shadow of excuse as precision military-objective bombing. When the guilt of having done this catches up with us, what will it do to us? Or will it be better than this horrible callousness that covers all of us now: "They had it coming," we say placidly as we sit back in our comfortable chairs. And the fliers lost—bringing about this hell.)

Finland is refusing Russia's peace terms. We are urging her to accept them and guaranteeing her nothing in exchange.

People are "waking up" but Europe has been destroyed in the meantime. "The child is dead."

Wednesday, March 22nd

Charles comes home. I am just leaving the trailer when I see him, lanky blue figure tumbling down the hill from the house to find me.

It is so strange to see someone like that, whom you love, suddenly coming down the steps in all his warm bodily reality, to catch sight of him before he sees you, and to feel suddenly, in one of those incredible flashes of vision in life: "How much he means to me—all of life is coming down the steps to me."

And then the vision goes with physical closeness, with the familiar "coming home" to one's husband.

As usual the house comes to life with him. He throws Anne up in the air. She eats with us. C. is glowing with good spirits. Happy about the book (for the reviews on the whole have been good and the advance sales good). Happy in his work and because he has been talking with people who see the world picture as he does. Happy to be home and with the children, but chiefly, I feel, exhilarated because it looks as though he might get to the Pacific. (How male! I think with a grim female bitterness.) "How long will you have?" I ask quickly (here before he goes). "Oh, a week!" Well, we have a week. We go out and walk and talk; Jon, with glowing face, catches up with us and walks along with us.

April 5th

Two weeks have gone by without writing. One week with Charles (his last one)[1] and one without him. The week with him —knowing he was going off, crazy to go!—was too intense. Packages all over the floor, boxes going off, clothes put away, business cleared up—all so ominously final. C. was happy and full of energy; I apprehensive, not showing it. Peace in walks with him over the muddy fields to "our" orchard hill, or at night to Cranbrook. Now it has all vanished. I can't remember any of it. Nothing seems real except the future—when he comes home again. How greedy one is of life.

The last day I could not go down to the trailer but sat on my bed watching him pack and sewing buttons on his raincoat. (A button cut off *my* raincoat. It was the only one of the right color I could find and I was secretly pleased to have it going with him, like a charm.) I seemed so lost, unable to do anything else, not

---

[1] C. A. L. had received authorization to go to the South Pacific combat areas as a civilian adviser to observe in action the planes he had been testing. See Introduction, p. xxvii.

gloomy but just suspended, that he sat down on the bed beside me and I laughed and said, "It's no use—I won't be happy until you're gone!" "I know," he said, "I know just what you mean." "This is the worst part of it."

I dreaded his going and yet I knew I couldn't settle down and adjust until it was behind me.

One of the worst parts of it seemed to be the lack of significance —when someone is going off on a trip that may become dangerous, the last days should somehow be significant, beautiful, like a landscape before a storm. The grass an unreal vivid green, the sky purple. But these days were not vivid or significant. Because I was tired from the extra work in the house? Or because they really were *not* significant?

All this time I have been trying to do half the work of the children with Hilma—because I thought she was overtired and overworked. So I got the children up, washed and fed them, and made the beds before going to school and then again washed and fed them, read to them, and put them to bed at night.

And then the time spent writing, telephoning, to find a new nurse. Miss Hanky came from Pittsburgh for the day to see us. She arrived late one night in a snowstorm, cheerful and solid and ageless looking, with a bunch of snowdrops in her hand she had picked that morning. I liked her immediately. The next day I was not very open to impressions because I had the children alone. (But it all went beautifully.) Miss Hanky following me around and C. downstairs with a great beam on his face because he'd got his authorization and was going off "tomorrow"!

"Tomorrow"—I felt shaken by it and went through the routine with pounding efficiency to cover what I didn't want to face. Why did I have to make the decision on a nurse on a day like this? She is warm and loving. She is intelligent and perceptive, and probably sentimental. She seems adaptable, sympathetic to my point of view.

Will she have the elusive power to control Anne? Not to nag at her, not to give in to her, but be positive with her? That I can't tell. She comes in to Anne with a tiny pussycat as a present. Anne is sitting up in bed. Miss Hanky says, "I've brought you a pussycat, Anne. I thought perhaps you liked pussycats." Anne bent her fair head down, smiling with shy delight. "Miow," she said under her breath! No need to say *"I like cats,"* or "I'm so glad to have this cat"—so much more immediate just to *be* a cat in answer: "Miow!"

And C. goes off. "Don't forget your lunch!" I call as he goes down the stairs. But he leaves it behind on the hall table.

The days that follow I throw myself into hard physical work, care of the children, scrubbing the bathroom floor, washing dishes, washing out socks, bibs. Very tiring and not altogether satisfying.

Friday the children start their vacation! Land and Jon perpetually fighting and underfoot.

In the meantime letters and reviews, comments on my book keep pouring in. They move me, they agitate me whether good or bad, so that the pool is continually ruffled. And I am not alone enough to quiet it down.

That is it, I am not alone enough, I feel too naked, too vulnerable, touched by too many people. Even when I don't get the letters I *feel* the people's thoughts. (Or seem to—wild as that sounds.) I *feel* people are thinking about me, touching me, and I vibrate to it unsteadily.

The most deeply satisfying reaction has been from Mina [Curtiss]—a long and wonderful letter understanding everything (almost everything). It was a letter which showed me where I was, from where I had come, where I could go to next— a warm, generous, and illuminating letter, creative, feeding, strengthening.

And I have no time to write back all the letters I want to write, stimulated as I am by these touches from people.

This has been a very close time at home—very much turned in—to children, self, and the immediate people in my household. Mary, the cook, gets sick. Jon is moody and restless, Land gay and rambunctious, Anne fussy. But I have had two evenings out. One with Charles—at Janet and Eliza's, with the Scheyers and a French professor[1] and his wife. The Frenchman is precise and scholarly, *"raisonnable."* The evening ends up in a heated discussion of Picasso's "Guernica"—chiefly between Scheyer and the French professor—Scheyer believing that "Guernica" was a genuine work of art and a great one; and the professor believing it was not ("Art is meant to please—and this does not"). They are never really arguing on the same level because they never agree on the function of art. I agree with Scheyer but am too tired to argue (besides, he is doing much more brilliantly than I could) and too tired and stimulated at night to sleep, strangely enough. As one sometimes feels: If only that pain in my tooth would stop, I could sleep, I felt: If only I could stop seeing that woman's terrible face (in "Guernica") I could get to sleep.

Tuesday, April 4th

One of those days that sometimes strike a household. Land and Jon bust up the furniture on the top floor; Anne messes up the bathroom floor after Hilma has just cleaned it.

I go off to class. Coming back at four I find both doors of the house flung wide open and, walking upstairs, the unmistakable smell of skunk. It is a long time before I can find anyone—as though a bomb had exploded, scattering everyone to their separate holes. Finally I find out that Jon and Land and Jay (Jon's friend) shot a skunk in the woods, dragged it home, and then ran all through the house to find people and tell them about it. To Hilma, who had just cleaned the bathroom floor for the second time, it was the last straw (poor Hilma, who hardly ever raises her voice and never loses her temper). She shrieked and rushed them into the garage, stripped off all their clothes, washed them, told them they'd have to stay in there for three days!

"Where will we sleep?" queried Land, round-eyed. "Oh, anywhere—on the floor!"

---

[1] André Delattre, Professor at Wayne University, scholar, editor of Voltaire letters.

"Will we get anything to eat?" asked Jon.

Then she sent them to their rooms. The third floor was full of skunk odor and Miss Brodie immediately took a shower and washed her hair.

The only serious part about it, I feel, is Jon using his gun around here. Since it is against the law and he could be taken to a juvenile court for it. I talk to Jon about it and he is chagrined. I then wash his hair, his belt, etc.

Little forgotten things still persist of skunk odor—the gun case, the rubbers.

I talked to Land and said, "Why did you come on rushing into the house when you smelled so?"

"Well," said Land, innocent-eyed, *"I thought it was Jon* and Jon thought it was *me!"*

In the middle of this, Anne's beautifully groomed and always perfectly-under-control teacher comes for tea. I explain our confusion but I'm sure she feels we're hopelessly bohemian and untidy.

Hilma and Miss Brodie have recovered their sense of humor but I am wilted and Jon is still plunged in gloom. I think of the book I read as a child called *Anne's Terrible Good Nature.* Anne always meant well, but somehow . . . !

June 20th

I have not written all spring—April, May, June—and now that there is a little free time I find it hard to begin.

April went in a trip to New York, where I met Mary Knollenberg. We went to the ballet, art shows, together. Actually, though, we were both tired and wanted not stimulus but *earth.* I wanted Charles and came back from New York curiously flat and dissatisfied. What I had wanted had been Charles all along, not New York. I came back and threw myself into finishing the head, working every day in the week on it.

May went into the last weeks of work in the studio, every day. The school had its exhibition and my head was in it. And again people and parties, at Janet's, at my house. Music and talk about books, art, writing, politics sometimes. It has been great fun for me and in a sense the first time I have ever done it naturally, freely. In this circle I can give my true self as I have never done to a group of people before. Certainly not when I was young and shy and it was a boy-girl game I could not play and was over-shadowed by Elisabeth. Certainly not in my marriage, because the groups we have entered have never been *my* people. In political groups, aviation groups, quite naturally everyone looked to C. But here I am perpetually my own self—and they like me!

Goodhue Road, June 24th

Dear Mary [Knollenberg],

Forgive me for not writing sooner, but for the past month I have had all the children, with no help, and have been getting Jon and Land off to camp as well—*and* visitors—Mother—Constance and her child.

Charles has been away now about three months. I really miss him terribly. There seems no place to rest or to ground oneself. I feel perpetually up on the ceiling somewhere like the light princess who had no gravity.

Because I have missed him I have thrown myself into finishing up work in the studio and at night—in people. I have really had a very good time. In a strange way I have never had such a good time with a group of people before. It has been fun and has given me a kind of social courage about going out without Charles—finding my own group, etc., which is perhaps wise.

It makes me hesitate, too, about leaving here for Connecticut. Am I going to find it again in those smug New England towns? I wonder.

Well, if Charles really wants to move we will move (since I am not any more for his being permanently wedded to the Ford organization than he is). But it seems more unlikely as the months go by and he does not return. One has to move before September and the beginning of school—if one has children.

Charles is apparently very happy and satisfied about his work and trip.[1] In a strange way I sense (through the photographs the posts have sent back rather than through the letters) that not since his barnstorming days has he had such basic and satisfying companionship with his fellow men. He is not a hero—he is working with them, he is really contributing, he is anonymous (the glory goes to the war heroes), and he is completely and warmly accepted as one of them. They love him.

I am guessing all this but I think it is true. I am very happy about it. It is strange, isn't it, and terribly frustrating how little a woman can do to give this sort of thing to her husband. Nothing she can give will make up for it and she cannot find or make the situation that gives it. She can only encourage him, when he does light on it, to go ahead and take it.

He has written me twice, urging me to meet him on the West Coast and wait at Margot's for him. Only I have really no idea of when to go—since in true masculine fashion he says only "pretty soon now." I have a lower on a train out July 2nd and plan to go then if I hear no further word of delay. I expect to be back here in August. To move to New England?

I have no idea. The lease on the house, the applications for schools, are all suspended in this uncertainty.

Like you—only you are working or will work when you get to Connecticut. If you can keep hold of that I feel everything else will eventually fall into place around it.

July 2nd, Train Chicago–San Francisco

Dear Charles,

I am on my way West. I hope to meet you. I feel madly extravagant and altogether quite mad, speeding over the country with not much certainty of when or where I'll meet you.

[1] "As a civilian technical representative in the Pacific, C. A. L. flew fifty combat missions to evaluate at first hand the comparative combat qualities of the Marine F4U Corsair and the twin-engine P-38 Lightning of the Army Air Forces. During his missions, Lindbergh was often under fire and he shot down one enemy plane. He also developed fuel consumption techniques which stretched the effective range of the P-38 by hundreds of miles."—Raymond H. Fredette, Lt. Col. U.S.A.F. (Ret.), July 11, 1973, Report for Veterans Day Award.

But I feel happy tonight. I have sat and watched the cornfields of Iowa darken, seen the homesteads pass by—a white house, a red barn and a brave cluster of green trees in the midst of oceans of flat fields—like an oasis in a desert. The glossy flanks of horses and the glossy leaves of corn. And I have been overcome by the beauty and richness of this country I have flown over so many times with you. And overcome with the beauty and richness of our life together, those early mornings setting out, those evenings gleaming with rivers and lakes below us, still holding the last light. Those fields of daisies we landed on—and dusty fields and desert stretches. Memories of many skies and many earths beneath us—many days, many nights of stars. "How are the waters of the world sweet—if we should die, we have drunk them. If we should sin—or separate—if we should fail or secede—we have tasted of happiness—we must be written in the book of the blessed. We have had what life could give, we have eaten of the tree of knowledge, we have known—we have been the mystery of the universe."[1]

Good night—

Dear Charles,

It is morning—all the fields have disappeared and the wide rolling plains have taken their place. "Oklahoma!" I thought waking this morning, but no, we are farther north than that and farther west too. These plains are greener—it is Nebraska and Wyoming. We have just left Cheyenne, and I can see the first faint line of blue mountains touched with white far ahead of us. I feel a touch of mountain excitement. "Look, look! The mountains!" I said to the little boy eating breakfast opposite me. But he didn't feel "mountain excitement." It takes a long time to love this country, to recognize in it what one loves. (It takes a long time to learn to love anything.) One must know it well, not just see it through the thick windows of an air-conditioned super-de-luxe train. One must have felt its heat, its inescapable burning sun, its endlessness, its dust, its sand storms, its tornado spouts of wind, its barrenness, but especially its endlessness—its endless-

[1] From *John Jay Chapman and His Letters*, M. A. De Wolfe Howe, ed.

ness and then and then—the mountains! "Look! there are the mountains!" Yes, then it means something. The mountains are certainly a symbol of something spiritual, of a deliverance from the everyday, of an ascent of man's spirit. And a deliverance through ascent. *"C'est là que l'on respire comme un prisonnier délivré"* ("It is there one can breathe like a prisoner who has been freed"). I think always of that line of the Bible, "How beautiful upon the mountains are the feet of him that bringeth good tidings, that publisheth peace."

We are climbing now, slowly up the foothills, and pine trees are dotting the bare slopes. The sky is wide, windy, and beautiful —I am quite drunk with it. I am thinking of that time in the du Noüys' apartment in Paris when they showed us movies of *Le Grand Ouest* and all the French people said, "Ah! oh! *Épatant! Formidable!"* when the pictures of these plains and mountains appeared. But I—I could only feel, "But it is *my* country, it is of me—and in me—those plains, those deserts, those endless distances, those wild rock formations, those twisted pine trees clinging to life on the stony slopes. It is my flesh and blood."

And then when the screen flashed back to Paris—the Dôme des Invalides, the soft lights of Paris, and all the French people relaxed in their chairs in a sense of familiar and comforting homecoming. Then it was *I* who felt a stranger, who said in my heart, *"Épatant! Formidable!"*

And it is you who have given me this country, this love. You have stretched my heart out of its New England shell, so that it now holds the curves of the Mississippi, the endless grain fields of Kansas, the bare ugly buttes of Oklahoma, and the green-gray rolling plains of this country—endless and monotonous in themselves but somehow exciting because they breed the mountains, pregnant and explosive with the mountains which spring from their borders.

And then the mountains—I wish I could paint. I would like to paint these criss-cross fences weighted down by red stones (snow fences?) which appear like fragile little toys of man against the endless rolling plains, the rise of blue mountains in the distance and the endless sky over all.

How right you were to urge me to come! (You *did* urge me, didn't you?! It is my excuse for coming!)

"One sees only through change."

Yes, you are right. I have been too long in the East. (And Detroit is still the East.) All this excites me so much. Everything seems unbearably beautiful to me.

"O world, I cannot hold thee close enough!" [Edna St. Vincent Millay]

> "I forgive it all its sins
> I kiss the scars upon its face." [Elinor Wylie]

We have just passed *Laramie*. This is Jon's country [where he went to camp]. I am so happy he is here and that this country is going to be his flesh and blood also.

We must never stay away from it for good, Charles. You are right. We must remember that this wildness and bleakness and expanse is in us. You never forget it but I do sometimes. We must not forget.

I think this is long enough—don't you—for a letter that probably won't get to you, since I *hope* I'll see you first. A letter I couldn't help writing—I wanted so much to say it to you.

July 3rd. En route San Francisco

Dear Janet [de Coux],

I am crossing over Salt Lake, Utah, and there are great one-faced cut-out blue mountains against an evening sky. The water is satin smooth, with not a ripple of life—fish or boat—in it. It might be a scene from Perelandra[1]—another planet. I left yesterday (can that be possible!) and will get to San Francisco tomorrow to stay at Margot and Dwight's and—I hope—to wait for Charles! I won't be here more than a month and perhaps shorter, should he come home sooner. Ever since I got on the train I have been filled with the most tremendous exhilaration. I don't know if it's just shaking off the "swarm of mosquito cares"

---

[1] *Perelandra,* a novel about another planet, by C. S. Lewis.

one always has at home, or whether it is the excitement at the thought of—perhaps—seeing Charles soon. Or whether it is just the joy of being alone and free to sink down into oneself, to find oneself, to taste the essence of things again. I have not started really to think much yet—I am just overcome with the beauty of the West, which I haven't seen for so long. Charles says, "One sees only through change." And I think it is true. Suddenly, moved from my environment, I see everything with a freshness and a vividness that is almost painful.

I started this really to tell you of the various bombshells that burst upon me the last day at Cranbrook, which perhaps may turn out not to be bombshells at all. But you should know about them.

Mr. Patterson wrote me that we couldn't have the house next winter. The lease expires the last of August. That means we'd have to be out and moved into a new house by September 1! I felt as if someone had hit me in the solar plexus. Just as I had decided I liked Michigan and wanted to stay. My mind whirled all morning—move to Maine? Leave children there while looking for house in Connecticut? Should I telephone Janet? Should I go to California at all? By afternoon we reached Mr. Snyder, the real estate agent, who took the line: "There, there—don't you worry. You won't have to move at all. He doesn't mean a word of it." He said that Mr. Patterson wants to rent a smaller house but hasn't found one yet. He thinks he will find one and then we can stay where we are. He says Mr. Patterson is just safeguarding himself.

Well, there it is. I decided to go to California, to be back by August 1st at the latest, in case we have to move. I am hoping no catastrophic change will occur. But I thought you ought to know about it.

At the moment, with these bare wrinkled mountains climbing up out of the gray sagebrush, nothing seems to matter.

Forgive this quite incoherent scrawl. If you were here we would not talk—just watch the rain squalls ahead blend the dark thunderheads with the darkening earth.

Dearest Con,

I am sitting in Margot's living room on the couch, listening for crying children while Margot has a nap in the guest-house. Dwight is off to recapture a cow.

They cried! And then guests came. It is now Monday morning. I have been here three weeks and I don't really know where it has gone. Sleeping, sitting in the sun, seeing people and trying to help Margot with the household routine. It would be complete bliss (and has been almost) were it not for the fact that I have been in this same state of pins and needles suspense about when C. is coming home and whether or not we are going to move and where. Trying to figure out from his succinct little notes when he might be coming, how long I can safely stay, with the pressure of moving squeezing me from the other end. And also trying to gauge from cramped little phrases of his letters all the delicate balance of desires, repulsions, pulls and stresses that one gets somehow from even a confused half-hour's actual conversation with one's husband. They are, I know, all imprisoned in his little phrases "better start the grapevine going to Connecticut" or, "If you have to move even a short distance . . ." "As you think best," etc. But I cannot unfold them—like those compressed pellets of Japanese flowers and fish one had to put into water before they opened. I cannot force them to unfold their secrets. They need the water of reality, presence, conversation.

To be practical: Marta [Brodie] has wired me that she thinks Mr. Patterson will not re-rent and we must get out by September 1. If he won't re-rent I shall spend a week looking in Bloomfield Hills, on the chance of something "just right" (very small chance). Then I shall jump on the train East and look in Connecticut, probably arriving August 19th and staying for a week. If I find something just right, I shall try to move the family there the last of August. If I don't and if I have to move them from Cranbrook I shall move them to Englewood or Maine and go on looking.

In the meantime I am also looking here on the mad theory that the war in Europe might be over quicker than we think, that the war with Japan is apt to go on longer, that activity may be centered then on this coast, that if C. is going to be doing this sort of thing off and on, it might be better to be here. That it is a very beautiful coast and that as long as I am here I might as well do a little groundwork for "my little gray home in the West!"

Consequently I am looking for houses in three different places at the same time (chiefly by postcard and telegram). Well well— "we gather as we travel—bits of moss and dirty gravel." In the meantime I have just about given up all hope of catching C. here. I see no guarantee that he may not be gone several months more. I am staying here till the last possible moment—August 5th—on the chance of seeing him, but I don't think it's a very big one. He has been with the Marines, is now working with the Army and has not yet had *any* time with the Navy, so I think he might be delayed indefinitely. I have written him regularly to countless addresses but he has not had any of my letters since April because he's been moving around so fast. I think he's very much absorbed in the work, though, and as happy as he could be in the world at this time. That means a great deal.

What a strange suspended life it is without one's husband! And then remove one's children, too, and one begins to doubt the truth of Mrs. Miles: "There's nothing like being a childless widow!" I think the children are all right—at camp and with Miss Hanky. (Heavens—four huge sheets of probable plans—I surely could have said it in four lines.)

And how about your long hot plodding summer? Are you getting through it? I hope the fall will give you what this trip has given me—a lifting of the lid off the kettle—a little time to think, a little space in which to analyze what it is one fears, what it is that presses on one. It is true, I think, that understanding is the only thing that frees one. But it takes time, and when one is rushed there is no time or strength to understand— and so one puts on the lid of control and stoicism instead (just in case there might be an explosion). Which, of course, only postpones any real solving of the problems. One is always bartering awareness for self-control because there isn't time to be aware enough.

DIARY   *July 29th*
                              [*In California, with Margot and Dwight*]
More months have gone by without writing. There is never a vacuum. One must always clear the ground which has grown up with weeds and briars in the meantime—before one can start again.

How to review it seems difficult if necessary. Four months— April, May, June, July—without Charles. The first three went into active living, into work, into people, into family. The last one out here, with Margot, has gone into—at last—some thinking about the first three. Some summing up and inquiring into what I've done or learned in those months. What I've done does not seem important but what I've learned offers some possibilities.

For the first three months I avoided at all costs writing, thinking, or being alone. I think chiefly this was because I did not want to face the vacuum caused by C.'s being away. And partly, perhaps, it was just the general reaction once one has finished a book. I wanted life and people, felt on the whole happy at the success of the book and wanted to give this happiness and freedom directly to people. I felt full of life and wanted to share it and C. was not there to share it with. April went in work in the studio on the head and a trip to New York (April 12–19), where I went to the ballet and heard a Busch concert.

Back to Detroit—decided that I really preferred its atmosphere to New York. Seeing people in the evenings. The Scheyers, the Delattres, the Sepeshys, talking music and books and writing. A lovely evening at Carl's. Olga saying, "But I have waited all my life to have an evening like this, to have a circle of friends like this!"

I felt the same—at last at home in a group. It was with some shock I realized—when Svea pointed it out to me—that I was the only American there. They were all European.

It was a happy spring. One felt ashamed to be taking such happiness in the midst of world upheaval, and yet it was such simple happiness. Only friendship and talk and music. It was not gross or forgetful of the world and the war. Being Europeans, they never can forget it, only they are not violent and full of pressures.

June was friendship and sharing of thoughts and talk tempered by the physical care of the children—a very satisfying combination.

The only day that stands out was Invasion day. A day which shook even the far-away peace and smugness of Bloomfield Hills. One's daily life and thoughts seemed no longer significant. And one dropped through the crust of the everyday onto some more basic level. One went about one's business somewhere else, as though someone one loved were very ill.

It was strange, too, how much hope it brought. One did not realize how long the blind had been down, locked tight. But with this news ("My God, they've done it! They're actually there!") the blind was lifted just a crack ("Will there ever be a morning? Is there such a thing as day?").

And one started to whisper to oneself, incredulous, "It is possible, then. It might end, the war—the world might be peaceful again, France might be free. It is possible."

The blind was lifted and a crack of light fell in—on France.

I felt in some strange way that this was the great day of the war to all Frenchmen, that never again would it be equaled. This was the day of deliverance. This was the promise which would never quite be fulfilled. Before the delivered discover the burdens of being free. Before the invaders discover the problems of peace. There has been this day of hope, of ideals, of sacrifice. Perhaps to die for an ideal is in some way to give it validity.

The sense of that sacrifice, that suffering, was with me all day. Of course there is sacrifice every day, suffering constantly each hour of each day. But for once I felt conscious of it, I was involved in it, I felt humble before it. All day I remembered. (How terrible that one can ever forget, ever be unconscious. Though I am not sure one is ever quite unconscious. The fact that this day gave such hope made me realize what a constant cloud I had been living under, hardly realizing it.)

When I heard the news, coming down to breakfast, I went back upstairs immediately and went to the window and was on my knees. I felt too moved, too incoherent, to say anything, to find a prayer, but it seemed as though I should stop everything. It seemed as though I should be on my knees.

TO E. L. L. L.   *Fairfield, Connecticut, Tuesday, August 22nd*
Dear M.

Last night Mother called up from Maine to say the children had arrived all right and were sleeping peacefully. I am very relieved to have them safely there and wanted to let you know.

Then yesterday I had a cable from C. from Brisbane, Australia. It said, "Plans unchanged is everything OK reply Hotel Lennon Brisbane Australia."

I have really no idea what "Plans unchanged" means. But I hope it means that the news in his last letter still holds and that he'll be starting back soon. I cabled him back that it was impossible to re-rent Patterson house, that I was looking in Connecticut and for him to wire if O.K. and if he had any preference for locality and that "all well." It cost me $11.00 but I would have paid more to get assurance from him that I was doing the right thing.

And so I am now waiting for an answer! !

It was wonderful to get that direct word from him anyway, to know where he is.

Colonel Truman Smith here says that he hears the most wonderful praise of C. from all quarters. That he is doing a wonderful job, that it is being appreciated.

I have found a nice house here that would do for us. It will have to be partly furnished however. (Thank goodness for your two bureaus!) But it looks like us and has apple trees and a brook for the children and lots of room for Jon's goldfish and cocoons!

I won't do anything however until I get word back from C.

We would be a little over an hour from New York by train and five miles from Bridgeport and the United Aircraft factory there.

TO E. L. L. L.   *Fairfield, August 24th*
Dear M.

I was house-hunting all day yesterday in New Haven and came back here last night. Just before I left I had the cable back from Charles. It said, "Connecticut OK. Leaving here future address unknown. Home September."

"Home September"! That sounds wonderful to me although I'm not really counting on it yet. They might still find some reason to delay him out there. But it was wonderful to get direct word from him, so quickly, and to know that Connecticut was right.

But chiefly just to have the first *real* contact since March!

I am planning on going back tonight or tomorrow night.

I will see you soon. I just wanted you to get this news.

September 7th. Train from Rockland to Portland
Dearest Margot,

It was lovely to find your letter waiting for me on the hall table in Maine when we arrived a week ago. Betty B. M. [Baird Murray] and three children, I and Jon and Land, Con and D'Arcy—all somewhat bedraggled for one reason or another. We all look very different after our week in Maine. My four children have been left behind while I go down to get a cook, furniture, and start to move into an unfurnished house I have taken in Westport, Connecticut. So much has happened in the last month that it is hard to catch up, and not really very interesting. Packing, planning, looking for houses, traveling on trains, saying good-bye, moving, etc. I finally got a cable from C. from Brisbane and was able to cable back. The house we have taken is a little small and unfurnished but it looks rather like us—settled down among trees and a field and a brook. I think the community is going to be good for the children—quiet, healthy life, good schools, swimming and boats—like Lloyd Neck. I am inclined to think that Connecticut is perhaps best for this winter. Charles said that he would have to be there *most* of the time and I now feel that decides it for me. I am so tired of the half-life of being separated from my husband and the thought of all of us being together in our own house, with *our own* furniture, makes me quite giddy.

I must send this off and get off a note to C., who may be arriving any moment! I wish I were all moved in. I can see him arriving when we are half in Englewood and half in Westport, with no cook, no furniture, and all his clothes and files lost in Quirks' van! What a homecoming! But it will be wonderful to see him anyway, only I should have liked to present a beautiful clean fresh tidy home for him—all the children settled, our pictures on the walls and a delicious steak dinner on the stove—and C. A. L. stepping in the door smiling and saying, "My, this is wonderful, how did you do it!?"

As it is he will probably arrive in time to drive the heavily overloaded trailer to Connecticut and be met by fussy children falling out of the sleeper from Maine. "My," he will say, "how did you get into this mess—you certainly need me around!" Which is true. Good-bye for now. After September 15 (I hope!) we will be at Tompkins House, Long Lots Road, Westport, Connecticut.

Englewood, before breakfast,
Saturday, September 16th

TO E. L. L. L.
Dear M.

It has poured for three days—along with storms ("the hurricane"). All plans, moving, etc., have been held up. The van from Detroit which was supposed to arrive Wednesday or Thursday has not turned up yet. No cooks have come in to the agencies. And, of course, now his homecoming is imminent, I wait hourly for Charles, though I suppose it might be anytime in the next two weeks. There is a special anguish to waiting.

However, everything is all right here. The children are safe and sound and getting on all right here, though anxious to see the new house and their father. Jon was delighted with the "hurricane" and spent yesterday (which was clear and calm) going around the grounds counting, sawing up, and dragging away fallen trees and branches. Everyone says Scott looks like Daddy. Land, of course, looks just like C. Jon looks like himself, and Anne like no one one ever dreamed of!

DIARY   *Long Lots Road, Westport, October 8th*
Two more months gone by without writing. It is three months, really, because I have not written about the Western trip—July, August, and September. July was spent on the trip and at Margot's. August in moving, packing, good-byes, finding a new home. September: a week in Maine and three in Englewood, New York, and Westport, moving, shopping, collecting furniture, unpacking, looking at schools, for cooks. Feverishly.

And in the middle of all this, three big events in my life, in my heart. Three which moved me deeply and which—because of this torrent of moving, planning, and petty activity—I have hardly had time to plumb. C.'s return, St.-Ex.'s loss, and the liberation of Paris. I want so much to get to them, to know deeply what I feel before I start life over again. As I feel I am doing now, must do at this point in my life. But before I start I must catch up, I must let "my soul catch up" with me. And that I can only do by long quiet hours in the trailer—writing. For the trailer is up. It looks across the meadow to a flamelike tulip tree. There is soap in the basins and bathroom glasses in the bathrooms in this new house. The rugs are not down and the curtains not up and no mirrors are hung and a lot of furniture missing. I haven't a chair in my room but I have my big bed and a light to read by and the radio, where I can get the WQXR concerts.

And my desk is up in the alcove off my room and there is a chair for the desk and a lamp, and pen and paper and blotter and ink have been brought together there, too—what it means to put pen and paper and blotter and ink together! For all come packed in different boxes.

The Sikorskys came the first night and brought bread, salt, and a picture of the Virgin. They said one must bring those three things to a new home, as a symbol. To me it is pen, ink, blotter, and paper which are the symbol.

I must go back to the trip West, which was a wonderful experience for me. The extraordinary freedom and independence of it. I hadn't been entirely on my own like that, it seemed to me, since before I was married. This was not only because I usually travel with C. but more than that—an escape from the unreal newspaper personage of Mrs. Lindbergh. Traveling alone is not only escape from daily life to me, it is also—far more precious—escape from that artificial hedged-in, trapped newspaper personality. When I travel with C. I am immediately known. The Midas touch, the Medusa head. Life freezes around me. It is no longer unconscious, it is no longer life.

But to travel alone is to be incognito and myself. For no one recognizes me alone (or rarely). And I found that, unlike the days when I was young and shy, before marriage, now I could freely give and take and that I had much to give and much to take and that life was feeding me and I was hungry, as though some vitamin had been lacking from my diet.

I was intensely moved by the crowds of soldiers and sailors and wives in the stations. The officers and wives moving together, tired and worn, insecure, and yet, setting up a kind of housekeeping, a kind of security in their sections, with their knitting, their papers, their sparse words of understanding.

So different from those wistful tired women—suspended—back from seeing their husbands or going to join them, like me. I felt a kind of happiness in being one of them and a kind of pride. A secret joy in being ordinary, in being let in a door I have never been allowed in before. "Yes, my husband is in the South Pacific. Yes, I'm hoping to see him."

And yet, even in this there was separation from life—because, of course, since I got my tickets through Ford, I was on the super-de-luxe train (I said I would go on *any* train but they got me the best, thinking that was what I'd like). It wasn't quite as bad as it sounds because, although there was a good section of rich Hollywood, overdressed, loud-talking people (like the crowd on one of the prewar de-luxe liners, the *Normandie,* perhaps), the train was chiefly full of service people. Officers and their wives, Wacs, Waves, being sent to new posts. That made it real. And I found it easy to talk to them all.

The Wave who was studying therapy and the red-haired boy with the saxophone going to join the merchant marine. I crossed Chicago in a crowded taxi with him. Four servicemen and I and that boy; they all dropped out except the two of us. He was so pleased when he found I was going to San Francisco, too, and so dejected when he found it was another train.

There was a wonderful feeling of good nature, comradeship, friendliness in these war crowds, in the stations, on the trains. You could speak to anyone. Anyone could speak to you. We were together in it. The barriers were down. This good the war has done. I suppose any emergency does it. But does it last?

So many things have separated me from life. First, money. For money certainly does it. The camel through the needle's eye. But in this case the "Kingdom of Heaven" is life; money insulates you from real life (yes, and lack of money, too). And fame has insulated me from life—the Midas touch. And then, finally, *"Par délicatesse, j'ai perdu ma vie."* I realized on this trip how hungry I was for life, starved for it, fell on it ravenously, all the little scraps. People would laugh at such scraps; they are precious if one has starved.

Charles, of course, too, has been separated from life, by fame, by riches. But he has always been aware of it and resented it bitterly, fiercely, and fought his way out of it. His feeling of resentment at Englewood was this and his escape to the flying trips was this, and now his going to the war was this, too. One could not keep him from life; he breaks through to it. As St.-Ex. did. St.-Ex., like me, hungry for life, and again, like me, having to cross the barriers of breeding, education, and *délicatesse* to get it. Finding it in spite of everything, finding death, too, for it is all in one. Fighting those who wanted to protect him from it, from life and also from death. He knew they went together.

I realized, crossing this country by train that C. and I had crossed so often by plane (in dust, in heat, in cold, in wind, fog, storm, snow, early mornings, late nights, sitting on a parachute, the wind coming down my neck, my nose red, so many times), how the flying life had compensated C. and me, too, for the "life" fame had taken away from us. (And St.-Ex., too, did he not reach here what he could never reach on the ground?)

The glow of the beauty of the West lingered over my month with Margot. The dry golden hills, the gray live oaks clustered in hollows, the gorse, the sea—all seemed another, idyllic, world. Also dimly reminiscent of Brittany. I steeped myself in it. We lay in the sun, we ate outdoors. I helped Margot with the children. We talked—long sharings, constant sharings day by day. And physical work—care of the children, housework, helping Margot solve her household problems.

I contribute very little except an express wagon to drag the groceries uphill. And talk—the luxury of talking over everything with a sympathetic person—a luxury she gives me, of course.

I went to Margot's Inter-Racial Committee. It was very moving. The little crowd of men and women of good will seated in pews of the small white meeting room of the Monterey Town Hall. Like a New England church meeting it was—everyone rather shy, decent, glowing with good will. Negroes and whites sat, on the whole, in groups of their own race but smiled and made room for each other cordially. White, Negro, Filipino, and Chinese spoke. It was quite moving, especially the Negro. I was impressed again as always by the eloquence of the Negro, by his deeply moving qualities, his humility, his warmth, his generosity. So ahead of us in all these qualities of heart and spirit.

And how we have pretended to give them freedom, equality, the vote, and in reality have given them no equality, no decent education, no decent living quarters—no chance to earn a decent living.

What is the solution? Complete equality, complete intermixture? Certainly the Negro has things we would be better off with. He is superior to us, I feel, in many ways—artistically and spiritually. And yet the principle of complete intermingling looks forward, it seems to me, to a state of sameness all over the world, as though one grafted peach and pear and apple and plum together and came out with just one fruit in the universe. Would the universe be better off with just one fruit? Must differences always make for conflict? I suppose all *separateness* makes for conflict, as Krishnamurti[1] says. But is there no middle ground between a world with no differences and a world of conflicts? I do not know.

And over and on top and underneath all of this sharing of Margot's life ran a quality of suspense, during this month spent waiting for C.

I felt very close to Charles, in spite of lack of communication. I felt as if I knew what he was going through, a little, and what it meant to him. A little what I had on the train trip, but *much* more so. Being a part of his generation, having their experience, the experience all men seem to want to taste, to feel they are equal to—war.

And I was frightened for him, too. Where was he? What was he doing? I had a pretty good idea that he was going off on all the missions. Why should I believe he would be immune? Why was I so sure he would come back? I had felt so sure of the coming joy of seeing him as I took the train—but now I didn't know.

Sometimes in the middle of the night or early morning I would wake with a sudden sharp awareness of what he was and what I should lose—if I lost him. It was not a vision of him; it was not memory or thought, but a kind of sudden instantaneous piercing awareness of the essence of him—like a narrow beam of light, a concentration of light, not big—narrow as a pinpoint —but piercing as the point of light from a burning-glass. And in this awareness there was an intensity to the point of agony.

Yes, we both of us were hungry for life. We must definitely work to get more of it. No, it was not in Michigan for either of us. Not for C. in the production-minded Ford plant. Not for me in the Ivory Tower of Cranbrook, in spite of that wonderful circle of friends.

At any rate I felt sure that a time had come for a change in

[1] Jiddu Krishnamurti, Indian-born Hindu teacher, speaker, writer.

our life. I didn't know to what but I knew there must be a change.

I felt this all in a much more tangible form when I changed trains to Chicago. Every interesting face left the scene when I got on the train that went only to Detroit. I looked around the car and felt profoundly weighted down, suffocated. It wasn't just that these people were nouveau-riche, that they were over-dressed, talked too loud, got too drunk, bawled out the Negro porter. It was that they were so smug about all this. That no glimmer of the Negro porter's sensibilities had ever reached them, and no glimmer that they were not perfect, and no glimmer about Detroit's slums or problems. No glimmer of anything else outside of their own complacent comfortable lives. I felt with a kind of physical revulsion, no, we cannot live in Detroit another winter.

Then back in Detroit, the decision to move. (Mr. Patterson had as yet found no house he could move into and therefore wanted his own.) A sudden reversal of all plans, speeding up, thinking, planning, working. Tickets, railway accommodations, letters to friends on houses. Agents. And all this does not give the real parts of that month—the good-byes, in the midst of all the plans and packing and busy-ness.

Scheyer's gratitude and sadness, all coming out in a flood, at my leaving. Very moving in its open simplicity and sincerity. All this was said one evening I had with the two of them alone, and Mrs. Scheyer seemed to join in it. I suppose that is something—to have helped through sympathy, through understanding, through appreciation.

Yes, I shall miss them—his warm quick understanding, and his subtle, sensitive mind. And her quiet understanding, her calm strength and everything she says in her music. And Mrs. Bromley—kindly understanding and homely wisdom and courage—and Janet and Eliza. How I shall miss them, their values, their strength, their understanding to count on. What a luxury to live alongside of values like one's own.

But the others—the Scheyers—will politics and our different views separate us? The Delattres—whom I never knew as well as I wanted to. How I regret that fruit never tasted, snatched away. And the Milles'—old and weary and resigned—so sad to have us go, and I to leave them.

And Mrs. Lindbergh, frail in the driveway, waving good-bye. Frail and so gallant—I felt I could hardly bear it. I shall never lose that picture from my mind.

In the middle of all this moving and planning, on August 9th, I opened the paper to find a small paragraph in the *Free Press*. "Author-pilot missing over southern France—Saint-Exupéry." A brief notice. On a lone reconnaissance flight. He had just gone back into action after months on the ground teaching. He was 44.

Reading it, I had the feeling not of shock, exactly, because I had thought about it so many times, expected it for so long. It was the shock of recognition. There it is. You have known it before, but there it is, in black and white. Wipe it away, as you have wiped away the vision of it so many times before. No, it is there. Antoine de Saint-Exupéry. It was true.

And no time, no space in the moving to get away and think about it, to know what it meant to me. Nothing but that dull ache that I carried around through all the packing, that would occasionally wake to the sharp thrust of remembering what the ache was about. "But he is dead, he is lost, on a lone reconnaissance mission over southern France." As though by repeating to myself the words I could get closer to the reality, know it once and for all and not have to have the thrust again.

It was this way with the baby and with Elisabeth, I remember now. The heart will not take it all at once; it rejects it, it has to be told—a fresh telling, a fresh shock, a fresh thrust over and over again. And each thrust is as sharp, as cruel as the first, because in between the heart rejects the realization, it disbelieves, and then it must be hurt all over again. How slow a heart is to learn, much slower than the mind. So stupid, the heart, so tenacious, so heedless of hurt.

And even though my mind was on a thousand practical things, at every turning I would run up against this blank wall, this emptiness, and stop short—with the shock again—"But he is dead." Of what use to write if he were not there to read it, perhaps, sometime, somewhere? And my last book, which had gone out like a letter to him and never reached him, of what use was that? No one could really understand it, not as he could have. You write, and if there is one person in the world who you are sure will understand it is enough, and what you write glows with some kind of inner life, some life of its own. It has an ear to hear.

When I looked forward to my life, to the struggle and strife of our time, the separations, the tearings-apart—and he not in the world to shed a little light, to speak with compassion, to bridge both sides, to free us a little, to say, "We must not put one man's truth against another's"—I felt incredibly alone.

I felt like this at Elisabeth's death—completely alone to the end of my life—but that was personal. This is something more. This man's beliefs and his voicing of them made it possible, just possible, for me to live in the world as it is today, as it will be to-morrow. All the joy and the beauty in the world is somehow weighted with his loss. And the people rejoicing in the streets of Paris rejoice without him. And all the planes in the sky are going nowhere.

But, of course, I will live and relish life—my feeling for life is very strong. And I have a pattern for life, a good one. I have a husband I love. Nowhere could I find, could I have found, a better husband—a husband to whom I could give so much, who gives me so much—no marriage as good. A husband, a good marriage, is earth. Charles is earth to me, the whole world, life. St.-Ex. was not earth but he was a sun or a moon or stars which light earth, which make the whole world and life more beautiful. Now the earth is unlit and it is no longer so beautiful. I go ahead in it stumbling and without joy.

And then my mind fighting over it, arguing. After all, he wanted to die for France. He wanted to make the supreme sacrifice, he went back for that. Now his guilt (toward those who had suffered more) is appeased.

But it wasn't necessary, I cry out in rebellion. He had no need to feel guilt.

At least, the struggle is over for him, no more being torn apart, no more "If-you-are-not-with-me-you-are-against-me" decisions for him. He is above the civil strife.

But he could have helped so in that civil strife. He is desperately needed.

But perhaps illumined by his death, his words may take on more brilliance, be a torch to more people, like Péguy.[1] He will be the Péguy of this war. By his death his words have been made valid, somehow, beyond questioning.

But it wasn't necessary for him to die in order that they be made valid. They were valid anyway.

After all he would never have been satisfied with the rest of life. Only death could satisfy him. The pull to death was very strong in him.

*Yes—but it was wrong—*life is good. He should not have wanted to die. There was still much for him in life.

The night at Truman's when I could not sleep, the night we found the notice in *Time.* "Fifteen flak-riddled missions in a P-38."

"If he was flying a P-38," Truman said, "there is very little chance of his survival—the percentage of men getting out from P-38's is very low. . . ."

There is something terrible about "lost." It has a special agony of its own, quite distinct from death. Death, after all, is certain. There is a kind of tangibility in its very intangibility. One knows where they are, or where they are not. Destruction is complete, yes, but it is possible then slowly, brick by brick, to make up the new edifice. One can make of him *"un véritable ami mort."* But "lost"—neither here nor there, neither living nor dead, suspended, pale, insubstantial, faceless, like those souls in Dante drifting about between Heaven and Hell.

Aviation is full of this anguish. I have seen it in the faces of others; I have felt it myself. The TWA plane, crashed on Mt. Williams, that C. and I looked for early in our married life (I can still see that father's face, twisted like a tree in the wind, from anguish over his daughter, stewardess on the plane). And

[1] Charles Péguy, poet, social reformer, and Christian philosopher; killed on the Western Front during World War I.

then, looking back over my life, a succession of "losts." My own baby, and Amelia Earhart and Nelson and Phil and many others. I know the pattern well—the first shock, then the false hopes, and time passing, passing. There is never any answer—just time passing. The person you love is a hostage, a hostage to fate. One pictures the worst horrors and one is powerless to do anything about it, even to hope, even to pray. Even my prayers seem to bounce back to me as though there were an impenetrable wall. Does one pray for the dead?

And yet the wall seems to have cracks in it sometimes, as it has in life. That night I lay under the elm tree in North Haven and looked up at stars shining through its bare branches, so beautiful, the elm's bare branches, fruited with stars, hung with the heavens. The heavens, milky with the brilliance of many stars, veined with the dark branches of the elm. And there was a shooting star—right across the heavens—tearing it in half, ripping a great white gash in it.

At times like these one feels that one slips through—almost— and then those terrible doubts as to the validity of one's own emotions, one's own experiences, of one's own perceptions even.

A hundred times these past months I have said to myself: How can you pretend to a closeness, even a spiritual closeness, to a man you talked with only once and whom you know only through his writings? (But his writings are real, aren't they? Perhaps the realest part of him.)

How can you build up a relationship on a single contact that was never renewed and as far as you can tell he never wanted to renew? (But that contact was real to me. Does it matter whether it was real to him or not?)

Are you going to look back all your life to an hour's conversation on a train with a stranger who could not even speak your language, and you only haltingly, his? But obviously he spoke "my language" better than anyone I have ever met, before or since.

I am sad we never met again. I am sad he never tried to see us, though I understand it; I am sad that politics and the fierceness of the anti-war fight and the glare of publicity and the calumny and mixed-up pain and hurt and wrong of my book kept us from meeting again. I am sad that I never had the luxury of knowing whether or not he forgave us for our stand, forgave me for my book. Although—doubter that I am—his forgiveness rings through every page of *Lettre à un Otage* and *Flight to Arras,* too.

Long Lots Road, Westport, October 27th

I still have not caught up with this fall, so full of emotions. Our move to the East. St.-Ex.'s loss. C.'s return. This last, the emotions and thoughts about it still so near me, still rippling on. It is hard to describe joy—so much harder than to describe sorrow. I think this is because joy is almost always immediately shared, given off, communicated directly—in action or in words, or just in joy—to another. Or not even communicated in any way that one can see, and yet given off, dissipated. The world is so thirsty for joy—always parched for it. It soaks it up like rain. And so it doesn't get into words.

There is so much joy in my life, always—with the children or with Charles, or anywhere, with anyone or anything. Every morning before breakfast—opening my window onto the birch trees, the yellow birch leaves trembling against a blue sky—and every night, the stars through the elm branches; a wet maple leaf, scarlet, on the grass; a smooth chestnut, glossy from its damp shell; Scott's arms around me, Anne's yellow braids, Land in the bathtub. Jon's eyes when they are happy—a kind of secret happiness, a joy he lets me in on for an instant. Anne's face lit up with that angelic smile like day slowly breaking over her serious little face.

It is hard now to go back to the days without C. To remember what it was like—that strange unbalanced creature that I was, never really at rest, suspended, never touching earth. The suspense that went through all of life, got stuck like a note. "When —when—when he comes back. When—when—when we begin to live again." And how I dreaded getting into that big lonely bed at night. And the sleepless nights and the early mornings. And the sense—with people—that one was giving *out* all the time and that no one was giving *back* to you, no one filling you up to the brim. Being a little thirsty all the time—that was it.

And the sense that time was going very fast. Spring and summer. (The birds all have mates.) And looking enviously at couples together, on the street, in a restaurant, on a train, trying to taste vicariously the quality of marriage, the stream in which they were flowing, through which they communicated in little gestures. The fluid security in which they were bathed and which they took for granted as their natural element. And I on the outside, I only knew how it could all be withdrawn, how one could be left parched when the tide went out. All this I have forgotten—now the tide has come back.

Even how it came back I have forgotten. With a great rush—overwhelming. The cable from Brisbane—my relief to be able to cable and hear from him directly. "Connecticut OK." My rush to get the house ready for him, my passionate desire to get moved in before he came. Ready for him, for our life together, for our children. My fear I wouldn't make it. (The hurricane.) Yes, I just could. His voice over the telephone from California.

As simple as that, as ordinary as that—this miracle.

Then the day he was to come. (The furniture just moved in, the children still in Englewood. We were to meet at Westport.) How I labored to put it in some order, to have one room to sit in, to make the beginnings of a home out of it—for him. And before I was cleaned up, the taxi at the door, the stooping figure inside. Quick steps past the sitting-room windows. And there he was, lean and brown, very young and taut looking, bursting into the room—like life always.

And then his joy at being home flooding everything, the house, the stream, the woods, the flowing fall weather—everything was perfect. The children—when they came. Anne tossed up in his arms. Scott, shy and round-eyed. The boys now at last free to vent their bursting energy. "This is what they needed—this!" I say to myself as I see them roughhousing with him, building a dam across the stream, or just sitting throwing stones and trying their aim against his.

And breakfasts together—breakfast is a wonderful family

meal—and walks in the golden woods and talks, finding we were following parallel lines all the time, that I somehow knew what was happening to him, his mood, his growth. And he knew what I was feeling about St.-Ex. "Yes, I thought of you," and again, "You have so little faith to mourn someone who is dead."

We are not separated from each other by our differing experiences but, rather, in some strange way, closer. Is this just a miracle of understanding? Or simply love? Or do we really both of us now stand at the same point, at the end of something, at the beginning of something?

Both of us are groping and a little lost—but we are together.

INDEX

Evening after you left. June 13th
1942
Seven Gates

Dear Claire,

Ann seems to be getting on all right. And the doctor said the boys would not get an acceptable shock if the 2 treatments were combined (as happens that sort [...] you). Apparently if you were to receive a wound this summer from which tetanus might result — he should be given the 2nd dose of Toxoid. This should prevent him from getting tetanus. If he should develop tetanus he could still be given the anti-toxin. But it very unlikely he would get it. I will check with